A TOMMY AT YPRES

A TOMMY AT YPRES
WALTER'S WAR

THE DIARY AND LETTERS OF WALTER WILLIAMSON
COMPILED BY DOREEN PRIDDEY

AMBERLEY

This edition first published 2013

Amberley Publishing
The Hill, Stroud,
Gloucestershire, GL5 4EP

www.amberleybooks.com

British Library Cataloguing in Publication Data.
A catalogue record for this book is available from the British Library.

ISBN 978-1-4456-1368-0

Typesetting and Origination by Amberley Publishing.
Map illustrations by User design.
Printed in the UK.

CONTENTS

FOREWORD

Walter is my grandfather and I am Doreen Priddey (née Williamson), daughter of Jim Williamson, Walter's son.

As I sit down to write this introduction to 'Grandpop's' diary I am almost at a loss for words to express how thrilled I am that Walter will come to life through his writing which, as you will discover for yourselves as you read his diary and letters, was always a great passion of his. Although we never met, missing each other by a few months in 1947, I feel a great affinity to him and whilst working on his diary that affinity has grown stronger and stronger, so my overwhelming gratitude goes to Sarah, Joe and all at Amberley Publishing for this opportunity.

Walter was born in 1888, one of nine children, seven boys and two girls, to John and Elaine Williamson, proprietors of a draper's shop in Oldham, Lancashire. I know little of his childhood other than he was born a twin, but his twin died at birth, and that Walter himself had rheumatic fever as a child. He met and fell in love with Amelia James and they were married at St Thomas Church, Heaton Chapel, Stockport, in 1913, and, as you will ascertain from his letters to her, which are intermingled chronologically, theirs was a truly loving relationship. As Mr and Mrs Williamson they moved to Cheadle Hulme, Cheshire, first to Heathbank Road and then on to 21 Queens Road, where they spent the rest of their married life. They had three children, Jim, my father, born in February 1914, Jean in 1919 and Elaine in 1921. From what I can remember my father telling me, Walter's working life was spent at Henry Bronnert and Co., shipping merchants of 56 Princess Street, Manchester, and on the outbreak of the Second World War he enlisted into the Home Guard.

There are a few affectionate and amusing anecdotes that have drifted down through the generations that give an inkling of his personality. The first one that comes to mind is that he was totally colour blind and, after coming home with a pair of bright pink socks thinking them to be black, Amelia decided to accompany him on all further shopping trips. Also Walter was very keen on new fangled gadgets and ideas, so he bought himself a pair of the latest trend in shoe-laces made of elastic – brilliant, thought he, no need to keep tying and untying them, that was till he was walking through a muddy, crowded field at a point-to-point race meeting, leaving his shoes stuck in the mud no longer attached to his feet! Another time when his fascination in all things new got the better of him was when he and Amelia visited what I suppose was one of the earliest Ideal Home exhibitions in Manchester. He spotted an automatic washing machine and, as nobody was around, pressed a few buttons; unfortunately for Walter it was switched on and in no time at all a crowd gathered round thinking he was giving a demonstration. And finally there was the time when he and Amelia, early in their relationship, were invited for dinner to her relatives. Being a little nervous and trying to be ultra polite to impress his in-laws-to-be, he laughed so heartily at one of his host's jokes that he rocked backwards with gusto on his dining chair, breaking its back and almost his own. These sorts of things just seemed to happen to Walter.

As a couple they shared many interests and especially loved the arts, music and theatre in particular. I now realise what a huge influence they have been on our family right through to the present generation, as two of his great-granddaughters and their families live in Cheadle Hulme and are members of the Players Amateur Dramatic Society, of which Walter's son, Jim, was a founder member. My brother, Howard, and I took it one step further and 'turned professional', starting our careers with the D'Oyly Carte Opera Company.

The diary starts as Walter is called to war in 1916 and we travel with him from Birkenhead to France and onward to the Ypres Salient, where his vivid recollections describe his part in the 118th Brigade's involvement in the Battle of St Julien at the opening of the 3rd Battle of Ypres, then on to the Somme and his return to Ypres. We meet his many comrades, his best friend Pat Nunn, and his commanding officers, all of whom come to life through his wonderfully keen observations. Walter was an educated man, not wealthy, but a gentle, sensitive, unassuming, loving family man with a warm humour that reflected these qualities, all of which in turn are reflected in his wonderful diary.

Within these pages lies the reality for a Tommy at Ypres: the bravery, the warm comradeship, the gentle humour, the strength of character and resilience, the sadness, the tragedy – *A Tommy at Ypres* reveals the true spirit of an outstanding generation. The values by which these men lived are perfectly expressed by Walter himself in a letter he wrote to Amelia, dated 30 March 1917:

> But dear old girl I do so miss you and would give worlds to have you in my arms again in our little home, I say worlds, but I must hedge a bit. If it was necessary to spend ten years out here to make sure our boy would never be called up to see the horrors of real warfare, I would do it gladly, aye and more …

So in conclusion Walter and Amelia, we, 'your family', are indebted to you in so many ways for the happy and fulfilled lives we are living today and we thank you with all our hearts. When I say 'your family', that is your five grandchildren, thirteen great-grandchildren, twenty-two great-great-grandchildren and one great-great-great-grandchild!

ACKNOWLEDGEMENTS

I must first of all thank Sarah Clover (née Phillips), without whose initial enthusiasm and tremendously dedicated hard work, this 'labour of love' may never have seen the light of day. So many, many thanks Sarah.

My heartfelt thanks to all at Amberley Publishing, especially Sarah Flight and Joseph Pettican, for giving life to *A Tommy at Ypres: Walter's War*, it is an immense thrill for me and all the family.

Sincere thanks also go to Major T. E. Pickering, Geoff Crump and Bill Preece at the Cheshire Military Museum, Chester. Geoff, in particular, has been a great support, always willing to answer my many queries, his research abilities being second to none and, on a visit to the Museum, he and Bill could not have been more helpful and encouraging. Bill even made me a cup of tea! Thank you so much.

We, that is the family, would like to express our thanks too to Alan Kennedy, Chairman of the East Cheshire Regiment Association, and his dear wife Rose for their kind invitation last August (2010) to the service at St George's church, Stockport, to commemorate the Battle of St Julien, 31 July 1917. They gave us such a warm welcome and we were all invited back to The Armoury for a most beautiful lunch. Everybody we met there was so kind and it is a day we shall never forget.

The family has all been very supportive of my efforts and I thank them for their encouragement; special family thanks go to my niece Alison (Walter's great-granddaughter) and her husband Paul for the innumerable hours that we all worked on the maps – they were supposed to be having a few days holiday with us away from the stress of work!

Finally, my love and thanks must go to Malcolm, my very dear husband, for his forbearance over the last two years whilst I have been 'on the First World War battlefields with my Grandfather' – he now can't wait to get his gardening assistant back!

GLOSSARY

AA MACHINE GUNS – anti-aircraft machine guns
AEF – American Expeditionary Force
APM – Assistant Provost Marshall
ASC – Army Service Corps
ASCMT – Army Service Corps Motor Transport
BANDOLIER – pocketed belt to hold ammunition
BANTAMS – Battalion of short men
BEF – British Expeditionary Force
BHQ – Battalion Headquarters
BLACK HAND GANG – a raiding party
BLANCO, SOLDIERS FRIEND & SILVO – cleaning materials
BOISSONS – drinks
BP – Billeting Party
BRABANÇONNE – Belgian National Anthem
CB – confined to barracks
CQM – Company Quarter Master
CSM – Company Sergeant Major
CURÉ – parish priest
DCM– Distinguished Conduct Medal
DERBIES – named after Lord Derby's Recruitment Scheme
DIXIE – large metal food container
DON THREES – cables
ECOSSAI – Scotsman
FACINES – bundles of sticks and small branches to support trenches
FFV – Free from vermin
FGCM – Field General Court Martial
FP – field punishment
FUNK HOLES – shelters dug out of the sides of trenches

HARRISON'S POMADE – treatment for nits, etc.

HE – High Explosives

HONEYDEW – tobacco

JAMES' – brand of cigarette (Family connection with his wife Amelia James)

JO – Junior Officer

JOHN BULL – magazine publication

KRR – Kings Royal Rifles

KRUSCHEN – cleansing salts to promote regularity and remove body toxins

KURSAAL – German word meaning spa or 'cure hall'

LA GRIPPE – influenza epidemic

LB & SC RAILWAY – London Brighton & South Coast Railway

L/C – Lance Corporal

MARY BULL – big gun

MG – machine-gun

MILLS No. 5 – bombs

MM – Military Medal

MP – Military Police

MRS GAMP – Character from Dickens 'Martin Chuzzlewit'

MUG TRAPS – booby traps

M4, a 3.4 … DV – map reference

OC – Officer Commanding

PBC – Revd P. B. Clayton (Tubby) of Talbot House, Poperinghe

PBI – Poor bloody infantry

PH (Gas Helmet) – Phenate Hexamine

POILUS – French Soldiers (literally hairy one)

POZZY – Plum and apple jam

QMS – Quartermaster Sergeant

'QUI VIVE' – on the alert, vigilant

RAMC – Royal Army Medical Corps

RE – Royal Engineers

RFC – Royal Flying Corps

RGA (Har Gee Hay) – Royal Garrison Artillery

RP – Regimental Police

RTO – Railway Transport Officer

RUBBER GUN – High velocity enemy gun

SAM BROWNE – military belt

SOLDIERS FRIEND & KHAKI BLANCO – cleaning materials

SRD – Supply Reserve Depot, jars for rum or lime juice
'SUFFICIENT UNTO THE DAY IS THE EVIL THEREOF' – Bible
quotation, Matthew Chapter 6 verse 34
SW – Small Woman
TM BATTERY – Trench Mortar Battery
WAACs – Womens Auxiliary Army Corps
WAB – William Arthur Bromley, brother-in-law
WATERS OF LETHE – River in Hades, Greek Mythology
WD Motors – War Department
VC – Victoria Cross

PEOPLE IN CHRONOLOGICAL ORDER

Volume One

(Cecil) **Pat Nunn** – mentioned throughout diary, Number 268164, consecutive number to Walter, p. 30.

W. A. B. **Walter Arthur Bromley** – brother-in-law, p. 31.

Adjutant Lieutenant **Naden**, p. 46.

Corporal **Jack Isaacs** – Lewis Gun instructor, Number 265604, killed in action 31 July 1917, no known grave, but his name appears on the Menin Gate, Ypres, p. 47.

Bob Smith – Bugler, p. 50.

Leather and **Speight** – on signalling course with Walter, p. 57.

General Sir **Hunter Weston** (Old Hunter Bunter) – Corps Commander, p. 61.

Revd **P. B. Clayton** – ran Talbot House in Poperinghe, founder of TOC H, p. 62.

Jock Mitchell and **Crole** (Black Watch) – on signalling course, pp. 65–69.

Jimmy Robinson – signaller, (first mentioned) p. 71.

"Nobby" Clarke – signaller, (first mentioned) p. 71.

Rowbottom – signaller, (first mentioned) p. 71.

Fred Swann (alias 'Little Hommer') – signaller, (first mentioned) p. 94.

Frank Collier – signaller, (first mentioned) p. 98.

Bob Atkinson – Lewis Gunner, p. 113.

Bob Cawley – battalion chiropodist and 'general factotum' from Hyde, Cheshire, Number 265037, p. 115–321.

Volume Two

Lieutenant **George Bleazard Cowpe**, p. 131.
Duncan – runner (from Birkenhead), p. 133.
Art Wilkinson – bomber, p. 136.
McKnight, Fernley and **Timms** – signallers, p. 138.
Harry Murphy, p. 145.
Bill Beswick – signaller (first mentioned), p. 147.
Quarter Master Sergeant **J. H. Pearson** – 'Q' Number 265538 – Orderly Room, (first mentioned) p. 155.
Len Graham (Young Len) – Orderly Room staff, (first mentioned) p. 155.
"Sammy" – signal officers batman, (first mentioned) p. 163.
Len Watson (friend from Cheadle Hulme), pp. 171, 174, 176.
Entwistle (nickname "Aunty") – signaller, (first mentioned) p. 187.
Billy Hobbs – bandmaster, p. 189.

Volume Three

2nd Lieutenant **Brooks**, p. 216.
Billy Wildgoose – Orderly Room clerk, p. 230.
General **Gough** – 5th Army, Somme, January 1918, p. 242.
Captain **"Tubby"**, (first mentioned) p. 256.
General **Feetham**, p. 278.
Brigadier-General **Bellingham**, p. 278.
General **Hubback**, p. 283.
Field Marshall **Haig** ("Backs to the Wall" appeal), p. 284.
Billy Hunter – corporal, (first mentioned) p. 311.
Billy Gee – batman, p. 311.
Captain **Nicholson**, p. 312.

Jim Murphy (Harry's brother), p. 312.
"Jud" Foley – runner, p. 314.
Gamble and **Bailey** – runners, p. 314.
Captain **Kenyon**, p. 314.
Sergeant **Speakman**, p. 314.
Sergeant **Marsh**, p. 319.
Signaller **McKnight**, p. 325.
Joe Hayes – batman to adjutant, p. 330.
Captain **Wood**, p. 332.
Captain **Yorston**, p. 332.
Bobby Howarth – runner, now RSM's batman, p. 335.
Lieutenant **Jimmy Holt**, p. 335.

MAPS

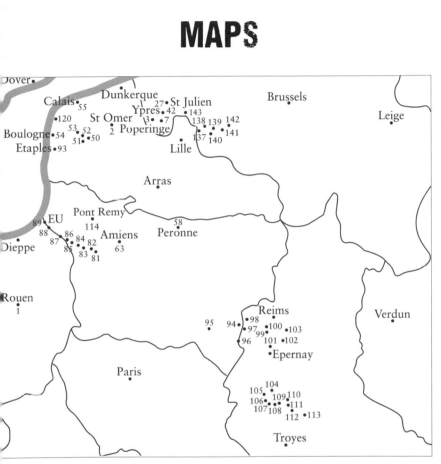

Map 1: Overview of Walter's wartime experience.

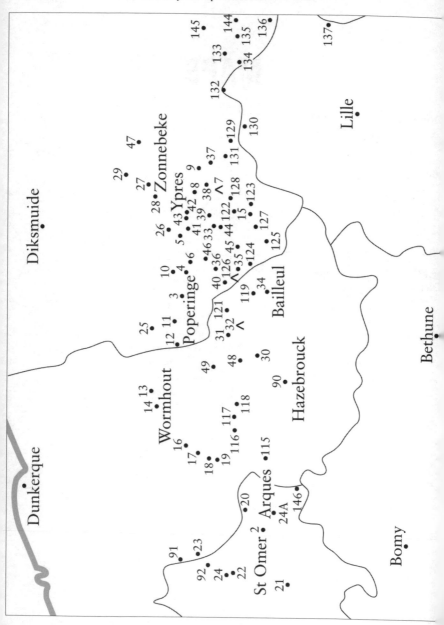

Map 2: The Ypres Salient.

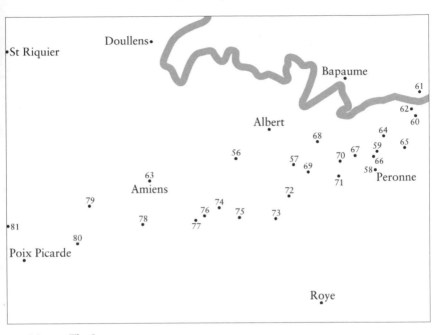

Map 3: The Somme.

Volume One

First route – Ypres (Volume One) – Map 2, pages 36–120

1–2–3–4–5–3–6–7–6–5–8–9–6–10–3–11–12–13–14–3–15–14–16–
17–18–19–20–21– (then Coulomby, Harlettes)–22–23–3

Volume Two

Continuation of Volume One route – Ypres – Map 2, pages 123–198

3–23–24–22–11–2–24a–13–12–25–26–27–28–29–26–10–30–31–
32–33–34–35–36–33–37–38–39–46–40– (La Brasserie – between 33
& 39)–40–41–42–43–42–44–45–46–38–39

Volume Three

Route – Marne and surrounding areas (Map 1), pages 293–298

93–94–95–96–97–98–99–100–101–102–103–104–105–106–107–
108–109–110–111–112–113–114

97.   Romigny
98.   Lhery
99.   Bois De Courton
100. Champlat
101. Hautvillers
102. Ay
103. Germaine
104. Fère-Champenoise
105. St Loup
106. Linthelles
107. Pleurs
108. Ognes
109. Corroy
110. Euvy
111. Gourganson
112. Semoine
113. Mailly (Mailly-le-Camp)
114. Pont-Remy

Route – return to Ypres area (Maps 1 & 2), pages 299–332

2–20–24a–115–116–117–118–119–(49 to 48 road)–120 (Rest Camp)–49–35–121–49–122–123–124–45–125–126–127–15–122–128–129–130–131–132–133–134–135–136–137–138–139–140–141 142–143–144–145–146

115. Le Nieppe (Nieppe)
116. Bavinchove
117. Oxelaere
118. St Marie Capelle
119. St Jans Capelle
120. Audresselles Rest Camp (Map 1)
121. Boeschepe
122. Wytschaete (Wijtschate)
123. Messines
124. Dranouter Ridge
125. Neuve-Église Sector (Nieuwkerke)
126. Mont Rouge
127. Wulvergem

Letters, 25 June – 8 August 1916

June 25th 1916 – Prees Heath – a ma femme

Dear little Woman,

There is only one thing wrong with this job. I do miss you and the lad terribly. I don't know what I wouldn't give just to have you in my arms just for 5 minutes even, and hold you tight to me, and kiss you on your hair all the way down to your chin in quarter inches, a dozen kisses to every quarter of an inch.

Then to have 5 minutes with that lad of ours, and squeeze his chubby little ribs and kiss his cheeky little face.

But it won't be long. Shan't know till the Friday before I come on the Saturday, but will let you know at once.

Keep on loving me kid, and then the world is still rosy.
Your lover, Walter

August 8th 1916 – Prees Heath

Dear Wife,

I got your letter this morning girl and a good letter it is to hold a man up and help him to make himself worthy of his manhood, his wife, his child and his Country. It is fine of you to say you are sure I shall go to France, and make yourself ready for anything that might happen. It is a great deal better than hoping and hoping till you get to think it a certainty that I won't go out, because then it would come so much harder for both of us. I don't know anyone that gets so much help from his wife, and I feel that if I do anything less than my best, in anything I do, I shall be unworthy, but as you know little girl, I am not one for any glory, only to do my duty to the best of my ability, and I know you and Jim would rather I did that, than try to make my way above other men for the sake of a little extra comfort.

When I feel a bit down in the dumps or lonely, I shall just read your letter again, it will be a good antidote for anything of the kind.

I just wish I could have been with you on Sunday to try those songs over with you, it seems such a long time since I heard you sing. I don't know any of the songs by name, though I possibly may have heard some of them down here as we get some very good singers and good songs now and again in the sing song huts.

I fear Jim has been keeping late hours lately what with staying up to see his Daddy, Uncle Arthur, Jack, etc. and was quite pleased to hear that he was in bed early on Sunday. You must get him off to bed early when you can and give that lively brain, and those lively legs of his as much rest as he will allow. Do you know, I can just fancy I feel his little fist hold of my thumb as he had last weekend. By the way I am putting in for a pass again this weekend, nothing like cheek is there, but I might just as well get it refused this week, as the week after.

I shall laugh if it comes off, but I wouldn't care to chance 2*d* on it.

You will be having some fine old gossips with your mother I expect. Hope you don't get squabbling too much about the respective merits of your soldier lads.

I will tell you the latest rumour that is going the round, but you will take it for what it is worth when I tell you that (by rumour) we should have already been in Bournemouth, in Ireland, finishing our training in France, Salonica and Egypt, and India and all these were really more likely than the latest. Now I have warned you fully, I will hand you the rumour. It runs that we are to go to take charge of the Camp at Handforth and relieve the Shropshires from there. I think its genealogical tree would work out about as follows

"The man who takes the swill from the cookhouse met a private who knew a man at
the Quarter Masters store who knew the man who sent a man to put up a tent for a
barber who shaved a corporal who had charge of some men on fatigue at the officers
mess, and one of these men heard the cook say that he knew the man who was a relation
of a waiter at the mess who heard the Colonel say the Colonel of the Shropshires was
grumbling at his men being there, saying it was no soldiers job, and the Cheshires ought
to be put on it."

I had a letter from Pat Nunn today addressed from Cheadle Hulme. His time farming in South Wales is not up till the 19th but he has evidently begged a week end off from the farmer. He is off back this morning. There are only 4 short in the hut now. I miss Nunn rather, for the walks in the evening. He seems to have found a good place, but says the work is hard and the hours very long. I must write him a line tonight.

We have all been dismissed early this afternoon in order to be able to attend the sports at Whitchurch, but as most of our hut are down for picket duty tonight, I have not gone down, but have stayed to help dress the picket. There are a few of them who havn't been in full dress yet and need dressing. You would be surprised at the many different ways we have of dressing ourselves up through a single day, and the amount of time spent in changing and rearranging our equipment. The first day or two learning how to bring a mass of straps, buckles, pouches and tools to a semblance of order is quite a business, and makes those who have got the hang of things (both literally and in its concrete sense) only too willing to help men get into their harness for the first time.

When you have once got all your tackle together so that you can slip it on your shoulders and fasten your belt and there you are, you absolutely dread having to put the thing to pieces again, until it dawns on you that you can't go for a walk in the evening till you get your belt off it, and then of course the whole thing collapses.

There is a big draft leaving here for Salonica tonight and it won't leave much of our Company. Practically only the men who came up about my time. Give the Jim boy a big kiss from his Daddy and a husbands love to Mamsy, from her loving husband   Walter.

1 DECEMBER 1916 – 29 JUNE 1917

268163 L/C (A/CPL) W. WILLIAMSON

6th Battalion

Cheshire Regiment

1 December 1916

It was 3.0 a.m. in the Draft Room at Birkenhead and we had just been roused from our slumbers (at least those of us who had slept). The sergeant's voice was unusually lamb-like and to be called "Laddies" was a thing that had not previously happened. Of course it does make a difference when you arc "draft", and then of course the sergeant was not going with us. We showed the necessary leg as requested, and the next hour was spent packing, and dumping everything that could not find a home in our packs.

It was warm work while it lasted, what with new warm underclothing, and the little locket containing "powdered rose leaves" to discourage the too pressing attentions of little friends we had not yet met.

At last we were packed, breakfasted and on parade for inspection, and were informed that we were a credit to the 3rd Battalion, the Cheshire Regiment. This was pleasant as, although we ourselves were aware of the fact, we were under the impression that such was certainly not the opinion of any N.C.Os or officers of the 3rd and it was quite nice to hear that their previously expressed opinions were evidently in the way of good humoured chaff. However, the Colonel had said it, and if the Colonel said it, it was of course equal to seeing it in "John Bull".

It was still dark when we marched through the big gates, led by the band. The Regimental Police of course turned out in strong force and marched alongside, or I should say, along each side. This was of course to prevent the hot heads from rushing off to catch an earlier train.

The band played "The Long Long Trail", "Swanee River" and many other excerpts from the classics but spared us "Tipperary", and one wonders now how we came to feel sentimental after a 3 o'clock Reveille on a cold December morning.

A war being on, of course drafts were always sent off in the darkness, and we supposed that the full Regimental band played us to the station to drown the tramp of marching feet, so that no one should hear us going.

Either the band failed to waken the housewives of the district, or they were under the impression that it was an early band practice of the Salvation Army, but there was not the expected rush to drag the front door mats into safety. This was always supposed to be done by a careful housewife when the "Cheshires" passed.

On arrival at the station we were not long getting more or less comfortably packed into the train, and as, (before starting out), we had been issued with (amongst other things) "Preserved meat, per two men – tins – one" much care was taken in getting into the same compartment as the man who was carrying your share of "Bully". As Pat Nunn carried our tin, I stuck to him like a leech. The Colonel then taking a flying start from the front of the train popped a long arm into each compartment and shook hands on relinquishing command over us, until such time as any of us should be so unlucky as to return for training again at Birkenhead. The next arm that came through was the Major's handing in morning papers.

The band then formed up facing the train, and as we started to move out, they struck up "Should auld acquaintance be forgot", – perhaps not, but we hadn't any particular desire to linger over fond memories of one or two recent ones.

After a bit of chat, and a few feeble attempts to organise glee parties to take up the offensive against the next compartment, I think most of us shuffled down and went to sleep, but not for long, as we changed at Crewe and joined a troop train which had evidently come from Scotland, and before getting on board we spent some little time picking up the language, and learning the customs of that wonderful country where they risk wearing kilts in a land where thistles grow.

Our search after knowledge was at last cut short by our Officer in Charge wanting to count his precious jewels. This took some little time as one gets a bit foggy about "falling in on the left" and which end was which end. Some would appear suddenly from some mysterious corner and push in to the middle of the rear rank, but eventually we were audited and found correct, and boarded the train again.

About noon we stopped for some time in Oxford station, and thinking we would like to stretch our legs a little, we were disappointed to find the carriage doors locked, no doubt to keep the "draft in". Failing exercise, we fell to investigating the hidden mysteries of Fray Bentos and trying our new Jack Knives and the bread, wondering meanwhile, what they fed Cadets on. It was evidently not time for their lunch yet, as many were busy working up their appetites with a constitutional along the platform. There also seemed to be a riot of them round the book stall, but we could not just remember whether it was the "Winning Post" or "Sunday Tales" that came out that day.

I looked for "W.A.B." amongst the crowd, but could not spot him. Perhaps he was strolling the banks of the Isis reckoning up the difference between the commission on a turnover, and the turnover on a Commission.

Southampton was reached late in the afternoon. We detrained on the dockside, and those who had been busy pencilling fond farewells in the train, made desperate efforts to induce spare soldiers about, to post them, but to no avail. Unlimited uncensored correspondence had now become a thing of the past. We were marched into a large shed on the quayside and watched other drafts blow in during the evening. A canteen in the corner of the shed soon began to do a roaring business though it was a "dry" canteen and sold nothing wetter than tea and coffee. The tea was much like the coffee, and the coffee retaliated, but neither of them were quite wet enough to wash down the cake that was sold there. Such cake cannot be obtained anywhere but from Army Canteens and no one but soldiers ever get hungry enough to tackle it. Made by a secret process, a careful analysis by a "private" analyst has proved (to the satisfaction of soldiers generally) the constituent parts to be Army workshop sawdust 50%, stationary department used blotting paper 50%, currants (if any) accidental.

Later a few of us managed to get outside the shed in the dark, on to the quayside, and were treated to a fine display of searchlights, which were used we believe, to guide zeppelins which had lost their way, to Southampton.

It was quite dark when we embarked on a disappointingly small steamer. Equipment was dumped below and everyone supplied with lifebelts. By the size of the boat and the accommodation, it was fairly certain that it was bound either for Ireland or France, but no further. For safety we preferred France.

We were soon moving down Southampton Water, no lights or smoking allowed on deck. It was interesting to see signals being flashed out of the darkness, and being answered from our boat, but a December night without a moon, and without a smoke not being over conducive to deck strolling, Pat and I decided for a smoke and a bit of warmth below. After getting warmed and having a smoke, deck seemed preferable after all, as the accommodation down below was of course not fit for anything but troops, and it was also evident that good soldiers do not necessarily make good sailors. We reconnoitred the deck for a warm corner, and settled ourselves near a ventilator from the engine room.

2 December

We awakened to find the boat in dock. It was a grey cold morning and not yet daylight. At the other end of the dock was a great hospital ship, lighted up from end to end, and the great red cross on its bulwarks outlined with lights. In the grey cold morning mist it looked almost phantom like. It was a huge ship and would perhaps hold three times as many wounded as ours would hold reinforcements. This caused uncomfortable mental calculations as to how long the British Army would last if the wastage and supplies bore any relation to this incident in the dock at Le Havre.

Pat's voice pulled me up with his "What about it?" "About what?" I asked. "Breakfast" he replied curtly. I had not heard him wake. I had heard him wake each morning for some months past, as he had a habit of saying his prayers rather vehemently before "Cookhouse", but invariably some minutes later than "Reveille".

His opinion of "Reveille" was that it was unmusical, uncouth, and a barbaric custom, and the man who first blew it, and every man who has blown it since should have his brains dashed out with his own bugle. As it had not been blown this morning, he was up before it for the first time since he joined the Army. I had the good taste (and good sense) not to remark about it, and we went below to see what could be begged, borrowed, bought or scrounged in the way of sustinence. At a little bar down below we managed to secure a cup of coffee and a sandwich or two. The bar keeper's chief business however, just then, seemed to be exchanging English currency for French at a rate of exchange that would have caused some excitement in the European money markets, and also accepting letters with a suitable fee, for posting when he returned to Southampton. Either the boat was sunk on the return journey, or this man must be comfortably retired from business, perhaps living affluently somewhere in the Isle of Wight, and thanking the gods that he got a job on a "Rooky" boat and not on a leave boat where such childlike simplicity and faith are not to be found.

The man has yet to be found who dared to offer such terms on a leave boat returning to France.

Things must have been quiet that morning on the Western Front, as there seemed to be no hurry about getting off the boat, though officers had left the boat early, no doubt to find out at which part of the line the British Army was being most hard pressed, so that we could come up and save the situation.

During the morning the boat was attacked by numerous vendors of picture postcards, on which many of the trusting ones immediately scribbled the latest news and map reference, and handed back to the sellers with a few coppers to cover postage and thirst caused by licking the stamps. These gentlemen were however, quickly bustled off the boat again, but not before they had disposed of most of their stock-in-trade.

Later in the day we disembarked and heard with feelings of pleasure, that we were to go to a rest camp for the night. Up to that day we had no idea that Le Havre was a much bigger port than London or Liverpool, but by the time we were clear of the docks, we felt convinced of it. Perhaps it was that our conducting officer wished to have a good look round the docks, or even may have lost his way. Such a thing has actually been known to happen. The tedium of our exploration was relieved however by our first acquaintance with the blue coated poilus. They had charge of German prisoners working at the docks. Most picturesque old gentlemen they were in their long blue coats with the lapels on the skirts instead of at the collar. Some of them had evidently put on flesh since their campaigning days of 1870/1. They have evidently treasured their rifles and bayonets too, as they looked quite businesslike despite their antiquity.

We really did envy them their beards, and we understood why they look so happy. The morning shave and chin inspections held no terrors for them.

On getting into the town itself, we were assailed by most of the youngsters in the immediate neighbourhood who demanded souvenirs in the shape of buttons, badges, biscuits and bully. It gave the idea that their knowledge of English was confined to words commencing with "B", but on being told to "Allez toute suite" we found that they were quite well up in many other words culled from the British Army Vocabulary.

After marching some distance through the town, we halted for a rest outside a huge French Barracks which looked very inviting, but that was as far as the invitation got. On the far side of the road was a little shop whose sign read "BOISSONS".

A few dared and dived for it, and N.C.O.'s were immediately sent in chase and they were brought out (after the N.C.O.'s had quenched their thirst). One poor soul who had not been, was heard confiding that he would have gone too, but thought "Boissons" was French for fish. His sorrow was alleviated however by those who had been, and declared that the sign should have read "POISSONS" or even "POISON".

We were soon on the march again, leaving the business quarter behind, along to the residential outskirts, along the fine promenade, past the Kursaal (now being used as a hospital) and on to the foot of the hill of Ingouville.

Wise authorities decreed that Rest Camps in France should invariably be situated at the top of a hill, the higher and steeper the better. This is to ensure that everyone who arrives is really in need of a rest.

The Officer in charge of the draft had been unable to find any transport to convey his kit to the Rest Camp, and it had been carried along in turn to the back of the procession, by men of the draft. It was a most inopportune moment for such a thing to happen as we were just pulling ourselves together for the last weary lap up the hill, but just then someone came along the ranks and asked if Pat and I had yet done a turn at carrying the kit. We endeavoured to look as if he was speaking to someone else, but his query was too pointed and well directed to miss, so we pleaded guilty and expressed our pleasure at being allowed to assist in any way that might bring the war to an early and successful conclusion, right the wrong of Belgium, roll back the invading Hun, and – er – carry the blessed kit. We were soon of the opinion that the officer had made a very big hole in his Kit Allowance, and had left nothing behind him.

We discovered his name on the kit and wondered if he would provide for our wives and children, should either or both of us die from a broken heart before we reached that Rest Camp. We were saved from this fate, being relieved by two more unlucky mortals who did not seem as pleased to see the kit, as we were, to lose sight of it. Eventually we reached the top of the hill and found the Rest Camp.

The most noticeable features of a Rest Camp are its latrines and refuse incinerators, then one notices that the tents are in bad repair.

We were numbered off into tents, care being taken to put sufficient men into each tent to prevent the canvas from shrinking. After being supplied with a meal we were informed that any letters for post would be collected for censoring in an hours time. Then brains were racked as to what might, may, should or could be put in a letter. Was the officer married or single? Callous or sympathetic? Would it be wise to address the wife as pre-censorship days, or would it be wiser to address her as "Dear Mary Jane" and stand the chance of her thinking that you were quickly cooling off? Enough information however was a way to let interested persons know that we had safely crossed the channel, and that no submarine had interfered with our affairs sufficiently to cut our budding military careers short, in favour of Channel swimming.

After finding out that there was no chance of having a look round Havre, we made for the next place of interest – the Canteen. One locates a canteen in a camp by the direction of the traffic. On arriving there, an enquiry for "Bass" elicited the fact that "Beer only" was sold. The French barman evidently was under the impression that what we required was a fish shop. The beer itself was distinctly discouraging, so we went dry and tried the coffee in the dry canteen. When this excitement palled, we returned to our tent and got into our blankets for the night. Having been unlucky in the scramble for places, we were fixed up near the tent flap, and made a capital door mat for the latecomers.

3 December

We rose to find that the winter had fallen upon us, the ground was frozen hard, and all water supplies in a similar state. A search round the ablution benches only discovered bowls frozen to the benches and a disconsolate batman bemoaning the fact that he could get no hot water for the C.O.'s bath. As a mark of sympathy with the C.O. we did not continue our search. Breakfast however turned up, and by going steady with the tea, a warm shave and a lather brush wash completed our toilet. We hoped that the C.O. was as lucky.

As we had nothing to do but await orders after breakfast, a walk round the camp found a fine view of the harbour and bay. Outside the harbour could be discerned, the funnels and rigging of three steamers, evidently victims of the submarines. After dinner, other drafts came into camp and our tents being required we dumped our belongings on the parade ground, and sat on them, so that we would know where to look for them when they were wanted.

At dusk we left the Rest Camp and marched to the Railway station, and found the journey down the hill much more to our liking. This happened to be our last railway journey in passenger coaches for quite a long time. Had we known this, we might not have grumbled at the wooden seats as much as we did. The compartments were marked "III" but it did not say whether this was "A.D" or "B.C".

4 December

The train eventually reached Rouen before shaking to pieces, but it was evident that care had to be exercised, as about 8 hours were taken over a journey of something under forty miles. We were marched through the town to the Infantry Base depot on the outskirts. On this side of the town we passed the fine Race-course, where the huge grand-stand was in use as a hospital, and there is a maze of hospital camps in the district. We soon found the Reinforcement Camp but had some difficulty in locating the Cheshire lines (not managed by the C.L.C.), but on finding them at last, we were marched on to the parade ground, and immediately ordered to lay out our kits for inspection. There we learned still another "Only correct way" to lay out a kit for inspection. After being checked and found correct by our Bill of Lading, we were allowed to be present at a dramatic recital by the Regimental Sergt. Major, of the 110 Commandments. They seemed to be divided into two parts, the one part commencing with "No man shall" and the other part with "Any man found". The penalties for non-compliance with these orders did not seem so terrible, as when all was said, there was no threat of "the sack".

We were marched off to our tents by a sergeant, and warned for a medical inspection after dinner. This caused the usual rush to the wash houses, but they were found to be locked, and we learned that they were only available at such times as would prevent a passion for cleanliness overcoming one's love of parades.

The medical examination proved that the travelling had not caused sufficient physical deterioration to qualify for discharge, or even for a job at the Base.

After inspections and parades were over for the day and tea disposed of, Pat suggested a stroll into the town. Nothing doing however. Passes were required and for passes, names must be handed in to the Line Sgt. each morning, so we handed our names in for passes on the next day, and that was all we heard about it. A search for amusement within the camp revealed numerous canteens, a cinema, and Recreation Huts belonging to every religious denomination one could think of, perhaps with the exception of Christadelphians and Particular Baptists. The first was passed over without a second thought, as Pat had relinquished all hope of finding a "Bass" in France, and we decided for the Cinema. Officers 1 fr. N.C.O.'s 50 ctms. O.R. 20 ctms. You cannot live above your rank in the Army, even after parade hours in your amusements. You cannot pay for your good seat and ruffle it with the best of them. If the poor officer is broke, he must still pay his franc and go in the stalls, if the "other rank" is "flush" he may only pay his 20 centimes and chance the splinters.

To keep us warm while waiting for the programme to start, the pianist struck up "Keep the home fires burning" and the boys joined in with such fervour that made one fear the results of such a defiance of the Governments demand for economy in coal.

When we were thoroughly warmed up, we passed onto the "Long long trail" and "Are you from Dixie" put the light out. The great "Charlie" then did the best he could for us, considering the prices of admission. Next, we were entangled in five reels of a French domestic drama, and as the letter press of the plot was in French, and the scenes quite as French, we reserved our sympathy for the wronged husband, until such time as we found out which really was her husband. As it was almost time for "lights out" there was a scurry for tents. Oh why are all tents alike, and why do tent ropes spread like the tentacles of an octopus, and tent pegs leave no room to tread, when it grows dark.

A few intrusions and a few uncalled for remarks in reply to our polite apologies brought us at last to our own tent, tunics, boots and puttees off, and "lights out" was beaten by a few seconds.

5 December

About breakfast time some excitement was caused by the appearance of a French lady newsvendor gaily tripping along the lines calling "Engleesh papaire, vaire good news". On making a purchase the English paper was found to be the "New York Herald" and the "vaire good news" purely a matter of the lady's own optimism, at least it could not be found in the paper by anyone whose optimism was not highly developed. That this lady looked well upon the bright side of things was proved by the fact that some months earlier, when England was staggering under a sudden calamity, she had been heard calling "English papers, very good news, Kitchener dead".

After breakfast we were served out with bully and biscuit and marched off to the famous "Bull Ring" for a full days training. Enquiry as to why this ground was called the "Bull Ring" elicited the information that it was <u>because</u> Napoleon trained his troops there. In 1926 the joke still eludes me. The "Bull Ring" is actually a huge natural parade ground, where, when we arrived, cavalry, artillery, infantry, and even squads of Officers were being drilled. The Indian Cavalry were a fine sight to watch when opportunity occurred, which was not often. For us there was foot drill, physical training, bayonet fighting, bombing and firing which were all gone through again in tabloid form. We were also given a lecture on the new Box Respirator which evidently was a great improvement on the old "P.H." gas helmet, whose chief safeguard against gas seemed to be asphyxiation. We were put through the gas chamber in the old "P.H." helmet however, and those who were in too big a hurry to take their helmets off after leaving the chamber, found themselves treated to a little dose of Lachrymatory gas, whose effect in a minute or two was not so pleasant as that faint odour of pear drops that we were inquisitive about in the passage leading from the gas chamber.

5–9 December

We spent the week training, one day being set apart for a special stunt, a miniature start of the Somme offensive. I was marked down as a casualty within a minute or two of the opening. My wounds were not too painful to prevent my enjoyment of the spectacle while waiting for the stretcher bearers, who did not seem in a great hurry. Casualties here, had their own choice of wounds, and they all seemed to prefer some wound which made it impossible to walk a step, much to the disgust of the stretcher bearers. After some argument with the stretcher bearers who came at last to attend to me, I was bundled unceremoniously on to a stretcher with my mess tin making itself unpleasant in the middle of my back, despite the fact that both my legs had been shattered (in theory).

Pat spent an exhausting afternoon jumping trenches and charging about, frisking like a lamb in May. When I met him afterwards, he did not seem as pleased as he might have done, at coming through safely, but would make unpleasant remarks about "scroungers" in general and particular.

The weekend found us served out with 120 rounds of ·303, gas helmets (old P.H.), fur coats, trench gloves and also our first pay in France – 5 francs.

Saturday morning was spent getting the fat out of the new rifles, cleaning the bayonets, and splitting thumb nails opening butt traps to find if the oil bottle and pull-thro. were where they should be.

10 December

Sunday morning, heard we were to leave in the afternoon for the 6th Battn. and from two boys in the tent who were returning from Hospital, we gathered that the battalion was last heard of in the Ypres Salient. What a nice cheery outlook.

Some difficulty was experienced in balancing a jerkin and two blankets on the top of a full pack but after dinner we were ready to start.

We thought we knew before, what Full Marching Orders meant, but we found we were mistaken. To Rouen station that day, was the longest march of two miles that I had yet dropped across, and I sat on my pack at the station and wondered whether we should ever have to walk more than about two miles again with the same load.

We had evidently now become goods traffic, as we used the goods siding, and our train was made up of covered vans. There was to be no overcrowding, that was plain, for each truck was marked with its holding capacity, which was 40 men or 8 horses per truck. That is where the horse has the pull. We were delighted to find that it was not to be a mixed freight, as 20 men and four horses in a van would be some proposition.

Although we had no horses in our van, evidence was not wanting that horses had been there. I have heard many discussions since then, as to why trucks were not always cleaned out after having horses on board, and the popular theory seems to have been that, during the war, many of the troops were much below the physical standard of – say the Grenadier Guards, and it may have been possible that the authorities were experimenting to find out whether "Bantams" planted in trucks at the Base, might add cubits to their stature on their journey to the line.

There is not much chance of choosing your spot when forty of you have managed to get in with all their equipment. The choice place however during daylight seemed to be at the sliding doors with the legs dangling out. This is not so dangerous on a troop train in France as might appear at first sight, as anyone dropping out while the train was in motion could usually join the train again, a few trucks lower down, after giving himself time to dust himself.

This position has all the advantages during daylight, one's legs hanging outside cannot be trodden on, then the scenery can be admired or otherwise as it deserves, pieces of biscuit can be shied at passersby, chat can be passed with "Ma" who deputises at small stations for hubby who is at the war. He is at Verdun of course. It is a peculiar fact that all the married soldiers of France fought at Verdun. This was proved from little conversations one often heard. "Votre homme un soldat. Madame?" "Oui!! Oui!!" "a Verdun?" "Oui!! Oui!! M'sieu".

Of course it may have been that they could not understand our French, and like us, when we did not understand theirs, they smiled and chanced "Oui Oui!!"

It was getting dusk and card parties in the inner recesses of the trucks were only carried on by the aid of stumps of candles stuck on the floor in the middle of each little circle. Efforts had been made to stick the candles on the sides of the van, but they would persist in getting jogged off and falling into someone's neck or pocket.

The advantages of a front seat faded when darkness fell and legs were tucked in and the doors rolled into their places. All other berths being taken up, the only thing now was heads or backs to the door and legs where one could get them without causing bloodshed. Eighty legs on the floor left no room for candles, so things were soon quiet and the only light showing being from cigarette ends, relieved occasionally by illuminating remarks addressed to those who had decided against taking their boots off. Legs were arranged more or less amicably and the rattle of wheels and doors soon became drowned in the opening bars of a Symphony of Somnolence. Those poor souls who were against the doors however found out that the only way to beat the draught that caught them, was to wrap their heads up in a blanket and jam a steel helmet on top of that, and even then it seemed that the engine had regained its lost youth, and made some speed solely to increase the draughts.

11 December

When daylight again began to show through the chinks in the floor and at the doors, stirrings and gruntings commenced, and anyone treating himself to a stretch quickly learned with some emphasis, that his ancestry (if he had any), be a clumsy footed race, and suffered from a lack of anything pertaining to intelligence or good morals.

Attempts to roll back the doors were hampered by a few who evidently thought it against all military precedence to rise before "Reveille" was blown, and failing "Reveille", the correct thing was not to get up at all. With a little moral persuasion however a move was made. We were all horribly stiff and sore, and failing room for a run round to warm our feet and loosen our joints, the flooring was treated to a stamping of 80 feet to the accompaniment of that famous song "What did I join the Army for".

Nobody had slept a wink, of course they never do, some had been so much awake to know that we had passed through Paris, some said Marseilles, another man was correct in saying that we had been travelling northwards, as he had seen the North Star all night, through a chink in the far end of the truck, evidently a cigarette end.

We tried to get our bearings from little stations we passed through, but there are evidently more places in France than appear on school maps. One man was bothered because all the stations seemed to bear the same name – "Dames – Hommes".

The first place we reached that we had heard of before was St Omer, and catching a glimpse of the ruins of the Benedictine Abbey there, we were guilty of our injustice to the Hun by laying the damage at his door. We were correct however in placing the damage visible at the station itself to those responsible. Glass was mostly conspicuous by the holes it had left empty in windows and roofs. During the halt here, a raid was made on the engine with mess tins and dry tea, for hot water.

The reason was now plain for the lack of speed, as we found out that the engine had evidently been running on tepid water.

Before we left again, a terribly long hospital train drew in from the direction in which we were to go, filled from end to end with bunks occupied by soldier debris. Who is it that has omitted to paint a picture for the War Collection, entitled "The up line, and the down line".

One lay by an open window and was hailed by an "up liner".

"Nice bloomin' return tickets they gives yer, chum". The "chum" turned his head slightly and found a grin for the occasion, and his reply was somewhat comforting. "'Ell of a sight better than a single". Those hospital trains seemed splendidly equipped and everything made for comfort, but somehow made us feel more content with our own accommodation, and as one man put it – "Better travelling 3rd with two legs, than first with one".

Leaving St Omer we were soon in Belgium, and were soon interested in seeing fields with innumerable stark hop poles standing in wonderfully straight lines. This was taken as a good omen, but it was eventually found out that Belgium beer was much the same as French.

The end of our rail journey was Poperinghe, about 6 miles west of Ypres, arriving there after 23 hours travelling from Rouen. Equipment and belongings took some sorting out, but we were soon formed up in the little station square, where we were served out with Iron Rations. These consisted of one tin of Bully, a few biscuits, and a small tin of dry tea and sugar. These are only meant to be carried about, to be produced for inspection when demanded. They are only to be consumed in the last extremity, and then only by order of an officer. It took us some little time to find out that the "last extremity" was often interpreted as "feeling like a bit of supper" and officers orders taken for granted, the fear of consequences being less in ratio to one's ability to "scrounge" the necessaries before the next inspection, or to tell a good tale.

A gaze round the square convinced us that we were getting somewhere near the war, and if that had been wanting, the rumble of guns would have done just as well.

On one side of the station stood the remains of a restaurant with a sign still left hanging, informing arrivals that "Bifstik" could be procured at all hours of the day, and opposite the station was a large YMCA hut. This was not open just then, but a few of us were lucky enough to obtain a drink of tea at the back door before being called back on parade.

Poperinghe, in peace times with a population of about 12,000, was then the last town of any size left in Belgium. The larger part of the population had left, but there still remained the courageous element with the business instinct, who found in Tommy a good source of income. Almost every shop then had stocks of chocolate at such prices as only a soldier could pay, souvenirs of Ypres were offered in great variety, silk table centres and handkerchiefs depicting Ypres Cloth Hall wrapt in most gorgeous flames and sprinkled over with shell bursts in colour schemes undreamt of by Brock. Real Brussels lace all the way from Nottingham, metal miniatures of German helmets, inkpots from shell cases, and above all, silk and lace postcards with loving messages addressed to any possible relation Tommy may have left behind him.

We soon learned too, what Tommy's special dish was on his evening out. Besides little eating houses, drapers shops, ironmongers and grocers shewed in their windows a card bearing the legend "Coffee, eggs and chips". Nearly all the estaminets too had cards in the windows with the information that English Beer, extra strong was sold within. Soon we came into the square, at one corner of which stood quite a smart modern Town Hall quite untouched by shell fire. The cellars of this place were used as a shelter during shelling or bombing, while almost opposite was a fine old church which had been badly battered by shells. Behind the church was a large brewery, the larger part of whose premises was used as a Divisional bath. This fact caused some misgivings about the qualities of that "English Beer, extra strong".

Passing through the square we soon arrived at our billet for the night, this was an empty convent, much knocked about. No windows were left. Some were boarded up, and others were hung over with sacking. Cookers had been sent down from the battalion and we were served with a hot meal. We were not allowed out of the billet, but in one room a Belgian woman and her daughter did a big business in coffee, biscuits and chocolate.

We were not long in getting down for the night and a few draughts did not interfere with a good night's sleep.

12 December

We had a blizzard during the night, it was still snowing hard when we rose and there was a fair amount of snow in the room. A hurried hunt at the back of the premises for wash, found a few bowls and a broken pump. In the hurry of ablutions, a square hole in the pavement was not noticed by everyone. Pat pushing out backwards from the washing bench polishing himself with a nice clean towel, suddenly disappeared from sight. When he re-appeared he informed us that it was a many times qualified coal hole. From his appearance and the appearance of his towel, we had already gathered that it was a coal hole, but we were quite interested to hear what a special kind of coal hole it really was. This was noted as the last time that Pat was ever seen with a clean towel. The next man who disappeared down the coal hole was more lucky, as the last we saw of him, a few minutes later, he was being carried off to hospital on a stretcher.

We left our billet in the afternoon, to join the battalion, back through Poperinghe, passing the station, and out by the Poperinghe – Ypres road. The snow had messed things up somewhat, and the road was a quagmire. There was no martial sound of marching men, but just a "swish swish" as we moved along. About two miles down the road we turned off into a by-way on the left which was even worse than the main road.

It was now getting dark, but we had not much further to go. We halted at a corner where we could discern a Church Army Hut, and a Church of England Hut, so sinners were evidently close at hand. Beyond, we could make out a wood and a few lights moving about. This was evidently "D" Camp which was our destination.

At this corner, a cart track struck off the road into the wood, but it was then in such a state that I doubt whether any vehicle could have got through it. Along each side of the track duckboards were laid, and after some delay, we endeavoured to make our way along these.

It is unfortunate when the acquaintance of strange duckboards must be made in the dark. They are much more friendly and better understood when met in the daylight. There is the duckboard who likes to "hold his end up" a few inches above the end of his neighbour, and the one that is "at a loose end" which loose ends playfully rattles your shin bone as you pass along. Then one who has lost a few ribs in the war and likes you to put your foot in the gap as you pass by. The most villainous duckboard of all in wet weather, however, is the one with the side slope. The unwary one in the darkness usually dances a few hectic steps on it and is then posted as missing till he cleans himself up in the morning. To be told to "get a move on in front" when you are trying to decide whether you left the duckboard on your right or your left as you fell off it, is one of the encouragements to calm and reflective speech, that one so often meets with in the Army. We successfully reached our objective however, which turned out to be company dining huts which was evidently the only accommodation available. Some tea was soon served and later on in the evening we were served out with our first rum ration, two spoons full which at that time seemed quite a lot.

Bed time caused some shuffling about, some fixed up on the tables, some on forms, and the remainder on the floor. Pat and I fixed ourselves alongside a brick fireplace in the centre of the hut, joining forces with our blankets making two into four. It was a nice warm spot, but we were a bit bothered during the night by a man who was lying across in front of the fire.

He had a troublesome cough and an unpleasant and frequent habit of expectorating at the fireplace. It was not his cough that troubled us, but the expectation of his expectorations missing the fireplace. Fortunately he attended sick parade the following morning and that was the last we saw of him.

13 December

We were up betimes as the hut was required for breakfast. First the usual rush and hunt for the ablution benches, with a feeling of thankfulness that we had not cleaned our boots first, as it was ankle deep in mud on the way to the wash.

Our hut was "A" boys' "Dining Hall" and soon the company came trooping in for breakfast. The battalion had recently come up from the Somme front and talk was of St Pierre Divion, Schwaben Redoubt and Thiepval and many hair raising tales were passed about, possibly with a little "pep" added for the benefit of the newcomers. We were however made very welcome, and knowing that the battalion had been in France since 1914, it was a pleasant surprise to hear no remarks about "Derbies".

As soon as breakfast was over, the new draft was paraded for inspection by the Colonel, a fine soldierly officer whom we soon learned to respect. He was accompanied by the Adjutant Lt Naden who looked an equally keen officer and who was to gain even more than our respect before we had known him long. The C.O. and the Adjt. followed up by the R.S.M. weighed up our visible merits and demerits and we were pronounced "a good draft" also duly informed that we had come to a fine battalion, and would be expected to do credit to it. Altogether a much better welcome than we expected, after experiencing a certain welcome to the 3rd Battalion at Birkenhead.

The four company Quarter Master Sergeants were on parade and the draft was divided into four portions, and each Q.M.S was given each a portion to march off to his Company Officer for a further inspection. Our portion was destined for "A" Company and we were marched off to our Company Orderly Room.

This was a small hut, where behind a little table just inside the door of the hut sat Capt. "S" with his second in command. We passed to the door one by one, had our particulars entered up from our paybook and passed along, to be divided up again into platoons. Platoons were still further divided up into Lewis Gunners, Bombers and Riflemen. To finish up with, Pat and I found ourselves members of a Lewis Gun team of 6.

In the afternoon, the whole draft was again inspected, this time by the Medical Officer on a hunt for scabies. Scabies, we learned later, were little itching spots which first appear on the hands and chest. If judiciously encouraged with a stiff brush, and kept out of sight for a few days until fairly ripe, they are reckoned worth at least 10 days in hospital.

14–24 December

The next day we commenced our training on the Lewis Gun under 265604 Cpl. Jack Isaacs from Stalybridge and soon learned enough about the gun to call him "Jack". We took our instructions in the dining hut with the gun lying on the table between us, and it was about the softest job in training that we had yet struck. We soon knew enough about the gun to be able to smoke and listen to yarns until some intrusive officer or Sgt. Major was heard about, and then we at once got busy juggling with the radiator and talking learnedly about pistons, cams, ejectors, return coils and whatnot. A safe way was always to take the gun to pieces first thing, and then in case of surprise, it was either being "taken down" or "put up".

The monotony was relieved one day by someone forgetting that a charge had been left in the breech, and pulling the trigger. A Lewis Gun may miss fire at times, but never yet when it wasn't intended to fire.

Jack Isaac's expletive sounded almost like a second round let loose. The bullet disappeared through the end of the hut and we all expected an immediate rush on the hut and an immediate arrest, but no one seemed to have heard it, so we quickly scouted as far as we could along the line of fire, but found no one in trouble, then patched up the bullet hole in the wall, and kept quiet about it.

Friday December 15th 1916

Dear Mammy,

I have been served with my first green envelope today, so am making use of it straight away.

I am keeping just tip top and if the Army folks were not so long in getting your letters along to me, I would be without a grumble. There was a big mail up last night and I think we all dreamt of having nice long letters from home in the morning, but there was nothing for our lot when the bag got sorted out.

We are about 4 miles behind the firing line here, and things have been very quiet in this section lately, in fact the boys of our battalion who came out of the trenches as we arrived tell the yarn that they took a line over from the French, and as most of them came from this part, their wives used to take their meals up to them. However things began to hum yesterday and all last night our artillery were giving the Allemands some awful wipers. A big thunderstorm was like a penny pop gun against the row.

We are living in a wood and considering all conditions, are wonderfully comfortable, but I wish now I hadn't grumbled so about the mud in dear old blighty, t'was such a trifle after all. We find very soon out here, that training is a comparatively cushy job at home. We get plenty to eat and of course we can sleep when the time comes, and really the only thing we badly want is some clean water to have a wash. Of course we do wash in a kind of water, and if we whirl it about quick enough, we finish a shade or two cleaner than when we started, but I have seen no one brave enough to wash his teeth with it yet. We get tea twice a day, but no drinking water. You can quite understand this if you could see the poor horses dragging the water carts here from a distant town.

Nunn and I have, since we came to France, become closer friends than ever, as from sleeping in beds next to one another, we have now come to sleeping in the same blanket, so when I come home, if I happen to bring any small but affectionate friends with me, you must blame him, as I am sure he will do the same to me.

Both of us have been picked out for Lewis gunners and are on the same gun team which consists of 6 men. We are busy learning all about our new gun before the battn. goes in again. We are already getting adept at taking her to little bits and putting her together again, and I feel sure I shan't have to take my watch to the jeweller in an envelope the next time I pull that to pieces. She is a wonderful little thing (much better than Billy's big awkward things) and she can pump out 600 to the minute if we can only feed the brute quickly enough. We have a little cart for her when there is room, something like a little bakers errand boy cart, but we are open to give any errand boy at Heaton Chapel, half the length of the Moor in a race. Of course she has all the nasty tricks of her late rival (rifle) and will I suppose get jammed occasionally, but as we have now got 6 of us to swear at her she may prove quite docile, and then we are to carry revolvers instead of rifles, so I should know something about firearms soon. They are very useful things to carry on your shoulder too, as our instructor shewed us two nasty marks on the gun case caused by shrapnel while he was going "over the top" with it on his shoulder, so they make a very decent muffler.

We are finding that the nearer one gets to the war, the less one knows about it. I haven't seen a paper since I left the base, when Lloyd George had just fixed up his new cabinet. Up here this is the sort of thing we hear – "Has anyone seen a paper?" "No, but a chap tells me that Lloyd G. has just refused Germany's peace terms, and all the others have accepted and are going to fight against us." and so on Ad. Lib.

I think I gave you my address in my last letter, but in case you havn't got it properly I give it you again. Pt. WW No 15362. No1 Platoon. A Company 6th Batt., Cheshire Regt. B.E.F. France. You must put France although as a matter of fact we ain't, but of course we may be moved to any part of the line as wanted. You may find 'un clé' to this on the first page.

The weather keeps very wet here which doesn't improve the state of the ground, but it isn't very cold with it which is a comfort.

Now I am just waiting for a nice long letter to turn up telling me how you all are, and what you and Jim have been doing with yourselves since I left you both at Preston.

Just fancy 10 days only to Christmas. I could have done with just another week or two in the old country to see Christmas over, but I musn't grumble, but for goodness sake don't stuff Jimmy with my share of pudding and turkey or he will be sick for sure, but you can try it yourself if you like. I should be glad to hear that your appetite was as good as ever.

I should dearly like to know too how Joe is getting along, although I expect you have written. Give my love to Granny, Madge and Nancy if she is still at Mayfield, and if you and Granny Williamson swap letters, this is as far as she is permitted to go.

Give the boy a big kiss from his Dad and a loving husband's hug and a dozen for yourself,   from Walter

About a week later we heard that the Commander-in-Chief – Sir Douglas Haig was to inspect the Brigade. The day before he was expected, a dress rehearsal was held near the camp. It was a pouring wet day and in "full marching order", the Brigade was paraded and went through a few evolutions, and splashed about generally. Senior

Officers even could not do things right the first time, and the ranks hugely enjoyed seeing junior officers trying to do their best with what little they had not forgotten about "Review Order", and being drilled till they managed it better. After a march past in six inches of mud we spent the rest of the day in getting clean again for the next day.

The following morning found the camp a bit hectic and everyone was busy seeing the camp and huts were made as like a garden village as possible, but the rain still poured down and the camp seemed to sink lower into the quagmire.

All equipment was spick and span again and ready to be put on, but no one seemed to know what time the parade would be. The afternoon came with news that there would be no parade, but the Commander-in-Chief would inspect the men in their billets. If he did not turn up quickly, he would have to carry a candle round our hut, as it was dark even in the daylight, and what little bit of daylight there had been that day, was quickly disappearing. Each company was collected into its own dining hut, and shortly afterwards we heard the "General Salute" sounded (Bob Smith got a stripe for blowing it well that day).

We were lined up round our hut and presently the "R.S.M." "shunned" "A" Company into a lot of statues, then round the hut whirled a quick procession of red tabs and gold braid followed up by our C.O., Adjt. and R.S.M. and disappeared through the door again. Only a few minutes later, and the "General Salute" sounded again, he was gone. That was how the "C.I.C." came to "D" Camp.

An event of perhaps more moment to us than to the O.C. this time, happened a day or two later. Due warning was given out in "Orders" the previous evening. "A" Company will parade for baths 9.0 a.m.

There was no trouble to get the men "Fell in" for that parade. There was a divisional Bath close to the camp. There were no baths at the "Baths" as a matter of fact. "Wash-houses" they should be called but I suppose the word "Baths" has been kept as an encouragement to newcomers. A dozen or so overhead sprays usually (and some strong soap) completes the actual "bathing", after "peeling", and a reminder to a heap of clothes to be good and still till you come back, there is a wild skating along wet duckboards round a partition to the showers. The rush is to get under a shower if possible by oneself if only for sufficient time to get wet all over before being joined by four or five others. If you manage to get at a shower with no more than four of you at it "your jams in". The short man has rather a rough time of it. Even under the centre of the shower with the taller men round him, he can keep as dry as a bone, while the other four divide the available water between them. His only chance is on the outside catching the splashes, meanwhile keeping a sharp eye open for the first man who drops his soap through the duckboards, and then to dash in.

There is no such thing as waiting for a place till the others have finished. No one ever finished yet in a Divisional Bath. Too often has one just got nicely soaped when the water is turned off and the stentorious voice of the Scottish N.C.O. in charge of the bath orders "all Hoot". (Note) "(A Scottish N.C.O. is invariably placed in charge of a bath to see that the water is not wasted.)" Another slither back round the partition, a good rub down, and the B.E.F. man then whistles to his old underclothes which get up and follow him affectionately round a corner, and run up a partition and are caught in a grip of iron by a man behind an opening, who has been specially trained for this work. He drags them in and by virtue of long practice, recognises them as Shirt, Pants, Vest and Socks, and drops them into a heap for the lethal chamber, and in return, to the late owner, he hands out four small checks marked respectively "S" "P" "V" and "Sox". There are people who still maintain that our "Staff" work in France was anything but brilliant, but the "Sox" reputes the unkind aspertion. Someone evidently knew that "shirt" and "socks" are both spelled with an initial "s" and to avoid the chance of any man being issued with two shirts in exchange for a shirt and a pair of socks, or two pairs of socks, this clever plan had evidently been thought out. One can easily tell whether the waters of Lethe at the local Lethal Chamber have been on the boil, by looking for any signs of life in the little black specks on the fresh garments. Then long men commence to struggle into short pants, and short men get lost in big shirts. The thin man invariably gets served with anything over a forty inch vest, and the big stout man's luck in vests should be marked with a big S.W.

Socks are all one size for guardsmen or bantams any variation only being caused by the different styles of darning. Bathing is evidently considered a risky business judging by the time that is allowed for a bath, and by the time that is allowed to elapse between them, also by the fact that we were served out with rum again that evening.

On December 22nd, Christmas services, ditto pudding and extra rum engendered a suspicion that further celebrations on the 25th would not be of too festive a character.

Our suspicions proved correct as we had orders to move on the 24th. The morning was spent in loading up the Lewis Guns and ammunition on the little Lewis Gun carts, and the Lewis Gunners were to drag these up, while the remainder of the battalion took trains from Brandhoek to Ypres, our destination being the reserve line on the Yser Canal in front of Ypres. We started off before dark, each gun team with its own cart, one man at the shafts and the others at the ropes. The place in the shafts was not a comfortable job, as, the carts being without springs, every bump seemed to rattle one's bones. We made good pace along the roads, but when it came to cross-country work the fun commenced. It was a blessing for the man at the shafts, that the position there was not a permanent one, and that each took his turn at it. It was his place to see that the cart ran on its wheels and not its head, his place to see that it ran into no shell holes, although dragged there by the men at the ropes, his place to steer clear of ruts and holes, his place to yell "steady" and be ignored. No matter what accident happened to the cart, his was the blame. As darkness came on, things began to get quite interesting as the only way to find ruts and shell holes, was by getting into them, and the cart itself turned out to be a sleuth at the job, and did not seem to be able to miss at all.

Once it lost a wheel, once it broke a shaft, and once or twice it lay on its side, and scattered our packs which we had put aboard, into the mud.

Eventually we arrived with it on its wheels to a road running along near the bank of the Yser Canal. What a jumble of horse and motor transport, Lewis Gun Carts and infantry here. Horses breathed steamy nothings down one's neck, and were none too careful with their feet. Backing politely to give it a bit more room one would get the choice of a big "W.D." motor without lights, and decide quickly that the horse was not so bad.

We were halted at the ruins of a building that was known as "The Red Heart Estaminet". It was difficult to imagine it as a convivial spot. Plenty of orders were being given, but not for drinks. The road here was churned up ankle deep in mud, horses champing, stamping, and slithering against one another. Limber wheels were getting interlocked and drivers quoting wholesale from Deuteronomy. To add to the gaiety of things a few shells screamed overhead into Ypres. At last we got moving again and pulled our carts round to the rear of the estaminet and unloaded them. Putting packs on, and carrying the guns and ammunition, we set off in Indian file. My load was two or three panniers of ammunition, and I immediately floundered into a shell hole up to my waist in water. I managed to scramble out quickly and join on the end of the line again. We reached the canal bank, slithered down a steep path to a footbridge and crossed to the further bank. Half way up this bank, numerous dugouts had been made and a duckboard track laid along the front of the entrances. After groping some distance along the duckboards, we found an empty dugout, and flung ourselves down with our baggage, dead beat, muddy and bad tempered. Someone sticking up a candle we found ourselves in what was termed an "Elephant" dugout. Perhaps a dozen men could lay down in it. The roof was lined with corrugated steel and floored with duckboards, under which water lay. A portion of the flooring had evidently been used up for fuel, but as we could all find room on what remained of the flooring, we did not worry. We had only been in a few minutes when an officer of the "Black Watch" put his head in, and inquired who and what we were. On being informed, he ordered us out again, as it appeared that we were in a dugout allocated to his battalion, and we found ourselves out again on the duckboards, hoping that we should find our right dugout before we slipped off the beastly duckboards into the murky waters of the Yser Canal. We were in luck's way however and dropped across our platoon sergeant who soon shepherded us safely into the dugout where we found our platoon already comfortably ensconced, a much better dugout than the one we had left, perfectly dry, and quite roomy enough for the platoon.

After drawing rations, arranging gas guards and hearing the morrow's orders read, we settled down for the night, or at least for what was left of it, and were quite undisturbed by any carol singers.

25 December

Christmas morning heralded nothing special in the way of festivities. There was the usual difficulties in making "dixies orderlies" understand that it was their turn for duty. After breakfast, some cleaning up, rifle inspections, and some speeding up drill with the new respirators which had been issued to us before we left camp.

The Lewis Guns then had to be taken down and cleaned, ammunition magazines emptied and the ammunition all cleaned. This was quite a good job and could usually be made to last out other people's inspections etc., if a quiet corner could be found.

In the evening we heard that we were for a sandbagging fatigue up the line. Darkness found us in "Fighting Order" wending our way along the canal bank by the duckboard track. Turning off into a deep communication trench we were immediately startled by a notice board with the cheery notice "Wind Dangerous" and we fingered our respirators to make sure that they were at "The Alert" position. We did not know then, that the notice was there continually, wind or no wind.

The guide is usually less burdened than the party he guides, and he usually makes a pace that keeps the men behind him fairly warm. The new beginners amongst us find our first trip along communication trenches, quite an experience. The duckboard at the bottom leaves a space each side of the trench for drainage, and just wide enough to allow of a leg slipping down without skinning it more than one side, nor higher than the thigh, then a turning every few yards gets monotonous till one gets dizzy and in time, simply progresses by the momentum gained from bumps first one side of the trench and then the other, and from a horrible fear of losing sight of the man in front of you. When the guide gets tired, he halts and enquires if all are in touch, and the enquiry "All up?" goes down the trench dying away round the corners, and soon the answer comes up from the rear in the same words "All up", and off the procession moves again. Travelling some distance along this trench we came out on to a road which was in a state of repair that did not encourage anyone to hang about, and we quickly dropped into a continuation of the trench across the road. The further we travelled along the trench, it seemed to get into a worse state of repair. Duckboards which up to now had proved fairly friendly, now became a snare and a delusion, and instead of finding them more or less firmly fixed, they cropped up in places simply floating on a couple of feet of water, and as time does not allow of testing each board before trusting it, other things than ardour got considerably damped. In places, the sides of the trench had collapsed under the too pressing attentions of a shell, and here we had to scramble over a heap of mud mixed with broken timber and wire netting. It was up here that we dropped across "Broad Street" where no doubt the famous "Broad Street Brawl" was practised.

Our destination proved to be Hill Top Farm. We recognised this as a farm by a few bricks in the sides of the trench, and the stumps of two trees. Work was in progress here. A deep sap was being excavated, and, with the bags of smelly slob coming up mysteriously from the bowels of the earth, we were to strengthen the trench and make a strong point. This was no pleasant task. Sandbags full of wet Flanders bog are no light weight, and to get these to the top of the parapet already seven or eight feet high, sorely taxed what bit of muscle some of us had. An additional joy was the way the beastly stuff trickled in little icy rivulets down one's sleeves while trying to thrutch the bag over the top. During our work here, we could hear mysterious clankings, bumps, and stifled curses up above on the back of the trench. On investigation it turned out to be another fatigue party running rations up on little trucks on miniature rails. The exciting part about this job was the fact that one never knew what would happen to the truck when it came to the end of a rail section. There may be another section attached to it, or there may not. Twenty yards without coming off was reckoned good going. To return to our own job however we got so heartily sick and tired of it in an hour or two that we positively jumped at the chance of going out on the top of the trench to straighten things up a bit there. The Boche livened things up a little later by throwing over a few shells in our direction, and the corporal in charge ordered us into the mouth of the sap for cover.

As the shells were not falling particularly close, and the corporal in charge happened to be our friend of the Lewis Gunners, I fancy he thought it an opportunity to make good use of, so we had a little rest. After another spell of work the welcome order came at last "Get dressed".

This does not mean that we had been working like miners, but only referred to our equipment which we had taken off. After being counted and found correct we set off on the return journey to our dugouts in the canal bank. On the way back no one troubled to inquire whether we were "All up". I suppose it is taken for granted that instinct will prompt the way out of the line, but not up to it. We arrived back at the canal just as dawn was breaking on Boxing Day and found the cookhouse open with some hot soup for us, also some rum. There did not seem to be any teetotallers in our party, and even the novices were now able to manage the whole of their ration without the kind assistance of the sergeant.

26–28 December

After a sleep which dried our clothes somewhat, they still gave off an unpleasant smell and at mealtimes, every movement seemed to shake dried mud into our mess tins. In reply to a question as to why the mud should smell so, someone who was evidently after dinners that might be left, murmured "Bagged Boche".

This was our work each night that week, the only variation being in the weather, which treated us to everything but daylight and sunshine. Two nights of it were icebound and ice on duckboards is a state of things that leaves one without sufficient breath to express one's opinions at the time. Pat had a particularly heavy fall on the return journey one night and was quite unable to express his feelings fully till breakfast time the next day.

29 December

We were busy cleaning the Lewis Gun after breakfast when the Orderly Sgt. appeared, collected me, and marched me off to the orderly room. There were 3 other men on parade there, and while waiting further events, compared notes, and none of us had the faintest notion what the "jump" was. The Colonel, Adjutant and R.S.M. however emerged from the Orderly Room and eyed us over. Asking if we could write, we all pleaded guilty, but being only privates of course we could not be believed without proof. The Adjt. handed us his notebook and pencil and asked us to write down our names and regimental details. Three of us "passed" but the fourth man was "plucked", his plea that he "wasn't uster' writin' standin" being ignored.

A runner was then called to take us over to Brigade Headquarters to the Signal Officer there. Bde. H.Q. were in dugouts under the west bank of the canal. We were taken into a dugout and rather startled to find four or five wired beds and decided that a job on Bde. H.Q. would not be too bad. Here we met men from the Black Watch, Herts, and Cambs Regts, a battalion each of these, with our own battalion, composing our Brigade (118th). When the Signal Officer turned up, we found that we were candidates for a course of signalling. He was also inquisitive as to whether we could write.

After finding that we were so far advanced with our education, he gave us a dictation test. All passing, we were informed that we would be leaving the battalion on the following day for a signalling course at the 8th Corps Signal School. Reported back at our own Orderly Room, and on returning to the team, was met with a hurricane of enquiries. "What is it? 28 days scabies, or a course?" On hearing that it was "a course", the general opinion seemed to be "Mugs for luck". Pat seemed to think it was just as well, as he had given up hope of making me into a soldier.

30 December

11-15 a.m., the orderly Sgt pushed his head in the dugout and murmured sweetly "Williamson. W. parade Full Marching Order and two blankets orderly room 11-30 lucky b_ _ _".

Pat helped to put my "clobber" together and strapped me to it, warning me never to take it off again till I returned, as I certainly would never be able to put it together again without his help. Prompt at 11-30 found the other two men, Leather and Speight at the orderly room, where we were handed the usual nominal roll of ourselves, addressed to the "O.C. Signal School, "V" Camp" and instructed to get the Vlamertinghe Bus at 2.30. If it had been anyone less omnipotent than the "R.S.M." we might have had courage to ask for a little more information about the Vlamertinghe bus, but as we were dismissed and told that we had plenty of time to do it in, we left it at that.

The first thing to do after crossing the canal was to find the Brigade Canteen which was a much better affair than our own, and stock up with chocolates and biscuits, seeing that we had been paid two weeks pay before leaving. We decided that the Vlamertinghe bus must leave Ypres for Vlamertinghe, and as it evidently did not leave Ypres till 2.30, we thought it a good opportunity to have a look round Ypres, which we had not seen yet at close quarters.

On reaching Ypres we unanimously decided against having a look round, and thought that a bus much sooner than 2.30 would suit very well. Ypres neither looked nor sounded at all healthy, and like all good soldiers, we were very particular about our health.

Peeping out of the cellar we espied a worried looking "traffic bloke" and having regained our breath we sallied forth to ask him about the

Vlamertinghe "bus". He grinned, but was good natured enough not to ask "When did you come up". He pointed out the Vlamertinghe Road and told us that "anything" going that way would get to Vlamertinghe (with luck). We made tracks along the road, and in our callow inexperience expected the first motor going along to pull up and ask if we wanted a lift. The motors seemed to be in as big a hurry to get away from Ypres as we were, and it was quite a long time before one good soul pulled up his big "WD" wagon sufficiently to let us scramble on board, then we found he was short of cigarettes, that accounted for it. During the ride we developed the brainy idea that the Vlamertinghe bus actually started from Vlamertinghe, and tentative enquiries from our driver elicited the pleasant fact that a pal of his was picking up a party at Vlamertinghe church, or what was left of it, and at 2.30 prompt, a big "WD" drove up and picked up the party that had gathered there about 30 strong. Rifles and equipment were thrown in to make a comfortable foundation, and what was left of us, sat on top of it, and off we went.

We were expected to report at "V" Camp before 3.30 p.m. and the driver reckoned half an hour would do it. If we travelled at the same speed we came from Ypres we looked like doing some distance in the half hour. We were not long in reaching Poperinghe and through it into the heart of the 8th Army Corps Headquarters. We passed lines and lines of transport, motor parks, and camps of all letters but "V". When we had nearly reached open country again, the driver decided that we must have passed "V" Camp, so turned and drove back, making enquiries along the way, without result until we reached a cross road where we heard that if we took the road to the left, we would find our camp. The road here was not passable for big motors, so we unloaded ourselves, and the motor drove off and left us to our own devices. It was now half an hour after the time we were due to report at the Signal School. Before we set off as directed however, we made a further enquiry from a passer-by who upset things by being convinced that "V" Camp lay down the road to the right.

Tempers began to get short, and the remainder of the British Army, "A.S.C.M.T." more especially, appeared to be a lot of blithering idiots. We decided not to lose touch with that corner until it was definitely settled whether "V" Camp lay down the road to the right or down the road to the left. While we were having what must have sounded like a real good vestry meeting, a staff officer came along and wanted to know what all these men were hanging about the road for, and if we had no N.C.O. in charge.

We found we had a diffident L/C in the party, but he seemed at the moment as if he would willingly sell his dizzy rank for a mess of pottage or any other mess than the present mess. He was ordered to take us off the road and to send two men to Corps H.Q. at the Château Louvie a short distance along the road, and get the location of the camp from the Orderly Room there. It was getting dark when they returned with the information that the Orderly Room Sgt. there laid it down distinctly, after referring to a map, that we should take the road to the left, so we took it. We tramped on in the darkness, and found the road a particularly vile one, and the further we went, the more we were convinced that no camp lay in that direction. When at last the road led into the fields and disappeared altogether we squatted in the field and swore long and lustily. The two unfortunates who had been sent to the Château of course came in for special commendation. As nothing was to be gained by sitting there, out of the track of possible information, or even a less possible lift, we retraced our way. A passing cyclist could give us no information, and nearly lost his life by wishing us "A happy New Year when it comes". A second cyclist came along, and we were fully prepared to dash his brains out if he ventured to wish us the usual compliment. He was however of an enquiring disposition and asked what we were looking for. Various replies were tendered such as "Tickets", "Nuts" and "The end of the war". We despaired of asking for "V" Camp any more. We were beginning to think like Mrs Gamp, that "There 'ain't no sich thing". Evidently to pull his leg someone asked "Have you ever heard of a camp called "V"?" He actually knew the camp, having been there on a signal course. Strong men almost wept and the weaker ones grew hysterical. We were sobered by the remark that it was an 'ell of a way. It appeared that we must make our way right back to the main road, and take the other turn that had been in doubt from the start, and then keep straight on. An alternative was to call again at Corps H.Q. signals where they might run us up by motor. We got back again to the main road and found the Signal Office. Our N.C.O. went in to find the office while we dumped ourselves down outside. Of course we got no motor, but were provided with a guide to take us a short cut through the Château grounds. In the daylight and under other conditions we may have admired the grounds, but only the question of finding that blessed camp could be considered at the time. The guide at last passed us out through a big pair of gilded gates on to another high road, and according to his directions we should have been at the camp in ten minutes. Unfortunately for the ten minutes however, someone crossed the road to investigate a light that shewed through a chink in the shutter of a little building that loomed out of the darkness. A wild yell of "Beer" and the road was suddenly left quiet and deserted. Later when we resumed our journey, spirits were much brighter, and a few lights appearing down the road, we found at last to belong to "V" Camp. We reported at once to the S.M. who seemed to be labouring under the delusion that we had been spending the day in riotous living in Poperinghe (on ten francs) instead of reporting at 3.30 p.m. We of course stated the facts (with reservations regarding the estaminet along the road). We were handed over to a corporal who put us in a nice new Nissen hut, so new in fact that we were told to sweep the joiners shavings up before we did anything else. Some tea was supplied from the cookhouse and we settled down in the hut for the evening and made a closer acquaintance with our new friends, which included men from the Black Watch, Cambs, Herts, Kings Royal Rifles, London Scottish, Rifle Brigade and Sussex Regts, not to speak of a sprinkling of Artillery. The Artillery could easily be recognised by the fact that they arrived on horseback and seemed to possess an extraordinary amount of kit, a gunner in the Artillery seemed to possess a kit equal to that of a "Q.M.S." in the P.B.I.

Only one man of the Artillery seemed to have landed in our hut, but he evidently felt lonesome or unsafe amongst men who only possessed two blankets, and deserted us to join his own chums in another hut. We soon settled down for the night and left it till morning to find out about the camp.

1 January 1917

We were up betimes and the camp was explored whilst looking for a wash. It consisted of only about a dozen Nissen huts, a larger hut for dining, the ever present incinerator and the usual etceteras, but what pleased us most was, to find in the enclosure, a little cottage occupied by Belgians, where we could get coffee, chocolate, biscuits and various odds and ends.

After breakfast we were all paraded in the dining hut and made a fuller acquaintance with the Sgt. Major and our instructors. The instructors appeared to be a very decent set of chaps, but the Sgt. Major could be simply described as a Sgt. Major and left at that. He took a roll of names and when he saw my initials he hoped it was not a "h'omen", as "W.W." was a signal abbreviation for "Washout". Very Cheering. It was impressed on us that we were there for work, and not for a rest.

"Returned to Unit" was the penalty for doing those things which we ought not to do, and leaving undone those things which we ought to do, or in any other way annoying the Sgt. Major. On hearing the list of parades there did not seem to be much time left for getting into mischief. 7-0 to 8-0 a.m. P.T., 9 to 12-30 Signalling, 2-0 to 4-30 ditto, 5-30 to 6-30 lamp signalling. After that we were free till roll call, about 9.30 p.m. Seven "ack emma" (we are at a signal school now and don't forget it). "A" has suddenly become "Ack, "B" – beer, "D" – Don, "M" – Emma, "P" – Pip, "S" – Esses, "T" – Tock, "V" – Vick, and woe betide anyone forgetting in front of the Sgt. Major, and though "Thompson T" was always called on the roll as "Thompson, Tock", poor "Mitchell. J" was never heard called out as "Mitchell, Jock".

As I was saying – 7 a.m. Monday morning found us paraded on the road for "P.T.". This started off with a double along the road till out of the Sgt. Major's sight and then spells of quick step and double. While out we sighted the Château that we had met before and heard that it was the Château Louvie and head-quarters of Gen. Sir Hunter Weston, our Corps Commander. It was not a bad billet anyway, and we felt we could win the war if only we had a billet like it.

Later on we met "Old Hunter Bunter" as he was called. He would sometimes be out for a constitutional on his own, and on sighting him, of course everyone was put on the "qui vive" for a smart salute, as a smart salute to a general seems to be the one thing that makes a good soldier. On returning to camp there was a rush to the cottage in the camp, for coffee. Here we made the acquaintance of Rosie, her mother, father, and little sister. Rosie was the linguist of the family, she spoke a little English and a deal of "Army Talk", and was not afraid of the whole British Army. She served out the coffee and kept the troops in order, while "Ma" counted the biscuits out and collected the money. Pa's occupation was stoking the stove, grinding the coffee and keeping the pot boiling. The big coffee pot seemed to have been cleaned last about the time of the last great war. Rosie's leanings (if she had any) seemed to be towards Scots, as kilts seemed to occupy the warmest corner near the stove. This of course may have only been sympathy on account of the cold weather and the bare knees. One man alone seemed to be specially favoured, sometimes even allowed to grind the coffee, and it was rumoured that he had been seen squeezing her hand. The poor girl was sadly deceived as he was a bit of real cockney in the London Scottish and three poor Dundee lads of the Black Watch were filled with disgust every time Rosy called him "Écossai". Too much time could not be spent over the morning coffee as breakfast was served soon after returning from "exercise".

After breakfast classes were formed and work commenced. Lamp parade after tea finished work for the day. Choice of recreation afterwards was more plentiful than the time at our disposal. There was of course, more coffee to be had at Rosie's in the evening, and just outside the camp were two estaminets where one could endeavour to get hardened to Belgian beer. Most of the men however made straight off for Poperinghe where one was not limited to two or even twenty estaminets. For the "non-swimmers" there were as many "egg and chips" shops as estaminets, or a visit to "The Hollies" (the 39th Divisional Concert Party) who were then giving a good show in Poperinghe. For a quiet read with a dip into a good library, a game of chess, or billiards, or a quiet chat, "Talbot House" was the place.

A large house in Rue de l'Hôpital, it was one time residence of a wealthy Poperinghe brewer, whose dislike to the place dated from the day of the arrival of a shell from the direction of Pilkem Ridge, which was the means of forming an ornamental lake in the garden at the rear of the house.

The house was called after the Rev. N. S. Talbot. M.C. late Assistant Chaplain General to the 5th Army, who was the moving spirit in obtaining the premises and starting it as a sort of "Everyman's Club".

The presiding genius at that time was the garrison Chaplain of Poperinghe, the Rev. P. B. Clayton M.C. who will long be remembered by the boys who used "Talbot House". His genial wit and the seams of his tunic were always bursting forth, and with the finances of the "House" as with his "Sam Browne", he was always trying to make ends meet.

It was to "Talbot House" that we were marched down each Sunday morning to Church Service, which was held in a large hop warehouse at the rear of the premises. This room was used during the week for Concerts, lectures and debates organised by "P.B.C.". After service, the men were marched back to camp but Communicants had permission to remain behind for Celebration. The Chapel where Celebration was held and where Evensong was held each evening, was a wonderful place, and was the pride of "Talbot House". It had a comforting peaceful beauty of its own. It was situated in the loft and was reached by a very steep and awkward little staircase. Gifts from Units, Officers and men, and the loving labour of "P.B.C" with willing helpers had made an "Upper Chamber" that will not be soon forgotten by thousands of the "B.E.F." who knew it.

Many received the sacrament there for the first time, and many for the last. A confirmation chair in the Chapel there was given in memory of a boy who was killed in 1917, and who had been baptised, confirmed and received his first Communion there within six weeks.

"P.B.C's" room was on the floor below the Chapel, a card on the door bearing the legend "Abandon rank all ye who enter here." Sunday afternoon he dispersed tea, cakes and chat to Colonels and Tommies alike who had the courage to beard the timid man in his den. If cakes ran out, it was not always a Tommy who ran off to the confectioners for a further supply. There was worldly wisdom after all behind those great spectacles, behind which "P.B.C." hid himself. If it was an officer who went for the cakes, of course P.B.C.'s ten francs went to some other good cause within or without the house.

Only one fee did he charge for invading his sanctum, and that was your name and address, military and civilian, in his visitors book. With the exception of a few whose writing was too illegible to be deciphered even with the aid of his great spectacles, all who signed his book are still at his mercy.

Affairs at the Signal School moved along quietly while the instructors grew more friendly and the Sgt. Major grew more disliked.

17 January

After a big fall of snow the weather became intensely cold. The pond from which we dipped our water for washing became a safe short cut to the incinerator where a few moments warmth outbalanced the outrage on one's olfactory nerves, and the only happy men in camp were the lucky mortals who were detailed for Sanitary Fatigue, whose duties (onerous but not odourless) permitted them access to the one warm spot in the camp.

The man who was seen one morning chopping a fine washbowl out of the ice on the washing benches, with a hatchet borrowed from the pioneers, and later found attacking the ice on the pond with the same bloodthirsty looking weapon was strongly advised to "go sick" and be examined by a mental expert.

Breakfast took less time nowadays, just long enough to get back to the hut with half your tea ration still hot for shaving, and a wipe over visible skin with a warm shaving brush, completed the morning toilet.

At night before returning to rest, it was wise to remove the icicles from the inside of the corrugated roof that hung anywhere above your downy couch to avoid accidents should a sudden thaw turn up during the night.

1 February

Three enemy aeroplanes appeared over Poperinghe this morning whilst we were busy at Flag Drill. They were soon in the midst of a cloud of little white puffs of shrapnel shells from our anti-aircraft guns.

Three of ours suddenly appeared from nowhere and there was soon a ding dong fight going. One plane was brought down in flames, but the other two made off for home. An unpleasant sensation for the first time to see an aeroplane come hurtling down from the blue. Though the fight seemed directly overhead, we heard later that the plane dropped at Elverdinghe, a couple of miles away.

3 February

Detailed for Sanitary Fatigue today with Crole and Mitchell of the Black Watch. Made friends with "Spud" surnamed "Murphy" O.C. Incinerator. Quite a character and looks due for his old age pension but as he says "Smells is 'ealthy". An old Dublin Fusilier, and being good boys and listening to his tales of soldiering peacefully, we eventually persuaded him to warm some ice up for a wash.

6 February

Drury Lane Drama as performed in hut 3, any odd evening (after rum ration).

slow music on the empty stoves with entrenching tools.
(enter first Jock breathlessly) – Have you heard the news boys?
(Omnes) No! What is it?
(First Jock) The Squires Daughter is in the water
(Omnes) Howls "Who will save her?"
(2nd Jock dashing through the crowd) I will
(Crowd cheers itself hoarse)
(first Jock – after cheers have subsided) And who are you?
(second ditto – triumphantly). I'm Jolly Jack the Sailor!!
Mad cheering with "Inferno Dantesque" on the stove fortissimo, while Jolly Jack dances a Reel under the impression that it is the Hornpipe, till someone unfastens his safety pin.
"Curtain"

20 February

The cold spell breaks suddenly and rain falls heavily. Headquarters issue orders to at once cut down heavy traffic to minimum to save the roads. Many roads closed altogether to traffic. Heavy traffic evidently consists of rations and post.

23 February

Poperinghe tonight crowded out with Brass Hats and Tabs. A big conference has been held at Talbot House. It seems as if things are going to hum a bit in the near future. All coming out of Talbot House seem to be putting away note books with recipes for cooking the German goose. One can almost hear the fat frizzle.

27 February

Passed exams and lost no time in decorating myself with crossed flags which I bought cheap second hand from Jock Mitchell, thereby saving some centimes and an amount of labour in cleaning. Spent the evening in Poperinghe hoping that if I moved my arms quickly enough, flags might be mistaken for crowns, but no one seemed to mistake me for a Sgt. Major. Called at Talbot House to shake hands with "P.B.C". He has a wonderful knack of making you feel that you will be really missed.

28 February

There was a jam at breakfast time at the door of the dining hall, mess tins and their owners jangled furiously together. About 160 men could find their way through that door in two minutes in the ordinary course of things, but when each man had to stop to read the notice pinned on the door, it messed things up somewhat.

"There will be a Whist Drive held this evening in the Dining Hall. Tickets 50cts. Refreshments free."

While breakfast was being disposed of, speculation was rife concerning the refreshments. The general optimism seemed to be

Sandwiches. Boeuf preservé – Fray Bentos – per man.

Biscuits – a L'armeé Anglaise.

By judicious enquiry round the precincts of the cookhouse, however, we learned that it would at least be Ham Sandwiches and tea.

The school instructors (<u>not</u> including the Sgt. Major) had been invited by No. 3 Hut to a little festive gathering at a near by estaminet, the previous evening, where all evening we seemed to be mutually agreeing that "when on parade, you are on parade, but when you are not, well, there you are". It may not sound very lucid, but it sounded less lucid as the night wore on.

The tit-bit of the evening was the rendering of the ancient masterpiece "Knocked 'em in the old Kent Road". This was given by one of the instructors who had assured us earlier in the evening that he only sang when he was drunk, and that Belgium did not hold enough beer to get him to that state. Jock Mitchell also delighted us with a Scottish song which we listened to with the appreciation most of us give to Italian Opera, that is, we admired the noise but wondered what it was all about. It was something about either the "Lakes" or the "Links" of Montrose. Montrose must have got to Jock's head, as on the way back to camp he decided suddenly that he wanted to get home, and dashed for a Red Cross train passing over a level crossing.

We managed to retain his company by superhuman efforts and with the loss of a piece of his kilt. The Whist Drive tonight was to take place at 6 p.m. We were in our hut just after tea when instructor Cpl. W. (our bosom friend since the previous evening) walked in, and announced that a barrel of real "Blighty" stout had been procured and would be retailed at the Whist Drive at 3*d* per gill.

Then a terrific argument broke out with Mitchell, Finlay and Crole as chief speakers, as to whether the stout should not correctly come under the heading of "Refreshments" which were announced free. Argument however was useless, and the case was lost. Consternation reigned as the hut was in a state of bankruptcy after the previous evening. Suddenly Mitchell dived into his haversack and drew forth a German Helmet, bayonet and belt that he had treasured from the Somme, and disappeared with them. He returned in half an hour with 50 francs and a lucidly expressed opinion of the meanness of an A.S.C. man who would pay no more than 50 fcs. for the chance of going home on leave with evidence that he had seen the war. Jock kept 10 fcs. for himself and loaned the remainder out at 5 fcs. per time simply on a promise to send it on when times were better, and I verily believe that Jock Mitchell made no bad debts on that occasion, but I doubt that he does business on such terms in peace times.

The Whist Drive went with a rush, as did the stout and the refreshments, and it was found that a reserve barrel of stout had been procured in case one did not suffice. The N.C.O.'s acted as waiters and the Sgt. Major as M.C. The waiters later in the proceedings seemed to be getting a bit overcome by the fumes of the stout they were serving out. The barrels were carefully screened however to prevent the fumes reaching the players free of charge. Our M.C. somewhat startled us by getting into a merry mood and cracking jokes which fell on a deathly and ghastly silence. We could not forget his daily greeting on parade for the first two months, and his particularly choice remark on our first parade a bit bedraggled out from the line. To be told that we would disgrace a company of b—— Landwehr got through some thick skins and still rankled. We didn't mind his adjectives a bit, but we did not like the "Landwehr".

Not that we knew quite what they were anymore than he did, but being something German was sufficient.

As the end of the Whist Drive drew nearer, inquests on games became more furious and many came near to the fate of the man who led the 13th trump. The officer in charge of the school (a fine chap) turned up to give the prizes and was given three rollicking cheers. Then the Sgt. Major received three ("ironical" as the parliamentary reports say), with plenty of sand in, and cries of "What about the Landwehr".

The officer gave us special dispensation in the matter of lights out till 10.30 and we dispersed to our respective huts.

Various of the younger end against the advice of the older and more matured, had saved up their last few nights rum ration with the intention of having a last night "beano". They were soon disposed of and put to bed.

Crole, nicknamed "ma chérie" for his pretty face, opened the programme with an exhibition of toe dancing in the manner of Pavlova, till he was unfortunate enough to come in contact with the stove, parting it from its flue and smothering himself and others with soot. We dusted him well and put him to bed singing "Annie Laurie".

"The Marquis" then took on the programme. The Marquis was a waiter from London Town who one night in a torrid state of sunstroke during the cold spell, told us in confidence that he had "waited" on the Marquis of Clauricarde whose chiefly claim to emminence according to his waiter was, that he wore a dirty shirt with diamond "cufflinks" worth £1,000. The Marquis also "knew something" of a famous "Mrs. C. W." that he would divulge to no one, as a well paid waiter was the soul of honour, and "noblesse oblige" and all that sort of thing, and thereon proceeded to give us details.

His speciality was Vesta Tilly songs with his entrenching tool as a swagger cane. He usually was allowed plenty of room for his performances. His turn was broken by the door opening and instructor Cpl. D. inquiring if he was alright for No. 3 hut. On finding he had some bottles of beer in his arms it was unanimously declared that it was quite alright. He was assisted to a place of honour on the dismantled stove, but soon found a safer place on the floor. He had come with a little gift for the boys of No. 3 and to assure us that when he first saw us on parade he knew at a glance that we would make fine signallers, etc., etc., ad-lib. Compliments flew as the beer disappeared and the Corporal to show that he really loved us decided to sleep in the hut with us. As he could not get up from where he had settled, it seemed wise.

The next arrival was the Orderly Sgt. who appeared carrying a broom. He said it was a wonderful help along the duckboards, though he was a long way from "blind". He had come to inform us that it was time for "lights out", but sighting the beer, he forgot the business on hand. Two more corporals arrived then, one with a drop more rum and the other demanding three or four mess tins to bring some more stout, Jock Mitchell going along to see him and especially the stout – safely back again. Things were getting mellow and we were in the midst of another rendering of "Knocked 'em in the Old Kent Road" when the door opened sharply to admit the Sgt. Major, armed with a rifle. We were never quite sure whether he carried this in self defence, or in self support as the Orderly Sgt. did with the broom. He made a short, curt speech which improved our opinion of him slightly. He said "I don't mind you taking a bite at me on your last night, I may be no gentleman, but our officer is and I will not allow his orders to be ignored – hiccup". We assured him that all lights would be out in a shake, and he left. The door had hardly closed before he seemed to be entirely forgotten again, till the door opened and the officer himself appeared with an electric torch in his hand. He just turned it round the hut in silence then said "Now boys, you have had a good time for your last night, I want all lights out now and silence," and he stood there waiting. Someone whipped a blanket over the sleeping form of Corporal 'D', the Orderly Sgt. and his broom had already disappeared quietly behind the Officer while the two other corporals whose strategic positions were not so good, made a ridiculous attempt to look as if they had spent all the evening trying to get the lights out. In an incredibly short space of time however, everyone was down and the last candle blown out. The Officer then gave us a "Good night boys and good luck" and went out. Darkness and silence reigned for quite five minutes when the Officer's car was heard to leave the camp. Jock Mitchell's voice broke the silence and his candle flickered again. We sat up and looked round to see what things looked like, and found that within that five minutes about fifteen of the party were already fast asleep. The remainder debated the matter of Corporal D's removal to his own quarters without waking him from his beauty sleep. We were just preparing to carry him back when the door creaked. The corporal was dropped and we disappeared under our blankets again. Then we heard a plaintive voice asking if we had any stout left, as the barrel had run dry. Investigations were made, and it was found that the mess tins had tumbled inside the stove during the excitement of the Officer visit. As the Corporal showed signs of making a noise about it, Jock admonished him. "Hae ye no had plenty ce soir, gie a hand wie that puir limpit "D" and let's hae him aben," so four of us rolled the somnolent form in a blanket, and like another famous soldier "we carried him out at dead of night" – and laid him in his own quarters. Then down to it, and at last "Lights Out".

I laid awake thinking over the evening. Some people may say "Disgusting". The same people very likely think War is an uplifting thing. They don't know "The Salient", where the uplifted ones live in mud, die in mud, eat it and breathe it. "P.B.C." called it "A nightmare fit for Cain". Back into the Salient tomorrow, all of them, after two months of comparative peace, good clean huts, good food and plenty, and best of all regular sleep. And all to end tonight. While the ink is hardly dry on my number, the great majority at the school were 1914/15 lads, and now 1917, and back to it tomorrow with a light heart.

May I meet in England someday "Jock" who when asked to speak English would howl "Blimey Bill", "Ma chérie" who should have been a ballet girl, "Finlay" whom we called "the quiet one" till we knew his name. "Old Moore" of the "K.R.R." whose pendulous countenance and weighty speech would have suited the "Woolsack" quite as well as "The Chair" at the local estaminet, Marquis of "Cufflinks" and all the other boys. Good luck to them all.

1 March

We dispersed from the Signal School at 10 next morning to join our respective units, with the foggiest possible information as to their whereabouts.

It was a beautiful morning, much too warm for March and a pack that had not been worn for two months. Passing through Poperinghe of course we had to call at Talbot House, and there decided that the day was too nice to spend perhaps the whole of it in full pack looking for the battalion, so we dumped our baggage there and had a good look round "Pop".

After a good feed of eggs and chips and enough coffee to sink a ship, we collected our luggage and set off. We were lucky in falling across some of our transport soon after leaving Poperinghe and reached the Battn. in time for tea. They were out of the line at Toronto Camp, quite a good camp, and a great improvement on "D" camp, the last camp we were in. Reporting at once to the Signal Office, we found that our school reports had preceded us. The Signal Sgt. however decided to test our knowledge first hand and sat us down to make a diagram of the circuits of a Fullerphone, – my weak point of course. This was a new instrument and not then in regular use in the line. I did my best which looked more like a Coconut Whirl than an electric signalling apparatus, and as the Sgt. was not too critical about it, I decided that his knowledge of the instrument was not much more extensive than mine.

I found Pat still with the Lewis Gun team, looking rather seedy after a bad cold. The team generally and Pat in particular were at pains to tell me what trouble they had to hold the enemy back, whilst I had a good time at Poperinghe.

2 March

Signallers were detailed to their stations for the next turn in the line. Jimmy Robinson, "Nobby" Clarke, Rowbottom and myself detailed for "A" Coy's signals. Battalion is to move up to the front line tomorrow night. I had settled down for the night when a runner came in with orders to report at once to the Signal Office. Putting on the few clothes I had taken off, I dashed off to the "Signals" and received orders to get ready at once to proceed to the line with a party of signallers, to take over the signal stations in advance of the battalion's arrival. Dashed back and found Pat awake wondering what all the disturbance was about when all decent people ought to be asleep. As he was making sure that I was not forgetting either my rifle or my rations, a signaller popped his head in to say that a mistake had been made and that I was not going up the line till the battalion went up the following night, for which respite I tried to look more disappointed than I felt and got back to my blankets.

3 March

The battalion left Toronto Camp after dark to take over the front line, on Observatory Ridge Sector from the Black Watch. Relief nights, either going in or coming out, are a nerve and temper destroying institution, and going into the line, one is positively glad to arrive there.

If the enemy opposite was aware that a relief was in progress, he knew it was just the best time for a "strafe" or a raid. We nearly always had good luck with our battalion reliefs, and put it down to perhaps managing our reliefs on the same night as the people opposite, which made for a mutually quiet evening. Reliefs from the support lines to the front were bad enough, but when it came to a long march from a camp, in the dark over bad roads or across country, the men were tired even before they reached the tortuous trenches. Secret orders for reliefs would contain a passage "Guides will meet incoming unit at M4, a 3.4" though "D.V." might have been inserted with advantage after the map reference. The odds were against the guides having seen a map, and most likely would be given verbal instructions by some Sgt. Major, where to meet the relieving parties. The instructions may have taken the shape of "You know the corner where there was a smell of dead mule when we came up".

On the one hand, the smell may have been removed, and on the other hand, smells would not be shown on the map which the officer in charge of the relieving party would no doubt carry, so the chances of the guide treading on the officers toes suddenly in the dark, were not very great. Many cases however, have rarely been known of guides actually being found where expected, and even of relieving parties being up to time.

The Black Watch and our battalion were the "chummiest" battalions under ordinary circumstances, but one would never have imagined this to be the case if they had met a platoon of each, blocked in a communication trench on a dark night, one trying to get to the front line, the other trying to get out, while enemy Verey Lights flared up, and odd Lewis and Machine guns rattled off to assure "Fritz" that there was nothing special going on, that everyone was on duty and on the watch, and that no such thing could happen, as half of two battalions to be mixed up, and unable to move one way or another, for sometimes a quarter of an hour at a time.

When our company eventually arrived and got fixed up we found our signal station in a huge sap, a good twenty feet below ground, a black, wet, smelly hole. Long dark tunnels, ankle deep in water. The signal office was a shelf dug in the side of the tunnel, and shut off for privacy with a blanket whose lower end disappeared into the black water in the tunnel. Our "office" would hold three of us. In getting in and out we had to be very careful with the blanket which had a trick of coming from its fastenings and disappearing into the water, then it had to be fished for and re-hung. To touch this blanket at anytime gave one the horrors, and movement on the shelf was restricted.

The whole tunnel was shelved in a similar manner and found shelter for as many of the company as were off duty at a time. There were two entrances to the tunnel, but one of them was used principally as a flue for the officers' mess cook's fire, which he had made at the foot of the steps of this entrance. The officers of the company had their quarters at the end of the same tunnel.

As our signal office would only hold three of us, (two sleeping and one at the instrument) we held council and decided that we should each take a turn to sleep further along the tunnel, when Rowbottom settled matters by saying that he would find a "kip" along the tunnel permanently during our stay. Robinson and Nobby argued about it, which I thought was in very bad taste in view of Rowbottom's self sacrifice.

I found later that Jimmy R. and Nobby knew Rowbottom much better than I did.

When we arrived there we had found Nobby in charge. He had come up with the advance party to take over the signals. He was just picking his dab of chewing gum off the wall where he had stuck it for safety while attending the instrument.

After explaining the different station calls, plan of stations of H.Q., the other 3 companies, the battalions on left and right, and in support, he handed over to Jimmy who took over duty. Two spells each of 3 hours each day were arranged as with four of us on the station, we were well manned. I found that the proper thing to do when not on duty was to sleep.

My first spell on duty came 3 to 6 a.m., and I was instructed that at 5 a.m. I must get the "Situation Report" and direction of wind, from the Company Officer and forward it through to H.Q. At 5.0 a.m. prompt, I groped my way along the tunnel to the officers quarters, I found Capt. S. there sound asleep. He had a heavy time of it during relief, and would have to see all posts safely taken over, and manned, and all in apple pie order before he could turn in. I shook him gently, but found gentle methods useless, and had to use some energy before I so much as disturbed the regularity of his snores. After some time I was so far successful as to get him murmur "What is it?" and immediately he fell to snoring again. A further shaking brought him up on one elbow, so I immediately yelled "Situation Report Sir" into his ear.

I at last managed to make him understand that it was 5 a.m. and the Situation Report was due at "H.Q". He then startled me by asking "Where is the wind?" Military Medals have been given for less than refusing to reply "Up" to a question like that, but I replied that I did not know. After asking if I was a new signaller, he informed me that I should have made this enquiry from the gas corporal, before coming for the report. I dashed along the tunnel for the stairway and up in to the trench where I found the gas corporal and obtained the desired information. Stumbling down again, of course I found the Capt. asleep again, but not so far gone this time. On rousing him he told me to write out the report with today's wind and yesterday's situation. Back to the signal office, I found the instrument buzzing frantically. Tumbling over Jimmy and "Nobby", and grabbing the receiver, I made out a message from H.Q.: "EXPEDITE S.R." I puzzled over "S.R." "Service Rifles" "Soldiers Rum", and ran my mind over the miscellaneous signal signs without result, so I kicked the smaller of my two sleeping partners, which happened to be Jimmy, "What is "S.R" Jimmy?" I yelled frantically.

"Do you mean "S.R.D."" Jimmy replied. "No just "S.R."". "Let's have a look at it". I handed the message to him "Oh Situation Report, what time is it, 5.30. Oh 'ell, haven't you sent it in." I explained my difficulties, and said I had got the wind alright but what was yesterday's situation. Jimmy said "Oh just put "situation quiet" and chance it."

So the situation was quiet on "A" company's front that morning, and I breathed normally again after I sent the message off, though Jimmy who was a bit of a pessimist, said that "H.Q." would play 'ell about the report being late.

At 6.0 a.m. my turn on duty finished and Rowbottom should relieve me. He had not turned up at 6.15, so I decided to hunt him up and turn him out. I had no difficulty in finding him, but compared to Rowbottom the Captain was a light sleeper. It was seven o'clock when he groped his way into the signal office.

Half an hour before dawn "Stand to" was called and the tunnel emptied while all went on watch in the trench until "Stand down" was called an hour later. This period was supposed to be the most likely for a surprise attack. After "Stand down" came breakfast. Tea and bacon were brought up from the cookhouse which was in a gully some distance behind the trench. Deciding for a breath of fresh air before getting down to sleep, I had a look round up in the trench, and after some wandering about, found Pat with the Lewis Gun team at their post. The battalion had been on this sector previously, during the time I was at the Signal School.

Things were very quiet and Pat offered to show me the sights. He pointed out an interesting feature, a fair sized hill, a little distance wide of our front, which he pointed out as "Hill 60". I was rather surprised, as I had a recollection of a question being asked in Parliament, as to whether we or the Germans held Hill 60. If I remembered correctly, the reply was given that neither side actually held it, as correctly speaking, there was no Hill 60 left, as it had been practically levelled by shell fire and mines from both sides, and the actual site was at that time between the enemy line and ours. As replies to Parliamentary questions are no doubt always the exact truth, someone must have put up another hill to keep the war going. Things were fairly quiet during the daytime, and unless anything special occurred, the Lewis Guns did not fire during daylight as it was very necessary to keep the positions of the gun posts unknown to the enemy, but after dark they were kept fairly busy covering gaps in the wire, and searching.

On the left of our position there was a considerable gap between us and the next battalion, which could not be manned, and Lewis Guns were posted by the battalion each side of the gap, and the gap was further covered by Machine Guns in the rear, and such a peppering was kept up after dark, that a worm, much less a Boche, stood a poor chance of passing that way. The enemy had worked his trench very near to this gap, in fact at one point they were so near to our trench that neither side dared to bomb the other. It was near here that Pat asked me if I would care to have a look at the enemy's trench. "Just take a peep over here". I took a short peep – very short – and what I saw made me feel it would be rude to stand there staring for any length of time.

We had hot stew brought up each night. It was a good idea to bring it up at night, as the men seemed to enjoy it better in the dark than in broad daylight, when they could discuss the contents of their mess tins with an analytical fervour worthy of a Home Office expert at an inquest.

We signallers were rather fortunate in having the Sgt. Major's bunk only divided from ours by a blanket. He would have tasty bits cooked by his own batmen at the fire for the Officer's cook, and we benefited sometimes when his appetite was not up to mark, and occasionally even had a drink of that sweet and milky beverage known as "Sergeant Major's tea".

One night when both the Sgt. Major and his batman were out, I was just going on duty, while Nobby whom I had just relieved was getting down to sleep. Nobby had just stretched his long legs out and let his head drop, when he sat up again quickly with a curse, and rubbed his head. He had bumped his head on something hard just the other side of the blanket dividing our bunk from the Sgt. Major's. Investigation proved it to be a rum jar containing the surplus left over after the company had been served out with their ration. After a full debate it was decided that the Sgt. Major's water bottle must be full, and that of his Batman too, otherwise there would be none in the jar, therefore – well, it would be wise to leave enough in the jar to make a noise when shaken – so we did the wise thing.

There was the bread question too. Let the bread ration be big or small, we never had enough left for tea after we had finished breakfast, so during the day we were sure at some time to find the Sgt. Major and his batman both out. A good look-out was kept while someone crept under the blanket and hurriedly sawed off a slice or two from the plentiful supply. To allay suspicion, we would ask the S.M. as soon as he returned if he could spare us a bit of bread. Between what we took, and what we begged, we usually managed enough for tea.

7 March

The battalion was relieved at night and moved from the front line to support at Maple Copse.

We made our way there from the front line by a duckboard track across the open. Evidence was not wanting that some enemy battery could, and had made some good artillery practice on this track, and we hoped that it was suppertime with this particular battery. The artillery did leave us alone, but some restless machine gunner, seemed to have a "hunch" that he might bag something if he sprayed the track a little. He was putting his shots across some distance in front of us, we could hear them whipping across, then he cut off for a while. We made good speed then, and were mightily pleased to hear his next belt of ammunition crossing the track behind us. All he got, as far as we knew, was a solitary Jock, who by irony of circumstance was a stretcher bearer who was carrying a stretcher. He was sat on the duckboards bandaging himself up, not particularly anxious about the "Nice one in the leg", but wanting to get a help back before he got one that was not so convenient.

Maple Copse perhaps had been a copse I suppose at some time, but at present it was just a little ravine running off at right angles to the track, and what trees there had been, were now stumps blasted and riven out of all semblance of trees. The banks were honeycombed with little dugouts, and we were just stood about waiting to be detailed to our various holes, when that confounded machine gun rapped out again, and whether by good luck or good management, he got a beautiful enfilade right along the front of the dugouts. We were billeted in the twinkling of an eye, despite the fact that entrance to the dugouts could only be made on hands and knees. The only man left quite outside was the Sergeant Major, who had dived down behind a convenient tree stump.

Owing to the overcrowding in some of the dugouts, various legs for which there was no room inside, had been left sticking out, but it was noticeable that no heads were left sticking out. As with the ostrich, it was always the head end that took cover first. We soon were sorted out into our proper dug-outs when the M.G. gentleman finished his fun.

The dugouts were fairly roomy, but low, and after crawling in on hands and knees, if you forgot, and stood up, you at once sat down, as you ought to have done in the first place, but as a higher ceiling meant less earth on top, we did not mind. We had only one telephone line to look after here, and that only ran to Battalion H.Q. We had some difficulty in keeping communication up, as the wire went over the open where shelling was fairly persistent. My first venture out in the open, in daylight, was really a tame affair. "Jock" invited me to come along and see what was the matter with the wire, as we could not get through.

We climbed out over the top of the dugout, and ran the wire through our fingers, through water filled shell holes and mud, till, by a new shell hole, we were left with a broken end, and no signs of the other broken end. We searched and groped about without success, till "Jock" decided to go to Batt. H.Q. and follow the line back from there, whilst I stayed to look after the one end we had found. I sat on the shell hole and tried to feel unconcerned, and a shell or two passing overhead nearly shook my faith in the maxim that was taught us during training, that two shells never fall in the same spot. "Jock" was really not as long away as it seemed, and he eventually appeared in sight coming along the wire from H.Q.

The repair job that followed may not have been a perfect example of workmanship, but as a speed test, it would have taken some beating.

For three days we had a quiet time of it and I spent most of my time in the Lewis Gunner's dugout. They were having a great time cooking and eating pork chops most of the time, and to look in for a chat usually meant a little offering on the end of a bayonet. It appeared that when the Lewis Gunners went into the front line, they did so in advance of the battalion and took their meat ration with them to do their own cooking. "A" company were given a lump of pork which was supposed to be the ration for the other three company's gunners, in addition to their own. During the spell in the line, B, C, and D Coy's gunners either received other rations, or did not want the pork. Anyway they did not send for it, which they should have done. It was kept for them till the battalion moved out of the front line, when "A" Coy were practically isolated at Maple Copse, hence the "buckshee" chops.

10 March

The battalion moved back to reserve trenches. Signallers preferred if possible to move on their own rather than with the company, their duties often allowing of this. The signallers of the battalion coming in, had arrived early, and we were handing over to them when we found that the line was disconnected again. Of course the new signallers would not take over till the line was in working order, so we had to chase over the top to find the trouble again. We managed however to get away before the company was ready to move. We had not proceeded far on our way before we began to wish we had waited for the Company, as we could see the communication trench we were in, being nicely demolished by shells, some distance in front of us. We sat down and waited for a quiet spell and then made a dash for it, over the tangle of trench boards, wire, and debris with the acrid shell fumes still thick enough to make our eyes smart. We found our new quarter in a trench named "Ritz Trench". It was a wonderful trench fully fifteen feet deep. The bottom was well duckboarded over running water. About a foot above the level of the duckboards, little "roosts" had been dug in the sides of the trench. These were just big enough to sit in, and would accommodate 3 men lying down. We fixed up a hole for sleeping in, and one next door for the man on duty and the instruments.

Our first night here was rather unfortunate, as Nobby being rather long in the leg, and usually a restless sleeper, managed to kick our 3 fur jerkins out into the water under the duckboards, as we had laid them over our feet to keep them warm, as they were near the door.

It was at Ritz Trench one morning when off duty, I found Pat sat in his "Nugger hole" with his shirt laid across his knee, examining it intently almost thread by thread. I thought at first he had conceived an idea of changing his business when the war was over, and was trying to count warp and weft by the naked eye. When it really dawned upon me what he was doing, I felt a shiver of disgust, and could not keep it out of my voice when I asked "Are you like that?" "Like what?" he asked as he calmly cracked a fine one, and continued "I suppose you are not." On being hotly informed that his supposition for once was correct, he immediately challenged me to take my shirt off for his examination and a side bet of 6d. (These were days of limited means.) I returned to my hole later, less one days pay, and thought sadly of the Pharisee who said "I am not as other men are."

I wrote home that night, and in my letter casually asked for a tin of "Harrison's Pomade" and trusted that my wife would be sufficiently unsuspecting to imagine that I had belated hopes of my hair growing again.

13–15 March

We went into reserve at Ypres Cavalry Barracks. Ypres by dark was even more desolating than by daylight. Jagged ghosts of brickwork loomed up each side of us as we tramped through the mud of the streets that had been ploughed up by shells, and then churned to mud by the ceaseless traffic through the town by night.

Not a light was to be seen but the Verey Lights going up in the distance on three sides of us. The barracks had been a huge place, we entered by a narrow door, along a narrow passage until we came to a corridor which ran round the four sides of the barrack square which the building surrounded.

This corridor was packed with troops coming in and going out. Different battalions and companies seemed to get inextricably mixed, but I heard of no instance of any man of a battalion coming into reserve, getting up into the line again with a battalion going up. After a good deal of pushing and shouting in the darkness, our company turned into a large basement which was comparatively brilliantly lighted by a few candles.

Along each wall were two shelves of corrugated iron sheets on wooden supports. This was the sleeping accommodation, and seemed to work out at one sheet of corrugated iron per man, and there was a great clatter of shoe irons while the men staked out their claims, and a rush for the bottom shelf by those who did not feel energetic enough to climb on the second shelf. The bottom shelfers were sorry very shortly afterwards. Many pieces of the corrugated iron were much dilapidated and while the holes were not big enough to allow of a man to drop through, they were quite big enough to allow odds and ends of equipment, lumps of mud, and dirt generally to drop through, but the man who dropped his pipe down into another man's mess tin of tea, really felt quite as much aggrieved as the owner of the tea below him. We found however that corrugated iron sheets made a fairly comfortable bed after what we had been having. Daylight showed the barrack square to be fairly ploughed up with shells and scattered with bricks and masonry from the building itself. The upper part of the building was riddled with shell fire despite the fact that the walls were in places fully six feet thick of solid brickwork. For the morning wash, no water was available within the building, but out in the street a couple of hundred yards away, ablution benches had been erected round a well that had evidently at one time, been inside a house. The well had not been moved though the house had. In trousers and shirts plus steel helmets and gas masks, we did wonderful time in washing and shaving. The celerity of our movements was aided by a bitterly cold wind, and a suspicion that we might not be able to get our steel helmets or gas masks on in time, if a shell dropped in the close vicinity.

We spent 3 days here, and found that being in reserve meant going up the line each night armed with a pick or shovel or both, in addition to our usual arms and equipment, and returning by dawn, feeling as if we had neither legs nor arms left, but more feet and backs than we knew what to do with. It was on the return from one of these so called working "parties" that I first found that little sandbagged canteen under the Lille Gate, where one could get a jam tin filled with hot tea, which at such times, tasted worth its weight in radium.

On the night of Mar 15/16 another battalion came into the barracks, and after the usual mix up in the corridors, our battalion moved out, and splashed through the streets of Ypres, through the square past the ghostly ruins of the Cloth Hall, out of the town on our way back to Toronto Camp.

16 March

Marched down to Poperinghe for a hot bath and a change, then medical inspection on our return, and also on our chests. Scabies seems to be the chief interest of the M.O. again. The rest of the day was spent in getting "posh" again, with much use of khaki blanco and brasso, and the usual fervid expressions of love towards the man at the War Office who was supposed to be the secret partner in the firm or firms who sold these two commodities.

The next day we were back on the parade ground learning to "Form" anything from "fours" to "squad" and practising the noble art of "Presenting" and "Sloping Arms". This I suppose, to emphasize that we were still soldiers and not mudlarks.

It was a peculiar trait of "Tommy" that one day of Blanco and Brasso with Parade Drills could produce such a "fed up" feeling that a week of mud and shell fire could not do. Parades however, were not overdone and we had a fairly comfortable time.

There was a large "Y.M.C.A." hut in the camp, and a concert was arranged one evening and much enjoyed. "Knocker" Hayes's "I'm Toney" vieing with Lt Sparke's "I'll sing thee songs of Araby" for the star turn.

19 March

We were marched off for a working party. Calling at a big "R.E." dump where we picked up picks and shovels. We went on to an old disused railway siding near Vlamertinghe. Half the party were detailed to some workshops near by, to stack empty shell boxes under cover. They were the lucky ones, being quite close by an estaminet (which also sold coffee). They found a nice soft job and returned in the evening with plenty of firewood.

I was unfortunate enough to get in with the unlucky half of the party which spent a day on the siding in driving snow, digging up old sleepers and stacking them. By the time we had finished work we had seen too much of sleepers to bother carrying any back for firewood. Then we wended our weary way back to the R.E. dump, and handed in our picks and shovels which were counted carefully before we were allowed to proceed on our way back to camp. Counting out picks and shovels to the "P.B.I." was an important part of the R.E. work.

21 March

We left Toronto Camp for the front line again to hold the same sector as on March 3rd – Observatory Ridge. "Nobby" Clarke had proceeded up earlier to take over the Signals for our company, and we found him bemoaning a bit of bad luck that had befallen him. It appears that after "Nobby" had relieved the signallers, and they had left, he found their signal watch still hanging on the wall. Perhaps to put the matter more exactly, he had watched them leave it. He was chuckling over the "find" when one of the signallers returned to collect it. It will be recognised that "Nobby" was an optimist, when it is mentioned that the battalion going out was the ""Black Watch" frae Dundee".

Things were quiet again this time, and having by now, been initiated into a few of the inner secrets of "signalling" it was possible to get the "Situation Report" off to "B.H.Q." to time in the morning, and get it from the officer afterwards. On the 24th we were relieved from the front line, and this time moved back into support at Zillebeke Bund. The journey though short was a bad one. The night was pitch black and the duckboards seem to have lost all sense of continuity, and those that were not missing were muddy and treacherous, and we were glad when we eventually reached the "Bund".

The accommodation here consisted of quite good dugouts in the bank of Zillebeke Lake. They fronted away from the line, and we faced batteries of our artillery at fairly close quarters, and when they got to work, it gave us a queer feeling of being blazed at and missed everytime, and fervent prayers went up for "No shorts or prematures".

Then sometimes the enemy would start searching for the batteries with "heavies" that made the ground quiver and occasionally we would feel sick at heart, at unmistakable evidence of a shell "finding its billet".

After darkness set in, we could hear the transport pounding round Shrapnel Corner, which was a hot spot at that time. It was at the "Bund" that some keen follower (on a different plane) of Izaak Walton was seized with the brilliant idea of fishing in the lake above, with Mill's No. 5 Bombs. This not being officially recognised as "Recreation" in Army Rules and Regulations, he was quickly discouraged. The weather had been vile for some days now, incessant snow, hail, or rain till everything was a quagmire. Moving about, even on duckboards in broad daylight was difficult, and in the darkness, we simply floundered about recklessly, as it was useless trying to pick one's way. The general opinion seemed to be that if this was the sort of ground we had to defend, it would do the enemy a right dirty trick to let him have it, and smother himself.

25 March 1917

When the Orderly Sergt. came round during the day, reckoning how many men he could muster for duty, we did not need to guess twice that the R.E. wanted some work doing. We started off at 8.0 p.m. with the night as black as the proverbial bag. Timber carrying we heard it was to be. We slopped our way along the communications trench for some distance and then climbed out onto a road which seemed to be well over ankle deep where it was in good repair, and any unknown depth where it was not. Coming to some ruins which seemed to be all that was left of Zillebeke Village, a stack of timber loomed up out of the darkness. We lined up in single file, Pat being in front of me, and as each man came alongside the stack, someone on top slid a heavy plank down to him, which he shouldered and joined up a few yards down the road, to those who had already been served. The weight of the plank in falling, buried its end well in the mud, and it took of my best to wiggle it out of its mud socket and get it on to the shoulder that was not already engaged with my rifle. Judging from its weight, I reckoned my limit, about a hundred yards.

As soon as we were all loaded, the R.E. guide started off, and I felt straight away that I would like to change shoulders with my load, but too late, we were off, and I must keep Pat in sight (visible 5 yards in front) otherwise he might have been a thousand miles away, and I would be left like a lost soul ploughing my way through a "Slough of Despond" and misleading all the poor souls behind me.

We made semicircles round water-logged shell holes, did wonderful balancing feats on muddy planks over old disused trenches, in an endeavour to keep pace with that long legged R.E. guide, whose load consisted of an overcoat and a gas mask, whilst we were plank ridden in full "Fighting Order". I felt at last that my very soul's salvation depended on having my plank on the other shoulder.

I stopped short to slide it off my shoulder, but instead of it standing on its end whilst I got my other shoulder to it, the perverse thing slid into a shell hole and took me along with it.

One is at a loss for words at such a moment, which fact perhaps accounted for Pat hearing nothing of my misfortune, and disappearing into the darkness. The man next behind me, after sympathetic[?] reference to my disappearance, made haste to get within sight of Pat. I managed to scramble out, shoulder my burden again, and join on the end of the party. Bringing up the rear was a good friend in the shape of Jack Isaacs, Corporal of the Lewis Gunners, my instructor in that department, before I deserted it for the Signals. Like the good soul he was, he took over my burden for a short spell in exchange for his rifle. After a good breather, I had taken my timber again and we were all making a bit better progress over a bit better ground when a machine gun rapped out right across us.

Some dropped flat, perhaps to keep their burdens from harm, while others played bo-peep behind theirs. It only lasted a few seconds, and though that Boche machine gunner had been lucky to find such a good target by chance in the dark, that was as far as his luck went, for we had not a single casualty. We got along appreciably quicker with our burdens after that. Barring an occasional further rattle of machine gun fire, which was not again in our direction, things were very quiet, the artillery seeming strangely quiet.

We dropped into a trench soon afterwards, and after negotiating a few awkward corners, we reached our destination at the head of a big sap. Here we dumped the timber, while an R.E. made an effort to count the planks to see if they had all turned up, while our N.C.O.

was concerned to know if all his men had also turned up. I found Pat here and his expressed opinions would have found some difficulty in getting into the Church Monthly, or whatever Sunday reading he takes in.

We were not overjoyed to find out then, that we had two more loads to bring up before we had finished for the night. On the second journey, I managed to get hold of a piece of more manageable weight and dimensions, and had quite a decent journey. Half way on the journey with the third load the evenings work came to a sudden and unexpected finish. All in a moment the quietness was torn to shreds with a howl of shells with an accompaniment of machine gun and rifle fire. Infantry training rules for taking the prone position quickly, were beaten to a standstill. I found myself lying full length in a ditch with my head well entrenched behind Pat's feet. "What's Up?" I enquired of Pat's feet.

"Not been out in a strafe before, have you? We were doing this while you were holding 'em back at Poperinghe" came the cutting reply, so for a while I lay and "enjoyed" the earthquakes, mud volcanoes, and firework display, and tried to avoid making any further silly enquiries. Then a big shell seemed to drop just on the other side of the hedge, and the world's end seemed to have arrived in a lump.

Someone seemed to be making a sudden rush and then a queer sound seemed to come from Pat. I was just putting my head up to see if he was hit, when a horrible crushing weight hit my helmet, and my face sank in the mud. The weight lifted as suddenly as it had fallen. When I could speak, I ventured an enquiry again, but found him this time only anxious to give a lucid and forceful explanation of this latest surprise. It appeared that a man lying in the ditch along in front of Pat, had been suddenly seized with a keen desire for a better hole, and had rushed along the ditch and done his best to tread us in, on his flight.

It was evident by now that a raid was in progress on the Black Watch and the Herts battalions, who were in the line in front of us, and what we were catching was the usual barrage put behind the line to keep reinforcements from getting up.

After a time one seemed to lose interest in the flying shrapnel, nosecaps and general ironmongery, and prayed for the awful noise to cease. A mouthful of fresh air too, would be a treat in place of lyddite fumes. We seemed to have settled there for the "duration", when Pat suddenly sat up, and suggested as things were quiet now, we might move. "Quiet?" I yelled, for the din was awful.

"There is nothing coming over now, that row is our guns" he assured me.

This put a more cheerful aspect on things, and we sat up and listened to our shells going over, and no reply coming back. Fritz, whatever had been the result of his raid, was getting it hot now. (We heard later that he got it hot altogether, and never reached our trenches, and the bigger part of the raiders never reached their own trenches again.) Our party (without its timber) was collected, and our only casualty appeared to be a man who had knocked his eye badly on a tree stump in getting down.

25 March

We had only lain in the mud for an hour and a half, though it was only the darkness that made us feel sure that it was not a day and a half. The timber was left where it fell and we were ordered back to the Bund. The remainder of the Battalion had been warned to "stand to" during the raid, but had not been called upon to move up, as the "Jocks" and "Herts" managed their own job in their usual business-like way.

As a special treat, rum punch was served out, and getting into my blanket I laid my aching head down, and thought that, after all, a Wagner night at The Halle was only a tame affair.

26 March

Of course we expected it, so we were quite resigned when we were ordered out at night to collect all that timber we had lost, and deliver it safely to its proper destination, but it was not the destination which most of us would have consigned it to, if we had our own way.

28 March

Up again to the front line, this time by way of a change, to the Sanctuary Wood sector. There was a Ridge at Observatory Ridge, but we could find very little of either Sanctuary, or Wood, here.

Some humourist had named the trench in which we found the signal dugout – "Lovers Walk" but we found nothing of that going on. The only reason we could think for the name, was the fact that a couple of lovers would have to mingle fairly closely to walk side by side up this "Lovers Walk".

We came across a gap in the trench going up, and it certainly was not a little cupid with his bow and arrow who had got his weapon nicely sighted on it. Our dugout here was an awkward little affair, and the best way to get in seemed to be to sit on the doorstep and shuffle in backwards. "Nobby's" legs were a nuisance as usual and he always seemed to be knocking someone's mess tin over, just as tea was up. Our company cookhouse was just a few yards further down the trench, and the first day the cooks received a warning from Fritz that they were infringing the local "Smoke Abatement" bye-law, thereafter the tea leaves never sank in the dixies.

One day here, an Artillery officer came up and took up a post of observation just outside our dugout, along with his signaller who tapped the artillery wire in the trench to telephone the fire orders to their battery. We were just having some tea and were greatly interested in the proceedings, and feeling quite delighted when, after two trial shots, his order went down the wire "Repeat" which meant that the guns had found the target and were busy making a thorough mess of it. Fritz however, after some time, must have observed the observer, so presently, a shell came hurtling to what we opined was going to be uncomfortably close quarters. The officer ducked and dived for our hole, landing in on his knees with each hand in a mess tin of hot tea, while his signaller charged him in the rear, mixing us all in a heap, breaking our telephone from its connections and putting out our candle.

"Nobby" of course improved matters by yelling from the bottom of the mix-up, "Come in Sir and mind the tea". The shell had landed just short of the parapet, and did no particular damage, while the officer made ample amends from his cigarette case.

30th March 1917

Dear little Soul,

I have got a green envelope at last and can now have a good chat with you, but this must be quite your own. I got such a nice letter from you yesterday dated 24th which I replied to by ordinary post. You are so good to think my little efforts in the episode line worthy of the praise you give them, and though of course your opinion is biased, you make me feel proud of myself, as no one else ever could. Am afraid the latest isn't quite up to the previous one, as I wrote it rather hurriedly. Funny thing happened over the last, I had finished it and put it away, as we were going into the front line that night, and I don't like putting them through during busy times, preferring to wait till the officer has more time on his hands. I happened to shew it to our corporal who was in the strafe with us. When he recovered, he told me all sorts of things Cowpe had said while I was away, but he was under the impression that it was poetry or some serious stuff. I laid down to have a nap and was wakened up in the middle of it by the Corporal asking for the Episode for Cowpe to read. I blessed him and Cowpe in no uncertain terms for waking me, and told him that "C" could just wait till I put it into the post in the ordinary way. Then to my dismay I found C in the dugout saying "Come now "W" those things are much too good to keep in your pocket, let me have, it and I will see it goes off first post." So I parted with it. I saw him later and he pronounced it good, and I have now permission (or perhaps it was a request) to hand them to him personally for censoring (or perusal, which?). He repeated the remark that you were so inquisitive about before. I'll let you have it this time despite my blushes and protestations. "Your wife is a lucky woman", fancy me as a luck bag.

But what annoys me, I hadn't time to get Pat's appreciation of it this time, so please save it, especially as it is the first time I have called him 'Pat' (behind his back).

I am glad Jim boy is keeping so merry and bright. Do keep him in mind of his Daddy. Wouldn't I just give something to spend "a bunch" of days playing with him. He will be grown out of all recognition, but I think I would know his eyes and his merry little face anywhere, even in a thousand years. Am almost afraid to come home before his little ribs are strong enough to bear the hugging I would like to give him. May God grant your wishes after the war, and let us have a house full of such sunbeams to drive all cobwebs away and keep their lucky parents ever young with them.

We are lucky little girl to have such a little chap and he to have such grand parents. It makes me so contented out here, to know you are so happy with my own folk, and can see your own too every day. I am only afraid your Mother may be grudging you not being there, but you will know by now how my Mammy and Dad like having you and the boy. Mother never misses in her letters trying to make out that Ivydene is all the more like home with you and the boy there.

Arthur keeps falling in lucky doesn't he. I would like to hear from him, but I suppose he hasn't much time.

Hope to goodness there won't be a wedding before I get home as I must be at the CEREMONY, invitation or no invitation.

Doesn't it seem strange that I should be out here now for four months before either of them and being last to join too.

We have had a fairly busy time of it this month, and have practically only had 7 days out of the trenches since I came from the school.

It is a wonderfully cramped sort of existence, and when one gets back for a rest it is right pleasant to be able to stretch oneself and walk in the open air. For instance at present, we (4 of us) are residing in a dugout, of the type we call "Baby Elephant". Cushy as things go. The roof is semicircular steel shrapnel proof with a boarded floor. The highest part in the centre is 4 feet high. The length is such that by lying flat I can touch both ends by my head and feet, width a little less. A quarter of the space is taken up by the instruments and another quarter by our equipment.

This is how we manage – 3 of us lay down while the operator squats at his intruments tailor fashion. When he has done his spell, he falls down on his back and rolls under the next man to him who rolls over him, and sits up in his place, and so on. We only get outside as necessity demands, because anyone doing so causes such a frightful disturbance finding his helmet and respirator, that he isn't too anxious to have the others' showers of blessings on his head too often. To add to the fun, the candle has a trick of falling over with fright every time a shell bursts anywhere in the vicinity, and usually gets into an awkward place in some cranny behind the instruments. Then the only light comes from the illuminating remarks of the crowd of us.

Billy would be tremendously interested if he was here just now. There is an RFA officer and two men observing and sending instructions to our batteries. They are using our wire and we find it quite exciting. They are just having a little target practice on places of interest on Fritz's line, just with one gun. We hear "No 1 gun, action." Then comes back "No. 1 in action". Then all kinds of technical detail about kind of shell and aiming instructions, reply comes "Ready Sir", "Fire", reply "Fired Sir", then we hear a big boom, and the scream of the shell over us, then a bust up further along. Then "Drop 50" reply "Fired Sir".

Then the observer calls out "Target. Repeat". Then we all smile and know the RFA have got it second shot and are proceeding to demolish some nice gun emplacement, that may have taken weeks of work, in as many minutes. It may even be a cookhouse, then of course that is nasty, but there is a <u>rumour</u> going about that one of our cooks was recently blown into a dixey of stew, but I think that the rumour got its foundation from an argument that took place over a piece of meat in the stew that one man swore was a piece of leather belt.

We find the work easier in the front line than in a support trench, as in support there are not always signal stations for each company. Then there are always heavy fatigues to do in the night time. Carrying rations, RE stuff, digging and all sorts, that must be done at night.

Taking it all round, it is much safer and easier in the firing line than in supports.

That pomade you sent is wonderful stuff. Though the war is not yet over, I have had peace on my own since the first application. Don't know where they have gone to, but my enemies have retired precipitately.

Talking of the real war, I really don't think it can last long, as we do really seem to hold the upper hand with him (the Hun). The strafe that we were caught in, was what he put over to our trenches preparatory to making a big raid, but when he came over, our artillery swept his trenches and no man's land backwards and forwards to such extent that not a man reached our lines. Our front line now always feels quite safe with our guns backing us up.

The Germans may make a stand on their new line, but nothing short of their retiring again can save them from being battered out of it, and so it will go on till they are ready to want peace at our price and not theirs.

The worst job of signalling is when the lines get broken by shell fire, or from any other cause. Then we have to get out and find the damage and get it repaired. It may be in the trench, or it may not. There is an old saying that a shell never drops twice in the same place, but that isn't much comfort if one drops a yard out of it. Anyway it is a job we don't dawdle on, not being paid by the hour.

The great thing that bothers me is not being able to have a glimpse of you and the boy even for a moment.

The discomforts, work, and risks are small things compared to being away from you so long, but then I think of the men who have been out over two years and try to think how lucky I am, then I get your cheery letters, then I sit down and scribble cheerful nonsense back, and it bucks me up tremendously.

Getting letters and writing letters are my chief comforts. Most of the men stick persistently to Field Cards (Whizz-Bangs we call them) as soon as they get in the trenches. I shall stick to a sheet of notepaper as long as I am allowed and find opportunity. I can't get much recreation out of a Field Card. The explanation of "Whizz-Bang" is that the WB is a particularly vicious kind of shell that you cannot hear coming and gives one the jumps. I fancy the Cards do the same thing to some extent at home, but it isn't at all wise to take it for granted that a man is in the trenches when a Field Card comes. It is often enough when he thinks he hasn't anything to write about, or is no man for writing letters.

You would be surprised at the quantity of men who find nothing to say except such things as would not pass the censor. If anything makes me feel ratty, it is a want of opportunity to write, and not a want of something to say.

Most of them think me a very quiet sort of chap out here, but I can talk their hind legs off with a pen.

It is the only way I have of chatting with you.

I know my letters are very empty of actual news, but the war is here, and I like to keep it here, and there will be plenty of time to talk of the war when I get home. Then I expect you will soon get your fill of it. Most folks at home I know like to hear about the war, but we like to hear a talk about home things. Apropos of nothing in particular, I haven't seen a civilian since leaving the school, so you will see how it comes that other topics than war are pleasant.

But dear old girl, I do so miss you and would give worlds to have you in my arms in our little home again. I say worlds, but I must hedge a bit. If it was necessary to spend 10 years out here to make sure that our boy would never be called to see the horrors of real warfare, I would do it gladly aye and more. I know that when he grows up, he will almost surely have to join the Army in some shape or form, and it will be a fine thing. And I know that if another war broke out, he would be one of the first lads to volunteer like his Uncle Joe, and I know too that you and I would be proud of him and let him go. But if my little bit can do anything towards making that eventuality an absolute impossibility, then let me stay here till that impossibility is beyond doubt. Then I shall have proved myself worthy of you and him. Bless you both.

Your loving husband, Walter

1 April 1917

We returned to Reserve in Ypres barracks again. The enemy's artillery feeling kindly disposed, Pat and I decided to have a look round Ypres. The destruction was frightful, and the remains of many fine, evidently religious institutions, added to the horror of it all. Of one fine Church, all that remained standing, was a piece of the gable end wall, still holding in a niche, a great stone crucifix, seemingly untouched.

Here we picked up a piece of paper that caught our eye, written in Latin and Flemish. From the little we could decipher, it appeared to be a page from the marriage register dating in the seventeenth century. We were not allowed into the square to have a look at the remains of the Cloth Hall and the Cathedral, though we had been through a few times in the darkness.

The next day we spent doing some warm tunnelling work in the Ramparts of the city. Evidently, the billets in the town were not considered healthy.

3 April

Left the Barracks by night for Toronto Camp, and on the morrow Khaki Blanco and Soldiers Friend were much to the fore, and we were soon looking something like soldiers again.

5 April

The morning of the 5th found us all paraded spick and span. The Brigade was going back to Herzeele, just over the French frontier for a short rest. The four battalions of the Brigade were timed to meet on the Ypres–Poperinghe Rd. near Brandhoek. We arrived by a side road through Brandhoek with some time to spare, and had a rest till the Pipers of the Black Watch were heard in the distance.

Our Battn. moved to its place at the head of the Brigade, as the senior battalion, and after much galloping about of Adjutants, the Brigade at last got on the move towards Poperinghe.

Before reaching the town itself we turned off taking the new switch road which skirted Poperinghe. This road had been made by the troops to relieve the traffic through the town. At that time it was a fine new Macadam road and had not yet received the attention from the enemy artillery that it received later. Along this road we met the Brigadier General taking the salute and noting shortcomings in dress and turnout, remarks on which would soon reach the commanding officers of each battalion, and eventually end in company inspections on the morrow with more Blanco and Brasso. This road brought us on to the Proven Road, a short distance along which brought us to that deeply and many times cursed cobble road which led through St Jan-ter-Biezen and Watou. A great road for knocking one's feet to pieces. Marching by the right of the road, the right hand man of each file marched with his left foot continually six inches higher than his right, except at such times that it skidded down the slope to knock corners off the right ankle. At the halt, the right hand man of the file crossed over to the left of the file for a rest. This road was a sore trial to the Band, but cut lips did not interfere with their eloquence during a halt, on the subject of whether Belgian road-makers should be shot on sight, or merely have their brains battered out with their own road material. Along this road near the two camps "Y" and "Z" many Belgian refugees had made their new homes, and queer structures some of them were, some made of biscuit tins and others just light wooden structures, and all seemed to be engaged in Belgian's staple industry, "Eggs and Chips, with coffee", with Chocolate and Silken Postcards of Ypres as side lines. Watou was soon reached, and the band, reserving its wind for half a mile before reaching it, did their best to blow all the windows out of the village. They could always be depended on to make themselves felt, in the narrow streets of a village. The inhabitants always dashed out, whether in fear of their homes falling about their ears, or to hear the music, seemed a matter of some doubt. Watou also noted for its "Eggs and Chips with coffee". After leaving Watou some distance behind us, the third halt brought up the Cookers, and dinner was served out. Generally, a fairly decent stew could be managed on the march, as the fires had to be lighted before the march commenced, and the meal was usually well cooked by the time of the dinner halt, which usually happened about the middle of the afternoon. This longer rest told its tale when we got to our feet again. Blood had commenced to circulate in our feet again, after being hammered out by the cobbles, and the next mile was seemingly walked with bare feet on red hot needles with business ends upward, but there was a better time coming soon, so we heard from those who had been this way once before. We soon reached the French frontier. A little stream evidently divided France from Belgium at this particular point and the cobbles came to a sudden end at the bridge, while on the other side commenced a beautifully level meadow road which felt like walking on velvet. On the French side of the bridge was the little Customs Office, and a "Poilu" on guard gave a salute that a first week recruit at Birkenhead would have got 7 days C.B. for. We made no remarks about it however so long as he was allowing us to come on to his road. Herzeele was soon reached after this, but "A" Company was more than disgusted to find that their billet was another good mile out of Herzeele. We were taken through some fields where snow was still laying, and a handful or two snatched up and rubbed on the face, or jammed into one's mouth was wonderfully refreshing.

We at last reached a farm where we were to be billeted, and weary legs found some difficulty in lifting heavy feet over the bottom of the barn door. Once inside, the deep straw was too inviting to wait till we had divested ourselves of our equipment, as it is quite as easy to do it while laid on the back. We had not been there more than five minutes however when someone disturbed the general serenity by putting his head in at the door and informing all and sundry that beer was to be had at the farmhouse at one penny per glass. Legs that had boggled at the barn door, now took it in their stride till the door got badly jammed.

The platoon sergeant, a little later, took it for granted that the whole of his platoon would be found where the beer was, and went there to detail two men to bring tea from the cooker. The few who stayed in the barn actually too tired to move out even for beer, look upon this as their consolation, as the cooker was a good half mile away.

Just after "Lights Out" someone was heard to remark to the darkness, that if heaven was a farm billet with plenty of good straw, he would give up swearing forthwith.

6 April

In the morning Jimmy Robinson and myself were transferred to another farm billet with the company "specialists" and there found Pat, and the old Lewis Gun team. Here we found a signaller who had just returned from Hospital. Fred Swann, alias "Little 'Ommer".

He seemed a shy lad, but of course I did not know him then. Henceforth, Jimmy, Freddy and myself were to be "A" company's signallers. This was even a better billet than the last one, and although beer was not available, eggs could be bought and boiled for 20 centimes. We had a man with us in the billet who could speak French fluently, and he was appointed at once "Egg Secretary" and saw to all orders for breakfast and tea. After some pressing as to where he gained his fluency, we learned the surprising fact that he had for a year or two, been an English barber in a Parisian hairdresser's establishment. There was a great joy too when it was found out that beaucoup French bread could be bought at the little village of Bambecque which could be reached in a few minutes from our billet. It was not that the French bread was better than our own – it was not nearly so good – but to have sufficient bread by one, to be able to have a slice when feeling that way, without having to go short for tea, was a great treat. Headquarters of our company were billeted at the next farm, and much amusement was caused there by an old Frenchwoman who swore good round English oaths at any Tommy who came near her.

Whether she was actually expressing her feelings, or just airing the only "English" she knew, was a matter of much speculation. At this farm we found two dogs doing the churning, running endlessly round inside a boxed wheel. In the mornings the same two dogs were harnessed to a good big milk cart, and evidently did the morning milk run. France and Belgium are evidently no places for dogs.

7 April

Billeted with us, we had the Headquarter Bombers. They were the bombing instructors to the Battalion. The cause of the whole affair of course was Pay Day. After pay parade they had received instructions to go down to Headquarters at Herzeele for bombs, for instructional purposes. We saw nothing more of them until late that night, when most of us were getting down to bed in the straw. We heard them coming carolling across the fields from the direction of Bambecque, and judged from the sounds of merriment that the estaminet keepers in Bambecque had been doing good business, and that next pay day would be welcomed at an early date.

They eventually arrived at the barn after safely negotiating the little footbridge over the stream at the back of the farmhouse. It was evident that they had supped "not wisely" "but too well" but had not gone too far to forget to bring home a couple of bottles of cheap champagne for a "pick-me-up" in the morning. On turning the bombs out, one of them would insist on giving us an exhibition of juggling with a couple of Mills No. 5. On being yelled at to put them down, he genially remarked "wind up, boys – Eh?" and proceeded to pull out the safety pin from one of the bombs. A Mills bomb with the safety pin out, in the hands of a man in his state, was enough to cause a little excitement.

It was useless to attempt to take it off him, for if his grip slackened, five seconds would prove whether it was fused or not. Everyone shouted at him to put the pin back and not be several kinds of fool. He still smiled benignly on us, and murmured "Alright boys, it isn't fused" and forthwith he let the lever fly. Whether he suddenly remembered, or whether he heard the fuse actually fizz – but he suddenly screamed "Hell! Look out" and flung it to the roof of the barn while we flung ourselves down in the straw. The bomb exploded with a noise like the crack of doom. The "hero" of the affair caused further excitement by fainting outright, and sobering his friends who were under the impression that he had been killed outright, and they had his clothes off, looking for his wounds, before he came round again. We made a rapid search to see what damage was done, and to see that no straw had caught fire or was smouldering. The barn door appeared to be the only casualty, and with the aid of mud we made his wounds look old enough to have dated back to the last war. Then we got down to bed again to await the appearance of the officers from the next billet, where we felt sure they must have heard the explosion. Now could it have been that same pay day was responsible for the strange fact that nothing more was heard of the matter, till the day we were leaving, when the farmer demanded compensation for the damage to his door, and our officer would not listen to him, as the damage was evidently an old one and not done during our occupation of the billet.

8 April

After Church Parade in the morning, Pat and I decided to have a walk to Bambecque in the afternoon. Pat was anxious to buy a little silver crucifix, and not being able to find exactly what he wanted in the little shops of the village, asked where he would be likely to obtain one. He was recommended to see M. Le Cure. I was taken along as a guarantee of respectability[?] and we found the house of M. Le Cure opposite the church. He was a fine old gentleman and he shook hands most affably, and then our troubles began. Pat started off in careful English, but we found the worthy old gentleman could make nothing of it. This was Pat's chance, that he had really been waiting for, and after coughing and steadying himself, he led off in the classic manner of the "First French Reader". The "Cure" stood it very well, crossing his hands resignedly across his rosary and he looked appealingly at Pat to stop it. At last he could stand it no longer and groaned "No spik Engleesh, Monsieur."

Pat grabbed at the top hook of his tunic, and felt a little better when he had rested a little. Then we let the old gentleman himself have a try, and we managed to save a remnant of Pat's reputation as a linguist, by deducing from the horrid noise the old gentleman made the fact that he was pure Flemish and understood neither French nor English.

He however, fully entered into the spirit of the game, and eventually, with much pantomime gesture, and a bit of shouting, he got an idea of what Pat was wanting, but was desolated at being unable to oblige him.

As we were verging on nervous prostration, we only waited till we were out of sight from Monsieur Le Cure's window, before diving into an estaminet for a stimulant, then called at the baker's shop and purchased some rolls of bread to console us.

11 April

Our Easter holiday was over and we paraded in the morning to march back to "The Salient".

The weather took a turn for the worse, and driving snow and sleet the whole of the march, made the roads in a frightful state. Tired and wet, we reached "O" camp, on the Poperinghe–Ypres road in the evening. The huts here were in a poor state of repair, and we blamed the severe winter for the fact that much of the lining and fittings of the huts had evidently been used for fuel.

We were no sooner into camp than a big party was detailed to proceed within the hour to Ypres, to work for the "R.E." (bless 'em).

12 April

Off early to work for the Canadian Construction Boys, making light railways. As someone put it – "An "<u>offensive</u>" odour about this".

The size of the Canadian shovels we were served out with, made us turn pale, but our colour soon came back when we started to use them. I am not surprised that we were able to stick to that part of Belgium. The trouble really would be to get rid of it. A shovelful seemed to have the tenacity of good glue, plus fly-paper mixture, black treacle and bird lime, and, if ever those railway tracks were finished, they ought to stick alright.

This was our chief occupation for a fortnight, part of which time Pat spent at a Lewis Gun School learning theory, after practice. An Anti-Aircraft battery in the vicinity supplied the only little diversion we had here, though a little excitement was caused one day by gas from a local Gas School blowing our way whilst at work without helmets with us. Even topping this for real excitement, was another "Bath Parade" down to Poperinghe.

28 April

We retired from Railway Construction work and went into the front line again, on what was known as "La Brique" sector, our particular locality being "Bilge Trench". Swann did not join us after all on our signal station and charge was taken by Collier of "D" Company, with Jim and myself making up the trio. Collier was already decorated with the D.C.M. for fine signal work on the Somme, during the big offensive in 1916. The instruments were fixed in the Company H.Q. dugout and while off duty, we had a little hole of our own to sleep in, close at hand. As our little home was not over strong in the roof, we were not averse to taking on a little extra duty where the sandbags were thicker, and it was a common thing to find us all there on duty at the same time.

Our Company Commander at that time was a good sort, a prosperous looking gentleman, pet name of "Theo", who was always the best dressed officer in the battalion, but whose uniform could never make him look anything else but a regular Church attender. He had rather a "sweet" tenor voice which always took the lead in "Who killed Cock Robin?" "Three blind mice", or "Who will o'er the downs so free?" one of which was religiously performed each evening after dinner.

He looked upon the signallers with an approving eye and did not at all object to having us in his quarters. "Very intelligent body of men, the signallers" he used to remark "Communication, most important thing" and so on, and of course we agreed with him, which proved that we were at least – intelligent.

Artillery on both sides was very active in this quarter, and the first night up there a message came through the wires from Battn. H.Q. giving warning that our Artillery would carry out two "Heavy Shoots" during the night on our immediate front, and giving the times for each "Shoot".

We knew what that meant. Collier explained it tersely in "Our guns blows 'is blinkin front line t'ell, then his guns blows ours after it".

As trouble was certain to occur with the telephone lines, and as we had taken a sudden strong dislike to our dugout since the message came through, we decided to all go on duty together during the shoots. Pat would be on duty at the Lewis Gun post, and a hot spot it promised to be.

Our barrage dropped to time and enemy S.O.S. went up immediately in expectation of a raid behind the barrage. Their Artillery answered the S.O.S. very quickly, and the din now beggared description. "Theo" was very anxious and feared that we should not be able to keep in communication with Battn. H.Q. and we were kept busy testing the wires till the inevitable happened, and we could get no reply.

The shelling was not quite as hot as the few opening bars, and leaving Jim and myself in charge of the instruments, Frank Collier disappeared from the dugout. Continually trying the line we soon found ourselves through to Battn. H.Q. again and reported to "Theo" who was delighted. We waited anxiously for Collier's appearance which occurred with a suddenness that startled us, accompanied by a big noise "off" as the prompt book puts it. He was quickly rewarded with a tot of rum, and Jim and I were also "totted" along with him. After a second break and a second tot, Collier evidently began to think that "breaks" were a paying proposition, and a few times that night, Collier went out to mend breaks whilst Jim and I pretended to be making frantic and futile efforts to get through to Battn. H.Q. on a perfectly sound wire. I refused my tots after the first, not from any conscientious scruples, but knowing that it would be my turn for duty when things had settled down, and Frank and Jim would be off to bed. When peace seemed to have been declared for what remained of the night, they went off to their little dug out in a frame of mind that might have taken them over the German lines to inform them that they could shell as much as they liked. Serious casualties were wonderfully few, though a good many men had been knocked about by trench collapses and flying sandbags. Pat's post had a rough time of it, two of the team being wounded and the remainder had to spend most of the time sitting on another member of the team who was an old sufferer of shell shock, and usually went "off his chump" as soon as any heavy shelling took place. An hour or two after the time I expected to be relieved, I left the phone to look after itself for a few moments, to go to see what had become of Frank and Jim.

I was shocked on reaching the dugout to find Jim lying half in and half out of the dugout with his face on the duckboards, with his arm dangling in the mud below. I rolled him over quickly and was horrified at the look in his face. "Where are you hit" I gasped. "Aint 'it, old man, I've losht my falsh teeth under the duckboard."

Having rescued his teeth and washed them for him, he got back to his downy couch where I found Frank sleeping soundly, and looking as if it would be a waste of time to try to get him up just then, so I left them to slumber awhile longer.

It was not long however, before Frank turned up with my breakfast and a little bit extra, as Jim did not want any breakfast that morning.

We had quite a good time for the remainder of the five days that we spent here, and "tit bits" from the officers' table were always welcome. Frank's only grumble being that he thought it an aspersion cast upon his honesty, the fact that he could never find out where it was that they put their whisky when all the officers were out.

An amusing incident happened the day before we moved, perhaps more amusing to us, than to the enthusiastic young officer who was the victim of his own excess of zeal. This officer dashed into Company H.Q. just before dawn, with an armful of tape. "What do you think of this Sir?" The Captain looked at it as if his wife was asking him to appraise the value of her purchase at the Spring Sales.

"What is it?" he asked dubiously. "Boche Tape Sir" was the excited reply. "They must be going to make a raid" he added. Then the Captain commenced to get excited too. It was often necessary in those times, when a raid was to be made in the dark, to lay out tapes a little earlier, which would act as a guide back to our trenches in the hurry of returning from a short raid.

The Capt. phoned down to Battn. H.Q. that he was coming down at once with urgent and important news, a message came back that the C.O. was out, and the Adjt. was already on the way to our Company H.Q.

As soon as the Adjt. appeared the news was hurled at him. "Where do you say you found it?" he asked, and after learning full details of the location, he surprised us by bursting into loud gaffaws.

We knew him as a fire eater, but never thought he would waste time sitting there laughing with a raid imminent. We were enlightened however when he remarked "Say, you had better get that tape back again tonight where you got it from. The Corps R.E. were up last night marking out a new forward trench, and the sooner you get it back, and the less you say about it, the better".

"What about a drop of whisky Theo?"

2 May

The battalion came back into support at trenches known as "X" lines and Irish Farm and 2 platoons of "A" company to a "strong point" called "Wilson's Farm", Frank, Jim and myself taking over the signals at this place. It consisted of a short well built trench, containing a deep sap which led down below fully 30 feet to the signal office and the sleeping accommodation. Down here we found the strongest point of the strong point. It was the smell. As yet, there was only the one entrance and no through ventilation, and the heat was terrific, and as we sat on our shelf we shed everything but tunics and trousers in our efforts to keep cool. As this failed and the smell became unbearable, we moved the instruments up into the trench where they were having glorious sunshine. "Nobby" Clarke who was now on Battn. H.Q. visited us one day to inspect [?] instruments, etc. While he was chatting with us, the Fullerphone buzzed off.

"Gas alert. Strombus horn heard on our left".

Everyone dashed for Gas Masks to see if they were in working order, which of course should be done every day. "Nobby" was horrified after unloading his gas mask case of candle ends, to find his mask short of an eye piece, which of course put the mask entirely out of action. We loaned him a good old "P.H." bag mask, and he flew off as hard as his long legs would carry him, to get back to Battn H.Q. before the gas caught him.

We heard later unofficially, that it was a false alarm. A new and inquisitive Sgt. had arrived in the line with the Battalion on our left front and had inadvertently started the strombus horn, and every telephone in a large area had immediately sent the alarm far and wide.

Here, we were in dire straits for cigarettes, and having managed to get hold of a packet or two of issue shag we fell to making cigarettes with it, using leaves from official message pads for cigarette papers.

The day before we left, Pat was sent away with a man Entwistle, for the same signal course that I had, and my opportunity came to get a little back for his remarks about giving up soldiering for signalling.

6 May

We went into reserve on the banks of the Yser (Eyesore) Canal. Here only Battn. H.Q. required signallers so went and billetted with No. 4 platoon of our Company and worked with them. We were put busy at once digging new dugouts in the bank for the next war. On the other bank of the canal others were busy on light railway work, the good work which we had started had now reached that far, so that both banks were at that time positive hives of industry. Enemy aircraft took particular delight in coming to inspect our progress and return to their quarters and report, and I suppose, give a hint that we were working far too hard for the amount of pay that we were drawing. The enemy artillery had both banks ranged to a yard, and when he decided that we should stop work he simply put a barrage down that drove us in a big hurry across the footbridges into the tunnels on the West Bank. His barrages at that time being a nice mixture of High Explosives, Shrapnel, and Gas shells, and casualties were heavier a deal, than actually in the front line.

A night or two was also spent cable laying, practically to the front line. This confirmed our suspicions of a big offensive coming in the near future, as cables usually only came as far forward as Divisional Headquarters, and front lines would have to travel forward very considerably to leave room for Div. H.Q. at the end of those cables.

12th May 1917

My own sweet wife,

Just the usual little gift with all the love it will carry, to make you think that we are still together, despite the miles that lay between us.

What I may be doing this day, I do not know, but whatever may be the task, it will be lightened and sweetened by thoughts of you and our little son, who was surely sent as a little companion.

May you be happy on this the fourth anniversary of our wedding.

Your lover and husband,

Walter

To my wife:

> Sweetness herself
> her sweetness imparts
> Love such as hers
> makes fast beating hearts
>
> Sweetness and love
> Two things worth untold
> And counted such riches
> Not bought by earth's gold
>
> Add to these
> Mother and Wife
> She is my mate
> My help, my life. W. W.

14th May 1917 – Cheshire View

Dear little Woman,

The enclosed letter got missed when the Post Corporal came round for letters this morning, I can get it away by the same post as this will not need censoring here.

Now little lady you mustn't get jumpy because you don't get a letter for a day or two. All kinds of things happen with letters nowadays, even yours arrive in bunches sometimes with a couple of days interval.

I had a letter from Mother written later the same day as yours, saying that two letters turned up after you had written.

There is no big fighting going on where we are, as there is in some sectors, and we are hoping to be clear of the line again very shortly for another spell of training, or rest as they call it. I expect your letter tomorrow will be as chirpy as usual.

It is fortunate you have optimistic Jim along with you at times.

You will have had my letters long before now I expect, telling you that I had got your parcel, mother's too, and the note you sent. Letters seem to take longer to get through nowadays, for some reason or other. What I keep hearing of the boy from everyone that writes to me makes me so anxious to see the little chap.

I feel at times that when I do come home, I shall be almost afraid to pick him up, fearing to crush the little man to pulp. You are lucky to have him all to yourself all this time, but when I do come home, you will have to run short a bit. Next thing, Joe and he will be having great times together. Wonder what Joe will have to say to Jim's argument vide Cheshires and Lancashires.

Half of Edie's letter was about the boy, and as I never fancied Edie took much notice of youngsters, I fancy Jim must have been at his best.

Hope his Dad doesn't go and spoil all his good upbringing when he comes home. Are you going to take him swimming again this summer with Mabel, hope so, let him have as much of the water as he can get while the weather is warm. He ought to be swimming soon with those little webbed toes of his. Am glad really that he has had this chance of having a spell of his Mam's influence alone, Father's roughening can come in later. Madge tells me he is such an open, fearless, straightforward little soul, and Edie tells me that he has such a sweet way of talking to anyone. There is his mother all over.

I suppose you will be horribly jealous by now, but you know, one never thinks of a gift without thinking of the giver. I sometimes begin to think I once had a lovely dream that I had a wife and a little son, then things crop up to prove it, and then I am alright again for a spell.

It is a funny thing, but when Nunn gets away from me, he seems to take Cheadle Hulme away with him, then I begin to miss you and Jim and feel lost a bit and alone amongst so many good friends. I don't however often get in that state, as it doesn't do. It is a funny thing that when things are hottest in the line, the lads are the most cheerful. In my case it is a quiet night spell on the telephone, nothing to read perhaps, or no letters to write, and nothing coming through, that tells.

The worst strafe I have experienced yet, brought a most hilarious evening in the Signal Office, while the said "Office" did its best to stand on its hind legs. This time up the line we have had a young D.C.M. signaller as head man on our station. He is an absolute scream and during the bombardment kept us and the officers who were in the office in a continual chuckle. He got his D.C.M. on the Somme for running out a telephone line under heavy shell fire to a position and got communication with 10 minutes of a position being captured.

He has a funny trick of carrying a pair of India rubber running shoes in his pocket. Of course our wires got broken, and he whipped the receiver off his head, and yelled "Get this on your 'dome' Walt" kicked off his big boots and slipped his rubbers on. The Capt. asked him what he was going out in 'those things' for. He naively remarked that they were not for going out in, but for coming back when he had found and mended the break. He slipped out like an eel while I sat continually trying the line. Five minutes and I got through, two minutes later, accompanied by a terrific crash outside, our worthy came through the dugout entrance like a stone from a catapult, remarking "Missed me again you old!!!!!" The officers present were simply roaring while he asked me if I was through. Then he turned to the Capt. and solemnly announced "All lines working Sir" and in the same breath "Let me come on that bloomin' 'oojah' Walt". The Capt. looked at him helplessly and passed him a good tot of rum. I was offered the same, but knowing that I was to do a good long spell of duty when things became normal again, decided to forgo it.

Then we were kept busy sending reports down to Hquarters as to how things were going, till our Artillery knocked Fritz into silence once more. After another tot, Collier (the worthy D.C.M.) passed the "oojah Kumpivvy" over to my charge, he passed out of the "office" and as the curtain dropped behind him we heard him sniff very audibly and remark "Phew!!!! t'ell of a stink" and truly the atmosphere smelt about a thousand times worse than at the fireworks at Belle Vue on a wet heavy close night, and it wasn't clear 24 hours later.

Our Captain asked me all particulars I knew of Collier, and we talked about him for quite a time and it was peeping dawn when the Capt. "got down" after deciding that he was a "character". I fancy he would like to get him transferred to "A" Company from "D" Company to which he really belongs.

I hope too that Collier's presidency of "A" Company's signal station when in the front line is a permanent and not a temporary business.

At present "A" Company has no station, and we don't see quite as much of him, as he is now on Batt. Headquarters.

We are quite a merry lot however in our present quarters. Though officially belonging to "A" Company Headquarters, for rations etc. we go along with No 4 platoon, and at present we are living with the platoon in one big dugout. Number 4 platoon sergeant who lives with us, is the nicest sergeant one could meet in a thousand years. He lives at Gatley and I think works at Moseley's Bleachworks at Cheadle. He has been out here since 1914 without getting a scratch and tells us of some of his terrific experiences with a quaint little stammer and a sense of humour that keeps us in one continual chuckle. And his experiences of a less serious nature, come from him in a way that makes us sore.

He is an immeasurable help to his lads and even to officers when hard times come to them in the front line. He is one of those men who is a hero to everyone but himself.

His tales of home are exquisite. It appears that he is an expert cornet player, and plays in the Didsbury Prize Band in peaceful times. He was asked particularly to play in a band contest on a certain date, and, promising faithfully to do so, he jotted the date down and did not notice till some time later that he was to be married that day. Two hours after being wed he was blowing his heart down his cornet in uniform and blew his band into the first prize.

His next comes when a little daughter came. A motherly old neighbour pushed him out of his own house into hers, where she told him he would find his dinner ready, and he wasn't to come bothering till he was sent for. He ate his dinner as he said to pass the time away, and mooned about till the Doctor came in and told him he could go and have a look at his daughter. Of course he shot off then and stayed awhile with them, till he was told he had been there long enough. So he went downstairs and proceeded forthwith to express his feelings on his beloved cornet.

The old neighbour came bustling downstairs to know what on earth he was thinking about. He said he thought the missus might like it, and on enquiries being made, it was found that he was quite right and the baby seemed to like it too. After the missus was "up and about" the nightly picture was to be seen of our cornetist seated in front of his music stand, cornet in one hand, baby nestled in the other arm, being played to sleep by cornet. When War broke out, the little girl was having her first lessons on the cornet. He has another baby about 3 months old which he reckons he ordered the only time he was on leave. You can guess he is simply living (not dying mind you) to get home and see it.

He tells a very funny tale of a working party he was once on. They were working in the open some distance from a tunnel and had one barrow in use. Fritz commenced to shell the party "like 'ell" as he has it. He then gives a graphic description as to how he bolted for the tunnel and must perforce charge into the barrow though there were scores of yards to spare round any side of the barrow. "There was Fritz "sniping" at me with Black Marias in my idea and I couldn't get past that barrow at 6 tries, so like ... I got hold of the handles and wheeled it out of the way, and then to put the finishing touch, climbed over it and finished with a wild sprint into the tunnel knocking down an officer who was coming out to see what the matter was."

He has us screaming with this yarn, the way he tells it.

I have heard the tale from other sources, and the barrow incident is true enough, but he omits to state that he was in charge of the party, and nearest to the lines of Fritz, keeping a look out when he saw the shelling commence, in the shape of a moving barrage which threatened to wipe the whole party out if they couldn't reach the tunnel in front of it. By his warning the men got there first, and Sgt Bob being advance post, was now rearguard and was caught in the barrage while seeing that all his lads got clear, and all he tells about it is what he calls his damn tomfoolery with the barrow, and the boys could do nothing but peep out of the tunnel expecting him to be blown to bits, as they swear they could see nothing but bursting shells and "Bob" wrestling in the midst of it with the unruly barrow. They say that he couldn't stop laughing when he got to safety, but they soon found out that his laugh didn't sound healthy. A terrific dose of rum shut him up and his first question was "All the lads are in, aren't they?".

I do hope I can get him to come and see us someday at Cheadle Hulme.

He has no decorations at all, beyond his sergt's stripe. We don't wish him any. The very fact that he hasn't got any, makes us think the more of him.

He doesn't look a soldier. A little stammer, a soft voice, a bit round shouldered though squarely built, a mild looking face, with a very downy attempt at a moustache. So you see that a perfect military figure, flashing eyes, fierce eyebrows and ringing voice, are not essentials. Another type is our R.C. Chaplain. Absolutely worshipped by all the boys, R.C. and C. of E. combined. If there is anything doing, he is found in the front line. If they are sheltering in dugouts, he is bobbing in for a chat in one and then another, if they are on the fire step, tense and too busy to talk, he will walk at the back of them saying "Aves" for their comfort. On the Somme he lost an eye bringing the wounded in (although an old man) and refused to be attended to although in awful agony, while there were others. Of course he was taken no notice of and the boys got him down to the dressing station in quick time. I am told that everyone thought his wound would prove fatal, or at the least total blindness. News came through when the Batt. was out of the line, and was read out on parade, and I believe the men shouted themselves hoarse.

He came out to us again as soon as he could get, and I suppose he got a terrific reception.

The night of our worst strafe up the line last, after all was over he came strolling into the Officers' Mess where I was on duty on the phone. He had been along with the lads. After a little chat with the Officers, he seemed to me to come to the point, "Can I beg a cigarette, do you know I am afraid my nerve isn't what it was, a cigarette soothes me wonderfully and I have run out". Consternation. The Officers' Mess absolutely out of cigs. Others nerves had evidently wanted soothing. I came to the rescue and he asked if he could take two with a smile that deserved 2000.

He was off again immediately on hearing of 1 casualty, which he caught up before the stretcher bearers had reached the dressing station. A couple of hours later he was back to the boys particular chums with a reassuring report from the doctor. Soon after coming back to the Batt. from hospital, he wanted to go over the top with the boys on a big attack to help the first wounded, saying that he would be quite alright if he wore his surplice. He was not allowed over till the attack had fairly progressed, much to his impatience.

Now breathe it not in Gath, he once (owing to some difficulty in getting the wounded away) offered to hold a man's post if they gave him half a dozen bombs handy.

It is getting bedtime now Mam's (no work tonight), or I could fill a volume with characters out here.

We have had quite a lazy day today, a little warm rain and lots of sunshine.

Tell Mother I have her letter too, but you have taken up all available time tonight, so you will have to stand down tomorrow in favour of Mother.

A kiss for that boy and one for yourself from

Your loving husband Walter.

The weather at this time was beautiful, though the warm sun did not tend to sweeten the odour from the canal, and it was almost possible to believe the tales of what the canal was supposed to chiefly contain. One drawback to summer to some of the men, was the withdrawal of the rum ration in favour of lime juice, and the lime juice was not "cordially" received, as one man said as he picked bits of wood out of his ration, "Well, if it bites lumps off the inside of the cask, what is it going to do to me?".

15 May

We left the Canal Bank without many regrets, in the darkness, and before dawn reached "O" Camp, in the same wood that we were in at "D" camp in the previous December. We found it a very different place with the trees in leaf, and dry underfoot. Railway work commenced again at once, and we were quite delighted to find little "puffing billies" running about where we had first commenced to level Belgian mud.

The first day we climbed aboard trucks of stone ballast, and the little engine set off at a gallop, doing its best to rattle us off it, but to the "P.B.I." a ride is a ride, and we were not to be shaken off. When we reached as far as the metals were safe, we found a fairly soft job pushing the ballast out of the trucks, till a Canadian Sgt. came along and presented half a dozen of us with a crowbar each, and sent us further along the lines to straighten them out, and before the end of the day, those crowbars nearly straightened us out. I promised myself that next day, if I saw that Sgt. looming in the offing, I would glue on to the spade and get lost in the crowd, instead of looking as if I was wanting a job.

20 May

About 300 of us were marched down to Poperinghe in the evening for a free show of our 39th Divl. Entertainment Party. It was quite a good show. Divisional staff were thick in the front rows, and there was enough gold braid to serve as footlights. They received many sly digs from the stage, referring principally to Leaves, Baths and Divisional Rest.

On getting back to camp that evening, I found a letter from Pat saying what a good time he was having, and informing me by postscript, that the huts at the Signal School had been limewashed since I left there. I have not yet known him long enough to judge whether this was unconscious or deliberate.

25 May

Off at 5–15 a.m. for road making. We finished early owing to the fact that early in the afternoon an enemy observation balloon rose, and had a nice view of the proceedings, and asked their artillery to send a message or two over. The one officer in charge of us was not anxious to have any casualties amongst the men (or officer(s)), so we struck work. In order that we should not arrive back at the camp too early, he took us to a bathing pool he had noticed on the outward journey, and as it was a sweltering hot day, we enjoyed ourselves immensely for an hour, the absence of A.S.A. regulation costumes, and towels troubling us not a jot, in fact shirts felt pleasantly cooler after being used as towels.

The following day, we started off at the same unfeeling hour, boarding a train of alternate trucks of rails and sleepers. Unluckily, with some others of our platoon, we were packed onto a pile of rails. As soon as the train started those rails commenced to joggle most uncomfortably. On arriving back at the camp there was a search instituted for blood blisters, and although none were found, we decided next morning to raid a truck containing sleepers.

28 May

The Battalion marched out of camp at 7.0 a.m. It was hot even at that early hour, but when we were still marching through Herzeele at 4.0 p.m. with no signs of stopping for the night, the temperature and the language too had reached "Torrid".

We finished however at Wormhoudt, a few miles further on and a good barn billet was some consolation.

We were allowed to rest the next day, and in the evening, everyone wended their way into Wormhoudt. It was quite a nice old place, with the usual big church, town square (with bandstand complete), plenty of shop windows (to gaze at) and the usual crowd of cafes and estaminets (to sample).

Our own band immediately commenced to blow the cobwebs off the bandstand, and the inhabitants flocked into the square, and the boys were soon busy instructing the girls of Wormhoudt in the correct pronunciation of the word "Cheshire" keeping a sharp look out on their cap badges at the same time.

Work on the morrow consisted of building a rifle range, and this created an illusion that we were to be at Wormhoudt for a long spell of training.

31 May

The illusion vanished into thin air as the Battn. paraded to march back. Rumours were rife that G.H.Q. or some other H.Q., or perhaps the War Office, had, in view of the good weather, decided to commence that offensive which seemed to be in the air.

It was even hotter on the march back, than on the march out, and many of the men were badly distressed and fell out of the ranks. This is not a good thing to happen on a march. As long as no one falls out of the ranks, many thoroughly beaten men will stick on, and on till the end of the march, but when one man gives way and gives the lead, these men will lose their fortitude and roll out of the ranks on to the roadside, and thus a rot commences.

The Army Authorities know this well, and strict rules are laid down in this regard. When stragglers finally arrive at their destination, they are permitted a medical examination, and only when the Medical Officer is satisfied that they were justified in leaving the ranks, do they escape punishment. We were lucky in having an M.O. who was sympathetic, except where he found malingering, and then woe betide the malingerer. We eventually reached a canvas camp on the old Race Course near Poperinghe, and we were allowed to lay down at once, and have tea even before being allotted to our respective tents, and all stragglers were in within the hour.

1 June

We found to our disgust that we were the only battn. of the Brigade to return from Wormhoudt and as we knew our Colonel for a bit of a sport, we feared that the Colonels of the Cheshires, Black Watch, Herts and Cambs had been tossing for it, and our Colonel had been unlucky.

On a railway siding which ran alongside the camp we noticed a big gun, and going to have a look, found it was the famous "Mary Bull". We admired her ample proportions and felt quite pleased that she was on our side, but we wondered where she had left her husband.

The battalion was set working in two portions, one for day work unloading on the railway siding, and the other night working, taking shells up to our gun positions in front of Messines Ridge, where, according to rumour, things were likely to happen very shortly. Our platoon was on day work at the siding, and although it was heavy work, it was much preferred to the night work. The enemy felt something was in the wind, and he took to shelling Poperinghe and district fairly well each day, but only one day did he disturb us.

It was those observation balloons of his. One particularly clear day, he must have spotted the activity at the Railway Siding, and gave it us hot and strong. A cottage near, was levelled and a mother and two little children were killed outright. One big shell fairly hit a big W.D. motor which was just leaving the siding and there was very little left of either wagon, or the two men with it. Two cows in an adjoining enclosure, seemed to have escaped actual injury, but it looked as if the poor beasts would have to be killed, as they seemed to have gone mad. On the railway siding were big joinery workshops where many civilians from Poperinghe – old men and young boys – were employed and they stood the shelling like heroes.

On the night of the 6th the night party did not turn out, and in the early hours of the morning, long before daylight, a deep rumble was heard followed by a tremendous artillery duel.

Messines Ridge had been captured.

I managed to secure a pass for Poperinghe one afternoon, and looked up Pat at the Signal School. The men of the Signal School were not allowed in Poperinghe at that time on account of the shelling, so I accepted his invitation to tea with him at the school, and adjourned later to an estaminet close by to talk small beer.

10 June

Reveille 3.0 a.m. Parade 3.30, all equipment clear of the camp and breakfast at 3.45 a.m. Camp to be struck at 4.15 a.m. Battn. ready to move off at 4.45 a.m.

There was a big scutter of course after breakfast but at 4.13 everyone was standing by, waiting for the bugle at 4.15 when all tents went over and in 20 minutes they had been folded and packed on wagons and the ground cleared up, and there was nothing left to show that a camp existed, except the incinerator, which was working overtime.

At 5.0 a.m. we were well away down the Switch Road on our way to rejoin our Brigade at Wormhoudt, which place was reached in time for dinner, having finished the march before the worst of the heat. After an immediate foot inspection, we lazed the remainder of the day in the fields, in anticipation of more marching the next day.

11 June

We continued our march, passing through Ledringhem to barn billets near Arneke, only about 10 miles today in view of a big march to come.

Having a look round with Bob Atkinson, a Lewis Gunner, we were delighted to find what we judged was quite a decent bathing pond. Bob tried it with a pole, and finding what proved to be the only deep spot in it (which we did not realize at the time), said there was any amount of water, so we stripped and dived together, and buried our noses in black slime at the bottom of 30 inches of water, and to add insult to injury, the farmer came along while we were trying to clean ourselves again, and screeched some most terrible French at us, and being patient with him, we eventually managed to understand that he did not allow dirty soldiers to use his clean cow's clean water, or something to that effect, and the only thing we could think of in reply was to ask him if he kept eggs, and finding he did we first ordered ours for tea and then warned the others that eggs might be had at the kitchen.

12 June

We were on the march again at 6.0 a.m. passing through the little villages of Ochterzeele and Noordpeene, then skirting the Fôret de Clairmarais where we had dinner on the road side. Continuing towards St Omer we found a prettily quaint part, where wide dykes ran along each side of the road, and narrow dykes cut off at right angles into the fields. These dykes were almost covered with water lilies, and little punts bobbed about these dykes at varying speeds, according to whether it was some old man going to work in the fields, or young boys having some fun with someone else's punt. Little bridges connecting the little houses with the road completed a picture.

Passing through St Omer we had our first vision of W.A.A.C.S., and very well they looked, but not at us, and there was a deal of talk in the ranks about getting transferred. As we passed the big railway siding at the station, a gang of German prisoners stopped work to watch us march past, and they were met with some good natured chaff, principally with reference to the shape of their heads, and their nice soft job.

We passed out of St Omer by the main road to Boulogne, and were beginning to feel the heat badly. Orders were given to open out, and each file of four spread across the whole width of the wide road, to get air through the ranks.

A mile or two out of the town we found a battalion of the Grenadier Guards, just falling out to their billets, whilst we had still six or seven miles in front of us. They looked as if they did not want any more marching that day, though they had only come from the same district. They gave us a cheering "Stick it Cheshires" and we plodded on our way. It had been practically all uphill work from St Omer, and the heat was terrific and to get a little relief we were ordered to open our tunics as far as equipment would allow. The boys were sticking it wonderfully well, but when we had done over 30 kilometres men began to faint, and drop in their tracks.

We had been looking at our watches, watching the fingers crawl their slow way to ten minutes to the hour, the time for a halt, though however we should get started again, if we did halt, none knew. Just on the minute that we expected the whistle to blow for a halt, the band struck up a tune, which meant that we were not halting. Shouts of protest actually went up from the men. This was the last straw. We knew our Colonel as a strict soldier, but always fair to his men, and we had never known him to march us over the 50 minutes in full equipment before. Men were just on the verge of defying all discipline when we suddenly turned a sharp corner down a steep hill, and found Setques in front of us. The band changed its tune to the famous Regimental "March, March the Twenty second". We tried our best to pick up a step and straighten ourselves out, but it was no use. Eyes were half blinded with smarting perspiration, and feet simply slithered, men from the rear unable to control their legs bumped the men in front and set them going and we reached the bottom of the hill, a broken rabble, and many men never knew how they got into their billets or how they arrived at Setques.

The Colonel had not been unmindful of us after all, as we found that someone had been sent on in advance and got in a plentiful supply of beer, which the officers immediately served out. For those whose thirst was not quenchable with a pint of beer, there was unlimited milk to be had at our billet, some even had both with no dire results, which speaks volumes for army training. Then of course the M.O. was round again admiring our pedal extremities, followed by Bob Cawley, the battalion chiropodist with his insignia of office "big brush rampant with iodine pendant and scissors on field of cotton wool".

After tea someone mentioned a river at the bottom of the field behind the barn, investigation followed and we were soon disporting ourselves. A heavy thunderstorm disturbed the proceedings, and there was a wild scramble for clothes. Bob Atkinson decided that he was not coming out for any thunderstorm, and I stayed for company, enjoying the sensation of bathing in a heavy thunderstorm. A peculiar idea occurred to us that we might be struck by lightening, and the thought of the lightening catching us without clothes was more than we could bear, so we climbed out, and found that instead of swimming about just near our clothes, we were a good fields length away. Our clothes were soaked through, so we picked them up and dashed for the back entrance to the barn, and spent the remainder of the evening in our overcoats, while the good lady at the farm dried our clothes.

13 June

It was 9.30 a.m. before we were on the march again. We took a by-road for a couple of miles which seemed all honeysuckle and roses, until we came again on to the Boulogne high road. This is one of those roads for which France is famous. A great broad white road, perfectly straight, lined on each side with fine trees at regular intervals. It rose gently and disappeared away over the sky line like a thin white thread. As we rose, we had fine views across the valleys on each side, and on reaching the highest level, a fine panorama opened out, but what pleased us most was a nice cool breeze that we found there.

The Colonel and the Adjutant had galloped away in front of us some time previously, and we now saw a little black dot on the whiteness of the road a long way in front of us, which eventually grew into the Adjutant returning at a swift gallop. We heard him instruct the Signal Officer who was leading the battalion, to take the first turn to the left.

This might have meant anything up to ten miles on those roads, but this particular road turned up quite suddenly, to our pleasant surprise, and we found a zig-zag road leading right down into the valley, and at the bottom we could just espy a pretty church spire peeping up through the trees. Half way down, the battalion drew into a field for dinner and afterwards proceeded down the hill to the village of Coulomby. When we arrived here, things were in a bad way with us. Cigarettes seem to have given out in the battalion generally, and on the march, the last few Woodbines had been going the rounds, say four draws to the original possessor, and three draws each as far as it would go round, also at breakfast time, most of us had decided to have a good breakfast and chance buying some bread at the end of the day's journey, for tea.

As soon as we arrived therefore, equipment was dumped, and an immediate search was instituted for bread and cigarettes. The village was one of the prettiest spots imaginable, but we could not smoke it, nor put jam on it and eat it. The place seemed to consist of about half a dozen estaminets, a few deserted barns in a very disreputable state of repair, a draper's shop whose stock seemed to consist chiefly of metal polish and chocolate, a farm that had no milk, a bakery that had no bread, a stream running through the centre of the village, with a bridge about every five yards, but no water to speak of, and lots of little kiddies who seemed to belong to no one in particular.

Completing the village was a beautiful old church big enough to put the remainder of the village inside. I was sat on one of the little bridges wondering where next to try for cigarettes while Jimmy was hunting bread, when a little toddler came and stood in front of me. He looked so friendly I nearly blurted out "Where can I get fags? Chum", but pulled myself together and tried the little chap very carefully in my best elementary French over the matter of bread and cigarettes. He seemed a bit overweighted with these economic problems, so I asked his name and his age, and where he came from, but found the poor little chap must have been no better at his French than I was. On only one matter did we reach a mutual understanding, we found that we both liked chocolate. Then a door suddenly opened and a shrill voice called something which was perfectly unintelligible to me, but was evidently thoroughly understood by my young friend, for he slid off my knee, and gave me a look that plainly said "must be going, sorry old man, but you see how I'm fixed", and I was left alone without the help of his silent sympathy.

We had not then all found billets, but I returned to where we had dumped our equipment to report lack of success to Jim whom I found in a state of excitement, as the first post for some days had just come in, and cigarettes were knocking about again. Jim had found us bread, so as hot tea was then being served out, we made a good tea on marmalade and cheese.

At 7.0 that evening our company and "B" company moved out again, as no billets could be found for us, and after climbing up out of the valley on to the high road again, we at last found rest in farm billets at Harlettes, a village on the other side of the main road.

At the front gate of our billet were two of the finest red thorns I have ever seen, but marching into the yard, a finer sight still met our gaze. It was the farmer's wife just finishing off her baking day, with piles of great round flat loaves all round the big kitchen.

We could hardly wait to be dismissed before making a raid on the kitchen.

A sweet rumour that we had reached the end of our journey, and would stay here for a spell of training, soothed us to sleep that night.

14 June

Our dream had come true. We were out for training and no one bothered their heads what the training was for, as long as we were there.

14–16 June

The weather was gloriously fine, and it was unfair to grumble at too much sunshine, though it was hot. Our billet was a fine one, the people at the farm, for a change, were actually interested in our comfort, to the extent even, of next baking day, baking a great pile of scones, and presenting the whole platoon with them well buttered.

In the evenings, if not laying out in the fields, we would foregather in the farm kitchen 'en famille' and regale ourselves with beer, milk or coffee.

Dixie Orderley's job which we took in turn, was eagerly looked forward to. Jim and I took our turn to gather up the fragments, tidy billet up and clean the dixies out. Then we made our way off to the village well to fill the dixies with fresh water. This was at the village cross roads, and looked in the distance like a little church, it had quite a fine front door and pews round it where the natives evidently sat waiting their turns in peacetimes.

A most monstrous double handled windlass topped the well, with a prehistoric break to stop it getting out of control. How the women folk and youngsters managed it, we never found out. After admiring the structure, we looked down the well but could see no water, then we childishly dropped stones down and nearly fell asleep before we heard them splash. After deciding that there really must be water in it somewhere, we fastened the bucket on, and let her go. The next game was to keep clear of the whirling handles while we hung on to the brake for dear life until the rope had run to a certain knot that we had been warned of, then we started to wind it up. When we were tired, we put the break on and looked for the bucket, but as it was not in sight, we sat down and had a smoke. We were quite pleased when we got the bucket eventually into view, and found that it would not require more than 2 buckets to fill the Dixie. I managed to get in the special good books of the old dame at the farm, by pretending that I thought she was the mother of her own grandchildren. This gained me a special invitation to go round the garden with her. This garden was forbidden ground hitherto. I admired her peonies of which she was inordinately proud, and was allowed to sample the garden peas. Strawberries unfortunately were not yet ripe.

Training consisted of four hours hard work each day, practising open warfare. Evidently dugouts, duckboards and trenches were thought to be going out of date.

17 June

Sunday, one or two of us decided to rise early and attend Holy Communion down in the valley at Coulomby, much preferring this quiet little service to the parade Drumhead Church Service. After the service, instead of returning up the valley by the road, we climbed up through the fields and woods, having a siesta on the way. The view across the valley was magnificent, and everything so still that it was difficult to imagine ourselves in a war stricken country.

Then we heard faintly the strains of the band and picked out the battalion taking the winding road down into the valley for Church Service. It was very hot again as we resumed our way to Harlettes, and passing the cookers before reaching the billet we were delighted to find that they had some cold tea left from breakfast, not ordinary platoon tea, but cook's tea, which is very different stuff.

Nearing home, we heard sounds of some great excitement, and hurrying in, we found the whole family, with the exception of the two small kiddies, busy in the garden. The bees had swarmed and they were busy playing tunes on tin trays, pan lids and other unmusical instruments. We immediately joined in the fun, covering an open flank with the latest ragtime on steel helmets with entrenching tools. The combined pandemonium soon procured the desired result, the bees settling on a big bush, while the expert members of the family finished the job off neatly, and soon had the bees safely housed again.

We were profusely thanked for our little assistance, and invited into the kitchen for coffee, whilst the old lady who forgot in her excitement that we were English, regaled us with a long tirade in French, on what we took to be "Bad Behaviour of Breton Bees". By interspersing her harangue fairly often with "Oui Oui" varied judiciously with "Oh, la, la!!" and shaking our heads portentously, we managed finely.

19 June

The whole brigade had a field day, and captured nearly every hill and wood in the district in quick time, and did not go back to billets till there was nothing left of any importance to capture.

A horrible rumour went the rounds during the morning that our company cooker had been captured but happily the rumour proved false.

20 June

Another big day capturing the few odd woods and hills that we overlooked yesterday.

We nearly lost our third objective however, through a wave of our infantry rousing a hare who seemed anxious to join in the attack.

One or two men had narrow escapes from bayonet wounds, and they all missed the hare after all. A couple of aeroplanes assisted. The signallers trying to receive messages from their Klaxon horns with but poor success, and the aeroplanes being no more successful in reading the messages from our aeroplane signalling sheet. We finished fairly early, having been warned for a long march the next day to fresh training grounds.

21 June

We marched away from that best of billets to our fresh training area, and after a march of 15 kilometres arrived at Moulle. This was a much larger and busier village than we had left. Various divisions were in the district evidently all training for the same business. We spent till the 28th here training hard each day. The first billet that our platoon had, was not one of the best. It was a poky little barn, and the straw was not of the cleanest. One had to be careful in stepping out of the barn, as there was only a path about a yard wide round the yard, the remainder of the yard being a manure tank, whose odour was always with us. Later on, the signallers were all transferred from companies to Headquarters, and all billeted together in a large loft over the empty stables of a large Château which was at that time being used as a French "Hôpital Complementaire".

There was a lake in the grounds on which the nurses and Polius disported themselves in a large punt. We bathed in a stream which fed the lake, and we were often annoyed by the Polius bringing the punt up the stream with the ladies on board, until one day as a protest, half a dozen of us seized the punt rope and towed it back to the lake again.

29 June

We left early in the morning, marching to Watten and taking the train, arrived at Poperinghe again, proceeding immediately to "B" camp, and the following evening took up our position in the front line again at Bilge trench. This time Freddy Swann joined Jim and myself on "A" company's signal station, which was not situated in the officer's quarters this time, but in a deep sap further along the trench. We were rather isolated from our platoon on whom we were dependant for meals, and being the junior signaller on the station, it was my duty at meal times to take the three mess tins and go in search of food. These excursions were usually attended with some little excitement. The enemy at this time was suffering from a severe attack of nerves, and was continuously giving us salvoes of hate, at most irregular and unexpected moments. Many times I arrived back more full of apologies than the mess tins were of tea, and a nasty mark on my tunic where I had clutched the bacon for safety.

It was a matter for much argument between Freddy and Jim whether I clutched it so, for its own safety, or as an additional chest protector. Once down in the sap however, shells did not disturb us much, and it took a heavy one on the top direct to put the candle out, which happened once or twice.

Wet weather had come upon us again, and the tunnel was ankle deep in water, and we were compelled to use odd planks and derelict petrol tins as stepping stones, which was rather difficult when we got beyond the rays of our one solitary candle.

Thirst troubled us a good deal down here in the stifling atmosphere, and to get water, we would hang a mess tin under one of the many dripping places in our ceiling. This water did not taste bad at all, though the M.O. might have had words to say on the matter had he known.

Pat arrived back to the battalion from the Signal School while we were here, and was immediately put on duty as a lineman, and his job of keeping the lines in order between the companies and Headquarters was no sinecure.

Our station was used one night as advanced H.Q. during a raid which our boys were making. "Nobby" Clarke came up from "H.Q." to take charge of the signalling. We had the Colonel, Adjutant, Signal Officer, and the Artillery liaison officer, all here, and bringing their own candles, business was carried on in a blaze of light that was seldom seen on a company station, where it was difficult sometimes to even procure one candle.

The boys went over without any Artillery preparation, and were not long away and the half dozen prisoners they brought in, were brought down the sap for examination. The raiding party then made tracks back to the support line. When the enemy recovered from his surprise he battered our trenches cruelly, and for a couple of casualties in the raid itself, we suffered about 50 casualties from the resulting bombardment, one shell in particular dropping amongst H.Q. staff at the proper H.Q., causing terrible havoc, and it was nearly dawn before our Artillery sufficiently punished the Boche to make him quieten down a bit.

6 JULY 1917 –
3 NOVEMBER 1917

6 July 1917

We were relieved on the night of the 6th and came out from the sap, where we had lived for 6 days, by candle light, (and very little of that) with a feeling like pit ponies coming up for a holiday, until we found out that we were only going into a similar sap at "Wilson's Farm" again.

For the second time, we fell upon a cigarette famine here, and Freddy had to get busy at once making them from issue "Honeydew" and message pads until a post arrived. We always made a point of taking enough cigarettes into the line to last us till we came out to camp again, but we always seemed to make a sharper point of smoking them all before that time arrived.

8–15 July

We left Wilson's Farm and the whole battalion went into reserve again on the Yser (Eyesore) Canal Bank. Work on the Canal Banks had now become so evident that we were shelled continuously and had no peace day or night, on duty or off duty. The light railway had now been carried across the canal, and each evening about dusk, a light engine would bring up a few truck loads of men for working parties. We never knew what horse power that engine had, but we always reckoned its noise at three times its horse power. Some sporty Canadian backwoodsman must have been driving it, as we could not imagine anyone else fool enough to toot his syren before leaving.

Our dugout was just against the line where it reached the East Bank, and where the men left the trucks. This spot seemed to be the chief target thereabouts for the enemy artillery, and many times we felt it incumbent upon us, for our health's sake, to change our location till they had finished with this particular target for the time being.

Our dugout was safe enough from anything but a direct hit, but a direct hit often seemed more likely than not. One evening, a party was detraining here, Pat, inquisitive as usual, was amongst them, seeing who they were, and what they were going to do. On the floor inside the dugout, an oilsheet was laid on the floor, with a stump of candle stuck up in the middle, and devotees of "Pontoon" were sat round, when with a sudden horrible shriek, which caused us all to drop flat, a big shell landed right outside the dugout.

On rushing out we found that it had caused terrible havoc. One officer and three men of ours had been killed outright, and twelve of the arriving party of Royal Welsh Fusiliers. One man of ours was never traced at all, and it was surmised that his body had been blown into the canal. Pat staggered into the dugout badly dazed and shaken, and, asking him if he was hit, he seemed to have an idea that he was hit somewhere in the leg.

On searching him however, all I could find was a little white blister with a piece of steel filing sticking out of it. Men much further away from the shell had been killed outright. In a very few moments the stretcher bearers had done their work, the party had moved off to work, and nothing was left to show of what had happened but a huge hole outside the dugout, and two or three steel helmets crumpled like paper.

Each night we had some heavy fatigue work up the line, in addition to work on the Canal Bank during the day.

The first night we had just put our equipment on and were hanging about ready to be paraded for digging fatigue. We noticed an extraordinary number of what we thought "Dud" shells, falling mostly on the far bank of the Canal. While wondering at this, our noses suddenly solved the mystery, and there was a sudden grab at gas helmets, and for the next quarter of an hour, the inhabitants of the canal bank looked like weird beings from some other planet.

Gas or no gas however, we were marched off to dig at a new communication trench near Irish Farm. All the way to the job we were pestered with these gas shells. When we had reached the scene of our labours and were preparing to get on with the digging a heavy barrage opened, and H.E. and shrapnel were added. We were compelled to dive for what cover happened to be near, and were kept there for an hour without being able to get on with the work. An officer who dropped into a hole where Pat and I had beaten him by a short head had no idea where his platoon had disappeared to, and Pat offered to find out where they were for him. He disappeared round the corner of the old broken and disused trench that we had dived into, appearing again shortly afterwards with the desired information. It was decided at last to send a runner back to the Headquarters on the Canal Bank with information concerning the condition of things. Word evidently came back to abandon work, as later, we were given orders to get back to the Canal Bank as best we could, and some very good "bests" were done, but things were nearly as bad there. (I heard accidentally some weeks later, that a very hot query was received from Brigade H.Q. the next day, as to why the work had not been done, and that our Adjutant went across there to reply personally – very personally.)

The following night, a party of us were taken across the Canal to the Red Heart Estaminet whose ruins were used as a dump and general store. Here we were loaded up, each with two sandbags, each sandbag containing 3 seven pound trench mortar shells, which we were to carry to a battery position forward. Each pair of sandbags was tied together at the neck so that they could be slung across the shoulders, which made us an extra 21 pounds front and back, on top of Fighting Order equipment and rifles. I reckoned that I would be lucky if I reached the Canal with mine much less some unknown battery position near the front line. Pat was quiet about the matter, but I had a feeling that we would hear later from him. As soon as the whole party was loaded up, we started off, and were soon back across the Canal, and off on our way to find that T.M. battery.

Aching shoulders were soon complained of, and I would dearly have liked to change my load to another position, but decided to carry on until a halt was called. I never cared much for shells, either passive or active, and to have half a dozen hanging round my neck, and tapping each other continually at every step, was beginning to get on my nerves. At last a halt was called, and many of the sandbags were dumped to the ground with thuds that sent cold shivers down my spine. Evidently someone knew more about the things than I did. Familiarity might breed contempt I knew, but I did not feel either familiar or contemptuous with my little lot, and I let mine down gently. We were not allowed to rest long however, and were soon going along a road again in the darkness. We had not proceeded far when a sudden clatter at my heels made me jump. It was Pat in trouble. I knew it was Pat, for he never hurried himself over anything. He stood looking at his two bags which had suddenly parted company, and without haste, in emphatic and well chosen periods, he gave us his convinced opinions of night fatigues, trench mortars, Germans, dark nights, bad roads, army sandbags, and a few other matters appertaining thereto. Then taking hold of the sandbags by the neck, one in each hand, he jangled along rattling the shells to such a tune that I wished him anywhere but at my heels. When we arrived as far as Hill Top Farm we went into the trench there to wait until an officer and N.C.O. went on to find the exact location of the battery. This they were unable to do, and the shells were left there and we returned home to the canal bank. Another party the following night, was sent up to collect them and deliver to their destination, which had been located in the meantime.

We were not of this party, but found comparative relaxation in running truckloads of Mills bombs up to a magazine in the line. Just above the Canal Bank a number of flat trucks had been dumped and light rails (lightly laid) had been run up nearly to the front line. First we put the trucks on to the lines and from a dump, loaded them up with boxes of bombs. The journey was chiefly a matter of stopping and starting. Twenty yards at a stretch was a really good performance, and it was annoying when one had prospects of beating even this, to suddenly charge in the darkness, into a truck that had become derailed in front, and join it off the line out of sheer sympathy. The man who was jammed between the two trucks failed to see however, that we had anything to be annoyed about. In places, the lines were missing altogether and at these gaps we were compelled to unload and carry the truck bodily across the intervening space and then load up again. In other places the lines ran across trenches, and here great care had to be taken to prevent the truck hurling itself to the bottom of the trench. A halt was made near Hill Top Farm, where the bombs were unloaded and carried to a magazine that had been built in a trench close by.

Other nights of this busy week were spent in digging cable trenches. Strange obstructions were met with in these diggings in the darkness. One night, digging near some ruins, we came upon a thick brick-vaulted roof of someone's cellar, and it needed some labour to get through it. The man who, the same night, dug into what proved to be a dead mule, had not half the work, but did not consider himself lucky on that account, though the man who had been working hard with a pick on a 5.9" shell before he discovered what it was, confessed that he had been favoured by fortune.

15 July

After such a week we were not sorry to leave the Canal Bank in the darkness and make our way to "C" Camp in the wood off the Poperinghe–Vlamertinghe Road, where we spent the night rather crowded under canvas, but slept well.

In the morning we marched away to the new Railway Depôt some distance out of Poperinghe. This new station had been opened to cope with the big traffic of the coming offensive, the old station at this period being too well shelled to work all the traffic. From here we took a train to Watten and marched to Houlle, where our company was billeted in a large corn-factor's warehouse.

17–21 July

After spending a day cleaning up, and having the usual inspections, we were taken for a bathe. The Canal from St Omer ran by the village, and divided from it by the tow path, were two large pools, one safe in parts for non-swimmers, and the other for swimmers only, with a diving board complete, so there was a good choice of bathing places. We enjoyed the afternoon here immensely, as it was a hot day, and after the bathe, the tow path (which was also the public road) was packed with men taking a sun bathe, and taking the opportunity of cleaning as much vermin from their clothing as time would permit.

Of course the inhabitants of the village got wind of the interesting proceedings, and we soon had any amount of spectators. We stood it for some time, but when a young lady aired her knowledge of English by rudely shouting "Hitchy Koo", it was decided to cut the proceedings short.

Those little beggars who escaped annihilation that afternoon, and thought that they were to be left to live and thrive, received a rude shock two days later, as we then had hot baths, and clean clothing was served out.

Some distance outside Houlle, a plan of the ground we were to cover in the coming attack, had been marked out to exact distances.

The German trenches as far as they were known, were marked out, the village of St Julien which was to be captured, was denoted by a canvas erection surmounted by a little wooden cross, and the little river Steenbeek which had to be crossed, was marked out and labelled "Banks 5 ft high, width 10 feet" but failed to inform us what depth of water lay within those 10 ft.

We supposed it varied according to the weather, but anyway 10 ft was quite plenty to jump, in equipment, and did not seem to leave much room for a bad "take off". We were marched over the course in battle formation, and had all the points and landmarks explained to us at some length. The 116th Brigade were down to take the first objective on our Divisional front. This consisted of the German first line of defence of 3 trenches, known to us as Caliban Trench, Caliban Support and Caliban Reserve.

The second objective was to fall to the 117th Brigade, this consisting also of 3 trenches – Canopus Trench, Canopus Support and Canopus Reserve.

When these two operations were successfully completed, it fell to the lot of our brigade (the 118th) to take the 3rd objective. This was not so well defined or perhaps so well known. We were to pass through the 116th and 117th Brigades, and proceed forward, cross the Steenbeek, take the village of St Julien, and carry on forward again to the Langemarck Rd, where it was thought his third defence would be made. After taking this, we were to consolidate our new line beyond it, and hold this till a fresh division passed through us for the second day of the attack. Each succeeding day would see further advances. In addition to this, it was whispered (perhaps not officially), that a big landing of troops would be made on the Belgian coast, and take the enemy in the rear. Taking it all round, it appeared that the war would be a thing of the past, in a month or two. Freddy Swann and I were detailed as Signallers for "A" Company for the attack. Pat was to be on Advanced Headquarter Signals.

Swann was always known as "Little Hommer". The "Little" needed no explanation, but I could never get at the derivation of "Hommer". It was supposed to have some relation to his short bow legs, but that was as far as I could get in the matter. He was a cheerful young sprite and we got along finely together. His worst vice seemed to be "Spearmint".

We trained furiously while we were at it, but training hours were not long, and with the fine weather, we had some capital bathing in the evenings, or for those inclined that way, there were cheerful little estaminets in the village where Madame and Mademoiselle dispensed vin blanc, vin rouge and so-called beer. The band also played in the factory yard in the evenings.

The factory had a fine house just opposite the building that we were billeted in, and here lodged the Brigadier General with his staff, so our behaviour had to be of the best, and a sharp eye had to be kept on our hooks and buttons as we left the billet. A parade was held in the yard one afternoon at which the Brigadier presented decorations won during our last turn in the line. Two Military Crosses, two Distinguished Conduct Medals, and two Military Medals.

22 July

Training at last came to an end, and we thought that the only thing we did not know, was the actual date of the attack.

In the afternoon we marched to Moulle, where we boarded motors, and soon a seemingly endless stream of busses was on the move. We heard that our destination was "Y" and "Z" Camps at St Jan-ter-Biezen near Poperinghe. We passed through St Omer and Arques, and took devious ways to Herzeele and through Watou. It was dark by this time, and in the distance in the direction of Poperinghe, we could see signs of some excitement skywards. Searchlights in dozens were sweeping the sky and anti-aircraft shells could be seen bursting in the air, while tracer bullets from the "AA" machine guns flew upwards and disappeared amongst the searchlight beams, and bursting shells. Added to this was the unmistakable "crump" of aeroplane bombs.

To my surprise we were whirled past the comparative peacefulness of "Y" and "Z" camps, and continued on the way to Poperinghe, but on reaching the main road between that place and Proven, we turned towards Proven for a short distance, then a halt was made and we alighted.

The road here was wide, but was absolutely jammed with motors and troops, all lights were out, and not even a cigarette could be lighted. It was the biggest thing in air-raids that we had seen. Now and again, a beam from the searchlights would find a plane and show it up like a little silver butterfly, and shells and tracer bullets would seem to stream up the beam, but not for long could the beam keep its victim, and the bombs still fell with their reverberating crash and upward burst of flame. It was an awe inspiring sight, but we were not left long to watch it, as officers were quietly working sorting out their men. We were got together and loaded up with dixies and stoves of all kinds that had been brought along with us, as the horse transport would not arrive until the following day. We were turned down a by-lane in the darkness, and after much stumbling along bad tracks we eventually arrived back at "Y" and "Z" camps.

In ordinary times, each of these two camps would hold a battalion, but now we found that the whole of our Brigade was putting up here. The Cambridgeshires and Hertfordshires occupied one camp, while the Black Watch and ourselves joined at the other. Huts that held twenty men comfortably, now held double that number with comfort of course in inverse ratio.

We spent a few days here in light training, the signallers having quite a "cushy" time of it. This extra few days here was something of a surprise, (as a matter of fact, we learned later that the opening of the offensive was delayed a few days at the request of the French who were not ready to take their part on our left as arranged).

We usually finished work about dinner time and in the evenings sampled the eggs and chips in one or other of the cottages on the road.

Before leaving, the whole brigade was paraded and sat round the parade ground to hear the Brigadier talk about the attack. We heard what we were to do with any odd Germans that might be left over after the Artillery had finished with them, and were given a useful hint as to how a bayonet might be easily extricated from a seemingly hopeless jam in some unfortunate German's clockwork. The artillery figures that he gave us, and a description of the barrages that would be put down, gave us a feeling that we would only need to walk across to our respective objectives, and make ourselves comfortable till the cookers came up with dinner.

28 July

We left camp and proceeded by by-ways, keeping clear of Poperinghe to "O" Camp in the wood again, and the next day we were busy getting all equipment, ammunition and arms complete and another good look at the model in miniature of the ground of attack, that had been laid out here.

29 July

By dinner time everyone was completely fitted out. Overcoats and haversacks were discarded and handed into store.

In addition to his full ammunition pouches, each man was served out with an extra bandolier, two bombs, and a spade. The spade was carried fixed down the back of the valise with the blade upwards, making a protection for the back of the neck. Three days rations were served out, some chocolate and cigarettes.

To celebrate the occasion, a big lot of St Julien tobacco had been obtained. As signallers, Hommer and I carried in addition to full arms and equipment, signalling flags, a telephone, a coil of wire, a morse lamp and a signalling shutter.

A small nucleus of the battalion was made up and sent away from the line in charge of our company officer, and charge of our Company in the attack fell to Lt Cowpe, who was well liked by the whole company.

After dinner, orders were given for the men to get down to sleep, as it was not expected that there would be much rest for a day or two. The camp became very quiet for an hour or two, but I do not think that there was much actual sleep.

Old hands talked quietly of other big attacks that they had been through, and the others found that orders to sleep were somewhat difficult to comply with.

30 July 1917
The Opening of the Third Battle of Ypres

We left camp at dusk, by platoons, proceeding by one of the new battle tracks that had recently been made, towards the Canal Bank.

Near Brielen we passed by some of the heavy guns, and their crews shouted "Good Luck" and intimated that we would have more than their moral support in the morning. A little further along, things began to get a little crowded. All tracks and roads seemed to be leading to the Canal Bank. Guns, Limbers, Transport and many different units seemed in danger of getting inextricably mixed. Reaching the road we knew so well, near the Red Heart Estaminet, we found it jammed from ditch to ditch, and to make matters more uncomfortable, the enemy artillery commenced to search the road.

We managed to get through to one of the approaches to the Canal, when suddenly, as if the enemy had waited until he knew that the Canal Bank was packed with troops, he put down a heavy barrage that seemed to include everything he had but boiling oil. There came Gas shells, H.E. Shells, Shrapnel, nicely mixed. The beauty of mixing them so, was, that it was extremely difficult to detect the gas amongst the noise and fumes of the H.E. and Shrapnel. There was no mistaking it now however. Our platoon was just then wedged by the side of a strong concrete dugout, which was manned as an aid post. We were sheltered from the one side, but felt convinced that no shells were wasting themselves on the other side. The barrage was playing havoc in less time than it takes to relate, and the aid post could not cope with the casualties close at hand, and many wounded could not get to the aid post owing to the congestion. The night was dark enough in itself, but with gas helmets on, hardly room to move one's arms, and the cries of the wounded heard through the shriek and bursting of shells, seemed to make the night a black one indeed.

This too, seemed to breed a suspicion in our minds, that the morning's attack was not going to be the big surprise to the enemy that some of us fondly imagined.

"Hommer" was by my side at the time, and while the gas was at its worst, I noticed that he seemed to be in difficulties. The face of his mask flapped about on his cheeks which pointed to the fact that he was not using the breathing apparatus properly, and he was making a peculiar noise inside his helmet. I grabbed him by the arm and shouted through my helmet as best I could, to ask him what the matter was. I could get nothing from him but queer noises, and I was just going to make an effort to get him into the aid post, when he suddenly seemed to recover and inform me that he was quite alright, and had managed to get back his chewing gum which had slipped down the mouthpiece of his mask.

We eventually managed to extricate ourselves and made a dash for the wooden footbridge that crossed the Canal. This had already been badly smashed, and crossing it in the darkness with gas masks on, further casualties occurred. There was no hope for anyone who fell into the canal, as, weighted with ammunition and equipment as we were, the unfortunate one would sink like a stone and nothing could be seen in the darkness.

Once across the bridge on the eastern bank of the Canal, we were in comparative safety, and no time was lost in getting along to our "X" lines. Dropping into our support trenches we had a short rest, and then climbed out in front, with orders to make ourselves as comfortable as possible in available shell holes, for a few hours. There was no shortage of shell holes, and we were not long in getting settled down and making necessary structural improvements. "Hommer" and I along with a runner named Duncan, had found quite a good hole, but Duncan was not quite satisfied with it, and proceeded to dig a hole in the side to put his head in. As he was a runner, we pointed out to him that it was his feet that he ought to care most about, but he was not open to be convinced. Silence fell upon us for a while, only broken by the rustle of paper as Hommer unfolded a fresh tablet of his beloved "Spearmint". I accepted his kind invitation to join him in a chew, and we chewed away quietly till "Hommer" broke the peacefulness by asking Duncan, who was still digging, whether he thought he would reach St Julien quicker that way, than over the top. This led to a lengthy argument which eventually ended in "Hommer" remarking that he had never heard of Birkenhead as a town, and was under the impression that it was a little back street in New Brighton, and Duncan expressing himself with emphasis that even if a place called Glossop had appeared on a map, it had been a woeful waste of ink.

31 July

About 1.0 a.m., we began to miss our overcoats, and feel the damp night air, and thoughts turned towards rum, how, when, and where, and in what quantity it would be served out.

A few odd shells had fallen about, but had not done much damage, but we heard afterwards that the trench behind us had received a good thumping, and one officer was wounded and off on his way to "Blighty" long before zero. We hoped fervently that the cookhouse had escaped injury, as we expected something from there before zero, which was to be at 3.50 a.m.

Shortly afterwards, slabs of cold ham were brought from the trench for breakfast and then we learned with consternation, that rum and coffee had been served out some time previously. Our shell hole had been missed in the darkness, or we should have applied for it, at the huge shell hole where most of No. 4 platoon were domiciled.

I gathered our three mess tins together, and clambered out of the shell hole, with the intention of slipping to the cookhouse in the trench to see whether I could get any there, but before I reached the trench, I stumbled across a container which looked promising. These containers were a thermos arrangement to hold a couple of gallons, and were fitted to be carried on the back for trench work, and crossing rough country during operations. I dragged the thing along to our shell hole, and Hommer and Duncan carefully lowered it in. On making investigations we found the contents still hot, and sufficient of it, to make us forgive the man who had overlooked us.

As 3.50 a.m. drew nearer, watches were peered at every odd minute.

Some considerable time would elapse before we moved forward. The barrage was to open at 3.50 a.m. to pummel the first line of defence, and neutralize the enemy's batteries.

On the frontage apportioned to our division, the 116th Brigade were to take the German first defence line. The 117th Brigade were to follow the barrage forward and take the second line of defence. After further artillery preparation, our Brigade (the 118th) was to go forward, through the 116th and 117th and take the 3rd and last objective for the day. This included the village of St Julien, and then on to what was thought to be his last organised trench defence, along the Zonnebeke–Poelcapelle Road.

After capturing this line, we were to consolidate the position, and hold it until dawn of the following day, when fresh divisions would continue the attack.

About this time, a new type of shell was in use. It was a shrapnel shell whose burst all went forward, and troops could be practically underneath the bursting shells with comparative safety.

For our attack on the 3rd objective, and the subsequent digging in, we were promised such a barrage of these shells, as would eliminate all danger of counter attack, until we were fairly consolidated in our new line.

On the dot of 3.50 as per programme, we heard the boom of one big gun, and immediately the barrage opened.

We sprang out of our shell holes to watch the wonderful sight. Behind us, was one long line of rapid flashes, and looking forward, the German line, as far as the eye could reach, was an inferno of bursting shells of all kinds – H.E., Shrapnel, Gas, and climbing up through it all, and soaring high above the smoke, the enemy's "S.O.S." lights could be seen.

Our Brigadier had spoken truly. It was a stupendous barrage. The number of guns in action was sufficient to keep the firing like the continuous roll of drums. The sound was beyond description. One seemed to have the impression that nothing existed in the world but one great howling noise, a noise that hammered itself against one's flesh, almost numbing the senses.

The first signs of dawn were just appearing, though it was still dark, and the men were walking about now in the open, seemingly convinced that the enemy artillery had been annihilated at the opening of the barrage. One could be forgiven for having this feeling, as no reply, to speak of, came back, just a few straggling shells that no one seemed to bother about.

The only casualty that we noticed at this period, was a young officer who went off raving with shell shock. This is exactly what we expected would happen to him. He had not been with us long, having previously been in the Flying Corps. He had suffered the misfortune to be brought down by enemy anti-aircraft guns and had a bad smash. His nerves were all shattered, and some all-wise authority had either transferred him, or allowed him to be transferred, to the Infantry, evidently thinking that the quiet life with them would effect a cure.

Soon we could see that the barrage had moved forward, and we guessed that the 116th had now gone forward, and taken over what remained of the Caliban Line. Lt Cowpe then collected our company together, and we moved off in Artillery Formation, each platoon of the company moving forward as the four corners of a square, while company headquarters followed to the rear of the square. Companies "B" and "D" were leading with "A" and "C" companies in their rear, to close up together for the final attack beyond St Julien. We moved slowly forward, and passing over some old front line, we found it very heavy going. The ground had been shelled so furiously that there did not seem an inch that was not newly turned. What part of it that was not new shell holes, was loose soil thrown up by the bursts of H.E. and when we were not stumbling into shell holes, we were sinking half way to our knees in newly turned soft earth. The first enemy trench that we crossed, was hardly recognisable as a trench, and only saved its identity by the remains of its dugouts and facines, and what was left of its barbed wire defence. By this time the enemy had put down a heavy barrage of "H.E.", vile big murderous stuff it was, each shell screaming to make volcanic eruptions of black earth, fifty feet into the air. Evidently he had some guns left. This barrage was falling behind us, but creeping forward all the time, and we wondered which side of it Batt. Hd. Qrs. had managed to get, or whether they were getting the full benefit of it.

We heard later that they were actually advancing under it, by diving from shell hole to shell hole, while endeavouring to keep touch with the companies, the barrage advancing with them and keeping the companies moving in front of it. This was responsible for the companies getting along too quickly, and in advance of the timetable. After passing "Caliban" line and finding ourselves getting into close touch with the front companies, we halted for a little while in shell holes. Our Sgt. Major took his rest in a shell hole with "Hommer" and myself. He remarked that it was "devilish hot" as he took a pull at his water bottle. He passed it along to us with an invitation to take a drink, and after taking the drink we wondered whether he was referring to the weather, or the contents of his bottle when he said it was "devilish hot".

Starting off again, we reached the "Canopus" lines with surprisingly few casualties, considering the fact that the barrage had now caught us up, and machine gun fire was catching us from quarters that were unexpected.

We expected to find the 117th Brigade holding this line, but were amazed to find troops of the 55th Division in possession. This Division was supposed to be on the right of our divisional front. Some confusion arose, and it was found that we had lost direction, and moved too far to our right. We got quickly on the move again, inclining to the left to get back to our correct front again.

This mishap soon cost us dearly. Isolated Machine Gun posts had been missed on the ground that we should have covered, and these were beating a devil's tattoo in our rear. One or two tanks were now coming into action, and we hoped that they would quickly attend to them.

Young Art. Wilkinson, a bomber who was on C.H.Qrs with us, and had only just arrived back from leave, sank silently with a bullet through his head, and a stretcher bearer who was seeing whether he was beyond aid, met a similar fate. The platoons too were thinning out sadly, and we were not yet in actual touch with our objective. Even now, however, big numbers of Germans were rushing down from their lines with their hands in the air, and many of them were deliberately shot down by their own people. They needed no directing, had thrown down their arms and equipment, and were quickly putting as much space as possible between themselves and their old friends. We did not need to bother with them, as they would all be collected up further back, that is, as many as managed to get clear. Just on our right at this time, a terrific explosion took place.

The ground under our feet rocked, and when the huge fountain of earth had subsided, there remained overhead, a huge black canopy which hung there and slowly contorted into weird shapes. We judged it to be a mine at the time, and felt that we had been lucky to correct our direction, when we did. Casualties were already heavy enough without that.

What had actually happened was that a German shell had actually hit a dump of shells that he had left behind him when he left.

Our next obstacle was the "Steenbeck", but before reaching this, we were absolutely held up by Machine Gun and shell fire, and could make no progress against it. The company by now, was reduced to a skeleton, and no longer divided into platoons. A message was received here that the enemy was preparing to counter attack at once, and we were given orders to "dig in" with all speed, so spades and picks were pulled out, and no further incentive was needed to do some quick digging, and in a very short time, a trench of a sort was dug and manned. It was decided shortly after however, to try to move on again.

The Steenbeck itself did not present any difficulty as the enemy had left a few crossings, and also, as we found to our cost, he had them nicely ranged by his snipers and Machine Guns. Not much more than a platoon seemed to be left when we had crossed.

Just on our left lay St Julien, or what was left of it. All we could see, seemed to be two or three gable ends of buildings left at the cross roads. The left half of the battalion found three German guns here, and they were marked with the battalion sign and left for collection. It was evident now, that the enemy had got practically all his artillery safely away, and he certainly had not moved it that morning. Another matter that made us anxious, was the absence of our own barrage, that we were promised on our objective, and of aeroplanes, while the enemy had a fair number of planes up, whose pressing attentions were anything but pleasant.

We could not get forward at all here, and were held down again with the barrage of shell and M.G. fire. We were compelled to get what shelter we could in the shell holes, while our officer and the Sgt. Major tried to get forward to see what had happened to the other companies. This was the last we saw of them, as they were both killed.

Each occupied shell hole now seemed to be covered by either an M.G. or snipers, and we could not locate them. We were left here with no orders, but it became so hot after a while, that we decided to try to get forward again. The first man to get up instantly fell back in the hole, shot through the neck and died before anything could be done for him.

It was a single shot, and a sniper who was with us, decided that he had got the direction of the shot, and peeped up to see whether he could spot the source of trouble. Before he could find what he wanted, his cheek was laid open with a bullet. While we were trying to devise ways and means of getting clear of this rifle spot, a stretcher bearer dashed across from another shell hole, to ask if we had any first aid bandages to spare, as his supply was used up. We yelled at him to get in, but we were too late, and he fell in a crumpled inert mass on top of us, having given his life in aiding his pals.

The only way we could think of getting out of the hole with any hope of getting further, was to dig a trench out for a few yards, and make a dash one by one. We managed to get clear in this manner, but were of course compelled to leave the bodies behind, with a hope that searchers later would come across them.

We fell in with the front companies who had now been reduced to a few stragglers with no officers or N.C.O. in charge. From them we could learn nothing of our Officer or the Sgt. Major. From the second objective, we had covered a distance of something like 2,000 yards over the open through a withering fire, and there seemed now to be nothing left. We were wondering what had become of Battn. Hd. Qrs. and how we might find them, when we were hailed from a shell hole. Advanced Battn. Hd. Qrs. Signals were actually in front of us, and we made a dash and dropped into a shell hole, where Pat, McKnight,

Fernley and Timms had established themselves as a signal station, with no chance of being able to signal. Keeping them company were two badly wounded Germans, who were being patched up by Mac and Fernley.

While we were here, a stretcher bearer fell into the hole with a message from one of the Company Captains, and as it was hopeless to try to pick up H.Q. by signal, Pat decided to make a dash for it and deliver the message, he disappeared over the top of the shell hole, and we heard later that he was in such a state of exhaustion when he found the Adjt, that he was too weak to take his lips away from the Adjt's waterbottle, which the Adjt. pushed at him for a refresher, and the bottle was only secured again after some trouble.

When it began to look as if there were no men of ours left in front, and no good could be done by still holding Advanced HQ in this spot, it was decided to evacuate it and get to B.H.Q. somehow. Hommer and I left together, but having to make a sudden dive into a shell hole, before we had travelled far, I picked myself up at the bottom to find myself alone. I looked over the top but could see nothing of him, and hoped he had not come to grief. I shouted his name and was delighted to hear him reply from a neighbouring shell hole.

He said he was staying there for a bit, and nothing lost, I decided to rest also. When things seemed a little quieter, I left my hole to join him, but not a sign of him was to be found, but somehow, I did not feel anxious about him. I could now locate Battn. Hd. Qrs, by a little flag stuck on a mound and made for it with all speed.

The Adjutant was here in charge of about twenty men, which thus seemed to be about all that was left of the Battalion. The Colonel had been wounded early on, and was compelled to go down to a dressing station to have his wounds attended to. Hommer was not to be found, but some men were understood to have missed H.Qrs, and were at "X" lines. Adv. H.Q joined us here, and a further straggler or two dropped in. St Julien was still in our rear, and we were set to work digging furiously, to make a strong point if possible, to hold in case of counter attack.

Our Artillery was disappointing us terribly, and we were getting no help from them now.

There was no doubt on the other hand, that the enemy had his guns out of harm's way before our barrage had opened, as he certainly could not have moved them through it, and no guns had been found on our front, with the exception of the three small guns found in St Julien. Very few dead were seen in passing his first and second lines, and practically no prisoners were taken till they fled to us from their own third line. This pointed to the fact that his first two lines were but lightly held, and he had massed his defence at the third line with his full artillery at his back.

We could only hope that there would be no counter attack before morning, when we expected the fresh divisions would move forward again.

A couple of tanks now appeared on the scene and ambled about with the idea of being of some assistance.

As a matter of fact, they turned out a terrible nuisance. First, one loomed over the back of our "strong-point[?]" and we just managed to scramble out, before it toppled nose downwards into the great hole, with its caterpillar tracks churning up the ground, and making a clank that nearly drowned the noise of bursting shells. It finished up by bursting flame and smoke out of every hole in it, as the crew dashed out. Our strong point had now gone to glory, and with a tank on fire, another standing by, and a little crowd of men in the open, the enemy was presented with a target that we could not expect him to ignore, and our little band was quickly further reduced. Close by however, we found a large concrete pill box with a small trench round it, and it was quickly decided that this would make a much better strong point.

We found the place had two occupants. In the trench lay the body of a massive German N.C.O. He lay on his back with his arm upraised, still clasping in his hand a "Potato Masher" bomb, in the act of throwing it. Whoever had met him, had acted quickly, and made no mistake about it, as he showed a revolver shot wound squarely between the eyes. Inside the pillbox itself was another German, badly wounded in both legs. He was only a youngster, and he was patched up as well as could be managed and was very grateful and seemed quite cheered up by the prospect of getting to our "Blighty". In the trench we found a sample or two of German rations. The speciality seemed to be Linseed Cake. This awful stuff did not seem to compare favourably with the oil cake that cattle are fed on at home.

It was now getting well on in the afternoon, and had commenced to rain heavily. The sides of the trench having been badly smashed, the rain commenced to dissolve the sides slowly but surely, little rivers of mud began to trickle in, and in a short time we were in a quagmire half way to our knees. We hung on here long after darkness had fallen, when an order was given to fall back to a trench some distance behind, where a few more of the battalion had collected.

It was a black night and raining now in torrents. The clayey soil torn by the shells, and now sodden by the rain, had turned to a succession of great pools of mud. We were thoroughly tired out as we stumbled out of the trench, and round the back of the pill-box, and had but a faint idea where this trench was. We could not keep in touch with one another, owing to the darkness and the state of the ground, and to add to the unpleasantness, the shelling was still being kept up. As if this was not sufficient, machine gun and rifle fire was coming from the direction in which we were making, and we fervently hoped, that when we were spotted, we might have luck enough not to be mistaken for Germans.

My legs were by now getting too tired to pull themselves out of the mud, but I managed to stumble along sufficiently to keep a dark figure or two in sight, until I was unfortunate enough to make acquaintance with some barbed wire, and before I could extricate myself, I had completely lost sight of them. Stumbling on again desperately to catch up, I finally and hopelessly came to grief in a huge wet shell hole. I managed to scramble out, but seemed to have lost all idea of which direction to proceed in. How long I slithered about, sat down in the mud, and stumbled on in the blackness I don't know, but I began to feel that I would never get anywhere or see anyone till daylight came. At last however, I thought that I heard voices, and making towards them a huge form suddenly loomed in front of me, and growled "Who the 'ell are you?" and I found myself looking down the barrel of a service revolver. I was quite delighted to see it however, and thought I had found our lads at last, but my luck was out again, and I found myself in the hands of the enemy instead of friends. It was no German however, but a Sgt. Major of a battalion of the Sussex Regt. There was one of those wonderfully unreasoning antipathies existing at this time between the Sussex and the Cheshires.

They called themselves the "Iron Regiment" and we thought them a "Tinpot" lot, to put it mildly, and felt that any affair that they took an active part in, was doomed to failure, if it was not for the other units engaged. Their opinion of the Cheshire's I suppose only differed in detail, but not in substance.

Here was I, a lonely "Cheshire" in the hands of the Amalekites so to speak. After finding out that I was "A Cheshire" he made more or less polite enquiry as to where I might think I was going. I explained that I was going to find the Cheshire H.Qrs. He differed from me, and I found he was quite right in saying that I was not, for I found myself unceremoniously bundled into a trench where the Sussex men were busy trying to dig a trench in liquid mud, with flat shovels. I was presented with a shovel, and told to "dig like 'ell", and the men alongside me were given instructions to see that my work with the spade came up to their high standard of efficiency.

"Digging" here seemed to consist of a gallant attempt to put mud back on the top quicker than it trickled in again, with odds 100 to 1 against the spades. As we tried to shovel the mud back to the parapet again, it simply trickled down the handles of the spade, inside our tunic sleeves, into the intimate recesses of our underclothing and, as we were soaked to the skin long ago, it seemed to join in the stream that ran down our necks along our cold flesh to our boots, where it no doubt escaped by the lace holes back into the trench. We were expecting counter attacks in the darkness at any time, and great difficulty was experienced in keeping rifles in a fit state for immediate use. We tried laying them on our oilsheets on the parapet, but as the parapet dissolved, they had a trick of sliding down into the trench, and disappearing in the mud.

Our Artillery was still quiet, and it was only later that we heard, how, when they came to move forward, they found the ground and the roads so broken up by shell fire, that they experienced great difficulty in moving at all. Then the rain had commenced and turned everything into a huge quagmire.

Innocent looking pools on the roads turned out to be huge shell holes, and many guns were put out of action for the day, by disappearing into some of these traps. Off the roads matters were worse, and mules and men were actually drowned in trying to get along tracks in the darkness. The same conditions would however, make a counter attack in the darkness, on positions imperfectly known, a matter of some risk for the enemy, but we could hardly hope to pass the night without some effort being made by him, to recover at least some of his lost ground, before our positions were consolidated, and before he was attacked again at dawn, though we began to feel a little sceptical ourselves, about that programme, but still hoped for the best.

Shelling was still persistent, but the state of the ground, and the enemy's only vague idea of our positions, minimised the effect of his fire. As last orders were passed along to "Stand to", shovels were dropped and rifles taken up, and firing positions made, even the range was given out. Evidently the expected counter attack was at hand, and by the range given to us, he was to be allowed fairly close before we let fly.

We peered into the blackness with straining eyes, and thumping hearts, and that tightening of skin across the temples, but could make nothing out, when suddenly, from close in our rear, the air was rent with the rip of 18 pounders beating out a very devils tattoo. Such sweet music was never heard, and if our feet had not been so embedded in the mud, we could have danced with sheer delight. On and on they kept it up, and put such a barrage in front of us, that a counter attack through it would have stood as much chance of reaching us, as a snowball would, of rolling in the front door of Hades in midsummer and coming out at the back door.

These guns had been dismantled and carried up piecemeal by mules, and an almost endless chain of mules had been bringing ammunition up to them all through the darkness.

As dawn broke, we stood down with all fear of counter attack dispelled for the time being.

1 August 1917

There was no sign of any fresh attack going forward from our side as dawn broke, and during a bit of bustle in the trench, where some breakfast seemed to be expected, I slipped away. Getting clear and laying low for a while to see if I could get my bearings, I thought I could locate the spot some distance in front, where our remnants had gathered the previous afternoon, and felt sure I could see movement there. Making my way forward again I found about a score of our boys back there again, with the Adjutant and the Signal Officer endeavouring to make something of a trench that filled up as quickly as it was excavated. I was delighted to find Pat there and a few of the old friends, which made it feel like home again, though Hommer was not amongst them. The Adjutant was out in front of the trench with his coat black and dripping, with a soaked stump of a cigarette between his lips. He seemed to be strolling about picking up derelict spades, and dropping them into the trench. As we seemed to be getting more spades than we had men to use them, we were not sure whether he meant them to assist in making a solid foothold in the trench, or whether his idea was that we could get along better with a spade in each hand. What time he was not picking up spades he was searching with his binoculars for Germans, and every now and again coming to see how the trench was progressing, while he periodically informed us that he could find no trace of live Boche nearer than the Langemarck Rd., which was a matter of 800 yards away.

Near by, lay the two tanks that had caused us so much annoyance the previous day, derelict and deserted, one with its nose down in the huge hole and its tail in the air, whilst the other stood placidly by in silent sympathy.

Our trench made but poor progress till someone had a sudden brainwave and suggested draining it to a huge shell hole in the rear. When we had at last cut an opening into the shell hole, the tide in the trench fell quite a foot, but as one good soul said "The nearer yer gets to dry land, the more wetter it is".

From early in the previous afternoon, we had simply been a small isolated party, in touch with no troops on either flank. The actual new line had been dug and consolidated some distance behind us and west of St Julien, whilst we were still mudlarking in front of this place, and it annoyed us considerably sometime later, to find out from the official news, that St Julien was not held on July 31st.

Fortunately no attack developed in front of us during the day, as we were now about at the end of our tether, tired, hungry and with flesh almost as sodden with wet as our clothing.

Late in the afternoon we were rejoined by the Adjutant who had disappeared some time previously, also the Rgtl. Sgt. Major and a young 2nd Lt who, with the signal officer and the Adjt. himself, were the only three officers left of those who took part in the attack.

We were at last to leave our little trench and were sent off in couples. A ruin in our rear was pointed out to us and we were to make the best way we could to it, there we would find someone to whom we were to hand over our ammunition, and then proceed to another ruin further along, for orders. After watching two or three couples off, Pat and I left, and did quite good time to our first stopping place, although it could not be said that we raised much dust.

Dumping our ammunition as ordered, we made for the next stop. This turned out to be the ruins of a building on the St Julien road, where our Medical Officer had fixed up his aid post. Here, he and his staff were overwhelmed with dead, dying and a few hopeful cases. The place had simply been battered with shell fire and the road ploughed up, but this had now settled down to one horrible level surface of water and oozing mud.

Outside lay many bodies covered over, of men who had been wounded, had managed to make their way to the aid post, but had been killed by shell fire while waiting for their turn of attention. Stretchers with their pitiful burdens were brought out from the inner recesses of the ruins, and we were detailed each four to a stretcher.

The dead were to be taken down to a burial centre which we would find along the road near our old lines, the wounded, further on to where motor ambulances would be found on the road near our old "X" lines.

Young Harry Murphy, myself and two more men were detailed to a stretcher containing a badly wounded lad who was only conscious enough to feebly moan to us to put him straight in the boat. We heaved the stretcher to our shoulders, and started off that long remembered journey down the St Julien road. In addition to being weak and tired, our uneven heights made carrying difficult, and it must have been torture for the poor occupant of the stretcher. In the best places, the road was nearly knee deep in mud, and shell holes could not be located except by testing each foothold. Planks had been put down in places where the whole width of the road had been blown up, but these were now floating aimlessly about, and any attempt to use them would have resulted in a spill, and hurling our burden into the mud.

Rain still poured down unceasingly and the road was being shelled viciously. We could not well duck at the shells, with a badly wounded man dependent on steady shoulders, and all we could do was to plod through and trust to good luck. We had not travelled far down the road when we passed 3 dead Germans laying face downwards in the mud, and a yard or two behind them, one of our boys who had evidently been escorting them.

The road was a gruesome nightmare, bodies lay in the mud all along the road and burial parties were busy collecting them as best they could. Dead mules, horses, wrecked guns, limbers and all the terrible debris of battle lay in the mud.

We were getting now, that we could not carry the stretcher more than a hundred yards at a stretch, and each time we rested, we found it more difficult to heave it up again, but we plodded along with red hot shoulders and cracking backs, sometimes having to get nearly waist deep to find a foothold across some huge hole that stretched from one side of the road to the other.

Pat had not been detailed for stretcher carrying, as he was already loaded up with what seemed to be all that was left of the signalling apparatus. He gave us a helping hand where he could, and often saved us from disaster by finding the best footholds for us, and helping across difficult patches.

At last we came in sight of the burial party, busy on their gruesome task. Here a Padre in soaked surplice over muddy uniform, was reading a short service over a great open trench where men who had given their all, lay side by side. At one end of the trench lay stocks of equipment muddied and torn, and piles of boots, while the officer in charge was busy with note book and numerous little discs, paybooks, and little bags for "effects". That cold little word that covers all the intimate treasures found in a soldier's pockets, photographs of home folks and usually the last letter written home which had missed the post, and would usually contain those lies, finer than the truest truths, that he was having a "bon" time and that he expected to be comfortably at home in a month or two at the outside, with the war all finished with.

These are things that were not read of under the big newspaper headlines of August 1st which announced "Day of Victory in Flanders".

After leaving this scene, we soon sighted a row of motor ambulances, and by their side rows and rows of stretchers waiting their turn to be put aboard. The ambulances were moving off as quickly as they were filled, and we laid our burden down at the end of a row.

He was still moaning about the boat, and before we left him, we assured him that he would be on the boat in a few minutes.

From this point we found a duckboard track newly laid, which lead to our old quarters at "X" lines, from where we had commenced the attack. We found a few more of the boys collected here. Hommer amongst them. We were served out at once with overcoats, a hot meal, and a good tot of rum, and we laid down with our overcoats over our sodden clothes and slept.

2 August

The rain was still falling when we wakened in the morning, and we began to think it distinctly hard luck, that, if there was to be a second deluge on account of the wickedness of the Boche, we should be caught in it.

As the battalion had been so badly hit, we felt sure that we must be immediately withdrawn for re-organisation, some thought to Rouen, others more optimistic still, said it could not be done over in France, and that we would likely be sent to Stockport to recruit a new battalion. A damper was put on these optimistic meanderings when orders were given to draw fresh ammunition from the stores in the trench, and to get our rifles ready for inspection.

In the afternoon we were paraded on the top of the trench and proved 57 all told of those who had taken part in the attack, the casualties totalling 20 officers, and more than 500 other ranks. We had one Lewis Gun brought through by Bob Atkinson, but this was now useless.

Some fresh signalling equipment was found and Pat and Bill Beswick were sent off to take over the signals held by the battalion then holding the old German second line – "Canopus Trench". Later in the evening, the remainder of us were paraded under the Signal Officer and set off in the dusk, across the open, for Caliban Trench. We were still tired, sore and stiff, and we had now the additional weight of a wet overcoat which was not inconsiderable.

It had now rained without ceasing for well over 48 hours, and we hardly seemed to remember that it ever had been fine.

We were soon in difficulties as it grew darker. My speciality was barbed wire. I did not seem able to miss any odd barbed wire that happened to be about the district, and in a short while I had lost one puttee, half the other, and various pieces of my trousers.

Collier being my nearest call for help, gave his assistance cheerfully, till at last even his good humour waned and he at last threatened that if I got hung up again, he would be delighted to pass a .303 through me, and leave me there as a horrible warning to other silly blighters who wished to develop a perverted affection for barbed wire.

He did not say it in so many words, but this is what I came to understand from his sudden outburst of eloquence. The Signal Officer coming back to see what the stoppage was about, relieved me of a telephone I was carrying and which I was finding some encumbrance. It was an unfortunate thing for him to do, as his sympathetic nature was the cause of his arriving at Caliban Trench hung about with odd telephones, coils of wire and a couple of rifles. We tumbled into Caliban Trench, and after standing about in the mud, mixed up with the battalion that was already there, it was found that some mistake had been made, and we were to get back again to our old Front Line at Bilge Trench, and wait in the sap there for further orders. Arriving there we found the old trench in an undescribable state. It had been completely wrecked, and the once well boarded trench was now knee deep in mud. With some difficulty we found the entrance to the sap and climbed down through a stream of water to the bottom, and lit a couple of candles. All the old pumping arrangements had either been left, or had broken down, and the candle lights reflected in a foot of cold black water everywhere. A few ammunition boxes and petrol tins still showed their tops above the flood, and provided seats for a few of us, while the remainder leaned uncomfortably against the walls which were trickling with water and slowly crumbling away. No one seemed to be struck with the humour of the fact that we had been sent down here out of the rain.

We were ordered to remain here until the officer – (Bob we called him, out of his hearing) – went to obtain definite instructions as to where we really had to go. He returned after what seemed an age, with orders to get up to "Canopus" trench, not "Caliban". This was the old Boche second line, and to guide us, the Adjutant had fixed a signal lamp at the back of the trench where he was waiting our arrival. Crawling up again out of the sap, we could see the pin point of light in the distance, looking like one solitary star that had escaped being washed out, but was in imminent danger of giving up the unequal fight against the rain. Clambering out of the trench on to the road, we found Lt "Bob" had been looking for other things than orders.

He had managed to get a Dixie of Hot Tea brought up for us from the cookhouse in "X" lines, and this was polished off with avidity before we set off. Lt "Bob" again offered his services as a temporary pack mule, and he was quickly hung about again with a telephone or two, various oddments, and led off. With the lamp to guide us, we lost the fear of losing sight of the man in front. We were led slowly and cautiously however, and warning cries from the front, of "Wire",

"Hole on the left", etc., etc., helped us to reach the back of the trench, under the lamp in fairly close company. We scrambled over the back of the trench, and literally dropped in. I landed in a sitting position on an ammunition box, and felt so suddenly comfortable, that I sat there while the others disappeared round a corner of the trench, and was only prevented from falling into a sweet slumber by "Hommer" who had come in search of me. He informed me that he had reserved me a good "Kip" in a dugout, and we had time for a sleep before going on for a spell of telephone duty. A "Kip" meant sufficient room to lay down for the purposes of sleep, though a "Kip" itself was not a guarantee of sleep.

A "Good Kip" might mean anything. There were no standard values in "Kips" as their "goodness" varied according to the conditions preceding the "Kip". What could be honestly called "A good kip" under our present circumstances, would not have received any recognition at all as a "kip" in better times.

However, I followed "Hommer" along the trench till we came to a big concrete pill box which had escaped destruction. The entrance was not more than two feet high, and 6 inches out of these 24, were below water. We negotiated this on our hands and knees and found it fairly roomy inside. The floor was fortunately a little higher than at the entrance, while boards had been laid down and covered with old sacking, and this raised us just above water level.

By the light of a candle, we found sufficient room to lay down between the other somnolent figures, and we were not long before we were dreaming of "Leaves", "Divisional Rests" and other wonderful things that go to make dreams.

Two of the signallers had gone off to relieve Pat and Bill Beswick, who had been sent up to take over the signals before we left "X" lines, with a promise that they would be relieved in a couple of hours, whilst we had spent from dusk till nearly dawn mudlarking between "X" lines, Caliban Trench, Bilge Trench and finally to Canopus Trench.

3 August

Early in the morning, Hommer and I left to take our turn on the signals. We found the "signal office" some distance along the trench, in another concrete dugout, where with the aid of a few petrol tins, and ammunition boxes, an island was formed on which we could either sit with our feet tucked up, or dangle them in the water to suit our pleasure.

This dugout had a joke of its own. In the trench just opposite the entrance, were two floating planks.

At first, they appeared to be solid baulks of timber laid on a firm bottom, leading to the dugout entrance. Stepping on the end of them however, they simply sank and left us waist deep in water, while the further end came up and supplied a shower bath for that portion of us that was not already submerged, while a peal of laughter came from the dugout. After taking over duty, we began to enjoy the joke. Through the low entrance to the dugout, we could just see legs of passersby step on to these planks, stagger wildly and sink surely and suddenly. We took pains to conceal our mirth until we had heard the remarks of the victim. We had a great time, until an officer of the "Sussex" passed that way. We were unfortunate enough not to be able to distinguish officer's legs from the legs of other ranks, owing to the mud, and his remarks did not even give us an inkling of his rank. Our advice to him to "Pick 'em up" and our mirth seemed to cause him some annoyance, and an end was put to the joke by some men being set to work to move the planks, and get some draining done.

Then there came to be domiciled with us, a Sgt. Major from the Sussex, who were in touch with us at this point. He brought with him a petrol tin which he guarded jealously. After he had filled his water bottle from it, had a good drink and filled it up again, he went to the entrance and yelled "Headquarters – Rum up".

There was quickly a splashing outside and H.Q. trooped up, were served out with their tots, and disappeared again. The Sgt. Major returned inside and had his tot. We watched him at his "tot" with a gasp of admiration, which slowly turned to disgust, as he screwed up the petrol tin tightly and laid himself down to sleep without so much as "A bloomin' voulez-vous" as Hommer put it. We waited patiently until we judged the key of the sleepers snore to have reached the key denoting solid unconsciousness, then, whilst I kept an eye on the entrance, Hommer reached across for the petrol tin and shook it, and was delighted to find it was not as empty as we feared. He turned the screw stopper which of course screeched like a wild cat.

Hommer's suggestion for Supply Officers:–

"Stoppers, Brass, screw – of Tins, Petrol,

S.D.R. for use of – will in future be oiled"

The Sgt. Major however, was far past being wakened by trifles, and the contents of the petrol tin were quickly transferred to Hommer's mess tin, and the lid put on tightly. This was not for immediate use it appeared, as for our present requirements, we managed to extract sufficient from his water bottle without removing it from his waist.

I was "busy[?]" at the instrument as he wakened, but my busy partner held out our only available mess tin to the still sleepy Sgt. Major, and with all the pathos he could command (which was quite a lot), asked if he could spare a drop of rum, as we had very likely missed ours by being on duty away from our own Headquarters.

The worthy gentleman sleepily picked up the petrol tin, shook it and said he was sorry that there was none left. He then felt to see if his water bottle was safe, and fell asleep again.

Our relief, now coming on duty, warned us that rum was being served out at our own Hd. Qrs. We left them a drop from our store, with sufficient information as to its source, to guide their conduct, and hurried off to receive our tot at the hands of the R.S.M. To have missed this would have caused some suspicion, or a fear that we had become casualties.

After taking our ration, we proceeded to our dugout, and found Pat outside, looking as if his ration had been much too small to reach his rheumatism, which had now commenced to trouble him. He remarked that our ration had obviously done us some good, but when we showed the contents of the mess tin, he hurried us into the dugout where we received a warm welcome.

We had really not much to do here, beyond holding the trench in support of the troops now in front, though while we were here, heavy counter attacks were beaten off and St Julien was lost and retaken again, but we were not called upon to move up to their assistance.

Rain still fell continuously, and our legs and feet were becoming pulpy and sodden, as we had now been practically four days soaked through, with no chance of a change of clothes, or of even taking our boots off.

The bandsmen had been doing fine work, carrying containers of soup and hot tea up to us from the cookhouses in "X" lines. How they did the journeys through the mud and continuous shelling, only they knew.

4–5 August

On the fifth day the sun actually shone a little, and there was a great competition for corners in the trench where the sun caught. With the sun seemed to come the revelation that we looked dirty, unkempt rascals. The morning of July 30th had been the last time we had shaved or washed and clothing was in tatters.

Some sweet things in beards were to be seen, though their colours were somewhat dimmed by mud. Only this morning, as I was drinking my rum ration in front of the R. Sgt. Major, I was clumsy enough to let a drop trickle down my chin, which caused him to remark, that he liked to see a man drink his rum decently but could not bear to see a man soak his beard in it.

On August 5th we were at last relieved.

Pat who by now was hobbling about with difficulty was allowed to leave and make his way down in advance, as he could not hope to keep pace with the others. I was detailed to go along with him, whether as Medical Adviser or Military escort, I was not quite sure, though Pat would have it that I had been sent out of the way because the R.S.M. objected to the colour of my beard. This of course was pure jealousy on his part, and evidently meant to relieve a soreness that must have rankled from the days of 1916 at Prees Heath, when he was unjustly charged on parade with shaving his upper lip, and he dared not confess his inability to grow a moustache to his accuser.

Be that as it may, we looked a nice couple as we scrambled out over the back of the trench. Pat carried a pick shaft as an aid to progress, and I brought up the rear with my deficiencies in uniform made up by sandbags tied on with string. Altogether we looked as if we might be going on our first leave from the war of 1870.

Just as we were clear of the trench, three shells hurtled over. One landed in front of us and one at each side. We thought it rather a good omen, and felt that if we could not be caught by three shells at a time, we stood a really good chance with any single ones.

On the way down in a spirit of revenge for my sympathetic [?] remarks about his age and infirmity, Pat soon commenced to take a mean advantage of my well known aversion to shells – (dud or other). By the side of the track we had taken, any amount of shells lay about in the mud. When he could reach one with his pick shaft, he would poke it affectionately, like a farmer prodding his prize pigs, and would murmur "That's a beauty Walter". My threats to run a bayonet through him if he did not desist had no effect whatever. We were not long in striking a duckboard track leading towards Irish Farm and "X" lines, and the travelling was much easier.

Right by the side of the track, we came across a battery of 6 inch Howitzers, pumping shells across. We stayed awhile to watch the proceedings, and were interested to find that by standing directly behind the guns, we could actually follow the flight of the shells till they reached the highest point of their flight, and then it was lost to our view, though we hoped that someone else found them again. We were caught up here by a signaller, who had by some means become possessed of the Regtl. Sgt. Major's water bottle. After proving its contents other then water, we proceeded on our way, and near our old "X" line, were caught up by the other signallers. Not admiring their pace however, we let them pass by after hearing from them where we were expected to report. Making towards the Canal Bank we came across patches of level mud, acres in extent, and we were not now surprised that our Artillery had not been able to make forward as quickly as we had hoped. If it had not been for the new wooden tracks laid for the troops, it was doubtful whether even few men could have negotiated these horrible quagmires. Here we passed a battalion of the Oxfordshire and Buckinghamshire Regt. going up, and in answer to some of their enquiries, we assured them that we had spent a delightful weekend, that they had still a mile or two of pleasant country to go through, and that no submarines had appeared up to the time of our coming away.

We crossed the canal soon after and made for Reigersberg Château, Brielen. Just before reaching it, we came across one of our biggest guns, and on its name plate read "Crack of Doom". We hung about a little while in the hope of hearing what the Crack of Doom was really like, but business was over for the time being, and the gunners could not see their way to oblige us with one, just for our special benefit, in case the officer in charge, who was somewhere about, might possibly hear the gun go off.

In a field close by Reigersberg Château we found a bivouac camp where grass was actually visible. We quickly booked our births in a "bivvy" and then proceeded to peel our boots and socks off for the first time in six days, and paddled about in the long wet grass, just for the sheer joy of seeing our feet again. Bales of new clothing and equipment were waiting here for us, and a big bath was arranged. This consisted of a huge tarpaulin sheet, held up at the four corners, and fed with hot water from the boilers of a couple of traction engines. Into this we tumbled and rolled about, or sat as the sheet moved us.

The water was soon the colour of the rest of Belgium, but it was hot and our limbs lost their semblance to the surface of cold suet dumpling.

We slept here for two nights and on the 7th we packed up and moved across country to the little station of Brandhoek between Poperinghe and Vlamertinghe. Here we took a train a few stations back to Caestre, where we were met by motors and driven to Godeswaersvelde to farm billets, where we were joined by the nucleus that had not been in action. We were under the impression that it would take some time to reorganise us as a battalion fit for the line again, and visions of Base duty at Rouen floated before our eyes.

7–8 August

The day, however, after our arrival, reinforcements commenced to pour in. We were practically at full strength in a day or two, and busy fitting out again, the Q.M. Stores having a hectic time which played havoc with the tempers of the staff therein. The tailors shop too was doing a brisk trade in stripes. Many wanted their first, and many who had already one or two wanted one more. Privates burst forth in bunches to Lance Corporals, and promotions were fast and furious. On the second morning here, I was ordered to report to the Battalion Orderly Room and made a fuller acquaintance with that hitherto mysterious personage, the Orderly Room's Sgt, as a matter of fact he was a Quartermaster Sgt. and had that unmistakable 1914 (before you came-up-chum) appearance about him. By his waxed moustache, I took him to be an old Regular, but when he spoke to me without swearing, or asking me when I came up, I found I was mistaken.

It appears that there is an old suspicion in the Army, that a private who can write his name and address with ease, is something out of the ordinary, this was the second time in France that I had been asked whether I could write.

Pleading guilty again to being as far advanced in my education, I was ordered to commence work in the Orderly Room first thing after breakfast.

9–16 August

It was with mixed feelings that I reported this matter to Pat at breakfast in the barn. It appeared that he also had been offered a job as Company Clerk, but had declined it, or this is how he put it.

I expect the truth of it was, that he had asked so many questions about the job, that it would not be safe to put him in it. When the other signallers heard the news, they gave me strict instructions to get hold of the leave list first thing, and let them know where they stood. The Orderly Room was fixed up in a little outhouse on the opposite side of the farm yard from the barn in which we slept. A couple of trestle tables and boxes to sit on completed the office furniture. The Q.M.S. (known hereafter as "Q") was busy at one table with a pile of papers in front of him, while at the other desk was a new clerk who had commenced duty there only the day before. He was busy thumping at a big Remington which looked considerably war worn. The staff had suffered casualties during the push, and we were evidently reinforcements to fill the gaps. "Q" introduced me to my young fellow clerk who appeared quite a youngster. "Q" introduced him already as "Young Len". He was a most obliging young soul, and offered to show me anything he thought I might not know, from adding up figures to using the small "L" on the Remington for number one.

There was a great amount of work to get through, as many of the records had been lost owing to a shell having dropped on the Orderly Room dugout when in "X" lines. Company records had also been lost in the fighting, and great difficulty was found in getting details of the casualties.

The Record Office at the Base had furnished us already with a fresh roll of the Battalion. Working from this we first found out who were still present with the Battalion. Evidence was then taken from officers and men, of particulars of men known to have been killed. The list still remaining was then gone into again with lists received from Officers in charge of burial parties. Lists were also coming in daily from Casualty Clearing Stations. Still a long roll remained of men still unaccounted for. For the time being these had to be reported as "Missing", until such times as evidence came through that they were officially notified as Prisoners of War.

Of those that still remained unaccounted for, and reported as missing, after a statutory period, the casualty lists would contain their names as No......Reported Missing July 31st 1917 now presumed Killed in Action.

Many cases were known to us of men being slightly wounded, and having been seen on their way to the dressing stations, after which, all trace of them had been lost. One such case seen by both Pat and myself, was our Lewis Gun Instructor.

This was accounted for to a great extent, by the fact that the enemy had made deliberate attack by shell fire and aeroplane bombs, on every dressing station or casualty clearing station that they could locate. Many of these places, with rows of stretcher cases and walking cases waiting to be attended to, had been utterly destroyed, the staffs killed and records blown to atoms.

There was enough work for some days to keep us busy at it long after "Lights Out" for the battalion, who were now having an easy time of it, and finishing parades by dinner time.

As someone had to be on duty night and day in the Orderly Room, Len and I arranged to take it in turns to stay each night, and fix a bed up on one of the benches, adding the table blankets and the blanket used for packing the Remington to our own blankets, we could manage a nice comfortable "Kip".

Finding it rather lonely after a night each, we made our permanent abode there together, and found it much less work to get the table covers on, and the furniture straight, before "Q" came in after breakfast. The Colonel was back again with the Battalion for a day or two, but then left for England for a rest, the Adjutant remaining in charge.

One morning, enquiring of "Q" how the new staff were shaping, and "Q" giving us quite a satisfactory character, we were told to see the tailor and get a stripe each. After this, we could yell "Runner" with almost as much confidence in one appearing, as if "Q" himself had shouted.

When we had managed to get fairly straight with the work, we were allowed out alternate evenings. Borrowing a pair of binoculars one evening, Pat and I set out to climb the Mont des Cats, a hill close by. On the way up, we called at a farm house where Pat had been making friends the previous evening, to the extent of even assisting the lady of the house to lift a ham out of the boiling water, and had threatened to come up tonight for a slice. We really managed a good slice each, also an egg or two. We also tried the farm beer, but we much preferred the ham and eggs.

On the top of Mont des Cats was a fine old Trappist Monastery, the greater part of the building however, was in use at that time as a casualty clearing station, and a fine old windmill stood by. From the top of the hill, with the aid of the binoculars, we could see round a good part of the old salient. The Church Towers of Poperinghe stood out quite distinctly, and further eastwards we could pick up the white tower of the old mill at Vlamertinghe, and what we made out to be a few of the bigger remains of buildings in Ypres. Later, as the light grew dim, we could see the flashes of the guns, though we could not hear the reports.

When we returned to our billet, we found quite a number of youngsters busy selling chocolate. Going to the Orderly Room, I found "Q" in the clutches of a nipper of about seven years of age. To air his French a little when he had the chance, "Q" had opened a conversation in his very best style when the youngster interrupted him with "Speak English you Quarter Master Sergeant". Standing corrected he asked the price of a packet on the tray and received the answer pat, "A tanner". "Q" insisted that "Tanner" was not English and he did not understand. This brought a torrent of furious invective from the youngster in good "B.E.F." terms, and "Q", deciding that discretion was the better part of valour, hastily found a "Tanner" and got rid of the dangerous brute.

The village of Godewaersvelde was some distance from the billets, but we managed an evening there before we left the district. It was much like other Belgian villages. The usual crowd of cstaminets, egg and chip cottages, the usual big brewery (empty) and fine church.

17 August

On the 17th we left by motors for the southern side of the salient, proceeding by Bailleul, Locre, and La Clytte. Some distance past La Clytte we left the motors, debouching into a field for tea, before making our way forward to Ridge Wood. It was getting dark when we arrived here. In the wood itself great drains had been cut in all directions, and the ground being wet slippy clay with no vestige of grass, we did a fair amount of skidding before we reached our quarters. These consisted mostly of sandbag erections scattered about the wood, and a few tents. After finding out where the Orderly Room was located, Len and I went in search of the transport, collected our boxes, partly carried them, and partly slid them to the Orderly Room where we spent sometime scraping the mud off them.

The Orderly Room luggage consisted of 3 large black tin boxes, two wooden ones, and a wooden case containing the typewriter, and last but not least, the "Yellow Peril". This was a wooden case painted a brilliant yellow. It bore on its side the legend "Ellam's Duplicator", but had now fallen on evil days, and was used to carry as much orderly room stuff as it would hold, when the battalion went into the line.

19 August

On the 19th we left Ridge Wood Camp at dusk for the line, on the southern arm of the salient on the Battle Wood sector. When the battalion went into the line "Q" and Len removed the Orderly Room to the transport lines, while I took my first turn taking the "Yellow Peril" into the line.

We cut through the wood, past La Brasserie, and on to a wooden road which led towards the Ypres–Comines Canal. The mud was still thick everywhere, and in many places the wooden planks of the road were afloat. This road had been heavily shelled, and here and there were huge shell holes, where the planks lay shattered. This took us to a road that had a consistently level depth of mud of about six inches, but it was nice wet mud of a thin texture, that did not impede progress much. Things were very quiet till we reached the high bank of the Canal, where we had a few shells at uncomfortably close quarters. One particular shell that startled us, made a most peculiar racket, followed by smaller metallic crashes that we could not understand, till we found that the shell had actually struck a dump of empty shell cases. We made our way quickly down to the canal bank and, crossing a wooden footbridge, were kept waiting for a long time on the further bank, as guides had not appeared here as expected.

It was none too comfortable a place to hang about, as the enemy had a partiality for shelling canal banks, having a shrewd idea that darkness would be sure to find someone about. There were no dugouts here, but there were little "funk holes" in the bank here and there. They might have been useful during a shower of rain. We eventually got moving again, and took to a shallow trench. It seemed strange to be moving along a trench only waist deep, after the deep trenches we had been using on the other side of the salient, but this trench was not now under observation, fortunately, otherwise there might have been some doubt as to which end of our anatomy would be best to appear above the trench. After leaving the trench, we crossed some open ground, and dipped into a copse. A sudden halt was made here, as it dawned on us that we had suddenly become about half a platoon without any lead as to which way to take. Someone just in front had lost touch with the man in front of him. He had said nothing, hoping to catch up again, but having gone some distance without getting into touch, he suddenly began to wonder whether he was taking the right direction.

There was nothing for it but to sit down and wait in the hopes of being picked up by the next company following up.

We had not long to wait and were soon picked up again, and shortly afterwards arrived at the foot of the high embankment of the Ypres-Comines railway. Near the top of this, a trench had been cut, and little shelves cut into the sides did duty for dugouts. Two companies and Headquarters were accommodated here, while two companies climbed over the railway, and took up shell hole posts in front of the embankment.

My Orderly Room consisted of a gap in the back of the trench, roofed over with a sheet of corrugated iron and filled up at the back with sandbags. On my roof for company, I had the box with the signaller's pigeons. There was room to sit inside, but hardly room to lay down, and there were only two positions where I could find room for the "Yellow Peril", one was as a pillow, the other, on my lap as a writing desk.

Although there was not much work to do here, there was very little rest. Reports of one kind and another had to be sent to the Brigade Hd. Quarters at specified times, commencing with the "Situation Report" at 4 am. Runners came in at all times with correspondence, reports and orders of all kinds, some of which I could attend to, the remainder had to be taken to the C.O. or the Adjutant.

In a tunnel just opposite my "office" was the signal office, and all messages received were handed across to me, so that sleep could only be a matter of a snatch at a time.

20–25 August

Our late Adjutant now being in command of the battalion, a new Adjt. had been appointed. He was an officer we knew well, as he had been our platoon officer, and we had no great affection for him, to put it mildly.

My first day on duty under him was unfortunate, as we had a difference of opinion early on, as to the correct meaning of the word "business-like".

I could never get on well with anyone who pressed their forefinger on a pencil until the finger curled backwards. When he was a platoon officer, he had pulled me up one day, concerning the volume of my correspondence that he was obliged to censor. I had pleaded ignorance of any Battalion Order, Army Order, or any regulation limiting either the length or number of letters that might be written.

This seemed to have annoyed him at the time, but it was not long after this before Pat and I had a gratuitous offer from a more obliging officer, to hand to him personally any letters we had for censoring.

The Adjutant was a very heavy sleeper, and when I had to rouse him, he always wakened in a bad temper, and gave me the impression that he was not quite sure whether I had used unnecessary violence upon him, in my attempts to stir him to consciousness.

On the night of our arrival here, Pat and another signaller had been detailed at once to relieve two signallers of the outgoing battalion, who had a "visual" signal station on "The Mound".

Behind the embankment that we were on, lay a valley, which rose again in a hill that was known as "The Mound". From this place, they could pick up lamp signals from the embankment and transmit the messages back to Brigade Headquarters. They had traversed the valley in the dark, and found the two signallers in a little "nugger hole" with their lamp fixed up just outside. They made off quickly, and left Pat and his partner to carry on. Soon "The Mound" began to get well shelled, and they spent the night crouching as far as they could get into their little hole, while keeping a look out for signals.

When dawn broke, they found a little cross outside their shelter, to the memory of a signaller who had been killed at the post a week or so before, so for a week they had the little cross for company in the daylight, and for "comfort" in the darkness when the shelling commenced.

Each morning we could see Pat coming across the valley to draw rations. His speed across, or at least his want of speed, proved that he still believed in the idea that he might as well be hit by a shell, as die of over-exertion. After collecting his rations, he would attend certain secret rites in the signal office, where I had reason to believe a derelict jar of S.R.D. had been found. My reason for believing this to be the case, was the fact that Signaller Bill Beswick (an old reservist and chief of the "Black Hand Gang") would appear at the entrance of the tunnel at uncertain periods, glance up and down the trench, and if no one particular was about, he would shoot across into my office, hand me a grubby mess tin and hiss into my ear

"Hey! Walt. This'll do yer good, and bring the mess tin back when you've finished it."

Things were fairly quiet while we were here, though the valley behind us, and "The Mound" were well shelled and gassed.

It was so quiet and the weather so nice one afternoon, that the C.O. and Hd. Quarters officers decided to have tea out of doors, and the table was laid in the trench. All was peace, when suddenly a salvo of shells landed plump into the embankment just below the trench. Up flew a volcano of stones and earth, burying the table and all that was on it. When the party extricated themselves from the debris, the C.O. swore deeply, and glared back over the valley through his binoculars, then dived off into the Signal Office to speak pleasant remarks to Brigade Hd. Quarters, about that thrice blessed battery of 18 pdrs. in our rear, dropping "shorts" into our quarters. A day or two later, a rather annoying report came in from Brigade Hd. Quarters, with reference to the matter. It mentioned that the matter had been enquired into, and they were of the opinion that the shells came from an enemy battery which had been located at O18.d 7.9, which could enfilade our position, and that the battery would have their immediate attention.

26–28 August

On the 26th we were relieved by the Black Watch, and some little argument ensued between our signallers and theirs, as to whether S.R.D. was trench stores, or tenants moveable property.

The matter was amicably arranged by a little "give and take". On leaving the embankment, we made our way to the support line, which was a maze of old German Trenches, very badly knocked about.

In the darkness we seemed to cross and re-cross trenches without end, till we began to wonder when we would strike the right one.

At last, a voice from a trench at our feet complained that we were kicking mud down his "scarlet" ventilator. It seemed lucky that we had done so, or very likely we would have crossed the trench which happened to be the home we were looking for.

I had now lost my last shred of affection for the "Yellow Peril" and wished it might make the acquaintance of a 5.9 were it not that it kept me company so closely.

My home this time was in a concrete pill box. It was the same place that we had kicked the mud into, down the ventilator. Half a dozen of us were domiciled here. Timber had been laid over the flooded floor, and nothing prevented us from being quite comfortable, but the fact that the place was literally swarming with lice. As these were evidently of enemy origin, we showed no mercy till our energy was exhausted, and we fell to bemoaning our ill fate at becoming victims to German hate in this undignified manner.

Having a little time to spare the next morning, I had a walk round to see if I could find Pat, and found the signallers dugout, for once, a hive of industry, inside and out.

They were busy on a scheme of drainage, having evidently slept in the dugout first to dream of the plans for morning.

It (the scheme) seemed quite a success, but as I saw the stream of water pouring out of the dugout, down the trench, I wondered whose dugout would get the benefit of the deluge.

There was very little to do here, Pat was supposed to be "on the lines", but I suspect this was more or less of an excuse to roam about at his own sweet will, for one morning he looked me up to see whether I had time to come for a walk round to see the sights. I left word in the dugout that I had gone round to see the four companies over some question of "nominal rolls" and went off with him until four. We cut over the back of the trench. A short distance behind the trench was a road where the transport could come up at night with shells and rations, and where ration parties from the front line and the supports would meet them.

Beyond the road again was a masked battery of 18 pdrs. Camouflage curtains being lifted only during firing. As no one was visible about the guns, we dropped into some trenches close by where the gunners had their quarters. Pat seemed to be well known round here, though I could not learn of any telephone line between our battalion and the artillery, which might account for his presence over here. He popped his head in a dugout here and a dugout there, wishing them good morning, till at one dugout we learned that a new barrel of beer had arrived up the previous night, for their canteen. This was evidently "the line" that Pat was interested in hereabouts, as he did not then enquire the way to the canteen, but marched me off straight there to test the new barrel. The barrel and its attendant guardian occupied a dugout to themselves in solemn state. After testing the beer and murmuring "bon" more from habit than conviction, we moved off further to have a look at the old original front lines of this sector, previous to July. They were now battered out of all shape, but we could judge that it had not been a particularly restful spot to stay in. The German line was so near to our own, that it was impossible for either side to actually shell their opposing front line without their friends suffering in the process.

29–30 August 1917

On the 29th we were relieved by a battalion of the Sussex Rgt. Officers kits, cooking utensils and Lewis Guns were carried across to the road, and left in charge of a few men, until the transport arrived to pick them up. As the battalion was moving away, the road was a scene of activity. A string of mules had just arrived up with ammunition for the battery.

Not relishing the idea of carrying the "Yellow Peril" all the way back to Ridge Wood, I spotted "Sammy" the Signal Officers batman, sat on a pile of Officers' kits, awaiting the arrival of the limbers. I asked him, if I left the "Yellow Peril" in his charge, would he be good enough to put it on a limber with his stuff, and slip into the Orderly Room with it as soon as he arrived at Ridge Wood. Then I hurried up to catch the battalion, as I was not anxious to be left in the darkness to find my way back to Ridge Wood alone.

On arriving at Ridge Wood I found Len and "Q" comfortably fixed up in a big sandbagged Orderly Room, the battalion this time being in another camp, though in the same wood. I had not been in long before the Adjutant came in, and wanted some papers that were of course, safely stored away in the "Yellow Peril". I had to inform him how matters stood and he was furious. I began to wish fervently that I had carried the box down after all, or stayed behind, and come along with the limbers. He left the Orderly Room with a none too pleasantly expressed order that I must bring the papers to his dugout immediately the limbers arrived.

I patiently waited for "Sammy" but an hour or more had passed, and still no signs of him, so I went out to look whether the transport had arrived. I found that the limbers had arrived sometime ago. The Lewis Gun limbers had been unhorsed and left in the camp, still loaded, but the remaining limbers had been unloaded and left the camp for the transport lines.

I groped about the camp in the darkness on a hunt for "Sammy" and eventually found him comfortable in the officer's cookhouse, no thoughts of my box disturbing his serenity.

"What! Hasn't it come?" was all he could reply to my heated enquiry. After asking him how it could come if he had not brought it, I found out what had happened. It appeared that all our stores had been dumped on the road, right in front of that battery of 18 pdrs, and just as our limbers arrived to pick up our goods, the battery wished to commence business for the evening.

The limbers were ordered quickly away, and were sent off some distance back down the road, while the men in charge of the stores, made a wild scurry down the road with their goods and chattels. Sammy could not swear to picking my box up, but was convinced that nothing was left behind, and that it must have come down on one of the limbers.

Just then Sammy was called, and left to attend to his officer.

I went back to the Lewis Gun Limbers, unlaced them and unloaded the guns and ammunition cases, but could find no trace of my box, and with aching back, heaved the cases and boxes in again, only to find that they would not fit in as they did before. I persevered however, and managed at last to get them straight and laced up again. I groped my way back to the Orderly Room feeling how really inadequate the English Language is, to express one's deepest feelings at times.

I explained to "Q" what had happened, and it was decided that the only thing to be done was to get down to the transport lines, to see whether the box had been carried down there. If the Adjutant came again in the meantime, he would tell him some tale to keep him quiet. I started off with only the faintest idea of where to find the transport lines "Near the Scherpenberg" was the only information I could get. The "Scherpenberg" was over a small range of hills four to five miles away, consisting of the Scherpenberg, Mont Vidaigne and

Mont Rouge, to the west of Kemmel Hill. Passing through Hallebast, Millekruisse, La Clytte, and getting near the Scherpenberg I could find transport belonging to any unit but ours, but eventually found them snug in a little valley by the roadside. I laid hold of one of the drivers, and together we searched the limbers, but without result, and enquiries amongst the other drivers failed completely. Nobody had seen anything of the box. I walked back to Ridge Wood haunted by visions of a Court Martial or 28 days F.P. at the very least. The old tag that no one could be a real soldier till he had done F.P. held no comfort for me.

Len was still sitting up when I arrived back, and on hearing of my fruitless search, he was full of sympathy, trying to cheer me up by suggesting that if the "Yellow Peril" was lost, it was really a stroke of luck, as now we might indent for a proper despatch bag such as the O.R. clerks of other units carried.

We were quite agreed however, that it was no use worrying further that night either about Adjutants or boxes, so we took the blankets off the tables and made bed.

Morning however, brought anxious moments waiting for the Adjutant to appear.

"Q" had told the C.O. what had happened, and he had expressed what I thought was a very sane view of the matter, viz, that if the damned thing was lost, it was lost, and that was all there was about it. This sane view did not appeal to the Adjt. which of course proved, beyond doubt, that he was mad. When he appeared after breakfast, he ordered me off up the line at once to find the box, and not to come back till I had found it.

I was putting my "Fighting Order" equipment together – for no one was allowed near the line unless dressed in "Fighting Order" – when Pat poked his head in the door to pass his usual remarks about the two vilest things he knew of – the weather and the army. Noticing my battle array, he enquired the reason, and when I informed him that I was going to look for the "Yellow Peril", he asked "Not by yourself?" in a tone that led me to reply "Why not?" rather heatedly.

He disappeared and I mistakenly thought that I was rid of him. What happened was, that he went to the Regtl. Sgt. Major and guilelessly asked if it was in order for a man to go up to the line by himself. The "R.S.M." caught unawares replied "not if I know it". Pat then informed him that the Adjutant was sending me up.

The R.S.M., as Pat evidently knew, was not exactly on kissing terms with the Adjt. but gave himself away no further than coming into the Orderly Room to tell me to take a runner along with me.

Pat who had followed at his heels explained that as a linesman, he was out of a job at present and asked permission to act as a runner for the occasion.

Permission was granted, and we were soon leaving camp together, while Pat took pains to instil into my mind, the fact that he had not thought what a trouble I was going to be, when he gaily promised my wife to see me safely home again.

We trudged back along the way we had come the previous evening, till we reached a point where a difference of opinion arose as to which way to take. I knew that the way Pat wished to take was not the way we had come down, and I was all for the way I knew. Argument of course was useless, he always knew a better way, and his threat to let me go my own way alone clinched matters. I followed him by a track that I had not noticed before, and when we passed three dead mules whose presence would have not passed unnoticed if we had been blindfolded, I told him what I thought of his choice of route.

He pointed out that if my stomach was still squeamish after fifteen months of army "grub" I had my gas helmet with me. Shortly we dropped into an old trench, and making our way along this, we were about to turn a corner when we found a stack of shells taking up half the width of the trench. There did not seem room to pass without bumping them, and as their noses pointed our way, I did not admire the look of them. I knew all too little about them, whether they were fused or not, if fused, what sort of fuses they were. Pat would have it that they were not fused, though I do not expect that he really knew anything more about the matter than I did. I wanted to get out of the trench and go over the top, but just then Pat started off, and squeezed safely past without touching them. Fearing his remarks about my figure if I did not follow suit, I pressed my back into the side of the trench, and was so eager to get clear, that, as I neared the end of the pile, I made a sudden dive for the clear trench beyond, with the result that my bayonet and trenching tool handle caught the shells a resounding thump. My scalp tightened suddenly and I held my breath, when Pat broke in to remind me that he had said they were quite safe.

There are times when I feel sure that Pat will not die by the hands of the enemy, but I do not feel so sure about his friends.

We eventually came to the battery of 18 pdrs. whose acquaintance we had made before, and on to the road at the back of the support trench that we had occupied, cutting out perhaps a mile, which detail Pat did not allow to escape my attention.

Here, on the road, was where my box had been put along with the other baggage. We searched each side of the road for a considerable distance without luck, and Pat suggested that I should go over to our old Orderly Room dugout, to see if the incoming battalion (Sussex) had picked up the box, whilst he went and made enquiry at the Battery Head Quarters.

I searched shell holes on my way without result and dropped into the trench, not failing to first kick some mud down the ventilator into the Orderly room, in the hope that the Sussex Orderly Room Sgt. might get a neckful, which would be something in advance for the nasty remarks that would doubtless be forthcoming when my enquiries opened.

I was almost thankful to find that the Sussex had not found the box, and after an exchange of compliments with a corporal, I climbed out of the trench and kicked a bit more mud down the ventilator before meeting Pat again on the road.

He had been to the Battery Officers quarters without result, and it was decided that the only thing to do, was to see if there was any beer in the Artillery Canteen. We dropped into the trench where the gunners had their quarters, and Pat pushed his head into a dugout to ask how things were, when I heard him shout "where did you get that".

"That" was the Yellow Peril which one of the gunners had laid across his knee, and was using as a writing desk. He explained that after unloading shells the previous evening, he had noticed the box lying by the roadside. Taking it to his dugout, he had examined the contents and found out that it belonged to the battalion, and had kept it in the expectation of someone coming up to look for it, before handing it in to his Hd. Quarters. The contents were intact, and, adjourning to the canteen, we celebrated our success, before returning to Ridge Wood camp.

That same evening, when Brigade Orders came in, we found Pat's name amongst those awarded the Military Medal for gallantry and devotion to duty on July 31st. We sent the news in to the signallers dugout, unofficially, before issuing Battalion Orders and pandemonium reigned there, till we shortly saw Pat and a friend carrying a big empty tea Dixie towards the canteen, returning a little later with it filled with beer, when sounds of revelry broke out.

Pat appeared in the Orderly Room soon afterwards with an anxious enquiry as to whether it was permissible to bring beer into a self respecting place like ours, and we assured him that it would be quite in order if the C.O. or Adjt were not present. He disappeared and returned again with three mess tins from which we drank his health. He did not seem elated over his award, and was evidently afraid that he might get into trouble from home for not behaving himself. We cheered him up as best we could, by assuring him that any man who had the nerve to make such a hole in the contents of the C.O.'s water bottle as he did that day, deserved all he got.

2–6 September

On September 2nd, we left Ridge Wood for the line again, on the Shrewsbury Forest sector. Both Len and I went up together this time in charge of the Yellow box, and we found it as much as we could do to carry it in turn along the rough long journey in the dark, through Voormezeele, along the Mount Sorrel, and past the battered Hill 60 with its huge tunnels, to Shrewsbury Forest. We passed by big guns at intervals just off the roads and tracks, and sometimes the darkness would be split by a blinding flash and a stunning report that would leave us blind and numb for seconds afterwards.

Shrewsbury Forest was more of a desert than a forest, as hardly a vestige of a tree could be seen at dawn the next morning.

Headquarters occupied a large concrete dugout on the rise of a hill. Two companies held the crest by isolated posts in shell holes, while the remaining two companies were kept in support in a trench in our rear, across the ravine behind us.

The concrete Pill Box that we were in, was quite intact. It was a very solid affair, and on the top of its 3 feet of concrete roof, layers of steel rails and brushwood facines had been laid alternately. The interior consisted of four small compartments. Len and I occupied one portion with the runners, the signallers the second portion, Hd.Qr. Officers the third portion and the last compartment was in possession of the mess cooks.

The ground about was wonderfully dry considering the recent rains.

As soon as we arrived, Pat and his friend B.B. (Bill Beswick commonly known as Burglar Bill) had to set to work immediately running lines out, as this place had not been previously used as Headquarters. While running a cable out along a narrow trench, they ran into a party of the outgoing battalion, just as the enemy artillery opened out on the spot, and witnessed the horrible spectacle of practically the whole party being blown to pieces.

There was a great deal of aerial activity on this sector, and fighting in the air could be seen almost at anytime during daylight.

One of our aeroplanes was shot down here, and fell just in front of one of our posts, and despite the barrage that was, as usual, put round the smashed plane, the boys from the post went out and brought in the body of the young airman. After dark, the body was brought down to our quarters. He was only a youngster, but had put up a big fight against odds.

We got a message through to the squadron, and the same night two of his brother officers came up. They were greatly upset, as the young airman had only come to them during the week. The C.O. took them to gather what valuables they could salve from the wreckage. Four men were detailed to carry the body down to the nearest point to which they had been able to bring their car. For their services, the C.O.'s permission was asked to grant them 3 days holiday as guests of the squadron.

"Bill" provided a little excitement one day on his own account. He was seized with a sudden desire to get into communication with one of our observation balloons, and forthwith climbed on to the top of the pill box armed with a Lucas signalling lamp, with the result that after watching his efforts for a minute or two, we had to bolt into our holes like a lot of rabbits and sit tight till the enemy had decided that he had sent enough shells over, to make sure that such a thing would not happen again. Bill had managed to come scatheless through one "F.G.C.M." a few months before, and nearly landed himself in for another.

On the 6th we left in the darkness to make our way to Voormezeele. We had some difficulty in finding our quarters, as we seemed to have arrived in small parties, who were roaming about the village with no idea of where to go. Pat, Len, myself and two signallers had come down together, and had attached ourselves to various parties in the hope that they had some idea of where they were going. Having no success, we detached ourselves again, thinking we could do better by ourselves.

Someone advised us to follow a light railway track which he said would take us to a field which had been allocated to our battalion. We followed the advice and the railway track until we reached a point where the track divided. Here we sat down in disgust to argue which way to take. Every few yards along the track we had yelled "Cheshires" into the adjoining fields without receiving any reply. As we sat here we at last heard a voice calling back "Hello! Cheshires" and thought we had at last found home. Imagine our disgust to find it was a lone officer who had lost his way and also his platoon. He also thought that he had at last found a home, and his language, when he joined us, expressed our feelings exactly. Just as we had decided to divide forces and try both lines, someone noticed a light or two moving about some distance away, and we made tracks that way, and found ourselves practically the last comers.

The companies were accommodated in small dugouts in trenches cut across the field, while the officers and Orderly Room occupied sandbag erections placed at intervals round the field. How Len and I managed to get safely into the Orderly Room in the darkness, I never could quite understand, as, a few minutes later, when Len went out into the darkness to find the Adjt. I heard a howl and a splash, and rushed out in time to rescue him from a big shell hole of water, lying right outside our door. We hoped that before we left here, the Adjt. might take it into his head to visit us sometime in the darkness, and find it, but we were disappointed, as he saved his visits for the daylight.

8–12 September 1917

After spending two nights here, we left for Chippewa Camp.

This turned out to be one of the best camps we had found yet. It was a wooden camp and would hold a brigade.

The Orderly Room was more like a "Blighty" Orderly Room. The hut was divided into two parts, the inner sanctum was used as the O.R. proper, and where "Office Hours" were held each morning. The other portion was used by the runners when on duty. For once we had room to work in comfort. Len and I occupied a long bench across the end of the hut, where we could look out on to the parade ground, and thank out stars that we had no inspection to go through nowadays.

"Q" had a little table to himself which was used by the C.O. in the seat of justice at "Office Hours". All this extra table space entailed further blankets from the stores, as table covers, whereby Len and I derived extra comfort at bedtime.

The camp was on the main road between La Clytte and Reninghelst, and a great deal of traffic passed to and fro. Big new guns drawn by huge tractors could be seen daily, going up to replace disabled ones that came back by the same road.

On the opposite side of the road was a big casualty clearing station where one could judge from the traffic in and out, what was going on in the line.

The morning after our arrival, a big batch of reinforcements arrived and kept us busy in the Orderly Room. Most of them were returned casualties, many from other battalions, some from our own. The C.O. had a thoughtful way of dealing with these. He would call all men out who had been with the battalion previously, and put them in the companies that they wished for, so that they could get amongst their old friends again.

The remainder were then divided amongst the four companies to bring them as near as possible to equal strength.

It was not till the following day that there was any chance of having a look round.

Standing at the door of the orderly room that morning with nothing particular to do, I caught sight of a man standing in the door of a hut opposite, who seemed strangely familiar, and went across for closer investigation. It proved to be Len Watson an old friend of tennis club days. It was a mutual surprise and we immediately went indoors, made ourselves comfortable on his blankets, and had a good chat about old times and new. He had been awarded a Military Medal for good work during the capture of Messines in the previous June, but soon after had gone into hospital and had just come back.

This camp was such as soldiers liked, as along the road were one or two estaminets, and cottages where the ubiquitous eggs and chips were to be found.

After four days here, we packed up again and marched further back to what was known as "Kempton Park" camp at Westoutre. We expected great things from the name, but when we arrived we found it just a small field where we had to erect our own tents. After getting a tent fixed up for the Orderly Room we had to hunt round the stores to find what we could, in the shape of empty provision boxes, to make some sort of furniture.

12–18 September

A tent Orderly Room is not one of the least of life's trials. Given a small bell tent, six boxes of books and records, three tables and a typewriter, and there can be some excitement when work commences.

First "Q" wants some papers that he thinks are in a box on which Len has fixed his typewriter and started work.

Not finding them there, he decides the papers are in the box I am using as a seat. Search there proving useless, they must be in one of the boxes supporting his own table. After dismantling the table and not finding what he wanted, we would all be more or less delighted to find the papers on his table all the time. Add to these excitements a little breeze that would waft every unweighted paper out of the tent and across the camp, and one could realize that from the sounds issuing from the tent at times, we were not likely to be mistaken for a local branch of some Christian Endeavour Society.

When Battalion Orders had been issued that night, "Q" retired to the next tent where he slept with the R.S.M., guarded in the rear by their respective batmen who had built themselves a little bivouac at the rear of the tent. Then Len and I must pull all the furniture to pieces and stack it up, before we could find room to lie down. We made a bad blunder that day by not reconnoitring the officers lines by daylight and finding out where the tents of the CO, Adjt, or any other officers we might want, lay.

In the middle of the night, of course, a Brigade runner came in with a big bundle of communications. We lighted a candle and went through them, hoping that we would find nothing that needed attention before morning, but fate was against us, for we came up against that little envelope addressed to the "C.O." and marked "Urgent and Confidential". That of course meant finding the Adjt. at once. I would certainly have preferred to waken the "C.O." himself, but there was no help for it. I slipped into my boots and tunic, not having divested myself further, and made for the officers lines. First

I popped my head into the guard tent to see if by any chance they knew there, where the Adjutant's tent was. They knew nothing. I then walked quietly round a few tents, occasionally stumbling over the ropes in the darkness, in the hope of hearing the Adjutant's voice in some tent. There were however, only two kinds of tent here. One was silent – from the other issued snores of varying qualities, and I did not yet know the Adjutant's snore well enough to pick it out from the medley I could hear. There was nothing else for it, I must wake someone up, and chance the consequences. I rapped on two or three tents with no result at all. Evidently no notice was taken of tent rapping, so I called gently through the flys "Is this the Adjutant's tent, please?"

At each tent my question was evidently misunderstood as the only reply I received was another enquiry from the occupants, unvarying in its text "Is it Hell!!!" I thought of many smart repartees but decided to withhold them until I held a commission or was demobilised.

Trying another tent, I was startled to hear the C.O.'s voice call out "Who is that?" I replied apologetically that it was the "O.R." and was making off when he called me to bring the message in. This was easier said than done. Whoever had shut him in for the night had done it well. After fumbling for sometime with the fastenings I decided that it would be easier to crawl under. Misjudging distance on my hands and knees, I was surprised to find myself up against the tent pole before I thought I was fairly inside the tent, and getting to my feet, I felt myself knocking his tunic off the pole to the ground. I managed to push it up again before I struck a light, and lit a candle by his camp bed. The C.O. sat up and presented a rather startling appearance in a white linen skull cap. It gave him a monkish appearance that was not at all evident at other times. He opened the small envelope marked "Urgent and Confidential" read the contents out aloud, and remarked that everybody knew it, and it was about as urgent as next week. He wished me goodnight in a voice that made me feel he was sorry that I had been disturbed, I saluted and crawled back through the flys and made my way back to the Orderly Room wondering what sort of C.O. the present Adjt. might make if he unfortunately ever had the chance.

Len and I had to be up early in the morning as we had the furniture to put back ready for use, and the blankets back on the tables before anyone found that we had been sleeping in them. A further draft of reinforcements kept us busy during the day. The C.O. was delighted to find a couple of crack footballers and a good boxer amongst them. We had an important match outstanding with the Black Watch, and it was hoped to play this off before leaving our present quarters.

In the evening Pat came round with the interesting information that there was a pastry cook's shop in Westoutre, well spoken of, and worthy of patronage. It was even rumoured that custards and jam tarts were to be had. Pat himself was all for a change of diet, as an incipient boil had appeared over the collar of his tunic, which he feared was due to an unrestricted diet of eggs and chips while at Chippewa Camp. We found the pastry shop and stuffed ourselves to repletion in the manner more compatible with 14 years of age, than the age appearing in our paybooks, and strolled round the village with quite a strange feeling beneath our belts.

The village of Westoutre was then untouched except by a few bombs. Children played in numbers about, and very little of the population seemed to have left.

Before leaving here, the football match between the Black Watch and our battalion was played off with no more casualties than could be attended to by the combined medical services of both battalions.

On September 18th the battalion moved forward again into bivouacs at La Brasserie between Ridge Wood and Voormezeele, spending one night only here preparatory to going into action at Shrewsbury Forest. We erected a tent for the Orderly Room for the one night.

19 September 1917

The following day was spent in lectures to the men, as to what was expected of them in the coming action. During the afternoon Len Watson slipped in to the orderly room to ask me to take care of a few treasures, as I was not going up further with the battalion.

This was looked upon as a bad omen by many men of the battalion, but omens did not interest me particularly, and I took charge of them with some joke about omens, wished him luck and expected him to come and collect them again in a few days, little thinking it was the last time that I would see him.

The number of men to go into action was limited to the numbers laid down by Brigade orders, and the surplus (which we Christened the "B team") went into camp near Westoutre with the surplus from the other battalions of the Brigade.

Pat went down with the "B team" much to his disgust, and he looked forward to a spell of parades and inspections with small rations, with as much pleasure as a spell of neuralgia.

Our old friend Captain "Theo" was to be in charge of the B team camp, and he was known to be fond of Pomp and Polish when out of the line.

At dusk the boys went up, Len Graham going up this time with the Yellow Peril. After seeing them off I packed up the boxes, stowed them on to a limber, and climbed into an empty limber to return to the transport lines, where "Q" and I were to work till the battalion came out again. Riding in limbers was of course against all orders, but as it was dark, the driver said it would be alright if I laid down out of sight.

The ride was its own punishment for disobeying orders. I was sick, sore and sorry when we reached our destination. Limbers have no springs and of course no upholstery. Part of the journey was by rough tracks, and the road we reached passing Ridge Wood, was not of the best.

I would have given anything to get out again and walk, but I did not feel equal to keeping pace with army mules on their way home, and I did not know yet where we were bound for.

My first impression of the transport lines and stores the next morning was, that everyone seemed much bigger and fatter than the men in the companies, and much better fed.

I found at breakfast time in the stores, that the old rule of "One man one dip" into the bacon fat, did not hold sway here, and the feeling of repletion after every meal was something of a novelty.

"Quarters" and I had a table fixed up in the office of the Regtl. Q.M.'s office, but had very little work to do. Most of the day we were out on the road watching the traffic into Chippewa Dressing Station to see if we could get any news of our battalion. They were only supposed to be going into support, but from what could be gathered, everyone had already been ding dong into it, attacks and counter attacks following each other so quickly, that, as one wounded man who was waiting his turn informed us, you never knew whether it was your own attack you were taking part in, or whether it was Fritz's counter attack.

20–23 September

We heard a tale of our C.O. in support, not receiving any call, going forward himself to see what was happening, finding a gap between two battalions in front of him and then taking the battalion up to fill in the gap. In one day alone, eight attacks were made and a similar number of counter attacks were beaten off.

Beyond news picked up on the road, we could get no communication with the battalion. Rations each night were taken up by the transport and dumped at a given spot to be picked up by the battalion when and how circumstances permitted.

Pat turned up here one afternoon, being only about two miles away, and I walked across with him to see what kind of a place they were fixed in.

They were under bivouacs in a field just out of Westoutre. They were not having a bad time of it, though rations were small, and my account of breakfast at the Stores made his mouth water.

24–26 September

On the 24th the transport and stores of the brigade were moved closer up the line to a place called "Swan and Edgar's Corner", not far from Ridge Wood.

This corner was named from a ruined building at a crossroad where some humourist had painted the name "Swan and Edgar" across what remained of it. Here we began to get the first official news of the battalion from Len, in the shape of long lists of killed and wounded. On the very first list I opened to commence work on, I came across the name of Len Watson amongst the killed. As I packed his treasures up to post home, I vowed to myself, omen, or no omen, it was the last time I would take care of anyone's things again under similar circumstances. A good many men came to us at Swan and Edgar's Corner from leave, and schools, and we were ordered to send these men forward with the ration limbers at night to fill the vacancies. Many of these men never reached the line, and became casualties under the heavy shell fire that covered the roads and tracks day and night. Even at Swan and Edgar corner we came in for the shelling, and a staff officer was killed in his sleep at the camp, a piece of shrapnel coming through the tent.

I was surprised one afternoon when Pat walked into our encampment and invited me out to supper, and when he saw my sleeping accommodation he extended the invitation to staying the night with him.

Going along with him, I heard the tale.

At 6 o'clock one morning, ten of them including himself and Hommer had been detailed at the camp at Westoutre to pack up.

They were given a map reference where they would find an empty bivouac camp.

They were to leave at once to take charge of this camp, and be responsible for everything within the camp, till either the battalion came, or they received further orders.

They set off and eventually found the camp which was also in the vicinity of Swan and Edgar's corner. In the hurry of leaving the camp at Westoutre, no proper rations had been served out to them for the day, though for following days they had instructions to meet ration limbers on the road. As soon as they arrived of course, their first thought was where to get some "grub".

Pat and Hommer forthwith set out on a foraging expedition. There were many of these little camps about the neighbourhood, some occupied, some empty. They had the good luck to track a camp occupied by Australians.

The camp was carefully reconnoitred till the cookhouse was located. Then the offensive opened.

"Hello! Australia, – Hullo Chummy"

"Have you a chap named Johnson in your mob from Sydney?"

"Couldn't tell you Chummy, what Company?"

"I don't even know what Battalion. I know he came over with your lot, and I thought perhaps he might be with you."

From the war generally, by way of the weather, and the prowess of the Colonials, the question of rations was delicately approached.

Cheshire asks "How do you go on for rations in your mob?"

"Rations eh! Well, if we have to fight, we want feeding don't we? and we see we get it" says Australia.

"Oh!" replied Cheshire, in a way that invited further discussion. Australia fell to the bait straightaway.

"Why, how do you go on?" Pat of course went forward now, and wrung his withers with a tale of ten starving men, forgotten by the British Army and left to die a lingering death round the wilds of Swan and Edgar Corner.

Result. A sand bag with a goodly assortment of provisions. A similar visit to a camp of New Zealanders, was carried out on similar lines, with equally good results. A potato field in the vicinity was also a source of help.

When the stores arrived at Swan and Edgar Corner, they had to apply there for rations, but this was no reason why "Grub Hunts" should cease.

For cooking, they borrowed coal from engines passing along a light railway close by.

The only fly in the ointment was the fact that they were unable to cook all night, as well as all the day, as no lights were allowed to be visible after dark.

Three nights in succession, I returned with Pat when he came to draw rations in the evening, had a good supper and spent the night with them.

On the night of the 24th the battalion came out of the line, and between then and noon of the next day, they were arriving in batches.

They had been through a rough time of it, and their numbers were sadly depleted, and those that returned were thoroughly exhausted. Many had slept in the ditches by the side of the roads that were being shelled, rather than continue the journey in the dark in their exhausted state.

Len arrived with a couple of runners during the morning. They had slept in the ruins at Swan and Edgar corner, not knowing that we were within a stones throw. We tucked him away in the blankets, while "Q" and I got busy on further long lists of casualties. The battalion rested here, and for a couple of days did nothing beyond trying to get clean.

27 September–8 October

On the 27th we moved back to what was known as No. 4 camp Westoutre.

Len and I stayed behind to see the boxes loaded on the limbers, and set off later by ourselves, making the journey comfortably, with a feed of eggs and chips on the way.

We arrived to find the battalion fixed up in tents on a farm. H.Qr. Officers were billeted in the farm house itself, while the Orderly

Room made home in the shippon. It was actually a passage between the stalls where the cows were kept. This passage led right through the building, from the farmyard to the road outside, with a door at each end. When at home, the cows looked sadly at us through the openings and murmured their disapproval of our intrusion, while they chewed their cud, which seemed to be their chief meal. The door that led from the farmyard was used as an entrance, but the door at the other end had to be opened at the top to obtain sufficient light to work by. This made a through draught which caused some little excitement before we developed the habit of weighting all papers down. Documents of military importance had some narrow escapes of being devoured along with the cattle fodder.

After we had straightened up work for the evening, and "Q" had gone to his downy couch in a tent with the R.S.M., Len let me into the secret that on leaving the line, he had fallen across a derelict stone jar, marked S.R.D., and had filled his water bottle therefrom. Up the line, he had also been rationed with the R.S.M., and had managed to make a distinct profit on the partnership.

He had brought down some "buckshee" butter, bread, a tin of milk, and a few other useful commodities. We investigated the contents of his haversack, and after scraping the butter off the candles, and the tea and sugar off the butter, we found that, added to the contents of parcels that had just arrived, we had quite a good spread.

Len suggested that we might invite Pat round to supper to celebrate his "M.M.".

We looked him up and invited him to the repast. Len suggested making "Punch" with the aid of warm water and sugar, but Pat protested that this was spoiling good rum. Punch was however decided upon for Len and myself as being more safe and economical, so after making our Punch, we passed the bottle with the remainder unspoilt to Pat, wondering what he would do with it.

In the midst of the party, the door suddenly opened, and in walked the Adjutant, and we suddenly wished that the odour from the cows had been a little stronger. He sniffed suspiciously, but made no remark beyond asking for some papers that he wished to take to his billet.

Pat had stood to "Attention" when he appeared, but suddenly changed his mind, and sat down on his box again. The Adjt. soon disappeared again and we resumed our interrupted social evening. We spent quite a pleasant evening, till Pat, who was getting into the

"Thirdly" of one of his tales, suddenly remarked "Well!" to cut a short, short, story long." An immediate investigation was made, and we found out that it was as we feared. The water bottle was empty, so we decided that it was bedtime, and ordered Pat off to his tent. He told us the next day, that when he arrived at his tent, he found another party in progress. Bill Beswick had received a parcel, and would insist on Pat having a slab of cake before retiring, which somewhat upset his dreams for the night.

We wakened early in the morning and found that a few cows could add considerably to the density of the atmosphere in the course of a night, and we were glad to open the door and get some fresh air into our quarters.

The Camp Warden who lived in the stable next door notified his address to all whom it might concern by a little wooden sign stuck up in the rectangular swell opposite his door.

At the first glance it had the appearance of a small wooden cross. One day the Brigadier General came round with his Staff, and the Brigade Major suddenly pulled up, and put his monocle on to read the inscription, and then murmured sympathetically "Poor fellow, but what a place to bury him in."

A Brigade Parade was called here, at which the General presented ribbons to those who had been awarded decorations in the recent fighting.

I was unable to see the parade, but I heard before the parade was over, that Pat was likely to be the recipient of another award (which would not appear on the breast of his tunic).

Pat's version of the affair was, that he was stood forward in the square with the other men who were to be presented with their ribbons.

They were given the order to "Stand at Ease" while the General gave off a speech. The speech was rather long, and the weather rather warm. Suddenly someone yelled "Attention" so sharply that Pat dropped his rifle. No one seemed less upset about the dreadful affair than Pat himself. It was feared however that the Adjutant might have to be put to bed to avoid a stroke.

At the farmhouse where the officers were billeted, was a youngster, a little boy still in pinafores, who sat at the door continuously smoking cigarettes. Officers passing through the door would solemnly offer a cigarette from their case, and the little imp would take the cigarette just as seriously.

When making up the billetting account here, which had to be signed off by M. le Maire of the village, we were interested, and somewhat annoyed, to find that we were in France and not in Belgium. It was only a question of a few yards, but it entailed another hours work to make a fresh account up.

We did not forget to visit the pastry cook's shop again in Westoutre, and played havoc with their stock of custards. While in the village, we met one of the signallers who appeared slightly the "worse for wear," and took him safely back to camp and bed. During the night however, Pat was aroused from sleep by another signaller coming to enquire for the unfortunate one. It appeared that he had wakened in the night, and was seized with an uncontrollable desire to put himself right in Pat's eyes, by explaining that he was not under the influence of beer when we found him, but under the influence of love, having been overcome by the beauty of the fair maiden serving beer in the estaminet.

He had left his tent with the intention of calling on Pat, and putting the matter clearly before him. As he had not arrived at Pat's tent, search was made quietly in the darkness, till at last the "love sick" swain was discovered, happily sleeping, mixed up with the ropes of a tent not far from his own. He was put back to bed, and in the morning in penitent mood, received a fatherly lecture from Pat on the evil effects of beer, or love, whichever it was, on a constitution that could not stand either, or both mixed.

Business in the Orderly Room was enlivened one day by a little comedy. Investigating the post one morning, we came across a notification from that august personage, the "A.P.M." to the effect that No.... Pte.... of our unit had been reported by the "M" Police for having been caught in the act of stealing potatoes from a field. This matter was passed to us for disciplinary action, and to report the punishment ordered. I don't suppose the C.O. had any great objection to any man borrowing a few potatoes from a field, but he had a strong objection to any of his men being fool enough to be caught by the "A.P.M." men.

We looked through the roll, and found which company the man belonged to, then sent the communication to the Officer commanding the Company, with instructions that the man must be brought before the C.O. at office hours.

We were just debating what punishment the man was likely to be awarded, when Capt .... came in, wearing a very worried look.

8–14 October

It was our old friend "Theo" in a state of great perturbation. He took hold of "Q" and confided to him that it was a very awkward business. "Q" agreed, but when "Theo" proceeded to inform him that the man was cook to the company officers, and had been feeding the officers on the stolen potatoes, matters assumed an interesting turn. "Q" could see that the joke was too good to spoil too quickly, and insisted that nothing could be done to prevent the man coming before the C.O. and the whole of the facts coming out. Poor "Theo" who was a very "proper" officer was at his wit's end, and was aghast at the very idea that his Mess had been regaling themselves on purloined potatoes.

A couple of "Theo's" cigars however, brought the suggestion that if he would bring the "A.P.M's" communication back to the Orderly Room quietly, it could be kept out of sight for a day or two and see if any loophole turned up. Another cigar was forthcoming and "Theo" bustled off to bring the incriminating document along personally, so that it might not go astray.

As soon as he had disappeared again, "Q" sat down at his table and wrote to "A.P.M. ...th Division.

Ref. your .... of Oct..............

Pte.............. No........... has, since the date this offence was committed, been admitted to hospital and since evacuated to England and struck off the strength of this unit, and have therefore no indication of his present location."

This was pinned to the offending document and pushed in a pile of papers awaiting the C.O's signature.

The C.O. turned up at office hours as usual in a big hurry. After finding no prisoners for trial, he asked if there was anything to sign. "just a few routine papers sir" said "Q" who stood by while the "C.O." put his name to the papers "Q" put in front of him.

After the "C.O." had gone, "Q" picked the paper out and went to look up "Theo".

This was rather annoying, as Len or I was hoping to go round to calm his fears, although we had no great admiration for his cigars. The letter went off that night to the "A.P.M." and that was the last that was heard of the matter.

A sad tragedy occurred before we left the farm. Our sanitary department was always very efficient, even if rations were short, the sanitary dept. could always procure Creosol. A creosol tin which was not quite empty, had inadvertently been left in a corner of the farmyard, and unfortunately a French goose belonging to the farm, who of course could not read the English label on the tin, took it to be some English fattening food, and sampled it. That was the end of the goose, except for the claims department.

On October 8th we left our billet with regret, especially as it was a pouring wet day. We were met by motors near the camp, and proceeded to Kruisstraat, Ypres.

We marched through Ypres by daylight, by way of a change. This was made possible by our advance which had opened on July 31st. Going out by the Menin Gate, we proceeded by the Potijze road till we had passed by what remained of Potijze Village, when we turned off the road into a field.

It was a compliment to call it a field, as, before July 31st, it had practically been "No man's land", and was chiefly composed of shell holes, with very little space between them.

Here we sat about in the pouring rain wondering whether this was to be a camp with another fancy name attached to it.

After spending the bigger part of the day watching the rain come down, wagons appeared coming along the road loaded with nice white tents. I might say that this camp did not rise suddenly at the sound of a whistle, nor were the tents arranged in perfect lines. Tents were put up where they could be fixed, and a tent was lucky if it covered not more than a portion of at least one wet shell hole.

When the tents were eventually put up, the camp immediately became a home of pessimists prophesying the complete destruction of the camp by enemy aircraft, or shell fire, long before morning.

Looking round the camp in the gathering dusk, we looked a perfect target. Urgent requests were sent to Brigade Headquarters for Kutch, with which to stain the tents.

Some quantity of this was luckily forthcoming, but not enough to go round all the tents. The remainder were daubed with mud, which seemed quite as much use as the Kutch, and we eked out the disguise with brushwood and a small quantity of camouflage netting that was found lying about.

It could hardly be said that we had made ourselves invisible, but we had managed to make the camp look just a trifle less conspicuous than it was.

By the time we had got the boxes into our tent and lighted a candle to work by, three whistles sounded, which meant "Lights out" as enemy aircraft were over. This happened about every ten minutes, and made work rather spasmodic.

In the morning the battalion commenced work for the 2nd Australian Corps, on light railway construction, road repairing, and salvage, and we hoped that the Australians would not make the mistake of considering us a "Labour Mob".

The "Pièce de Résistance" of the Camp was furnished by the Hd. Quarters Mess. For their cookhouse, they had utilized a derelict tank, and by extending the hole that the tank had fallen into, they had made room for the Mess and covered it over.

We had a bad spell of weather here, and the camp quickly became a quagmire, both outside and inside the tents.

After dark the wind usually rose, and most of the time was spent either sitting inside in the dark, or making periodical dashes outside with a mallet, trying to induce the tent pegs to retain their altogether too precarious hold on the mud, and prevent the tent from leaving the "P.B.I" to join the R.F.C. The second night we were shelled, but came luckily out of it. One shell dropped between two tents without doing more than raise both tents suddenly a couple of feet.

The same night, Len had been trying to do a little typing, and was sat squeezed with his back against the canvas of the tent with the typewriter in front of him. Three whistles went, and out we blew the candle, and sat in the darkness. A minute or two later, shells began to fall in the camp. Suddenly Len gave vent to a great shout. Investigation proved the strange fact, that either a piece of spent shrapnel, or a flying stone had struck the tent a glancing blow, just at the point where Len's head was touching the canvas, producing a nice little lump on his head.

Searching for Pat one quiet afternoon, I found him ensconced in an old gun pit with "Aunty" Entwhistle and another signaller. The gun pit was nicely covered in, and with the aid of a ground sheet drawn across the entrance, they were never troubled when three whistles were blown, as no light could be seen from their abode. The only thing that I disliked about their home, was the fact that two of the walls were lined with shells.

Pat suggested a walk round to see the sights. We first examined a huge mine crater where the enemy had blown a mine under our old trenches after we had left them. Then we took a stroll along Oxford Road which ran just in the rear of our late front line.

This road was now packed with heavy traffic. Motor wagons were busy unloading ammunition for the guns. Coming on to the Potijze Road again, we found all traffic held up. Heavy fighting was in progress in front, and the stream of traffic had already been held up for some hours, and had not been able to get forward, while the line of transport was being continually added to in the rear. There would perhaps be a mile of transport in front of us, and we heard that the line continued as far back as Westoutre.

On our way back we left the road to investigate a Château. There was very little of it left standing now. A small burial ground had been made in the grounds, but it had suffered severely from shell fire and some of the bodies had been disinterred by heavy shells, which we covered again as best we could before leaving.

Making along an old trench from here we came across a unique sight. This was the remains of a long wall running round a place known as "The Vinery." In a few places here and there, there still remained short lengths of the wall showing its full height, which would be about eight feet. Enough of the wall remained however to prove the fact that the wall had been built wholly of champagne bottles.

15–22 October 1917

On the 15th of October we finished work for the Australians, struck camp, sent the tents back to where they came from, and marched back through Ypres, picking up motors at Vierstraat Corner. These landed us in Kemmel village in the darkness, and we climbed Little Kemmel Hill expecting to find a nice little camp, after the mud of Potijze.

We were disgusted to find ourselves marched into a field to a bivouac camp, in only a little less mud than we had left behind us. There were a few tents for the officers, and we managed to secure one for the Orderly Room. We had rather a startling reception on our arrival. As we marched in at one end of the field, eight aeroplane bombs dropped in quick succession at the other end of the field. We dared have no lights whatever for sometime after our arrival, and there was a deal of shouting, and passing of compliments in the darkness before the battalion was settled in.

Sometime after the battalion had got settled down Len and I were wandering miserably round the camp in the mud and darkness looking for our luggage.

The limber that had the Orderly Room boxes on board, had broken down on the journey and had not arrived.

We found "Q" and reported the matter to him. He decided that no work could be done before morning, and we might as well get to bed. When we left him, we groaned and looked blankly at one another, and our misery was great. When leaving Potijze we had been stuck with the brilliant idea of packing our blankets, rations, and anything else we could squeeze in, into the Orderly Room boxes, to save having to carry them.

This was of course against all rules, and without "Q's" knowledge, and we hardly knew him well enough yet to confess our predicament. Here we were, without a blanket or a bite, and expected to get down to bed.

We would of course go to bed without a blanket, but without a bite, was too much for us. We decided to hunt up the transport to find out if the limber had turned up. We found that it had just arrived, but orders had been given that the limber was not to be unloaded before morning.

We explained that we must have the typewriter at least, as some urgent work had to be done for the C.O.

We were allowed to unload the typewriter box, and bore it off triumphantly in the darkness. Getting it safely into the tent, we fastened up the tent, then extricated from the box, three blankets, some bread, and a tin of jam, and shortly afterwards went to bed as per orders.

The following day was miserably wet and cold. There was not enough room in the tent to work, without rubbing against the canvas, and everywhere we touched started a fresh drip, till the whole tent seemed about to dissolve.

After work it was quiet in the evening and Pat popped his head in to ask if I would like to sit round a nice warm fire. As it was getting dusk, and no lights could be shown, I thought he was simply being caustic about the weather. Going along with him, however, I found that his invitation was seriously meant.

Along with Entwistle and Hommer, they had settled down in a special little billet of their own again. Their "modus operandi" on getting to a camp of this sort, was to prowl about till everyone else had settled down, and then look round for some special corner for themselves, with a little more comfort and privacy. Having found something suitable, they would report to their officer that they could not find room in a bivouac, but had found room at such and such a place.

The officer would be usually tired and fed-up, and would perhaps just remark "Oh! alright if you are fixed up" and forthwith forget about them. This scheme, if worked with circumspection, meant missing quite a lot of parades and inspections.

Pat took me across the field to a small brick building, which might at sometime have offered shelter to a horse or a couple of pigs. The little apartment inside was shaped like a letter "L", and, by using the inner chamber and drawing a ground sheet across the angle, no lights could be seen outside. Inside, the chamber was a contrast to the rest of the camp. The brilliance of a couple of candles, combined with the warmth and comfort of a little red fire in the middle of the brick floor, gave a sense of luxurious contentment that could not be found elsewhere in the camp. The firegrate itself, consisting of a petrol tin, neatly and systematically jabbed with a bayonet, was beautifully red hot, but I had the good manners not to enquire too closely where the coal had come from.

The pleasurable sensation of sitting on a warm brick floor, in damp trousers, is not one of the least joys of campaigning.

Entwistle, who was affectionately known as "Auntie" on account of his domestic capabilities, was busy getting supper ready, while Hommer was engrossed in a fortnight old copy of the "Glossop Herald".

"Auntie" was rather an unusual character in the Army. While at the Signal School with Pat, he would spend his evenings after parades, "swotting" up signalling in his hut, whilst the camp had generally emptied itself into Poperinghe. He did not smoke, was a teetotaller, and never used a stronger expletive than "dash it" in his most excitable moments, thereby being a continual source of wonder to Pat and Hommer. After joining them in a little supper, Pat said that if I could get out the following afternoon, he knew where a good "eat" could be obtained, after arranging with Auntie that we would be back from the "eats" in time to allow of him taking Len to the pictures the same evening, as we had a cinema close by the camp.

The following afternoon Pat called in, and we set out to find where this wonderful "feed" was to be obtained. Getting on to the road and hearing that Locre was our destination, I suggested that it would be as well to step out if we were to be back in time to allow Auntie to take Len to the cinema. Pat, however, never walked where there was even a remote possibility of reaching his destination by less strenuous means. The end of the argument found us sitting by the roadside waiting for a motor to come along. When at last one appeared, we made a dash for the tailboard as it passed, and clambered aboard. We were going along finely, and had almost reached Locre, when the car turned off to the left, and put on such a speed that, as we dropped off we must have appeared like a couple of lunatics trying to catch it up again.

We covered quite a considerable distance before we were sure enough of our equilibrium to stop running. The driver of course knew that we were on board, and bound for Locre, but this was evidently what passed for humour in the A.S.C.M.T.

Locre itself was rather a nice place. There were many big houses used as Headquarters of one kind and another, and Brass Hats and Tabs abounded. Here we passed the Hospice, part of which was used as a Field Hospital.

In the pretty grounds of this Hospice, Capt. John Redmond was buried.

A little way out of the village, on the road to Reninghelst, we found the little cottage we were looking for, and found that the special line here consisted of a huge slice of roast pork, bedecked with chipped potatoes, onions and peas. We negotiated this with the aid of sundry cups of coffee, and then ambled out again into the village, Pat remarking that we might as well get back to camp and write home about the hardships that we were enduring.

Outside the village, we sat for sometime by the roadside waiting for a motor, before it began to dawn upon us that this was a "Traffic one way only" road. We managed to arrive back in time to relieve Len to go to the pictures with Auntie.

The following day we reversed the programme, and Len went with Auntie to sample the pork at Locre, while in the evening Pat and I went to the cinema, and saw Charlie Chaplin and Billy Merson for an outlay of 20cts each.

23 October

On the 23rd we packed up again, and the battalion marched forward again to Chippewa Camp. After Potijze and Little Kemmel, Chippewa with its good wooden huts, was quite a treat. It was evident that we were soon to be in the line again on some uncomfortable sector. We were suddenly being made a fuss of and there was only one explanation of these outbursts of affection.

25 October

On the 25th the big Church Army Hut in the camp was reserved for us, and a big concert arranged. The first part of the concert was to be given by the Divisional Concert Party, – The "Follies", and the second part by officers and men of the battalion, last but not least, refreshments were to be had free of charge.

"Q" and Len attended the concert while I looked after the Orderly Room. While the concert was in full swing, a batch of reinforcements turned up and kept things busy. When "Q" and Len returned with a full report of the concert, it appeared that the star turn of the show was one of our own men, a one time member of a George Edwards Company.

26 October

That meant of course that he would not be long with the battalion. Sure enough, next morning, orders came for him to report to Divisional H.Q. and the next we heard of him was, that he was one of the "Follies".

The Brigadier and his staff attended the concert, and were to dine at our H.Q. Mess afterwards.

We were just settling down after work was over for the evening, to get a few letters written, when the Adjutant came in to inform us that the band was coming to play in our hut during dinner in the Mess, which was next door. We supposed this was meant to get the effect of a hidden orchestra. The band was squeezed in, big drum included, candles were stuck up on the rafters, or any odd place they would stick, and the stands fixed up, while bandmaster Billy Hobbs borrowed one of our boxes to stand on.

We started off with dreamy waltzes with the soup, and got to something more solid in "The Maid of the Mountains" with the fish. Just then, word came in that the band could not be heard in the Mess. Len suggested this might be owing to the Adjutant being noisy with his soup, or failing that, the fish may have been "humming".

The C.O. however had sent word in that he wanted the "Bing Boys" with a bit of beef behind it. This suggested that they were getting towards the joint. Len and I had stood it bravely up to then. "Q" and the R.S.M. had managed to escape from the Orderly Room before the band was fixed up. We had heard our band play the "Bing Boys" in the open, but what it would be like with "beef" behind it, shut up in a hut, we could only surmise and fear. We tried to make a bolt for it, but found that we could not get out.

The man with the big drum spelt his "Bing" with the letter "a", and at every beat of his drum, the dust rose from the floor, and shook off the rafters. One candle who could stand it no longer, flung itself off its perch and just missed disappearing down the big bassoon. The man with the trombone nearly pushed the ear off the man in front, who was unfortunate enough to get in his line of fire. The little librarian was wriggling about on the floor rescuing odd loose pages of band parts that were being swept away in the tornado. The bandmaster's face was contorted, and streaming with perspiration, while his usually beautifully waxed moustache was in a state of complete collapse.

Relief came shortly afterwards by a message that the King's toast was about to be drunk, and the National Anthem was required. This brought an end to the services of the band for the evening. When they had cleared off, Len suggested looking round into the Mess Cook house, to see whether we could get anything to soothe our shattered nerves. The Mess Sgt. was there looking hot and worried, and it was rather an unpropitious moment perhaps, to tell him what we had suffered in helping to make his dinner a success.

His name was Williamson, but when he threw a lump of bread at us, and told us to "clear" we called him by quite a different name. A bottle of champagne came into the Orderly Room later, for the R.S.M. with the C.O.'s compliments. We sampled "Q's share of this, but were of the unanimous opinion that "Pop" as good, could be bought for 2*d* per bottle.

27 October 1917

On the 27th we left Chippewa Camp and were taken by busses to Shrapnel corner, through Ypres. Here, we were taken off the road into a shell ridden field to await darkness, before proceeding further.

Rations were served out here along with extra ammunition. When darkness fell, we set off to take over the sector in front of Tower Hamlets. Going some distance by the Ypres-Messines Road, we passed sign posts pointing to such interesting places as Bedford House, Stirling Castle, and Dumbarton Lakes. Taking a turn to the left led us along a timber road past Mount Sorrel. This road was badly smashed up in places by shell fire, and the enemy seemed to have it nicely ranged. Guns of ours had been drawn off to the sides of the road, and we had one or two nasty shocks as we made our way along. It was very dark, and we had no idea that they were in such close proximity to us, until one blazed out seemingly from under our feet. We were left blind and dazed for a second or two, though our speech was not affected beyond perhaps absorbing some of the explosive properties in the atmosphere.

The R.S.M. yelled curses out into the blackness asking why they could not have warned us before opening fire. Nothing could be seen of the gun however, and no reply came back from the darkness. This happened to us a few times before we got away forward beyond them. Passing below Canada Tunnels, which were dug into the hill above us, we rounded the hill and into a valley where the only road now was a narrow duck-board track crossing wastes of mud. Our guns were playing an unpleasant tattoo over our heads, while the enemy's guns were weirdly quiet. The taut expectancy of their reply at any moment was almost as bad as really being shelled. There was absolutely no shelter, and to leave the track meant being inextricably stuck in the mud, possibly smothered. Our speed along this track was wonderful, but it seemed endless. Still the enemy guns kept silence, and we at last reached a little ravine leading up to the ridge that we were to hold.

Here the moon broke through a little, and showed up a few ghastly stumps of trees, and here and there in the mud lay a few dead bodies that the burial parties had not yet collected.

The track was badly smashed up, and it appeared that these men had been caught by shell fire coming out of the line.

Some confusion arose here, as a stretcher party was coming out, and in getting off the track to let them have the best of the footing, we found ourselves waist deep in slime. This of course would be such a situation that required some shelling to complete, and by ill luck, the enemy chose the moment to search this part of the track with his shells. Just as we were scrambling up the ridge the man behind me had his face completely smashed by a big piece of shrapnel, and a few other casualties happened within a few minutes. They were quickly attended to by those wonderful men, the stretcher bearers, then after further attention of the Medical Officer, they were soon off, carried on stretchers along that awful valley track. We had a few more casualties, and the stretcher bearers were evidently in for a heartbreaking time.

The companies held the top of the ridge by a series of shell hole posts, as the ground and the position itself, made the digging of a trench impossible.

Headquarters of the battalion going out, was held in a concrete pill box just below the crest of the hill, and this was taken over by our Hd. Qr. Officers. Erected alongside the concrete wall of the pill box, was a "baby elephant". To the uninitiated, a "Baby Elephant" consisted of a semicircular corrugated steel roof covering a ground space equal to about the area of an ordinary lorry. This provided accommodation for the R.S.M. and his batman, two runners, two cooks and their utensils, and myself as Orderly Room staff with the "Yellow Peril" and four officers servants.

The cooking for the H.Q. officers was all done on a small "Pimms" spirit stove which had a silly habit of getting kicked over every time anyone moved. We all put our rations together with the officers, on a suggestion from the R.S.M. and ate out of the general fund. Such socialism from our point of view was a good thing. We, of course, could not tell what the officers' opinion on the matter might be, as they knew nothing of the arrangement. We found our accommodation rather cramped, as we could neither stand up, sit down, or lie down in comfort. We had a little extra room one day owing to our worthy adjutant feeling that his own private correspondence was sufficiently important to send "Bobby" the R.S.M.'s batman the double journey to the transport lines, to collect it. Bobby was put to bed by the R.S.M. himself when he arrived back in a state of utter exhaustion, and excused any duty for the whole of the following day, when the R.S.M. allowed himself the laxity of dirty buttons for one day only.

The runners decided that things were too cramped living altogether under the eye of the R.S.M, so they set to work and dug themselves a hole at the back of our premises where they were within call when wanted. This relieved the congestion somewhat, but we were crowded even then. Shells and weather permitting, those of us who could spent our time sat outside where we could look over the valley, and watch the track that came along it. It was not used much by daylight, but we would often see the enemy searching it along with shells, his favourite being overhead shrapnel.

At night, ration parties were sent along to meet the ration limbers near the Canada Tunnels on the wooden road, and would carry rations back along the valley track in sandbags. Not one single night did the ration party return without losing part of the men, and part of the rations.

Ammunition carriers and working parties were also out on this track in the darkness, and they all suffered heavily.

George, our favourite runner, was sat outside with me one morning, gazing pensively across the valley. Last night's ration party had again been unfortunate, and so had the rations. George came from Hyde, and was an asset in hard times. He could give a good imitation of most of the well known music hall turns, varied by parodies of Wilson Barrett in the "Sign of the Three Balls", Forbes Robertson in "The light that went out" or Martin Harvey in "The only way to do it".

George, looking across the valley, suddenly espied what looked like bags of rations lying beside the track. He stood up and smote his breast dramatically, and declaimed Ha!! Bread!! "It is a far far better thing that I do, watch me step. If the old swine will only keep quiet for a few minutes, the bread shall be ours, and the child shall not starve".

Before anyone could say a word he was off. We lost sight of him through the ravine, but soon picked him up making rapid progress along the track. We saw him reach the bags, pick one up, seem to hesitate, try another, and put it down again. Then he lighted a cigarette, and commenced his return journey empty handed. When he landed back we all yelled "Well!!?"

His reply was short and sweet – "Bombs" – and he sucked hard at his "Woodbine" and resumed his seat, and his pensive look across the valley behind us.

After a good deal of shelling one night we were, next morning, admiring the four feet of solid concrete on the top of the pill box, and comparing it to our double row of sandbags on our roof. The same evening we thought our end had come when a shell dropped plumb on top of the pill box next door. When we had recovered sufficiently to get outside and see what had really happened, we found the officers looking considerably rattled, and looking at a block of concrete that had changed its location suddenly from their roof to ours. We did not feel correspondingly safer in our abode on that account, as we had some misgivings as to whether our roof would stand the additional strain.

Pat and his friends were having a hard time of it up here trying to keep the telephone wires in order across the valley to Canada Tunnels, as the shelling was continually blowing the lines to bits.

30 October

On October 30th we were relieved. Outside our Hd. Qrs. had been stacked all the empty petrol tins that had been used by the battalion for water carrying during their turn in, and each man as he passed on his way out, had to carry one, or two, according to the number of hands he had vacant. These were to be taken down to be refilled for use of the relieving battalion.

We wasted no time again, returning along the Valley, making for Canada Tunnels. These were huge tunnels running in all directions cut into Mount Sorrel. At the foot of the hill lay the timber road, which was the farthest point that the ration limbers could reach. In the valley behind us, we could pick out the guns which had given our nerves such a shaking when we came up along that way.

Further back we could see the bigger guns with their light railway behind, where the ammunition could be brought along after dark.

The valley here was always well attended to by the enemy artillery, and we could often see that our batteries were suffering badly, and we saw more than one of our big guns blown into the air.

In the tunnels, Head Quarters of various units were fixed up. In one portion, shut off by the usual blanket, was the signal station of the Divisional Artillery, and passing along one day, an interesting but onesided conversation could be heard on the telephone.

It ran somewhat as follows:-

"Hello!! Hello!! Yes! Oh! Yes! What's that?
What's that? Oh! Shake up a bit, I can't make
you out, yes! Yes! What's that? Oh! Yes!

being blown to bits are you, Oh! Yes.
Well just get out and see what they are
and where they are coming from, and I'll
try to get something put on them. Yes!
Oh! Yes. Cheerio!!"

As I crept back towards my own quarters I felt rather pleased after all, with that Sergeant at Chester Castle who glared some inches over my head and informed me that the "Har Gee Hay" (R.G.Λ.) was not wanting me badly. "The Hinfantry for you my lad".

We were safe enough in the tunnels from shell fire, but the enemy, not to be outdone, and well knowing it to be a nest of troops in close reserve, regularly drenched the hill with gas shells. All arrangements of gas curtains at the entrances, could not keep out a certain amount of gas which percolated through. The atmosphere of the tunnels was so foetid however, that the gas was not easily detected, as it was not in such quantity as to make its presence felt at the time.

The "M.O." was kept very busy here with sick parades, as a great number of the men were suffering badly with Trench Feet, and there was a big trail off to hospital.

For every trench foot case, a long Army Form had to be filled up with full answers to a column of questions:-

"How many times had the man's feet been rubbed with Whale Oil?
How many times he had his boots off?
How many times he had changed his socks?
How many hot meals he had per day?
What was the condition of the trenches?"

Regulations were laid down that each man must rub his feet with whale oil, remove his boots, change his socks and have at least one hot meal a day.

The question of how a man could take his boots off, rub his feet and change his socks, while spending a week in mud, knee-deep, did not affect the matter. If it was put down that the man had not obeyed these regulations he was up against a Court Martial on his return from hospital.

If it was put down that he had not received at least one hot meal per day, then the C.O. would be in trouble, despite the fact that it was as impossible to get a hot meal in that sector to the men, as it was for the men to attend to their feet. So the forms were duly filled up that all the regulations had been complied with. This left us with the last question which we could answer with truth, and a little over as salve to our conscience for what Mr. Churchill would call, our "terminological inexactitudes" on the other matters.

We had so many cases of Trench Feet, that our available stock of forms ran out, and after "dinner" one day, the Adjutant ordered me off to find "Q" at the transport lines, and get a further supply.

Pat, having no telephone lines to attend to for the time being, was rushed in to fill the breach, and put to act as Orderly Room Clerk in my absence.

I looked forward to hearing some fun on my return as Pat's passion for facts would surely lead him to ask awkward questions of the Adjutant.

I set off for the Transport lines about mid-day, down the hill to the timber road. It was dark when we came up that way, and the road seemed even worse by daylight, than by darkness. In the mud, along each side of it lay the wreckage of limbers and dead mules, and working parties were busy repairing the road again, ready for the night traffic. Reaching the Ypres Messines Road, I made for Shrapnel Corner, passing that gruesome landmark, the skeleton of a German sniper complete in uniform, high up in the fork of a tree, where it must have remained for at least two years. It was getting dusk when Shrapnel Corner came into sight, and the place was just then keeping up its reputation. It was no place just then for loitering about wondering which way to take, so I bolted for a big sandbagged dugout which was then being used by the Australian Y.M.C.A. as a coffee stall. Here I was regaled with hot coffee, so hot, that I could scarcely hold the jam tin that served as a cup. When things grew quieter, I put Shrapnel corner some distance behind me, very quickly before the next "show" opened. I knew that the "B" team were at some little camp called "Beggar's Rest" near Voormezeele. If I could find this, I would very likely be able to obtain the exact location of the Transport. I found the ruins of Voormezeele in the darkness, but no one I met, seemed to have heard of "Beggar's Rest", though one pessimist said that the nearest thing he could think of was the burial ground in Ridge Wood. Though not on this man's suggestion, I kept on towards Ridge Wood, enquiring at every shack, light, or any moving thing on or off the road, till at last I saw a few tents and a glimmer of light in a field some distance from the road. Not being able to find the entrance to the field, I floundered into the ditch and scrambled through the hedge, making for the nearest tent where I could see a light. Small earthworks had been thrown up round the tents, but many tents had been taken down, which left the direct line to the tent something in the nature of a blindfold "Grand National", and I failed to finish the course without a few "croppers".

Reaching my goal at last, I poked my head into the tent, and when my eyes had become accustomed to the blinding glare of the candle, I found myself looking into the face of one of my late platoon officers. He was in charge of our "B" team, and I had evidently at last found "Beggar's Rest". The officer invited me to bring the rest of myself inside, and let him know what he could do for me. He offered a drop of comfort, and found me a "runner" to guide me to the transport lines, and I soon set off again from "Beggar's Rest", tired, but comfortable in the knowledge that the runner at least knew where he was going, and the nearest way to get there. By the time we had done the further four miles to the Transport lines, I had completely lost interest in the war, but managed to find "Quarters" and tell him that we wanted some more Trench Foot forms up the line and that I must get back at once with them, "vide" orders from the Adjutant. Len was away "On Command", and "Quarters" delved through his boxes in vain. Some forms, however, were procured from the Black Watch Orderly Room close by. As I was arguing (somewhat weakly) that I must set off at once with them, Capt. W., the Regtl. Q.M., walked in. What happened then was that I went to bed with a supper – à la stores – also a rum ration – à la stores – and the Adjutant could boil himself, so much I understood from "Quarters". I returned to Canada Tunnels the following afternoon, riding most of the way on a limber. As I heard nothing from the Adjutant with regard to my late return, I presumed Capt W. had taken on himself the responsibility for the delay.

As I expected, Pat had evidently been airing his views on Orderly Room work to the Adjutant. "What a peculiar chap your friend is" was the only reference he made to the matter. I asked him why he thought so, but received no reply.

Our last night in Canada Tunnels was quite a jovial affair. For some reason an extra large ration of rum was served out, evidently as an antidote for the effects of the gas in the tunnels which had now become very noticeable.

Everyone appeared to be very affable until the Adjutant joined us, then as usual, everyone quietened down, but strange to say, the Adjutant was also very affable, and was very soon joining in discussions on various subjects of much interest to soldiers, but far removed from warfare.

As the discussions developed, it at last dawned upon us that the Adjutant was evidently in his "anecdotage".

Up to this evening Pat's special point, as a friend, was the fact that he smoked a pipe, but never cigarettes, and therefore never "cadged" my cigarettes when he was out of smokes, and I could always feel sure of his cigarette ration, if I was "out". Judge my surprise when, during the evening, he thought he would like a cigarette.

Thereafter his faithful allegiance to his pipe was divided with what he had hitherto termed "Lad's smokes", and after that when I saw him coming my way, I began to wonder whether it was my soothing company he sought, or only that of "James's".

1. Walter in uniform, 1916.

2. Walter, *c.* 1912.

3. Amelia, née James, *c.* 1912, Walter's 'own sweet wife'.

4. Walter and Amelia's wedding, 12 May 1913.

5. The happy couple.

6. Amelia and Walter with Madge (on right), Amelia's sister, *c.* 1912.

7. Walter among family and friends. Front row from right: Walter, Amelia and Edith Lloyd (friend); back row: Margaret (Amelia's mother) and Madge (Amelia's sister), *c.* 1912.

8. Walter with his son, James (Jimmy), in 1914.

9. Walter with son, James, and daughter, Jean, c. 1920.

10. Walter in the 1930s.

11. Walter and Amelia in the mid-1940s.

12. Walter with his daughter, Jean, in the early 1940s; Walter is pictured in Home Guard uniform.

13. Walter with (from left to right) daughters Elaine, Jean, daughter-in-law (Jimmy's wife) Margaret and Amelia in the 1940s.

14. "Little Jimmy" (son James) in 1940 (RASC).

Cheshire View.
May 14. 1917.

Dear little Woman.

The enclosed letter got missed when the Post Corporal came round for letters this morning, I can get it away by the same post as this will not need censoring here.

Now little lady you musn't get jumpy because you don't get a letter for a day or two. All kinds of things happen with letters nowadays, even yours arrive in bunches sometimes with a couple of days interval.

I had a letter from Mother written later the same day as yours, saying that two letters turned up after you had written.

There is no big fighting going on where we are, as there is in some sectors, & we are hoping to be clear of the line again very shortly for another spell of training, or rest as they call it. I expect your letter tomorrow will be as chirpy as usual.

It is fortunate you have optimistic Jim along with you at times.

15. An extract from a letter from Walter dated 14 May 1917.

14/

Soon after coming back to the batt. from hospital, he wanted to go over the top with the boys on a big attack to help the first wounded, saying that he would be quite alright if he wore his surplice. He was not allowed over till the attack had fairly progressed, much to his impatience. Now breathe it not in Gath, he once (owing to some difficulty in getting wounded away) offered to hold a man's post if they gave him half a dozen bombs handy.

It is getting bedtime now Mam's (no work tonight), or I could fill a volume with characters out here.

We have had quite a lazy day today, a little warm rain, & lots of sunshine.

Tell Mother I have her letter too but you have taken up all available time tonight, so you will have to stand down tomorrow in favour of Mother. A kiss for that boy & one for yourself from
Your loving husband
Walter

16. An extract from one Walter's letters with regard to a Roman Catholic chaplain.

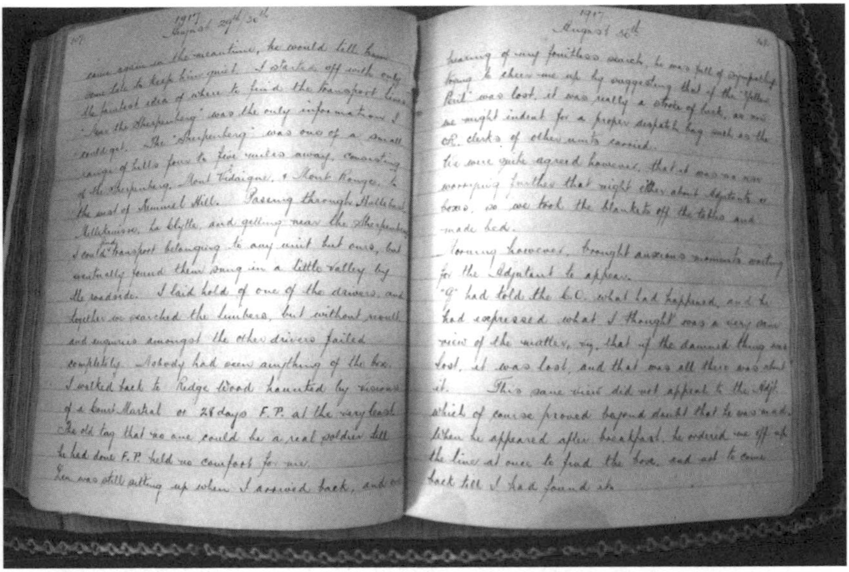

17. A diary page from 1917.

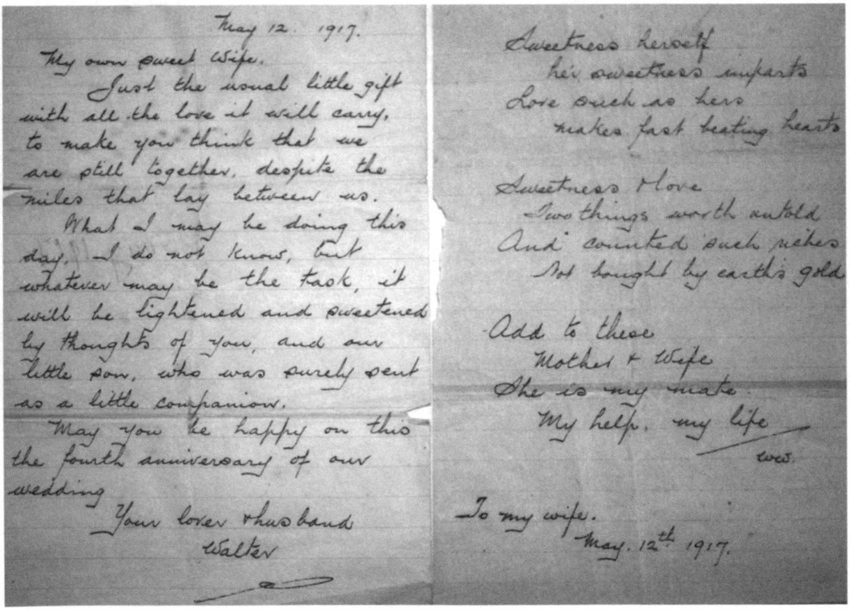

18. Diary letters dated 12 May 1917.

THE COLOURS OF THE
VI TH BATT. CHESHIRE REGIMENT (T.A.)
WERE PLACED IN THIS CHURCH
FOR SAFEKEEPING ON THE
OUTBREAK OF THE GREAT WAR
1914-1918
THEY WERE TAKEN TO FRANCE
ON DECEMBER 15TH 1918
CARRIED IN PROCESSION IN THE
ALLIED PEACE CELEBRATIONS
ON JULY 14TH 1919
BROUGHT BACK FROM FRANCE
ON SEPTEMBER 12TH 1919
AND WERE FINALLY HANDED OVER
TO THE VICAR AND WARDENS
FOR PERMANENT SAFEKEEPING
ON JULY 26TH 1925

19. A plaque dedicated to the colours of the 6th Cheshire Regiment, at St George's church, Stockport, where the following 'colours' are also held.

THE REGIMENTAL COLOURS.

20. The Colours of the 6th Battalion Cheshire Regiment.

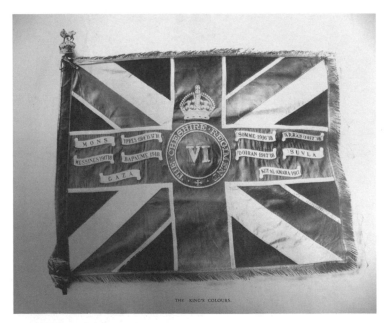

THE KING'S COLOURS.

21. The King's Colours.

22. A plaque at Stockport War Memorial dedicated to the 6th Battalion Cheshire Regiment soldiers who fell at the Battle of St Julien, 31 July 1917.

The War of 1914–1918.

Cheshire Regiment
268163 L./Cpl. [A.]Cpl.] W. Williamson, 1/6th. Bn. [T.F.]

was mentioned in a Despatch from

Field Marshal Sir Douglas Haig, K.T. G.C.B. O.M. G.C.V.O. K.C.I.E.

dated 16th March 1919

for gallant and distinguished services in the Field.

I have it in command from the King to record His Majesty's

high appreciation of the services rendered.

War Office,
Whitehall, S.W.
1st July 1919.

Winston S. Churchill
Secretary of State for War.

23. Walter's 'Mentioned in Despatches'.

July 31st 1917.
English Farm, YPRES.

20 Officers and 600 W.O.'s, N.C.O's, and Men assembled at Engish
Farm at 1 a.m. in preparation of the Advance at L 2OO, hour 3-50 a.m.
for the village of St. Julien, and the Arde Ridge which was to be
taken at 11-5 a.m. This was done, and everything was in order, the
Barage came down at 3-50 a.m. prompt, and the advance commenced. On
arrival at the Bosch front line the casualties had been fairly heavy,
but the advance was maintained. The Steenbechs was crossed at 10 a.m.
and the Battalion was re-organized for the final objective, intermittent
fire being maintained whilst this was going on. At 10-30a.m. the advance
continued, and the final objective taken at 11-5 a.m. punctual, but at
a terrible cost, there were 2 officers and 57 Cheshires, 11 Black Watch,
and 8 Herts left, out of 60 Officers and 1,800 men.

The total advance was three miles from the first objective. The
Cheshires had advances really too far, and had to retire 500 yards to
cognect with the 10th Liverpool Scottish on our right, the 11 Black
Watch and 8 Herts being the only troops left in our the 118th Brigade
on our left. We held on, and were finally relieved on the morning of
the 4th August, total Prisoners we took were 2 Officers and 101 men.

----------oOo-----------

We had, 3 Officers killed.
        1 Officer missing.
        14 Officers wounded.
        529 Men killed, wounded and missing.

? How many Cheshire went into action
Who was paid on how introdued & battle honours Come?
Why was not there a representation at the meeting
lecture were the 3 & 14 Bns

25. Walter's military medals. The bronze oak leaf at the top of the medal denotes his 'Mentioned in Despatches'.

3 NOVEMBER 1917 – 9 FEBRUARY 1919

3 November 1917

On the 3rd of November we left Canada Tunnels in small parties, making for Shrapnel Corner, where we were picked up by motors, and returned to Chippewa Camp. Two days later we vacated this comfortable camp in favour of some troops returning from rest, while wc went under canvas on a dreary waste of mud, known as "Bois Camp", not far from Ridge Wood. Since leaving Canada Tunnels, over a hundred gas cases had been sent into hospital. The remainder of the battalion were all suffering from the effects of the gas in a lesser degree, the chief symptom being complete loss of voice.

Pat's voice was completely gone, and nothing annoyed him more than being told not to shout every time he madc an effort to speak.

The loss of voice led to some rather amusing situations. The Brigadier General turned up suddenly one morning, and the sentry who was at the end of his beat from the Guard Tent, called "Guard Turn Out" in what was meant to be the usual stentorian shout, but which evolved itself into a hoarse whisper.

The guard of course did not hear him, and did not "turn out". In the meantime, the R.S.M. who was half way across the camp, had seen the General coming, and the guard giving no sign. The sight of the R.S.M. rushing towards the guard waving his arms madly and shrieking cusses towards the Guard Tent in a voice that could be perhaps heard a yard away, was well worth seeing. The General actually reached the tent before the guard was out, but the heavens failed to fall.

11 November 1917

On the 11th the battalion went into the line again at Polderhoek Château, Len going up in charge of the "Yellow Peril", while 'Q' and I stayed along with the 'B' team who were accommodated in a few tents at what was known as No. 1 Vierstraat Camp. The mud here was even worse than at Bois Camp. To get near the tents from the road was a problem. 'Quarters' looked inside our tent and shuddered, then thought he had seen some tent boards lying by the roadside as we came along. His batman 'Billy' and I went along to see if we could find any, and came across a set. After much labour and many mud baths, we eventually managed to get them to the tent and make things a little more comfortable indoors.

We had a new officer in charge of the 'B' team, and the first thing he did was to get at loggerheads with the Orderly Room, which is often as unlucky for the officer as for the Orderly Room.

The matter rose through the officer wishing to issue 'Battalion Orders' till 'Q' reminded him that he was not in charge of a battalion, but only of 'Details'. He knew of course that he was in the wrong, but took the well meant correction badly, lost his temper and threatened to do unto us many things that he knew he could not do, and knew also that we knew he knew he could not do, which of course made him more annoyed than ever.

If we had only known that before many weeks had passed, he would actually be in temporary command of the battalion we might have been nicer with him, but we did not know.

Thereafter, while he was in charge of the Details, he completely ignored the Orderly Room, and simply signed necessary papers that we sent to him, while he wrote out and issued his Daily Orders without bothering us, for which favour we felt quite pleased.

The weather however was enough to upset the best of tempers. What sort of a time the boys were having up the line could be guessed from the fact that rope life lines had been served out, one line to each ten men.

Len, before he went up, was bemoaning the fact that he had not thought to bring his rubber 'Water Wings' when he left England.

It was while at Vierstraat that 2nd Lt Brooks joined us, and left the next day to go to the Battalion in the line. I was quite pleased to see another Cheadle Hulme face, but that was the last I saw of him, as he was killed while returning from his first patrol.

Two days after going up, Len returned with a party for leave. They were caked from head to foot with mud, and had found the journey down very bad. Tracks were obliterated, and footboards across the streams had been washed away.

We were rather surprised to find Len amongst the men for leave, but we had overlooked the fact that so many men had been sent into hospital that the leave list was considerably reduced.

Pat again had been left in charge as Orderly Room clerk, the Adjutant having evidently developed an affection for him.

16 November

On the 16th the 'Details' moved back to Chippewa Camp, and the same night the boys arrived in Camp, back from the line, in a very exhausted state, with many more cases of 'Trench Feet'. Pat came stumbling into the Orderly Room with the precious [?] "Yellow Peril", and did not even wait to put the box down, before he had fully expressed his opinion of it and those it belonged to.

Len being on leave, Pat was taken on to the staff as a help. Oh! Help!!

We developed a wonderful spirit of patience and forbearance with him, in our endeavours to get him into a state of believing that all Army Orders were not made for the express purpose of being disobeyed, and to remember to clean his buttons regularly while in respectable company.

It was all useless, and we were left to pray to providence that we might escape the indignity of finding part of the O.R. Staff in the Guard Room some fine day.

20 November

On the 20th the battalions went into the line again in front of Gheluvelt, Pat's 'affection' for the Adjt. and the 'Yellow Peril', taking him into the line again as O.R. clerk.

When the battalion had left camp, we vacated the Orderly Room, and moved into a hut where the battalion's blankets were stored. We found this hut no haven of rest, as we found it somewhat tiring, writing with one hand, while the other hand was busily engaged in other 'pursuits'. One's own blankets are a source of worry at times, but to be shut up with the blankets of a whole battalion, caused us no little irritation. The one redeeming feature of our stay here, was, that the company's officers' mess boxes were also stored in the hut.

24 November

On the 24th the battalion came from the line, and the following day took train to Godewaersevelde, marching from there to the quiet little village of Eecke. At least it was quiet till our band commenced to play in the village square.

Orderly Room was accommodated in the front room of a cottage in the square and, with a table under the window, we had all the youngsters of the village peering in to see us perform on the typewriter.

Our first breakfast here, almost met with disaster. We had drawn some uncooked rations the night before, and Pat had taken the bacon to the kitchen to see if the lady of the house would be so kind as to cook it for us, for 7.30 in the morning. The lady had, however, retired to bed for the evening, but the husband was still downstairs, and though he could not speak English, Pat was supposed to have made matters clear to him, at least he was in the kitchen long enough to have done so. Later, we heard the old man lock up and go to bed, leaving the front door open for our use. It was some time after this that Pat could not find his pipe. After turning our room upside down without result, he suddenly remembered that he had taken it out of his mouth and laid it on the table in the kitchen, no doubt to give greater clarity and precision to his French when speaking to the old man. It is of course impossible to speak French fluently while sucking a pipe, and when he found the old chap could not understand his native tongue as he ought to have done, then I suppose Pat had need of both his hands as well.

I tried to persuade him to wait till morning for his old briar, but nothing would satisfy him on finding the kitchen locked up, but knocking up the old man to get his pipe. It took ten minutes to wake him and induce him to appear in answer to Pat's knocking on the door that seemed to lead upstairs. His appearance was rather startling, and he had evidently decided that if he was to be shot, it did not matter about wearing trousers. When he heard what the trouble really was, and rescued the pipe, the air became so thick with profuse apologies from both sides, that Len and I were disappointed when the old man went to bed again without kissing Pat.

7.30 a.m. next morning we could hear bacon frizzling beautifully in the kitchen, but when the frizzling died down and we heard nothing more but the clatter of knives and forks, and chairs being pulled to the table, a sudden chill fell upon us, and we looked at Pat. He made a sudden dive down the passage, and looked into the kitchen to find the family sat down to bacon for breakfast.

The wife could speak English, and when Pat could overcome his emotion sufficiently to speak, he asked about <u>our</u> bacon. Things were not so bad as appeared at first. Our bacon was still uncooked, on a plate in the larder, though the old gentleman had been under the impression that it was a present.

There were even more apologies about the bacon than about the pipe, but the bacon was quickly cooked for us and misunderstandings were avoided for the morrow, by conducting negotiations direct with the lady herself, and in English.

28 November

On the 28th after three nights at Eecke we returned to Poperinghe, and made home again in the ruins of the old Monastery.

We had heard that this place had been levelled by shell fire since July 31st, but we found it very little different.

With the Germans being now a little further away, perhaps some of the civilians had returned, as there seemed to be more people about. Even the clocks in the three big church towers were in use again, and it was a day or two before we became accustomed to the striking of the bells.

The enemy could still shell the place however, and though he now had no direct observation on the place, he could still do some good practice on it at times.

One particular high velocity gun interested us greatly. We knew it as the 'Rubber Gun'. A great crash would be heard in the town, and seconds later, a very faint report would be heard, and the shell which had already arrived, could be heard on its way. Close by the Monastery was a big gun of ours which would reply, and rock the district till we felt sure the old walls would topple down.

The Orderly Room occupied what appeared to have been a small vestry leading off the chapel, where the band was billeted. The furniture consisted of three small desks with seats attached, evidently from the infants department, and we did much penance to the flesh in squeezing ourselves in between the desks and the seats.

The room itself was in quite good repair, though the tiled floor was rather chilly. We found the tiles rather slippy, and wondered why, till we investigated the matter, and found a good coating of grease on the floor. The place had evidently been used during some hot spell as a Quarter Master's store of some unit, whose rank and file must have wondered what had become of the 'dip' belonging to the morning bacon.

While here, the battalion supplied working parties for the Artillery, and each night went up to Paaschendaele, carrying shells or making gun positions.

1 December 1917

On December 1st 'Quarters' left us for leave, with my best wishes for his safe and speedy return, as I was hoping to get my own leave when he returned.

Len had arrived back from England, 'fed up' and disgusted with everything but leave.

Thinking that if we made some effort to make a fire in the Orderly Room, it might go some way towards making him think that he was still toasting his toes at home, we found a petrol tin, did the necessary fancywork on it with a bayonet and scrounged some coal. After lighting it, we placed it in the centre of the floor to take the chill off. There being no fireplace in the room, and the windows being fixtures, the atmosphere soon became somewhat thick, or as the Flying Corps would put it 'Visibility seriously impaired'.

Of course Len improved matters by putting on some fresh coal just as the C.O. arrived to hold 'Office Hours'.

When he got fairly inside and found he could not breathe, he roared at us to take the 'damned thing' out, as he did not see why he should be gassed in Poperinghe.

To take it out was easier said than done, as the petrol tin was getting nicely red hot. Attempts to pick it up were not successful, and the C.O. stamped about and growled till we managed to find a stick to carry it out by. We set it down outside where the breeze soon improved it into a nice red glow, and as we warmed ourselves comfortably round it, we smiled to hear the C.O. and the Adjutant doing fancy step dances on the cold tiles to try to get their feet warm.

Our smiles faded however when the Adjt. poked his head out of the door and said we could bring the fire in again. Office hours continued for sometime, and as we stood outside and blew on our finger ends, we meditated on the waywardness of Commanding Officers and Adjutants generally.

When he left for leave, 'Quarters' spoke as if he was leaving us to a quiet fortnight, but the three of us found plenty to do.

Pat would have been a great help had he not argued so much, and asked so many questions. Another of his peculiarities was his way of making the 'Cookhouse' bugle do duty for 'Reveille'. His expressed opinion was, that the man who rose before 'Cookhouse' blew, was no soldier, but the man who got up before 'Reveille' had no business to be off a 'Sick Parade'.

We had not the pleasure of his company for long, as he left to go on leave, even then grumbling at having to walk to Proven, four or five miles from Poperinghe, where leave men were to entrain, as Poperinghe station at that time was receiving a fair amount of attention from enemy artillery. Even Proven station was not free from similar attention. A shell dropped in Proven station about this time as a leave train was loading up and caused severe casualties. The light side of the picture was seen in the case of an officer of ours who was picked up unconscious and placed on a stretcher to await removal. He regained consciousness just as the train was moving out, dashed off his stretcher and managed to scramble aboard, preferring to be treated for shell shock in Stockport.

6 December 1917

On December 6th we left Poperinghe again, returning to Eecke, and Len and I managed to secure the same billet as previously, in the house in the village square.

This was the day that 'States' went in to Brigade Headquarters each week.

'States day' was always a busy day in the Orderly Room. This was a certain army form which was tantamount to a stocktaking of the strength of the battalion in Horses, Mules, Wagons, Limbers, Ammunition, Officers, men, and all other impedimenta that go to make up the unit. Before attempting to fill up this form, one must have knowledge of various equations such as 'Horse – Heavy Draught 1 = Mules 2', and that a Mess Cart was a two wheeled vehicle, though a two wheeled limber was not, bicycles had a column to themselves.

Full particulars of all reinforcements that had arrived during the week, all casualties and every change in the personnel, stores or baggage had to be shown with as much reiteration as would be impossible on any form, other than that issued by some Government dept. Then, when we had at last got the final figures out, we had to find out (quietly) whether our figures agreed with the numbers that the Regimental Quarter Master was applying for, for rations. If the figures did not agree, it did not take a pair of City 'office boys' long to remedy a small detail like that.

What with being short-handed and moving during the day, we had not fairly started work at 6 p.m., the time that the forms should have been at Brigade Headquarters, then to help matters, the typewriter struck work, and required half an hour's tinkering before it would condescend to resume its labours. Then we had to put the 'States' on one side when the Adjutant came in to issue 'Battalion Orders'. When we heard that the battalion was moving again at 9.00 a.m. in the morning we sighed, but said nothing.

After completing the orders, it suddenly dawned on him that it was 'States' day, and that it was now 8.30 p.m. "What did we mean by it?" etc. etc. We tried to pacify him by suggesting that we might possibly have them ready by 8.30am in the morning. We worked hard at it till 4.00 a.m., when we seemed to be no nearer the end. We gave it up then in favour of a nap. At 6.00 a.m. we commenced again. At 7.30 the Regimental Quarter Master came in to say that he wanted the Orderly Room baggage in five minutes time, to be loaded on the limbers. We explained that it could not be done, as we had still some hours work to do. He was not a bit polite about the matter, and went off to see the Adjutant. He was back again in a few minutes with the Adjutant, also the C.O. The storm was just about to break, when in strolled the dapper little Staff Captain from Brigade Headquarters, looking like a new pin, and all smiles as usual.

"Just looked in about your States" said he. The Adjutant was as profuse in his apologies as he was with his perspiration, (Red Tabs scared him horribly), and he turned to us with a look that plainly showed that we had ruined all his chances of ever becoming a Field Marshal.

The Staff Captain cut in to say that he had just got States in from the Black Watch, Herts and Cambs, they were all late, "And of course you were moving yesterday, and I hear your Orderly Sgt. is on leave". The Adjutant took the nice polite hint that he was making too much noise, and shut up. Turning to us, he asked how long it would be before we could finish, and we told him we still had 2 to 3 hours hard work. Both the battalion and Brigade Head Quarters would be away from Eecke by that time, so he asked the C.O. if he would sign the uncompleted forms, and leave us behind to finish the work. When we had finished we were to deliver the 'States' to the Divisional Head Quarters, which was at Steenevoorde, about four miles away, and he would give us a note to a Staff Captain there who would have us forwarded, bag and baggage, after the battalion.

Len and I could scarcely conceal our chuckles.

The C.O. did not seem to like the idea, but evidently did not care to oppose the Staff Captain, and so later, when we had seen the Battalion march off through the square, and Brigade Headquarters follow, we immediately shut down work, and decided for some fresh air, a stroll round the village and something to eat. Fresh troops were already coming into the place, but we did not trouble about this until we arrived back and found our billet taken over by the orderly room of the Corps Royal Engineers, our own goods and chattels being deposited outside on the pavement. We went inside to investigate and found ourselves face to face with the most 'nutty' thing in Orderly Room Sergeants that we had met yet. Gold pince-nez, nearly white cord breeches, polished leggings and finished off with the 'toniest' of brown boots.

"Isn't he just sweet?" Len whispered to me as we gazed upon him. The orderly room furniture was at par with its sergeant. We looked at it in wonder. Folding chairs, collapsible tables, and the latest thing in index files confronted us. We must have looked like a couple of yokels suddenly finding themselves unaccountably in Buckingham Palace, but we came to our senses on hearing ourselves asked what the 'dayvel' we wanted. We explained that we wanted our Orderly Room. "Whose Orderly Room?" he demanded. "The 6th Cheshire's" we replied. He cuttingly explained to us that the 6th Cheshires had left Eecke some hours previously. The only thing of ours that had not been turned out were our arms, equipment, and the "Yellow Peril". We were gathering these together when the yellow box caught his attention. "What is that thing?" he enquired.

Len who was itching to get in a parting shot, replied "Oh you haven't anything like that, of course, it is a fighting mob's orderly room, that is" and as we passed out, he gave us a look that plainly said that he would immediately be sending for the 'sanitary men' to disinfect the billet.

We sat outside on the boxes, and cogitated awhile what to do, and Len was eventually left sat minding the boxes while I looked round to see whether I could find anywhere we could do a couple of hours work.

A little estaminet at the corner of the square had a little outhouse we could use if we wanted any beer. We did not want any beer, but we ordered some, and carried our impedimenta in, and commenced work again.

To help things along, Len became suddenly ill before we had finished the work. Our host happened to have some brandy in, but it cost the whole of our joint funds before we could get him to part with sufficient quantity to make a decent medicinal dose. Wrapping Len up in the blankets, I at last managed to finish the work, pack the boxes and left them to keep the draught off the invalid, while I made my way to Steenvoorde to find Divisional Headquarters. I delivered the forms at the 'Q' (Administration) Office, and was directed to another office to deliver my letter to the Staff Captain. Such a nice boy he was too, until I soured his life by worrying him. After reading the letter he smiled amiably, told me to report at Divl. H.Q. again, to Sergeant … and stay along with the 'Casuals' who would very likely move along with 'D.H.Q.' on the morrow. I told him that we had the Orderly Room boxes and typewriter at Eecke, four miles away. He was still nice about it, and said that I could go and bring them. Explaining that we could not carry them, he supposed our battalion had such a thing as a limber. This was one of the moments when sudden demobilization would have been a godsend, so that one could reply in a really suitable manner.

He suddenly seemed to remember that some reference was made to the matter in the letter which he held in his hand. He looked at it again, and rubbed his chin while he looked me up and down, evidently wondering why I had not carried about 3 cwt. of boxes, and a big Remington typewriter along with me.

The matter was beyond him, so he passed the letter to a Quarter Master Sgt. who had a sudden brain wave, as he said "They will need a limber Sir".

This led to developments, and shortly afterwards, I left the office armed with a 'chit' for the Transport Officer. Finding him with some difficulty, I was passed along with a chit to the Transport Sergeant, who then sent me to a close by estaminet to tell Driver … that he was wanted at once. Driver … was at that moment whirling a buxom Belgian wench round to the seductive strains of a gramophone and expressed his 'pleasure' at the interruption in terms that lost nothing in colour or vividness in their lucidity. He did not waste much time however, and we were soon out of Steenvoorde and on our way to Eecke at a most unorthodox pace for Army Mules. The driver evidently had hopes of being able to get back to the estaminet before the fateful hour of eight.

Arriving at Eecke we hoisted the boxes aboard, and set off back, but before we had proceeded far, the jolting proved too much for Len, who was still feeling very ill, and I had to convert myself into upholstery for the comfort of the invalid.

At Steenvoorde we crammed as many of the more important books and papers into the 'Yellow Peril' as possible, and took this into our own charge, while the more bulky boxes and the typewriter remained on the limber and were taken into the charge of the Transport Sgt.

Our quarters were with the 'Casuals' in a loft at the top of the building occupied by the Divisional General and his staff.

Whether the shaking up had done Len some good, I don't know, but he was feeling so much better that he suggested we might have a look round Steenvoorde before we turned in for the night. I could not but point out the futility of this, as we had liquidated all our available capital at Eecke, but as Len said "One never knows, does one?" and it was just one of those places where a few francs would have been handy.

No lights were showing, except through a few chinks of shutters, but there seemed to be quite a number of pastry shops, egg and chip emporiums, and estaminets. Our luck held, however, as we were just deciding to get back to our sleeping quarters and get away from tantalizing smells of egg and chips, when we suddenly fell across 'Ashy'. It would perhaps be nearer the mark to say that 'Ashy' nearly 'fell across' us. He was one of our signallers who, for some weeks, had been "On Command" at Divisional H.Q. Signals. We found that he had just arrived back to Steenvoorde from leave in England, and at the moment was both 'flush' and 'flushed'. In his sober moments 'Ashy' was known not to be unbridled in his generosity, but in his present state well "One never knows" as Len had said.

The average Tommy in those days of 'A tanner a day and a tanner for the missus' was not secretive of his days of pecuniary embarrassment and we decided to 'touch' Ashy's sympathy. At 5 francs we really had to stop him, and after seeing him safely home, we adjourned for eggs and chips to a shop near by, then home to our roost above the General.

We were up betimes in the morning as we were in some doubt as to where we were to get breakfast. After some enquiry, we found out rations for 'Casuals' were served out from a hut some distance away at 7.30 a.m., and as it was that time already, we had qualms.

There was a wild grab for mess tins, and a noisy rush downstairs, quite forgetful of the General, a sprint down the street, across the square, down past the Church (as per directions) till we sighted a wooden Army hut, arriving there breathless to find ourselves shut out in the rain, and breakfast not ready for another half hour.

After breakfast and a little polishing up, I made for the Orderly Room to make some enquiries about our getting away. I had a feeling that I only needed to mention the circumstances of our case, and we would find ourselves and our luggage being forwarded post haste in chase of our battalion. The fact, however, was that nobody seemed interested in the matter, and that we were twenty four hours away from the battalion, with all the battalion's papers, records and stationery, did not seem a matter of moment to any one. We had simply become 'Casuals' and as 'Casuals' we should go back to our quarters and wait until we received orders.

Despite our attempts at explanations we were kept there two days.

'Quarters' had gone home on leave before we left Poperinghe, and we could only faintly imagine the state of temper of our worthy adjutant, who was thus left with no Orderly Room staff, books or papers to work with.

10 December

It was the 10th of Dec when Divisional Headquarters and its impedimenta – including 'Casuals' – left for Nielles les Blequin. We paraded early in the square at Steenvoorde, and marched the four or five miles to Godewaersvelde to board the train which called at Steenvoorde a few minutes later. This was no doubt meant to give the troops the little treat of the extra train ride.

It was dusk by the time we arrived at a pretty village called Nielles-les-Blequin which was evidently to be Divisional Headquarters during the time the Division was out resting.

'Casuals' were billeted in an outhouse attached to a farm on the outskirts of the village. As it was the middle of December, we did not count it as an advantage that access to the billet could be gained through the walls without troubling about the door, but a plentiful supply of good clean straw to lay in, made amends.

We were told that tea would be available at the cookhouse in half an hour, and having first to find the cookhouse in the darkness, we set off at once with our mess tins. After quite a long search along roads which were now slippery with ice, we eventually found tea, and bread with cheese being served out through the window of an empty cottage by the roadside, on the farther side of the village. Feeling sure that either the tea would be cold or that we might even lose it before we reached our billets, we decided on sitting by the roadside, and making sure of the hot tea.

The next morning as soon as we had attended to breakfast, the 'Casuals' to a man snuggled down into the straw again, and hoped they might be forgotten. The hope was quickly dashed, as we had barely settled ourselves when a lance-corporal came in. It turned out that he wanted a party of men for work, building latrines for the officers. He proceeded to pick them in the usual manner. "You ten men come out of it" he shouted, indicating the line of recumbent figures lying along one wall. Eight of the ten rose slowly with a deal of grumbling. He eyed the remaining two forms, and Len being the nearer of the two, received a sharp poke from the lance-corporal's heavy boot. Len was only small, but he had a big temper. He suddenly sat up with all the dignity of his own stripe upon him, and demanded to know – with emphasis – how many lance-corporals he needed to look after his little party, and made him understand that we also stood on that same plane of eminence which he himself so worthily adorned.

After he had left with his party, we decided that it would perhaps be as well to have a walk in case a sergeant came round on a similar errand. On our way out of the village, we met the Orderly Room Sergeant and asked him if there was any hope of being allowed to rejoin our battalion in the near future. He glared at us, and promised to put us in 'blood-red' irons if we pestered him any more, so we left him and took to our walk. We kept clear of the village till dinner time, when we judged that work would be finished. On our way back we were hailed by our friend the Orderly Room Sergeant. It appeared that an urgent dispatch had arrived from our battalion, asking for information regarding their missing orderly room staff.

Result – we were ordered to obtain one day's rations from the cookhouse, and report at the Orderly Room at 9.0 a.m. in the morning.

In the morning we paraded punctually, and received a 'movement order' entitling us to travel by train to Desvres, and were told to enquire there from the Railway Transport Officer the location of our battalion.

We still had the precious "Yellow Peril" in our possession, and were promised that the typewriter and boxes would be sent on to the battalion by road.

Arriving at Nielles station we found it deserted. There seemed to be no Station master, Railway Transport Officer or any living soul about who could tell us what time there was likely to be a train for Desvres.

French civilians soon began to arrive however, and in time the station began to wear quite an animated appearance. This seemed to suggest that there evidently was a train to be expected. We did not bother to enquire about it, as we were not in much danger of taking the wrong train, as we had a fair idea of which was East and which was West.

It was about noon when our train managed to reach Desvres. From the Railway Transport Officer we learned that our Brigade Headquarters were stationed at the village of Alincthun, and from there we could get the exact location of the battalion which would be close by.

It was only about ten miles to Alincthun. Of course it is recognised that if an 'R.T.O.' answers one question, it is as much, or perhaps even more than is to be expected, so knowing this, we did not presume to ask him where Alincthun might be.

Instead, we enquired at a small shop in the square where we luckily found a young lady whose English – though far from fluent – was a deal better than our combined French. We learned from her the direction to take and that it was "Vaire longue and beaucoup up and down but vaire nice scenery".

If we had not been encumbered with the box and our equipment we might have enjoyed the walk, but as things were we would gladly have parted with the scenery to halve the distance. Soon after leaving Desvres the road ran through forest land, and did not belie the young lady's description. It was here we met a party of bearded old gentlemen evidently out for a little shooting. They had just arrived in a closed conveyance driven by a liveried coachman, and before proceeding with the shooting, seemed to be regaling themselves with wine and sandwiches. We wished them good health and good sport in the best French we could muster, but there was not the response to our salutations that we hoped for. They simply smiled, waved and called "Bon Jour".

Before we reached Alincthun, we saw a high dog-cart coming along the road towards us, and as it drew closer we found it was our 'C.O.' and the Adjutant evidently out for the afternoon. They recognised us as we saluted, and the Adjutant promised to see us later, in a tone that was evidently meant to put into us a fear that something dreadful would happen to us.

We could not develop a tremble between us however, as we were fast reaching that state when a Court-Martial would have been welcomed as a relief from carrying our box. We were now relieving each other at such short intervals that the blessed box could hardly remain with either of us longer than about three minutes at a spell.

We found our Brigade Headquarters at Alincthun and making enquiries there we learned that our Battalion was billeted at the village of Le Waast, about three miles further.

Before proceeding, we went into the state of our finances and found we had enough money left out of the sum we had 'borrowed' from 'Ashy' at Steenvoorde, to afford a little light refreshment. Finding a little cottage on whose window read 'EEFFOC', we went inside to see if it read what we thought it might. Finding our suspicions justified we ordered coffee and two 'encores'. 'Encore' and 'Comme Ça' were two popular drinks in France at that time.

We then felt we might be able to manage the rest of the journey. Shortly after leaving the village we came to the high road to Boulogne and were interested to find that we were only ten kilometres from that place. What disappointed us however, was the fact that the sign-post pointed in the opposite direction for Le Waast. Now being sure of our way we decided that there was no particular need to arrive at our destination before teatime, so we climbed through a hedge into a field, dropped the box, slipped our equipment off, and had a nap.

Later – a mile from Le Waast, we met one of our 'runners' who relieved us of the box while he regaled us with the horrible tales of what had been happening in the Orderly Room during our absence.

'Quarters' had not got back from leave, and the Regimental Sergeant Major had also been on leave. 'B' Company Sergeant Major was acting 'Regimental' and had pressed his Company Clerk into service for the Orderly Room. Leave allotments were coming in profusely, and no leave forms available. They had been sat up all night writing leave passes on blank paper, and were momentarily expecting leave takers to be sent back from the port for not being in possession of official forms.

Not having any 'leave roster' to work by, men had been sent out of their turn and the unfortunate ones were out for somebody's blood. Someone had said jokingly that all the Orderly Room staff had deserted, and all the familiar faces being missing, it had developed into a fact.

As we passed through the village square, Rowbottom (the runner) would amuse himself by informing all he met, that he had found us on the Boulogne Road making for the boat, and we were glad when we could get out of sight in the cosy little Orderly Room which had been fixed up in the village schoolmaster's house.

Here we found Sgt Maj. 'P' and Billy Wildgoose his clerk hard at work and looking very worried about it.

The Sgt Maj. greeted us with a torrent of his most picturesque, which we interrupted to ask if tea was anywhere about. He grinned and suddenly changed the subject to let us know what he thought of 'our friend' the Adjutant, and we quite agreed with him.

We emptied our "Yellow Peril" of its contents, and, after some tea, worked well on into the night getting matters straight.

The Adjutant came in during the evening, but for some mysterious reason, was quite affable, which we disliked even more than his usual offensive manner.

We found our quarters quite comfortable and cosy to work in, a big French stove to keep us warm, big cupboards where we could pack out of sight our equipment and bedding, comfortable chairs and a good table to work at.

Billy Wildgoose stayed on with us for the time being and added much to the gaiety of things in general, also, being able to draw his

'S.R.D.' ration from his company, as well as from Headquarters he was quite an acquisition in the evenings.

The 'H.Q.' runners, liking the look of our billet, suggested one should sleep with us, and so be handy for night 'runs'. When they found that the Orderly Room does not have its evenings all to itself when out of the line, they found their own billet quite comfortable again.

It seemed to us that Brigade Headquarters at this time, must close down during the day, and start work when we wanted to sleep. About 2 a.m. each morning, something would turn up. We would be roused up to receive a tug-of-war rope for a sports to be held some days later. Another morning it happened to be the battalion's allotment of Christmas Cards.

At the same early hour one morning word came in that the Divisional General would hold a parade at 11 a.m. that same morning, and at the parade would present decorations to the men who had been awarded in recent engagements.

A nominal roll of such men and a short account of the deed for which each man had been recommended was to be at Brigade Headquarters by 8 a.m. That meant getting the Adjutant out of bed, and getting orders round to the Company Officers. A wild hunt through our boxes for the 'Recommendation' file met with no success. There was no time for anything else, but making up a good tale for each man. We had a list of the men who had been awarded medals 'M.M.' and 'D.C.M.' and for each man we did our best, with no idea of what they were truly recommended for. The Adjutant made us tone some of them down in fear that the General might think he was handing out 'V.C.s'.

Everything went off well on the parade however, and though some of the recipients may have been a little surprised to hear how they gained their decorations, they were too well brought up to argue with the General about it.

The battalion was having a splendid rest at Le Waast, and as our Colonel was acting Brigadier-General at the time, matters went very comfortably and smoothly. 'Quarters' came back here from leave, and this put me into some state of excitement, as I was now able to look forward to going on leave to England with the next allotment, which was due on the 21st; thus allowing just nice time to reach home for Christmas.

There was a solemn rite before going on leave. When a leave allotment was received, passes were made out for the men, and in addition a typed certificate which read

This is to certify that

No .... Rank ....

Name................ Regt. ....

is free from scabies, infectious disease and vermin

(signed)..........................(M.O.)

Before going away the men were paraded before the Medical Officer to be examined, and to have their certificates signed.

There was never much doubt about any of the men suffering from the first two mentioned disabilities without the knowledge of the Medical Officer. With regard to the third matter, I never heard of a case in the battalion, where a man had been refused his certificate. This evidently speaks volumes for the general cleanliness of the men, or at least for the sporting spirit of the Medical Officer.

21 December

The 21st of the month duly arrived, and notwithstanding deep snow and hard frost, I do not think that any of those deeply concerned turned over in their blankets again when 'Reveille' sounded, and there were no laggards to hunt for when we were ready to start at 7.0 a.m.

Our village was within a couple of hours walk of Boulogne, from where leave boats left daily, but our tickets were only available via Calais.

First we had to report at Brigade Headquarters at Alincthun, three miles away, from which place motors ran us a twenty odd miles to St Omer, arriving there about noon to find out that our train did not leave for Calais till the next morning. We found a 'Y.M.C.A.' hut in the station square, where we could have a meal, and admire members of the 'W.A.A.C.' who came in with a rush for their dessert and hairpins. They looked very smart and prim, and had evidently been well brought up, or perhaps we did not look so respectable as troops on 'base' work at St Omer.

A stroll round the town and a look in at the Lord Roberts Memorial Club till closing time found us wending our way back to the 'Y.M.C.A.' in the station yard. It wasn't the warmest place we could find, but we began to wonder whether it was not too far from the platform, in case our unexpected train for Calais suddenly arrived. St Omer station at the time, had been very badly knocked about. Most of the roof had gone, and the pavements of the platforms and booking hall were all smashed up. We were not allowed on the platform so got what rest we could in a huge stone floored waiting room with a modicum of roof.

We were roused before daylight, cramped and stiff with cold, to scramble into the train which had arrived already packed. The usual accommodation of 40 per truck did not seem to matter for leave trains and no one seemed to mind.

I had visions that, in an hour of two, we should be steaming into the quayside station at Calais and step straight aboard the steamer. It will be understood from this, that it was my first experience of leave from France.

What really happened was, that we were unloaded in a dense cold fog at Fontinettes siding, outside Calais, and marched through the slums where the streets were broken up with bombing, and then splashed along through an ankle's depth of inky slush.

I was still optimistic, as, at intervals along the road appeared finger posts pointing in the direction we were taking and reading "To the Boat". My spirits sank however when we suddenly turned to the left, and the legend on the sign posts changed to "To No.1 and No.2 Leave Camps". We came to the leave camp which had all the appearance of a Prisoners of War Camp, so well was it guarded and wired.

The camp was on the sand dunes, and the tents looked anything but cosy in the snow. We were soon served with a good hot meal, and paraded immediately afterwards, and our leave papers collected. We were to remain in camp, and be ready to parade at a moments notice, and any infringement of the long list of camp regulations laid us open to the penalty of immediate return to our unit.

The thick fog showed no signs of lifting, but I was buoyed up with the fact that it was still 3 days from Christmas day, and that the fourteen days leave only dated from the day of embarkation.

Of amusements in the camp there were three. An easy first was the big canteen, second, the large 'Y.M.C.A.' hut, where there was usually a 'sing song' in progress, and a plentiful supply of magazines. The third was the Chinese Labour Company's camp which adjoined ours, where, through our barbed wire fence, we could enjoy the sight of Chinese coolies, housed comfortably in good wooden huts warmed by great stoves, while we stood in imminent danger of frost bite, our only really appreciated comfort being the fact that the water taps at the ablution benches were all frozen up, and we were unable to wash.

It was announced during the afternoon that Miss Lena Ashwell's Concert Party would give a concert in the 'Y.M.C.A.' that evening. Many of us decided to have our tea there in order to make sure of a seat. Long before the time announced for the commencement of the performance the huge hut was packed to its limit.

At last the Concert Party arrived. Amidst a storm of applause, they took the platform, and had just commenced an opening chorus, when three shrill whistles suddenly sounded through the camp, accompanied by shouts of "All lights out". An officer hurried to the platform and, after a hasty consultation, the Concert Party quickly left the platform, then, while lights were extinguished, we were ordered back to our tents.

On the keen night air came the well known drone of bombing-planes heavily laden, and soon came the crashes of bursting bombs falling in the town.

The next day leave boats arrived, but none left, and with the men returning from leave, and fresh trainloads arriving for leave, the camp became very congested, and three times in the day we were paraded, simply to move to another part of the camp, not to the boat as we each time fondly imagined.

Pat was amongst those returning from leave, and as soon as I could track him down to his tent, I called to see him. He assured me that leave was really the best thing about Army life, and he had quite a good time. Though sorry his leave was over he was full of good spirits, just like his water bottle. I was invited in for a few drops of comfort, and afterwards felt sure he would receive a warm welcome from his friends in the battalion.

24 December

Pat left camp for his unit early next morning, the 24th, and I had quite given up hope of reaching home for Christmas Day, when we were suddenly paraded, handed our papers stamped with the 24th as 'Day of Embarkation' and marched out of camp towards the boat.

On leaving the camp, we were set upon by hordes of urchins doing their best to induce us to part with our hard earned leave money for scrubby little apples at 4*d* each, worse oranges at 6*d*, and chocolate seemingly made of ground glass and clay at the rate of about one week's pay per packet. With the strong support of many members of Highland regiments we withstood the onslaught bravely, and gained the very fluently expressed contumely of the attackers. At the quayside we were served out with our jam roll, and one meat pie per man, and at last we were on the 'Blighty Boat'. We steamed out of Calais on the eve of Christmas in charge of two destroyers, and when close in to Dover, our guarding destroyers turned and as they passed us to continue their patrol, a signaller appeared on the bridge of the leading destroyer.

The captain of our boat megaphoned the message down to us. "The Patrol wish all on board a very Merry Christmas".

For the size of our boat, I think the Dover Patrol thought we had some good lungs on board, for the cheer we sent across the water to them was more than hearty, for few of us felt that we had ever so deeply appreciated the annual trite wish. Then we watched the Patrol swiftly disappearing away into the cold mist with the icy water plunging over their bows. We passed into Dover Harbour through the narrow opening in the big chain boom, and found a queer assortment of craft inside.

We were soon moored and there was a quick rush along the ice-covered quayside to the waiting train.

After being accustomed to troop trains in France and Belgium, the extra comfort of the 'L.B. & S.C.' Railway was appreciated, but counterbalanced by the nerve-wracking speed we made towards London. On the arrival platform at Victoria Station we met with a quite pleasant welcome. Long benches were laden with cups of steaming tea, coffee and cocoa, plates piled with sandwiches, bread and butter and cakes. Cries from the ladies in charge "Come along and help yourself Tommy". My natural shyness at being called by my Christian name by strange ladies, being overcome by the sight of the benches, I joined my thousand odd namesakes in the raid. At the exit from the platform stood an elderly gentleman in a smart uniform, bravely holding his own with the aid of a big time-table, against the simultaneous enquiries from a hundred impatient leave-men, for the time of a train to their home town. This gentleman had evidently been brought up on railway-guides from babyhood. I waited sometime to see if it was possible for him to fail. No. Quite impossible. He seemed to know all the trains for the bigger towns from memory. For smaller places his finger whisked furiously over a few pages, and the reply came quickly, time, station, and the way to get to the station. The next surprise for us was to be taken charge of by a wee girl guide who shepherded us from the station to the Army Pay Officer, and warned us against wicked people who laid wait for poor Tommy outside the 'A.P.O.' to rob us of those fabulous amounts that were supposed to be handed out there. Coming unscathed from the A.P.O. I found Christmas shopping in progress in the darkened streets. Finding the 'A.P.O.' solvent, and no fare to pay, and one hour to spare, I was minded to take home a present to compensate for my appearance, and the unearthly hour of my likely arrival.

Fate arrested my steps in front of a blouse shop, and summoning the necessary courage, I passed through the swing doors, which swung back again so quickly that I was afraid I had cracked a pane with my steel helmet strapped on the back of my pack. Turning quickly to see what damage I had done, I caught my rifle in a hanging festoon of trimmings and brought the arrangement down. This was a bad start and made me nervous, and when I found myself the sole male occupant of the establishment I was preparing to pretend that I had made a mistake and thought it was the tobacconist's shop next door. A duchess in black silk glided from behind the counter to pick up the fallen trimmings. She was quite nice about it, and instead of ordering me out, asked what I would like to see. I gave her to understand that I admired a certain blouse in the window, she brought it out on the model, and though did not say so, she gave me to understand that I had real judgement. Yet she made no effort to part with the blouse, caressing the dummy affectionately, until I was left in some perplexity. Was she wanting to sell the dummy along with it, or was she waiting till I turned my back while she de-bloused the figure. Suddenly she leaned forward very confidentially and mentioned that ladies usually wore something beneath blouses of that description. I restrained a mad impulse to agree that the weather was very cold for the time of year, and simply nodded while she brought forward a selection of 'Just the thing to go with it'. Murmuring an exhausted acquiescence we had almost reached the stage of parcelling up, when an old lady suddenly butted in at the rear to ask me if I had come from France.

Londoners are so frightfully keen. She could deduce evidently in a moment from the colour of my buttons and my beard that I had not just come off guard from Buckingham Palace. It was from no mere idle curiosity however, that she joined in. Just pure helpfulness to a poor male thing out of his element. She admired the blouse I had bought, and then turned a baleful eye on the lady behind the counter, and asked if it would wash. On receiving the reply that it would wash beautifully with ordinary care, she was quite satisfied, and turned a benign smile on me to remark "Men are so careless of such details", leaving me with a sense of my utter futility as a shopper.

I arrived home at 3.0 a.m. on Christmas morning and my wife never ever asked "Will it wash?"

8 January 1918

Leave finished, found us arriving at Euston Station in the very early hours, on a cold, frosty morning, scrambling for buses which we supposed would take us direct to Victoria Station. We were dropped off however at a Salvation Army Shelter, and provided with a hot breakfast followed by prayers, then we were allowed to make the best use of the place till nearer train time. That only meant one thing for most of us, viz 'more sleep'. We were roused in good time and found Victoria Station only just round the corner. The same afternoon found us back again in the leave camp in Calais where we spent the night. The following morning at dawn we were marched down to Fontinettes siding and entrained. A weary cold train ride in horse vans landed us back at Poperinghe. There may have been snow at Poperinghe, but it had simply added a little more to the mud. We were marched from the station to a new rest billet that had been fixed up there in an old mill, where, after a meal, we each booked our six feet of wire netting for the night by dumping our equipment upon it, and were then free till 9.0 p.m. We celebrated our return to France from the perils of leave, by a further meal – eggs and chips – at an establishment we knew well, and where wonders could be worked with the said eggs and chips with the aid of a piece of bread and a knife. A visit to Talbot House to write a quiet letter or two and 9.0 p.m. quickly arrived.

After our early breakfast the next morning we set out to find our battalion, with but vague instructions where to find their present location. "Through Ypres" was the nearest direction we could get. We got along through Ypres, passing over the canal, then found a peculiar sensation in traversing a road in broad daylight, that we had only been accustomed to going along warily in the dark, or in the daylight, bolting across like rabbits singly from a trench at one side to a trench at the other. On the ground, where some months before we had gone up for night work, building a strong post, we found the battalion in wooden huts at close quarters to a big ammunitions dump, to where a light railway was working by daylight. These were a part of the results of the third battle of Ypres in which we took a part in the opening on July 31st previously. I found Len looking much as usual, but I thought friend 'Quarters' looked particularly ill, till I found that his 'Top set' had come to grief one frosty night when he had slipped and come down heavily with his face on an icebound duckboard.

The battalion was just leaving camp as we arrived, and was going into the line at Poelcappelle. Pat was already up there with the brigade signals. The boys were not expecting a rosy time, as there were no trenches in that sector, it being impossible to cut trenches owing to the awful state of the ground, and to add to the discomfort, there had recently been heavy falls of snow followed by heavy rains and frosts, followed by quick thaws. The general opinion seemed to be that the chances of being drowned or frozen in were about even.

After watching the battalion move off, we packed up the Orderly Room boxes, and Transport, Quarter Masters, Company Clerks and Orderly Room struggled back over the canal and were accommodated at Siege Camp for a couple of nights and then went into Dambra Camp close by, which was empty and waited for the battalion coming down. On the 14th a foot of snow fell. This put a stop to Orderly Room work in favour of a hunt for fuel. In the evening it turned to torrential rain, keeping it up all the next day. A big railway siding across the road from the camp disappeared under three feet of water, the road disappeared, and so might the camp but for the wooden huts which appeared for all the world like a collection of Noah's Arks all afloat. The odds now on the battalion getting drowned as against frozen in, were stupendous.

The boys were expected down from Poelcappelle about midnight on the 15th. We heard that they were in a bad state owing to the terrible conditions existing up there, and arrangements had been made to bring them down on the light railway from the nearest point the line reached.

We heard from our end that the light railway had simply been washed away.

Risking enemy aircraft, lights were lit round about the camp to guide them as they reached the immediate neighbourhood.

Stoves and wood had been sent up from the Divisional Dump to the camp, and an attempt was made to warm and dry the huts, all available cookers were hard at work on hot soup for the arrivals. Everyone who could be spared was out in gum boots trying to get in touch. The night passed with everyone on edge, and it was not until dawn broke that the first arrivals turned up. The Medical Officer and another officer appeared and stumbled into the Orderly Room in a wretched state. The 'M.O.' was a lanky Scotsman standing about 6 foot 3 inches possessed of a pawky humour which even now had not deserted him. He said he was sure there was no need to worry waiting to report any more in, as he was sure he was the only man saved. He reckoned himself the tallest man in the unit, and he had been overhead half a dozen times.

Then the good soul went off at once without waiting a moment, to see that plenty of hot soup and rum was available, and that the medical aid post was ready for all eventualities.

Soon afterwards the boys commenced to arrive from all directions in small parties. Len arrived in a semi-conscious state, quite rambling, but still hanging on to his despatch case. We quickly made him completely unconscious, stripped his soaked rags off him, rolled him in blankets and put him to roast by a hot stove.

Not more than half the battalion had arrived by noon, but small parties, who had found some shelter till dawn, found their way down during the afternoon.

The battalion had returned in the darkness to find every track obliterated, footboards that had not lost their hold were feet under water, these were few. Most of them were floating about irresponsibly inviting people to step on them and disappear.

The Steenbeck and every other stream had lost their identity in the general inundation.

When the last arrivals had been made up, we were still some forty men missing, and fears were really entertained that these men had been drowned. They were accounted for however, a day or two later, as having been admitted to hospital, having been picked up by the relieving battalion, some wounded and some in a state of collapse.

Our old friend 'Aunty' Entwistle of the signallers retired from this narrative with a shattered leg.

Some eighty cases of severe 'Trench feet' were sent off at once to hospital, while practically the whole battalion was under treatment.

The Commanding Officer and the Medical Officer had some differences over this matter. Both the 'C.O.' and 'M.O.' were acting 'Pro tem' and were accordingly not inclined to have their 'temporary' status suffer any indignity. It commenced by the 'C.O.' expressing the opinion that the 'M.O.' was a bit too lenient in sending so many cases to hospital, and it was diminishing the strength of the unit unnecessarily.

The 'M.O.' took this as an unwarrantable interference in a matter that was under his (the M.O.s) control, and continued sending cases to hospital. The day after this we received an order from Brigade Headquarters to supply 200 men for working parties up the line.

The 'M.O.' happened to be in the Orderly Room when the order came in. He was furious about it, and there seemed to be more trouble brewing. The 'C.O.' insisted that the men must be found. The 'M.O.' countered this by placing the whole battalion 'Sick'. As the 'M.O.' was only acting 'pro tem' we felt pleased that there would be no lasting feud, as we always found that trouble at Headquarters eventually worked through to the rank and file who eventually suffered for it in some shape or form.

During this spell in the line Pat had been acting as linesman on the Brigade Advance Signal Station. Receiving information that the battalion intended to raid the enemy lines one evening at 6.0 p.m., they were particularly anxious about the telephone lines, and as fate would have it, a breakage occurred close upon time for the raid. Pat and another linesman dashed out in the darkness to find the break in order to have the line ready for urgent messages. Time was short, and by the time they found the break and repaired it, it was close on 6 o'clock. If they were short of time they had decided to make for Battalion Headquarters if they found themselves nearer there than their own station, as during a raid and for sometime afterwards, the back of our line would be shelled mercilessly to keep reinforcements or anything else from coming up. They found that they could not reach either station before 6 o'clock, so picked the best shell hole available, and trusted to luck. They waited and waited, every moment after six o'clock expected a tornado of shells, but nothing happened. They began to wonder whether a mistake had been made, and decided to get back to their station. Here they learned that the raid had been postponed and was to take place just before dawn. News came through later that the raid was cancelled in favour of a big Artillery 'Shoot', sometime during the day by the 39th Divisional Artillery.

At programme time the Shoot took place, and for a while our guns fairly pumped shells over without any retaliation. It was not long afterwards, while the gunners must have been cleaning the guns and putting all straight, when the enemy guns opened out.

From the sheltered side of their concrete 'Pill-box' the signallers saw our Artillery smothered under a hail of shells that blew guns, gunners and dugouts up into the air and, we heard, left very little of the 39th Divisional Artillery.

Later on the big Corps guns were heard at work, and kept at work for some hours, but we had no means of getting to know who came out best from the duel.

During the earlier part of their stay at this station, before the big thaw set in, ice still covered most of the shell holes. Drinking water was difficult to obtain. Pat had searched the immediate neighbourhood to find a shell hole with water that would at least boil for tea. Having found one that seemed fairly clean, he laid a trail by wire back to the dugout, so that they would have no difficulty in finding the same hole again. A runner going out one night for water arrived back in quicker time than usual, and on being questioned, admitted that he had not been to the chosen shell hole, considered it was a lot of fuss, and that one shell hole was as good as another. Pat and his fellow linesman decided it was not fit to drink and left it severely alone, while the remainder proceeded to make tea and drink it, deciding that it did not taste any worse than what they had been having. Three of them were taken off to hospital the following day.

Later when the ice disappeared, the shell hole from which the runner had obtained the water, was found to contain the dead body of a Bosche in an advanced state of decomposition.

It was now pretty well known that this was to be our last turn in the line in the Ypres Salient, at least for a while. Rumour had been rife for sometime that our division was to have a change at last and go down to the quieter front of the Somme for a rest.

The division had now been in the Salient from November 1916 to January 1918, a record held by no other division, though I feel sure no other division envied us the distinction.

We now heard definitely that we were moving down to the Somme to join the 5th Army under General Gough, under the arrangement that had been made to take over a further twenty five miles of front from the French.

26 January

On January 26th at 6.0 a.m. we splashed our way out of Dambra Camp singing a fervent 'Goodbyee' and hoped we had seen the last of the Ypres Salient.

We marched to Herzeele and in about ordinary marching time, despite the weak condition of many of the men. Here we found billets left in such a dirty condition by the last occupiers (a battalion of a crack London Regiment), that the unusual course was adopted of sending in a complaint about the matter, which would result in a severe censure reaching the battalion in question.

As soon as we had settled in, a 'pow-wow' of all officers of the battalion was called at Battalion Headquarters. We feared serious business was to be discussed, but it was much more serious than we had at first thought. A terrible thing had happened. We heard unofficially, but from a very reliable source, that one of our junior officers had actually failed to notice the Divisional General passing us on the road, during the march.

27 January

On the 27th the battalion marched back to Proven near Poperinghe to entrain for the Somme. Len and I worked the usual game by disappearing to the Stores with the Orderly Room boxes, and 'helping' to load up until the battalion had moved off. This of course meant riding to Proven instead of walking. We passed the battalion on the way, and tactfully drew the curtains at the rear of our motor wagon. We arrived at Proven railway siding in advance of them and, after deciding that loading Army Mules and transport into wagons was a much over-estimated recreation, we slipped off and found a canteen until the battalion arrived.

It was quite dark before stores, horses, mules, wagons and men in this order of merit, were all entrained. We decided that we ought to travel in the stores van in order to be responsible for the safety of the orderly room luggage. It was also a cold night and we had seen a little brazier and coal in the van.

The fire was burning nicely and we had made ourselves comfortable high on the top of a pile of blankets, where the warmth from the fire rose soothingly after an hour or two on the cold railway siding.

We were wondering what time we would leave when suddenly three shrill whistles gave the signal for all lights out, enemy aircraft over.

We were in a quandary. We could not and did not want to throw the fire out on to the line, and if we closed the doors we would get smoked out. While we were busy arguing about it, an officer's voice yelled "Put that ... light out" in a manner that made promptitude more than a virtue. We closed the doors at once and immediately afterwards heard the drone of heavy laden bombing planes overhead. We could hear the crash of bombs in and around Poperinghe and the shrieking of our anti-aircraft guns, and would dearly have liked to open the doors and watch, as we lay there gasping with the smoke. We hoped the raid might be over soon, or we stood a good chance of becoming martyrs for the sake of the safety of the Railway siding.

Those on the higher seats quickly repented of their eminence and sought room on the little floor space available in search of the little fresh air that came up through the flooring. Just as we were feeling at the last gasp, the 'All clear' sounded and we flung open the doors while we gulped mouthfuls of fresh air and the smoke belched out of the van.

It was not till our arrival at Méricourt l'Abbé at dawn the next morning that we found we were all as black as sweeps, and everything in the van was in a similar state including the beef and bacon for the whole battalion.

We marched from Méricourt l'Abbé to Bray-sur-Somme, arriving there about 2.0 p.m.

The billets here were of the poorest description. Many of the inhabitants of the village had left, and many buildings were available, but they were nearly all built only of wattle and daub. With bombing and long use as billets by French Senegalese troops one could walk in from the street or from one room to another without troubling to go through where the door had once been. Most of the daub had disappeared and a big part of the wattle had evidently been pulled out and used for fuel. To add to these discomforts, the village estaminets charged Fcs 1-75 for a bottle of very poor beer, and the same prices for a mess tin of worse coffee.

At Bray Pat fell across a cousin who was leading the higher life as chauffeur to a Brigadier General in the Tank Corps. Pat did not fail to fully explain to him what he really thought about Tanks despite the fact that good beer could be obtained at the Tank Brigade Canteen at a reasonable figure. On the 29th we marched out of Bray-sur-Somme with no great regret. Not far from the village we passed the Tank headquarters and practice ground where we saw some of the new Whippet Tanks at practice. They looked much less unwieldy and more nimble than the tanks that we had met with in the third Battle of Ypres. On the heights outside Bray we entrained again at the Plateau station for Peronne. The run to Peronne was most interesting.

The line ran along the Somme river and marshes the whole way. Alongside the new line we were running on, ran the old railway line battered out of recognition, and here and there wreckage of engines and wagons. In one place was a large field of agricultural machinery and implements of all kinds. These had been collected by the enemy during their late tenancy, and they evidently had not time to take them along when they retired.

We detrained at Peronne at the wrecked station and marched through the town. There had been some fine buildings at one time, but the place was almost in ruins. On every building left could be seen the German billeting marks. Every place had been marked with its billeting capacity, so many officers, so many men. Very few civilians remained in the town. It was bitterly cold when we reached a French camp at Haut Allaines after a long march, arriving in the dark and finding insufficient tents to meet the requirements of the battalion. When the men were eventually accommodated, the Orderly Room was still without quarters, and it was midnight before we managed to secure a tent and get it up. Long after the battalion was asleep we were busy there writing out battalion orders for the morning. The typewriter could not be unloaded and we had to do our best with frozen fingers and pencils, writing every copy out separately. We left camp again early the next morning, and during the march came across a typical example of Hun vandalism. The great high road for miles had been lined each side with great trees, every one had been cut down. Most had been removed, and no doubt made use of, but many remained just rolled into the ditches at the side awaiting removal.

At the end of the day we finished up at what had once been the village of Sorel-le-Grand. The place had evidently been blown up during the enemy's retreat. A few wooden huts had been put up since, and a large Y.M.C.A. hut erected. A good deal of Orderly Room work must be done that night, as we expected reaching the support trenches the following day.

The typewriter and boxes were unloaded long before we had found a home for them, and were dumped in the road.

We eventually came across a cellar without a house. The house was completely razed to the ground, but we found a hole amongst the debris which led us down a few stone steps into a strongly brick-arched cellar. We found a little fireplace and after making sure that at least some of the smoke would go up the hole where the chimney once had been, we 'borrowed' some coal and wood and soon had our quarters nice and warm. The smoke from the fire did seem to have some doubt as to which was really the chimney and divided itself about equally between that and the staircase.

To make our whereabouts known to those interested, we stuck up our little signpost at the top of the stairs, so that visitors would not make the mistake of entering by the chimney.

We were quite cosy inside however, and the smoke did no more than counteract the unpleasant smells that pervaded the cellar before.

Our arrival in the district had evidently been duly announced, as it had not long been dark before the three whistles were blown, and all lights were put out. We did not trouble to put our candles out after making tests from outside and found our light quite invisible.

A big number of enemy planes were out and commenced dropping bombs freely, but unlike the old Salient at Ypres where a bomb could hardly be dropped without damaging somebody or something, this district had any amount of spare room, where bombs could be dropped with safety. Most of the battalion spent the night watching the bombing raid, as it was much too noisy to get any sleep.

Investigations at dawn revealed the ironic fact that the Germans had been bombing the dead instead of the living. The only place close at hand that had suffered was the village cemetery where a number of their own troops had been buried. The condition of the graves was better left undescribed.

31 January

The next day (January 31st) we moved up to occupy support trenches behind Gouzeaucourt at the cheerfully named spot 'Dead Man's Corner'. It was a surprise to be able to take the limbers by daylight right up to the back of the trench, which was evidently not under direct enemy observation, as were the trenches in the old area.

The trenches themselves, though not in good condition, were dry. Part of the battalion occupied a sap, twenty feet below earth which was perfectly dry and smelled sweet compared to the wet, vile smelling saps we had been accustomed to. We managed a fine Orderly Room down here. Quite a big compartment with tables and forms complete, and to add to the general comfort four good wire frames which made capital beds. I felt quite sorry for 'Quarters' and Len who were at some unearthly spot very likely dodging bombs.

It was, however, decided that there was sufficient accommodation for all the Orderly Room staff and baggage, so word was sent down to the Transport lines by runner.

Len arrived the next morning when the Transport came up with the rations, wondering whether 'Quarters' had arrived before him. When he found that he had not arrived we were anxious, as it was quite dark, a strange neighbourhood, and part of the journey across country.

1 February 1918

Being a great favourite with the H.Q. runners, they set out to track him, but reached the Transport lines without meeting him on the way, to hear that he had left there only a few minutes after the Transport had left. It was eleven o'clock the next morning when he appeared, weary, footsore and hungry. His experiences of that night related in his now inimitable manner were highly amusing.

After the records of the Battalion having come to grief in the line the previous July, it had been decided that in the future, when the Battalion went into the line 'Q' should remain with the Transport in charge of the records, and had thus become to describe himself as a non-combatant, though in reality, Transport lines were often a deal more unsafe than being in the line.

When orders came for him and Len to bring the boxes up to 'Dead Man's Corner' Len had left with the limbers. 'Q' not being quite ready, was left putting a few odd books that had been left out of the boxes, into his pack, intending to catch up the limbers and put his pack on board. He delayed a little longer than he had intended, but thought he would have no difficulty in catching them up.

He started off in the wrong direction and, having travelled for sometime, eventually espied a Mess Cart going along the road in the distance. Taking it for granted that it belonged to our battalion, he made after it as hard as he could, but found the pace too much with his pack heavy with books. Feeling comfortable that he was in the right direction he decided to rest while the mess cart disappeared into the growing darkness. Trudging along in the darkness later, he nearly ran on to a sentry's bayonet. He enquired if a mess cart had passed that way belonging to the 6th Cheshires. The sentry had not seen the mess cart, and did not seem to have heard of the 'Cheshires'.

He was allowed to proceed and later reached a deserted village. He sat down to think things out when he heard footsteps approaching, and nearly fell foul of another sentry.

Asking this sentry where this road would lead to if he kept on, he received the startling reply "Doberitz".

When he heard that he was in imminent danger of crossing our front line 'Q' felt sure at last that he was in the wrong place. To convince him completely, the enemy dropped two or three shells uncomfortably near, and rattled a few machine gun bullets merrily along the village street. Considering that our Battalion was only in support, 'Q' was not doing so badly.

The sentry directed him to the H.Q. of the battalion there, and with becoming modesty 'Q' allowed himself to be led into a dugout with some of the men, to wait for daylight. 'Q' said they must have been rather a particular crowd, as they foisted him off to the Regimental Sgt. Major when they found he had too many stripes and crowns about him. He was given our location in the morning, and duly arrived, informing us that he had just come back from the front line.

Pat had not been feeling fit for some days, and was invited to bed in our room at night where there was a bit more comfort and space than with the signallers. The Signal Officer came in one night while we were working and Pat asleep in a dark corner, making weird noises. The officer cocked his ears and wanted to know what the noise was. I explained that it was Pat who refused to report 'Sick'. The Signal Officer walked over with a light to have a look at him, and then went away and brought the Medical Officer in to see the unusual phenomenon of a sick man refusing to 'Report Sick'. Result. Hospital first thing in the morning. He was very weak, but not too weak to spare me the usual flow of eloquence anent people who could not mind their own thrice adjectived business.

6 February

On the 6th we left our comfortable quarters at 'Dead Man's Corner' for the front line at Gouzeaucourt. It was again a case of reaching the front line for safety.

Gouzeaucourt itself was always being more or less shelled and swept by machine gun fire, more especially by night, as the enemy were aware that the front line in this sector could only be reached through the village itself, so he did his best to keep the traffic as low as possible. We entered the village from the valley at the rear, by a narrow gully that had once been fitted along both sides with numerous 'baby-elephant' dugouts. These had been shelled to such an extent that the gully was filled with wreckage, and it was a most uncomfortable journey scrambling in the darkness over the wreckage of duckboards and twisted corrugated steel roofs, and stumbling into shell holes, while shells fell in the close vicinity. Reaching the main road through the village, which we had to traverse for some distance, we found it being swept by M.G. fire and waited for the interval. There was no loitering during the short interval, and good times were recorded along the short stretch before we reached the shelter of buildings where we turned down a side lane.

The companies quickly took up their positions on the outskirts of the village overlooking another valley. Headquarters took over the H.Q. premises of the outgoing battalion in a sap dug straight down from the level of the road under a high bank. Here, in the darkness, the usual confusion reigned while the late tenants vacated, and we took over the tenancy.

Things were not too comfortable in the narrow lane, everyone was anxious to get indoors, the transport horses were restive under the noise of the guns. The two entrances to the sap were very low, and after squeezing down half a dozen steps, the angle of descent suddenly became steeper, and one found oneself suddenly jammed tight with no possibility of further progress without taking off one's pack, which was difficult owing to lack of space, with half a dozen followers close behind pushing and swearing in the blackness, unaware of the reason of the stoppage. Down below there was a fair amount of accommodation, though the atmosphere was anything but sweet.

I had the Regimental Sgt. Major for companion in a little two bunked cavity all by itself. During the week that we spent here, things were fairly quiet during the daytime, with any amount of shelling and gas after dark.

It was at this period that the Battalion of Herts was withdrawn from our Brigade under the new scheme that reduced Battalions in a Brigade from four to three, in order to make up new Brigades and Divisions.

Only two opinions were held amongst the troops with regard to this procedure.

The first and favourite opinion was that the War Office had badly overbought in Brass Hats and Gold Braid, and were suddenly compelled to appoint many new Generals to use up the stock, and Lance Corporals were supposed to be busy inspecting their 'housewives' to ascertain whether they still had sufficient needles and cotton to stitch another stripe on.

The other opinion seemed to be that it was only a game to bluff Ludendorff, who, when he saw new Divisions springing up suddenly from nowhere, would refuse to play any more because we were cheating.

From the bank above our dugout, we could see the village of Gonnelieu across the valley, with German troops passing to and fro, also in the valley three or four derelict tanks, and we could actually watch our shells dropping in the village opposite, raising somewhat of a dust, although at times we had to bolt for our hole when the enemy retaliated.

Some days it was quiet enough to have a walk round the village, bent on exploration. Our chief finds were the stock of a small drapery store, and a German Medical Store. Out with a couple of runners one day we found in a cellar a dump of German 18 pounder shells. While interested, we suddenly heard a shell coming with that unmistakable sound of 'a close one'. We flung ourselves down wondering what the sensation of going up with a shell dump would be like.

It fell twenty yards away. It was a 'Dud'.

The sap was not many yards away, but we found the difficulties of its entrance, for once, non-existent. Our nerves were not quite settled until we found that the 'R.S.M.' had gone his rounds without his 'water' bottle.

14 February

On the night of the 14th we were relieved by the Black Watch. Their companies had taken over and our companies had left.

Headquarters, both Black Watch and Cheshires were still hob-nobbing in the sap. It always took the Black Watch and Cheshires' H.Q. officers a long time to wish one another good luck etc. etc. It was late when the R.S.M., myself and two runners at last got away, still leaving the Colonel, the Adjutant and two more runners to follow. We were not going back into support at Dead Man's Corner but into reserve at Dessant Camp on the edge of Bois de Dessant near the village of Fins. Gouzeaucout was receiving its nightly shelling as we left the sap. Our way lay right along the highroad, and our desire to make a run for it could only be satisfied to the extent of treading on the Sgt. Major's heels as he stepped out at a smart pace which we considered not nearly smart enough. As we went along shells were dropping on the road behind us, and we wondered how the Colonel and Adjutant were faring in the rear of us.

Shortly we heard someone coming along at a smart pace in the rear of us, and they appeared out of the darkness, the C.O. carrying his steel helmet in his hands, so that he would not lose it while running. A shell splinter had taken off the corner of the attaché case he was carrying, but that was all the damage they had incurred.

We joined forces but it was another mile before we felt easy enough in our minds to slacken down from a really hot pace.

Dessant Camp near Fins was quite a good camp of 'Nissen' huts and here we found Pat back from hospital, where he protested he had been starved.

The camp was laid out spaciously in order to lessen casualties in the event of bombing raids by enemy aircraft, and outside most of the huts, small trenches had been dug. These would be considerably more safe than the huts during a raid, if there had only been enough trenches.

In Fins, half a mile away, the Divisional Concert Party was giving a pantomime, using as a theatre the ruins of the largest building in the place, patched up with canvas and timber. This held about 300 men, and was reserved for one night for our battalion. It was really a good show and hugely enjoyed.

When we left after the performance we found everywhere icebound, where two or three hours previously the roads were inches deep in mud.

On the following night a disastrous air raid took place. The camp itself was missed. At Fins, however, a big canteen had been erected and through a lighted brazier being left outside in the darkness, a concentration of bombs was dropped, wrecking the crowded canteen. Many of the battalion were killed outright, others mutilated to such an extent that identification was difficult, in fact impossible in some cases. A Roll Call in camp in perfect darkness was the only means of estimating and checking the casualties.

18 February

On February 18th the battalion left camp again for the line, on the sector left of the position held during the last turn in. I remained with 'Q' at the Transport Lines at Fins, while Len took duty in the line. From documents and orders passing through the Orderly Room from Brigade and Division we gathered that a big enemy offensive was looming ahead. Big stunts on night wiring, continuous patrols and raids for identification of opposing troops seemed to be the order of the day, or night would perhaps be more correct. Every night from the Transport Lines, air raids could be seen in progress, and we wondered nightly when our turn would come. The stores staff got busy digging trenches outside their quarters, and the stock of sandbags for carrying rations was sadly depleted to protect the huts. The strange sight was seen of store men oiling their rifles and actually putting ammunition into their pouches in the place of cigarettes. During this spell of raids our planes and anti-aircraft guns seemed to be conspicuous by their absence. One night however, the story gained credence that the raiders had reached as far back as Peronne and disturbed Corps Headquarters, for suddenly one night our artillery got very busy indeed, and it was rumoured played havoc with enemy aerodromes. Whether this was true or not, the fact remained that we had a little peace for the next few nights.

26 February

On the 26th the battalion returned to Dessant Camp where 'C' Company immediately commenced to practise for a raid.

It was at this time that Pat evidently thought that a little change of diet was necessary, in the signallers' quarters at any rate. He might have been seen walking stiffly out of camp, keeping a rifle out of sight beneath his great coat, making for Dessant Woods. In the evening savoury odours would be noticed emanating from the signallers' hut, along with a peculiar sibilant sound, which proved on investigation to be bones of pigeons and crows going through the last stage of polishing after the stew was finished. It was fortunate that signallers were not very often troubled with ammunition inspections, though no doubt Pat would have been delighted to explain to the inspecting officer that shooting pigeons and crows with a rifle was really splendid practice.

26th February 1918

Dear Kid,

Another nice long letter from you today dated the 22nd so letters seem to be coming through better at last. Sorry Jim's birthday card was a day late.

Am afraid he won't make his way as a sweet shop proprietor. His idea of eating up the stock to get sold out quickly isn't good business. Shall have to make an ironmonger out of him. But he is a lad thank goodness and not quite an angel.

I have missed two of his birthdays now, hope I don't miss anymore, as I don't want him to get too 'growed up' before I come home, I have seen little enough of his kiddy days yet.

The lads came back to camp in good trim last night. Times had been a little more exciting for them this time in, but nothing out of the way.

One company is leaving in the early hours on a hazardous game, while the remainder of us have that rotten job of sitting and waiting, wishing them good luck. They have been out a day or two practising the trick. We shan't sleep much till they come back for breakfast with us.

We have been giving them a good send off tonight. We have a big French hut in the camp (Joe will know what they are like) and we have made it into a concert hall for the evening. Got the band in there and plenty of talent, beer, smokes and eatables and have had a great time. Len is doing the whole concert through, while I did the first half, Pearson is there now for the second part of the programme.

Don't know what you will think of my letter writing lately, but if you won't show my letter round I'll give myself away just for once. As Pearson tells me 'the older I get, the softer'.

After the concert Pat, who is not detailed for the stunt, informs me that he is going to ask permission from the Signal Officer to go up. Of course we had the usual row about it, but I fully expected he would get snubbed for his pains. However judge my surprise when he came to tell me he was going up.

I was awfully mad about it, and said quite a lot of things I deserved clubbing for, and finished up by refusing to see him off and sticking in the orderly room in a sulk, like a kid.

Pearson had heard the row, and shewed his sympathy in the usual wrong way.

After they had gone off you can guess I was pretty miserable, and Pearson, I suppose for a joke plied the rum sympathy freely. Finished up by making a pretty rotten fool of myself, telling him in no complimentary terms what I thought of his job and mine, slammed my books about and walked off to the signallers, where I suppose I told them I was a signaller etc., etc. ad lib, much to their loss of sleep.

The weather too was enough to make anyone miserable and make it difficult for the lads that had gone up. I got away from there and went out to find the Artillery and waited to watch the barrage start, finishing up there by helping an 8" howitzer. When the guns finished I set off to meet the lads coming down again.

Goodness knows where I got to, and I began to wonder what had happened to the lads. Must have sat down to think the matter out. Anyway the rain had stopped and the sun was well up when I was wakened by someone calling me sweet names (I don't think).

From what I learned in a chastened spirit on the way back, the raid had been a huge success and Pat coming first of all to let me know all about it, and finding me not at home had hunted me down. I was also informed with vigour that if I hadn't been various kinds of superlative idiots, he would by that time have had his breakfast.

I reported in due humility to the Orderly Room, found them hard at work, Len looking anxious, Pearson highly amused. On Pat enquiring what should be done with me, he ordered Pat to take me away, wash me and put me to bed. I reported again about dinner time ready for work and Len, solicitous as usual, brought me my dinner, which I nearly threw at him when I saw it (stew), but I merely murmured that I was not hungry. Pearson suggested a tot of rum as a pick-me-up, well if looks could kill, his headstone would be up by now.

Call this an episode if you like, but it is not for publication.

However they must have annoyed Fritz terribly over the raid, as instead of going back for a rest, they rushed us all up today to hold him down and here we are again so to speak.

Am retrieving my reputation by leaving Len and Pearson behind. All is peace between Pat and I (for a time at least anyway).

Got another letter from you last night, also one from Madge. You mustn't get talking of leave in six months, as leave is quietening down again very much, and if we don't send more than we are doing at present, dates will get back again nearer 18 than 6, but of course the war won't stand that long.

Glad you have managed to let the house after all. It will be less worry for you, and an invitation to tea any time is a guarantee that things will be alright.

Glad to hear Mr Wheeler has absolutely got the sack from the Army. My congrats to him next time you see him.

Am in the pink (now). Postman just came up now and in a big hurry for back, so I must finish. Don't know yet whether he has anything for me. Hope so.

A big kiss each for you and the boy. Will try to write again tomorrow.

Your loving husband Walter.

29 February

On the evening of the 29th 'C' Company proceeded up the line for their raid. Pat, though not belonging to 'C' Company, persuaded the Signal Officer by some means to allow him to assist with the signals for the raid. I felt I ought to remonstrate with him, but was only laughed at for my pains. Feeling rather hurt at the way my remarks were met, I sought sympathy from 'Q' who poured it out with a lavish hand. Thus fortified I left camp in the darkness to see if I could see anything of the raid, or get any news of how it was going.

It was pitch dark and raining heavily. Our artillery was pounding away at the time, and I eventually fell in with a battery of 8 inch guns and watched them working. During a lull I enquired whether they were firing in connection with the raid. Learning much to my disgust that they were not bothering about our raid, but were firing right across to the Russian front, I left them and decided to go on and meet the boys coming out. The raiding party was busy having breakfast in camp when I eventually found my way back.

The raid had been a success, casualties small and they had accounted for a good number of Bosche. They had obtained identification of troops, some prisoners and had demolished a sap.

Hurriedly presenting myself for duty at the Orderly Room, I was immediately ordered out again to get myself clean and respectable, so I took the opportunity to have a nap in Pat's bed in the signallers' quarters while some good soul dried my clothes. I wakened to listen patiently (more or less) to a homily from Pat on the idiocy of my trying to find my way about alone in the dark, when I could not do it properly even by daylight.

The same afternoon surprise orders came to move up at once into support at 'Dead Man's Corner'. Everyone seemed on tenterhooks and communications from higher quarters seemed to have 'WIND UP' written all over them in invisible but plain type.

Things were quiet however, but too quiet to be comfortable.

2 March 1918

On March 2nd snow commenced to fall heavily and by noon all tracks were obliterated, everywhere was a white glare. That night we moved up into the line at Gouzeaucourt again, losing our track on the way, and having to retrace our steps about half the distance before we were put right.

Someone made the remark that we looked like the famous picture 'The Retreat from Moscow' but the language used as we continually fell into holes filled with snow was much more easily understood than Russian.

The first night on the line the enemy put a barrage round one of our Lewis Gun positions and collected the team and the gun, despite efforts to get to their assistance. Three men were killed and two officers and seven men were wounded in attempting a rescue. Higher Quarters let us know that they were distinctly annoyed about this incident, chiefly on account of the fact that we were unable to report the gun team as 'Killed' to relieve their minds. To make matters worse, the following night, a sergeant leaving a post after finding all well, left to visit the next post, but was never seen or heard of again.

Another serious affair cropped up at this time. The Mess Sergeant, who could hardly tell the difference between 'Cerebos' and 'Kruschen' without his spectacles, had a fall and broke his glasses. Considering him a source of danger in the Mess he was sent off to hospital for glasses, and was never seen with the Brigade again.

5 March

On March 5th one of three epoch making events occurred, such an event as stands out in one's memory. Pat was appointed Mess Caterer in place of the unfortunate Sergeant.

The post was no sinecure on the Somme. The nearest place to do his shopping was a large B.E.F. canteen at Peronne, twelve miles away. I kindly offered to work him a string bag for his shopping, he was also proffered much good advice and warned particularly not to forget himself and walk in some evening under the impression that he was at the golf club, pick up some officer's glass of whisky and commence telling the tale how he did the eighteenth hole (shell) in two under bogey.

As a suburban gardener, he might know the difference between a cauliflower and a calceolaria, but could he judge a salmon by the label on the tin? We felt convinced that the matter was fraught with serious perils both for Pat himself and the H.Q. Mess generally.

About this time leave of absence for 48 hours, to visit Amiens, was being granted to a few men daily. Great interest was taken in the tales of men returning from these excursions, all expressing the opinion that Amiens was a really 'bon' place.

Captain ... (affectionately known as Tubby and hereafter so called), Assistant Adjutant and Mess President conceived, with Pat, the brilliant idea that the Mess required refitting with crockery and that the only place to get what was required was Amiens.

7 March

On the 7th the enemy opened the day with a big artillery bombardment on the left of our sector and sent over big quantities of gas.

We thought that the expected big offensive was opening at last. H.Q. Officers were greatly excited, and one or two of them seemed doubtful of their efficiency with their revolvers so were hunting up spare rifles and bayonets. The matter, however, proved to be purely a local affair, nothing big developed, though we received a big dose of gas and spent most of the day in gas helmets. The gas expert on H.Q. was urged by the R.S.M. to get out on top to take a sample of the gas in case it was a new brand, but the expert, who was evidently not out for honours, was wisely convinced that it was the same old rotten 'Phosgene'.

When things were quiet, our quarters in the tunnel were quite comfortable, though like all underground warrens, that had previously been occupied by the Germans, it was infested with lice, which were anxious to become naturalised British at the first opportunity.

In a four bunk compartment, Captain 'Tubby', Captain 'Y' – Intelligence Officer, the R.S.M. and myself were accommodated.

Captain 'Y' had recently been home on leave and, whilst on leave, had been married. A picture of his bonny bride hung over his bunk.

'Tubby', from his bunk, would annoy his particular chum Captain 'Y' by throwing kisses to the lady and then demanding that she be placed with her face to the wall, whilst he took off his boots and tunic and wrapped himself in his blanket.

One of Tubby's accomplishments that we admired was his ability to shave himself while lying on his back in his bunk.

8th March 1918

Dear Milly,

Got two letters from you tonight posted March 3rd and 4th. I got no letters from you yesterday or the previous day, so these just fill up the gap.

Sorry to hear Mrs Lloyd at Sale is so ill. Don't they seem to have a lot of sickness in the house this last year or two.

Am waiting the arrival of the book you sent, with interest, and shall soon let you know whether you ought to read it. I may possibly agree with your mother. I can almost get the drift of the book from your few remarks about it. I think it is a fact as you say that a woman forgives a deal more than a man. That is a woman's mistake. She will take a man for what he is, what he is going to be, overlooking what he may have been. It is perhaps, after all, well that she does. But will a man do the same? Morally speaking, a young woman has as much right to sow wild oats before marriage as a man, or perhaps I should say, a man has no more right to do so than a woman. A woman from her nature cannot run the risk, a man from his nature, can, and none be the wiser. On the face of it then, does it not seem cowardly and unfair that the man should always demand so much more than the woman does. I think, however, if she did demand her rights (for it is her due) it would go a long way to doing away with the "wild oats" business, or on the other hand it might cause a shortage in husbands. In their hearts I know every man who marries a good wife will be of the same way of thinking. I don't know whether I have judged the drift of the book rightly, but I fancy so.

Fancy Percy not writing a line to his mother since last June, it is beyond comment, but one never knows, he may be in France, and Mildred blaming England for it, who knows. But if he is only going to write every time there is an addition to the family, I hope he will have many and often.

That little rumoured rest doesn't seem to solidify someway, we are still down the big hole, and though we move shortly, it is only a matter of a half hour walk and down another rabbit hole. Shall expect to find that little white tuft growing in a little while. I was out for a breather this morning, and it was a glorious morning. Just fancy hearing larks singing while shells are shrieking through the air. I would give something to be able to take a photograph and send you a picture of the utter desolation here. I stood on a little knoll this morning and had quite a birds eye view of the village we are buried under. Poor little village. There are signs of it being rather a pretty little place at sometime, with lots of little mud walled whitewashed cottages and a few big houses, but now there isn't a whole wall standing anywhere. There are boys with us now in the battalion here, who have at one time been billeted in the villages in front of us that we are shelling everyday. I was however rudely interrupted in my survey by being asked if I couldn't see Fritz's observation balloon up in front.

I do like to hear from you that the Jim boy is so fond of having his books read to him. It isn't every mother that will take the trouble. I shouldn't say take the trouble, I ought to say, it isn't every mother that finds a pleasure and a joy in interesting a youngster.

I may seem a bit soft, but you don't perhaps know how badly I feel, that he might perhaps be too big when I come home for good, to come on my knee and let me tell him tales of the big war, not gruesome tales, but interesting things that would hold him. Tales of fine men that helped the weaker ones, tales of brightness under hard times and tales of things that would mould him and hold his interest at the same time, for there are many such tales to be told. And here am I out here kid, while he is growing up, even talking of going to school, when I want to have him on my knee and help a little to mould him into what I would like him to be. You have a big advantage over me little woman, and I am missing the best of him. That is one of my troubles. You have given him to me, and here I am. But there is one thing good amongst it all. I think my experiences – what I have learned, and what I have felt, have made me more fit to be your husband and his father, than if I had stayed at home.

I know you don't feel jealous of a gift you gave me, but out here away from you all, his little supple body, his bonny face, his perfect health, well, he is such a perfect little gift, that I don't know whether I love his mother or himself the best. I think really after all I am a children's man, despite my relapse in not playing blind man's bluff at Christmas.

We must someday have that little Joan, and like you, I have a hankering after Alford, the smell of the red thorn, the lilac, the glow of the yellow laburnum, perhaps the lap of the water on the prow of the boat. She should be the counterpart of the Jim boy then, first healthy and strong, then pretty, then with a mind like her mother, a love for all things good and beautiful in nature, a cheerful youngster, perhaps a bit of a tomboy as will be needful as Jim's sister. But after all, if we can't afford such luxuries as Alford, what is the matter with Cheadle Hulme. We have the laburnum, the lilac, the apple blossom, and we are only short of the river. We could go and sit by the brook at Adswood near the bridges, and as you always tell me, imagination is a wonderful thing. I think it must be your two fine letters tonight, but I feel in a most contented state of mind. Feel someway, that I am making myself worthy a little bit, of all the good things that have been vouchsafed to me. A man doesn't deserve really to be so happy as I have been with you, without having to do something for it.

I feel you near me somehow tonight telling me to do my best, be always cheerful and wait till the end patiently, then come home and say I have done my best and have played the man. Then I feel I shall have deserved a little of the happiness that is waiting for me with the best little wife that ever God made, and gave to a man.

Everybody at Hqs is sleeping now except the sentries, the officer on duty, and the good old signallers, so I will get down along with them and tell Jim to say a word for the sentry lads watching over the soldiers. Things are very quiet tonight and it is such a lovely night outside. A big long kiss my wife and such a hug for you and the little man, from your loving husband Walter.

9 March

On the 9th we were relieved from Gouzeaucourt and went into support again at 'Dead Man's Corner'. Things were so quiet and the weather so pleasant that H.Q. officers fixed themselves up with a garden seat in the open at the back of the trench, and only once tumbled into the trench in rather a hurry, when a very unexpected salvo of shells fell in close proximity.

Two days later we were relieved from here by the 9th Division, and wended our way by darkness to Tyke Dump near Dessant Camp, where we were packed in open trucks on a light railway. It was a bitterly cold night and we were stiff with cold when we arrived at York Camp, Moislains, still in the darkness.

We were now a few miles nearer Peronne again and the humorists would have it that we had been given a decent start to catch an early train from there, when the next enemy offensive commenced.

York Camp had originally been a French camp and four huge huts held the four companies of the battalion. From communications passing through the Orderly Room from Brigade and Divisional Headquarters the next few days, it was easily gathered that the atmosphere was becoming electrical on the Somme.

Sheets of orders poured in giving minute details of what was to be done immediately on receipt of the signal 'Assemble', and precise particulars given of where the battalion was to move to at once. A tank was sent up to the battalion to perform some new evolutions, and the Brigadier General turned up to give a lecture.

There was something radically different between this speech and the speech he gave before we went into action at the 3rd Battle of Ypres.

After the lecture we knew that whenever the enemy offensive opened we had not a dog's chance of holding it.

Instead of hearing where we were to stay our advance and 'dig-in', we heard vague hints of good defensive positions rapidly being prepared in our rear.

Stereotyped phrases from previous lectures before going into action became woefully contorted

"We shall……."	became	"We hope to ……"
"The Artillery will……"	became	"The Artillery hopes to……"
"Our Aircraft will……."	became	"Our Aircraft hope……."
"Support will move forward"	became	Blank
"You will be relieved by"	became	Blank

After previous lectures the Brigadier had always bandied the usual hoary joke about 'Divisional Rest' afterwards. Even this was omitted. But the Tommies famous motto still held "Sufficient unto the day is the evil thereof".

Whilst in camp here Sgt H … arrived from Rouen. He was in charge of our Records at the Base Orderly Room. He had thought the time nice and quiet for a trip to the battalion for a little holiday with his old friend 'Q' but ostensibly to check the records.

Not much checking had been done however when I left the battalion on the afternoon of the 18th for 48 hours leave to visit Amiens in company with three others. Walking the six miles to the station at Peronne we hoped to get a train from there the same morning and gain a night in Amiens. Much to our disgust we were compelled to wait for a morning train and in the meantime make ourselves as comfortable as we could, with no blankets, in a big shed which had a good roof but whose walls fell three feet short of reaching the ground.

The floor was not even boarded and our uniforms, which had been specially 'poshed-up' for the occasion, somewhat suffered during our slumbers.

Amiens, however, came up to expectations early the next day. We had been recommended to a little hostel close to the station where we lorded it to the extent of ordering a bedroom each. A good meal was, as usual in such cases, the first item on the agenda, then we went out to see the town. We seemed somehow to remember electric cars and smart shops as things seen in some previous existence.

A fine feature of the arrangements made for the troops visiting Amiens was a splendid B.E.F. canteen, where really good meals could be had cheaply, served at little tables. This canteen arrangement occupied perhaps half the room, while a Cinema show ran in the remainder, and one could watch the show while having a meal or lighter refreshments at the tables. Strolling round the town in the afternoon, we saw crowds of people entering the large theatre to see a matinee show. Deciding to do the thing in style and join the throng, we paid a fancy price for seats in the stalls without bothering about the bill of fare. Judge our pained surprise when we found the stage occupied by our Divisional Concert Party, whose shows we had seen various times for nothing.

The only redeeming feature to relieve our pent up feelings was the fact that it turned out to be in aid of some charity. The theatre was crowded with many people standing, and we gained an undeserved and effusive expression of gratitude from some ladies by offering our seats and leaving in search of something more novel.

We spent the whole of the following morning in Amiens Cathedral. Though many of its treasures were covered by sandbag barricades, notably the glorious carvings at the main entrance and the twelve apostles in the interior, the beauty, nobility and serenity of the place gave one a wonderful feeling of peace and quiet, out of the noise, the dirt and turbulence of war. The beautiful rose window over the Great Altar was still uncovered at that time, and great shafts of sunlight slanting across the nave made a wonderful picture.

One of the party, who had not been with us during the morning, met us at dinner with the pleasant news that he had found the Public Swimming Bath, and we were so keen at the idea of going for a swim immediately after dinner, that we made only a moderate meal, remembering parental warnings of our youth about bathing on a full stomach, though one of the party thought a big meal would be safe in his case, as he usually swam on his back.

We returned from the baths in no amiable mood and expressed our feelings fluently to our guide who had been able to read the sign over the baths, without noticing the bill on the door informing the public that the bath was closed till further notice owing to the coal shortage.

20 March

Our little holiday quickly came to an end and the evening of the 20th found us back at camp.

There seemed to have been merry goings-on in the Orderly Room. The Colonel had received orders to proceed to England for some special course and had given a farewell night in the mess. Pat being in charge of the catering, it was only natural that some of the rum punch found its way into the Orderly Room causing some loss of orderliness thereto.

The Somme Retreat

21 March 1918

On the morning of the 21st the storm broke.

It was very early and very misty when we heard the guns commence to roar. A signaller's head soon popped into the Orderly Room with the expected message 'Assemble'. Within the hour the battalion was on the move to Longesvenes under Major H ... Orderly Room Records, Stores etc. were ordered to stand by for further orders. Len went with the Battalion as clerk whilst 'Q' and I remained with the Records.

Early on Pat had set off to Peronne to do some shopping for the Mess and on his way back met Sgt. H ... of Rouen making great speed for Peronne, from where – we heard later – he caught the last train that left there for many a long day. He had badly misjudged the time for holidaying on the Somme, but to this day prides himself in the belief that he holds the speed record between Moislains and Peronne. Pat on arrival at Moislains found himself faced with a further trip with H.Q. rations to Longesvenes. All the next day we stood watching tanks and artillery falling back and stores and dumps in all directions being destroyed.

We were under no delusions as to how matters stood. Light Artillery was coming back practically into the camp, slewing round and taking up new positions, pulling out again in a few minutes without firing a shot, and retiring still further back.

It was not until the evening that we received our orders to move. All records and as much of the stores as could be carried on the transport available was to be moved, and any surplus was to be destroyed. At 8 o'clock that night we left with the Orderly Room records and as much stores as could be carried with the first wagon, and joined the endless stream of transport passing through Moislains on the Peronne Road.

At Haut Allaines we turned from the Peronne Road. We were evidently not going back by Peronne which pointed to the fact that the enemy was there or near by. Instead we struck west through Feuillaucourt and Clery reaching Méricourt about 3 a.m. the next morning. Here was a large camp that had originally been French, but latterly had been used by our troops as a reinforcement camp and school of courses. All troops coming into this corps area from leave or from schools, and stragglers lost from their units were all being collected here. They were not sent to their own units but made up into Companies and Battalions composite of all units and sent into the line at once.

Major G … of our Battalion, returning from leave, was put in charge of such a battalion, and gained his D.S.O. for the good work he did with his mixed battalion.

During the following afternoon Pat arrived with the storesmen and canteen staff, all with sore hearts and sore feet. The canteen stock had been liberally handed out, but most of it had to be destroyed along with the famous work of art perpetrated by one of the Canteen Staff, consisting of a silk back cloth painted with a copy of the Theatre Curtain at Stockport, representing Bramall Hall, which was used to decorate the canteen.

Late at night a part of the battalion came in, with the impression that they were all that remained of the battalion. They had fallen back through Peronne and Clery, both of these places being now in the hands of the enemy, and from what we could hear the whole of the 5th Army front was giving way all along the line against big odds.

This same night the camp was furiously bombed by enemy aircraft, but surprisingly little damage was done to the camp itself, though the transport traffic on the road through the camp was badly caught.

24 March

On the 24th the whole camp was ordered to fall further back to Bray-sur-Somme, and in the confusion of leaving camp four of us managed to get clear of the awful dust of the column of transport and infantry on the white road, and made our way quietly to Bray following a much more comfortable route. Passing through a little out of the way village we came upon the poor proprietor of an estaminet, who was making ready to leave his premises.

Rather than allow the vile Bosche to find his estaminet nicely stocked, he had laid out all his stock at the roadside and invited passing troops to help themselves, evidently having full faith in the Government to grant him suitable compensation. We hope his faith has been rewarded, as we took him at his word and left with a bottle of champagne each. Len (who had arrived at Méricourt l'Abbé with the only part of the battalion that could be found) and I went into partnership with our two bottles and only cleared one bottle between us before we arrived at Bray, where we arrived before the column from Méricourt l'Abbé. On their arrival we quickly found a purchaser for the remaining bottle, and with the proceeds thereof, made somewhat extensive purchases of slab cake in Bray, where shops were clearing out their stocks at bargain prices as they had only just been given notice to evacuate the place at once.

While waiting orders in Bray we were interested to see a great number of German prisoners being marched through. We thought at first that the tide of the battle must have turned in our favour, until it dawned on us that there was a big prisoners of war camp at Bray, and this was being cleared and the prisoners taken further back. The prisoners themselves seemed to be aware of what was happening and grinned at us, some threw a cheering remark to us regarding our immediate future, but we only grinned back and promised to send along a few more of their pals shortly, if only in sandbags.

When our orders finally arrived, it was evident there had been a mistake made, or a sudden change of plans. The column was quickly formed again and we turned back on the road we had come but changing direction shortly after leaving Bray, we crossed the Somme and passed through Cappy, which had been evacuated, then out on to the high ground beyond the village, where the transport was unlimbered and men and horses had a couple of hours rest.

In the evening all men that could be scraped together were paraded, and set off with the ration limbers to find the other part of the battalion, which was still actually in the lines, if there was such a thing as a line at this period. We had a long, tiring tramp before we actually found the battalion on the bank of the canal between Feuilleres and Buscourt. Here in the darkness we could hear the movements of the enemy on the other bank of the canal. We could hear what was evidently the shouting of their transport drivers and the clatter of the transport. They were evidently doing the same as we were, getting rations and stores up in the darkness.

We arrived at the battalion just at the moment that orders had been received to fall back to Herbecourt. The limbers could not be unloaded, so moved again with the battalion to Herbecourt.

Before reaching Herbecourt a halt was made and rations served out. Later, on reaching Herbecourt we passed through the ruins of the village and occupied an old, disused trench cut across the open fields. Ours was a very thin, attenuated line, with no sign of troops on either flank and we had not the faintest hope of holding it in case of an attack or even a bombardment, for the trench was not more than waist deep anywhere.

Possibly the C.O. and the officers on the flanks knew where troops were on our flanks, but as far as most of the men knew, we might have been the only men for miles in that part of the country. This was not by any means comforting.

It was about this time that officers had evidently been instructed to commence the tale that the retreat was simply a trap to draw the enemy forward to fall into the hands of the pick of the French and British Armies, who were waiting a few miles back to utterly smash the Germans.

This tale utterly failed in its purpose, which I suppose was to hearten the troops. In the first place, the troops were in no need of it, and in the second place, it was a poor intelligence that brought forth the idea of telling the troops that the pick of the armies lay anywhere outside their own particular unit. The officers who had the job of retailing this poor joke fully expected to get 'the bird' and got it.

The transport had left again in the darkness and nothing particularly exciting turned up before dawn.

25 March

During the morning (25th) we were shelled a little, whether searching or ranging we were not quite sure, but as nothing serious followed, we felt fairly comfortable that it was only searching and that the enemy had not located us, otherwise they would have had no difficulty in blowing us out of our apology of a trench.

About noon we were mustered and made our way back again towards the canal. It was understood that the enemy had made a passage over during the night on the divisional front next to ours, and we were to take part in a local counter attack.

We were hidden under cover in a sunken road whilst the C.O. and some other officers went forward to make some arrangements concerning co-operation with troops who were evidently in front of us. They were not long away, and on their return we gathered from what we overheard of the instructions given to officers, that we were to move forward as soon as our Artillery barrage opened. The C.O. disappeared again forward, leaving the Adjutant in charge, and we waited, more or less, patiently for the expected barrage. From where we were we could see a couple of eighteen pounders close to Herbecourt and saw them rattle a few shells over, then limber up and disappear. We wondered where the guns were that the expected barrage was to come from. While still wondering the C.O. suddenly returned in a frightful temper, flew at the Adjutant, told him his character and fortune in a few choice and expressive sentences, and the troops were treated to the edifying spectacle of a row between the C.O. and the Adjutant.

We heard the Adjutant making efforts to explain that we were still waiting for the barrage, but we learned that the few shells we had heard actually constituted the barrage. Luckily, despite our non-appearance, the small counter attack had achieved its purpose of clearing our side of the canal bank for the time being.

It was dark when we returned again to the ruins of Herbecourt where we took shelter as best we could in cellars amongst the ruins. The ration limbers came up again during the night, Pat along with them with rations for the officers. They had come up from close by Bray-sur-Somme nearly ten miles away, and had to look forward to the same distance back again, with the probability of finding the Transport lines moved even further back during their absence. The

C.O. and Headquarters officers all occupied one rather large cellar, the R.S.M. found a little cellar, which we occupied jointly and called it the Orderly Room, after sticking up our little notice board, which I still carried as part of my equipment, along with the leather dispatch bag, maps, records, message pads etc., etc.

The R.S.M, who was having a heavy time of it, was dead beat, and lay down to snatch a little sleep, after instructing me to wake him up if anything fresh turned up. He was soon snoring, and I was trying to keep awake when I heard a motor cycle arrive outside and a Despatch Rider enquiring for the 6th Cheshires' Orderly Room. I went out and introduced myself, took the despatch and the rider disappeared again into the darkness, after expressing his opinions on war generally and the Somme Retreat particularly.

The village was being well shelled, so it did not take me long to 'stroll across' to Headquarters with the despatch. I handed it to the Orderly on duty and waited in the cellar passage to see if there was any reply or instruction, but only receiving a shout of "Alright Corporal" I scuttered back to my den. If I had known that the C.O. was at that moment holding a pow-wow with all the officers, I would have wakened the R.S.M.

I left him, however, and waited patiently expecting at any moment to receive some instructions to send round to the Company officers. Meanwhile the shelling grew worse, and at dawn it developed into a decent barrage all round the village. A particularly unkind shell landed somewhere above our cellar, rattling the place rather severely and covering us with dirt and dust. This saved me the trouble of waking the R.S.M. I told him of the despatch that had come in, and he decided to have a look round and see if there was anything doing.

He had scarcely disappeared when he returned with a rush with the news that we had the village to ourselves, but company might be expected at any minute. We grabbed our belongings and dashed up the cellar steps to find the battalion half a mile away from the village, falling back across the open in extended order, and German troops entering the other end of the village.

Regimental Sergeant Major and Lance Corporal did not stand on the order of their going, but each 'went' to the very best of their respective abilities.

We had covered about half the distance towards the battalion when something struck me heavily on the shoulder, causing me to come to earth suddenly with a force that I felt sure must have left an impression. The R.S.M. must have felt the ground shake for he turned to pick me up. This was his undoing, as I was up quickly and he lost his slight lead, and I reached the battalion half a head in front of him.

The men had then taken up a line, with Headquarters a few yards behind them in a big shell hole, and as there was a lull, they were having a bit of breakfast in the big shell hole.

The R.S.M., feeling very huffed at being left behind like a bit of 'buckshee' baggage, decided he would not join their breakfast table, so we found a good hole near by, and decided to breakfast by ourselves within sight and call in case H.Q. decided we might be wanted. Our rations were in one sandbag which had been somewhat shaken up during its rapid transit and were a little mixed. R.S.M.'s rations could not be distinguished (as they usually could be) from a Lance Corporal's rations, whereby said L/C gained a fall. After having breakfasted, we joined H.Q. and were met with a very uncalled for enquiry from the Adjutant as to where we had been.

The R.S.M had now quite passed the stage of being even nominally polite to the Adjutant who seemed to have altogether lost his head, and told him tersely, to the point and with considerable emphasis, actually where we had been. The Colonel seemed to be under the impression that we had been with them all the time.

Company Officers had just sent word that the men were short of ammunition. The R.S.M. thought he remembered seeing a small dump on the outskirts of the village, and immediately set off with a couple of men to try to get to it. This was the last I saw of the R.S.M for some days, though I thought at the time that it was the last we should see of him at all.

The battalion was falling back again under the attack, as we were not in touch with our troops on either flank, and on the right the enemy could be seen well in the rear of our present position.

At that moment a Staff Officer was seen galloping across country towards us from the rear, he pulled up at our H.Q., had a short conference with the C.O. and galloped away again. Orders had evidently been given to retire to some line that was being hastily prepared in the neighbourhood of Proyart, some three miles in our rear.

It was at this point that the C.O. noticed that the 'Orderly Room' was still with the battalion with maps, reports, message pads and suchlike deadly instruments of warfare, not to mention a bayonet, plenty of ammunition and no rifle, the rifle having become a casualty on our rapid journey from the village we had left.

The C.O. suggested to the Adjt. that an 'Orderly Room' was not much use and it might as well take itself off and try to find the transport and stay along with them. The Adjt. evidently did not like the idea of losing his staff, so I stayed along, quietly dumping a few message pads to lighten my burden a little.

The battalion was now extended in a painfully thin line, and fell back to keep pace with the movements of the enemy on our right, who at the moment seemed to be causing us considerably more anxiety than the troops in front of us, whose machine gun and rifle fire seemed a secondary matter as long as we could keep ourselves convinced that we were not going to get it from the back as well as the front.

We were thinking how finely our boys were working their thin line backwards when the same Staff Officer appeared again, cursing and raving that our frontage was not being held, and was shrinking inwards all the time. Considering that we commenced to fall back across the open with the boys scarcely within shouting distance of one another and had been peppered at for about two hours, it was hardly likely that our frontage could have been kept, and we considered the C.O. justified in losing his temper and swearing back at him. In fact, just after he had galloped away, we joined the C.O. and all cursed him roundly according to our varying abilities in that direction. We felt our cause was just, for the enemy evidently thought there must be something of importance near the spot where the Staff Officer had visited, so they treated the immediate neighbourhood to a little barrage of light shells, and we were all half smothered, battered and choked and left generally bad tempered, but all unhurt.

Thereafter, various of the party were fully prepared to snipe the Staff Officer long before he reached us, if he came in sight again. The fact that he himself must have been a fine target riding across the open all the morning with orders, did not impress us at the time, as we spat dirt out of our mouths and clawed mud out of our eyes.

By early afternoon we joined other troops on the high ground near Proyart, where they were busy digging in, we were put in and joined the good work. We had not been here an hour before fresh orders arrived, and we left the trench going still further back. The weather was now blazing hot, we were all tired out and the travelling now was very hard. The ground here was intersected every few yards with old trenches, which under ordinary circumstances could have been jumped without much trouble. We were not now in 'extended order', but simply scrambling along in what should have been 'Column of Four', and one can imagine the disorder caused by perhaps one man in three clearing the jump and the remainder falling into untidy bundles at the bottom of the trench.

The unfortunate ones who fell into the trench were much too tired to climb out unaided and those on top had to lend their assistance. The party (we still called it a battalion) then formed up again and carried on till the same thing happened at the next trench. We arrived near to the bank of the River Somme opposite a large village, which the C.O. thought was Suzanne, the 'J.O.' thought 'Bray' and the Adjutant thought 'Chipilly'. No one else seemed to mind as long as it was not Stockport.

While the matter was being discussed a fresh Staff Officer arrived in a hurry on horse back, to ask "Who the ...." also "What the........" we thought we were etc., etc.

We were evidently in the same parlous state as the unfortunate participators in the 'Charge of the Light Brigade'. "Someone had blundered".

The Staff Officer seemed to think this was an unusual occurrence in France. The men seemed to think it unusual that the Staff Officer should think such a usual occurrence to be unusual.

We were turned about and commenced the journey back again towards Proyart managing the trenches even more unsuccessfully on the return journey.

Instead of returning to the trench that was being prepared on the high ground outside Proyart, we proceeded down the valley itself. Proyart had every appearance of hasty evacuation by the civil population. Open doors disclosed pots and partly finished meals on the tables. Furniture that evidently could not find room on the available transport had been left lying about in the road. We passed through the village as it was growing dusk and beyond the village took cover in deep ditches on both sides of the road, remaining there for a couple of hours. Later, the battalion took up position on the south side of the high road to Amiens. Off the road we found a deserted Artillery Repair Depot with machinery and two big guns evidently in for repairs. There were three small huts in the depot which had been used as offices. The largest of the three found accommodation for the C.O. and H.Q. Officers, the second for the runners and 'R.P.', then the R.S.M. invited me to join him in the third, as long as we were left in peace.

During the night the ration limbers managed to trace us, and we were hungry enough to demolish most of what was supposed to be two days rations. The rest of the night passed fairly quietly, though one or two searching shells fell in the depot ground, fortunately far enough away to leave our little canvas huts untouched.

Matters were still quiet at dawn, when a message was received from Brigade Headquarters that an attack was to be expected about 8 a.m.

The R.S.M. having gone round to the companies, I joined No. 2 hut for company. Among the said company was a private under nominal arrest for overstaying leave and pending quieter times for trial, who was put to duty with the Sanitary Squad.

We were all sat round the hut with our backs to the canvas framework, and he was mentioning to me that he had read the small book I had just taken from my pocket. Someone opposite was cleaning his rifle. There was a blinding flash and an ear splitting report and the 'prisoner' fell across me. The bullet had caught him full in the chin and passed out at the base of the skull. The 'M.O.', who was immediately on the scene from the next hut, said that death was instantaneous. We buried him by the roadside and erected the usual little cross over his grave, which, before mid-day, was a few miles behind German lines.

The name was included amongst those 'Killed in action' during the day.

By 7 a.m. we were being badly peppered with machine gun fire from enemy aeroplanes flying uncomfortably low, but a little later French aeroplanes appeared, and gave the Germans something to distract their attention, much to our relief.

Our Intelligence department was almost exact in their forecast of the time of the enemy attack. By eight o'clock the enemy artillery was pounding away furiously and machine gun fire was intense, but from our side of the road we could not see the enemy infantry.

It was fairly plain again that the line could not be held. We had been in communication with Brigade Headquarters during the night, their Headquarters being located about a half mile down the road to Amiens.

No orders had come in from them since the attack opened, and things looked pretty hopeless. Receiving no reply from Brigade to messages sent by runners, the C.O. himself went off to see if he could get any orders or instructions. All the other officers were with the companies with the exception of the Adjutant, who had presumably gone after the C.O. to find Brigade Headquarters.

The expected soon happened, and we saw the companies compelled to evacuate their positions, falling back across the high road, and making towards higher ground in our rear, leaving 3 runners, 2 police, 2 sanitary staff and 1 Orderly Room corporal stranded in a well perforated canvas hut, wondering whether they ought to wait there for the return of the C.O. and Adjutant, or make a bolt for it and join the companies. A discussion ensued which was brought to an abrupt end when a perfect hail of bullets passed clean through the hut, without touching any one. It was decided that it was asking too much of Providence to expect a second streak of such luck, and H.Q. 'details' stood not upon the order of going, but went again.

Though the companies were not in sight, we knew which direction they had taken, and it was thought that the road would make for quicker travelling. Here we were mistaken.

The enemy machine guns had decided that the road should be closed for traffic and we complied hurriedly by diving off the road and immediately became entangled in the barbed wire mazes of an evacuated Prisoners of War Camp. Bullets were pinging on the wires and lengths of barbed wire whipped about like live reptiles as they were cut. We quickly decided that the best way out was the way we had come in, so we dived out again, circled the cage and made for the high ground in the direction the companies had taken. We did not find our companies but other troops on the crest of the high ground.

They had taken up their position with a wood at their backs and were blazing away merrily at the enemy troops coming up the valley. From this point we could see the German machine gunners with their machine guns strapped to the thigh, firing as they advanced.

Our troops here were without officers, and were working with a will under the direction of a Sgt. Major. A certain Captain/Adjutant appeared on the scene shortly afterwards and, after looking about him, demanded to know who was in charge. Then followed a scene which I still like to think was unique in the annals of the B.E.F. The Sgt. Major reported himself as in charge and the 'C/A' evidently gave some order that the Sgt. Major did not like, for the Sgt. Major rapped out above the din

"Get out to Hell and find your own 'B' Battalion."

The 'C/A' immediately whipped out his revolver, the Sgt. Major turned his back on him and ignored him and considered the interview at an end. The 'C/A' put his revolver back and also evidently considered the matter ended. He did not find his own 'B' battalion as the Sgt. Major called it, but in that unpropitious moment he spotted his Orderly Room Corporal. I thought he would have been glad to see even one member of his own battalion, but his welcome was anything but effusive. After finding that I did not know where the companies were, he decided that an Orderly Room Staff was fairly useless and ordered me to clear out with my records and find the Transport, and stay with them till I could be of some use. My enquiry re the whereabouts of the Transport made me decide that it was preferable to spend the rest of my days walking about France looking for the battalion transport than to spend my time in the company of a disgruntled Adjutant who had lost his battalion, his R.S.M. and all the other things that tend to keep an Adjutant in his right mind.

And so to find the Transport.

The Amiens road was sure to lead to something.

Making my way through the wood on the crest of the hill, I found the valley at the rear being well shelled. The enemy was evidently expecting someone else besides me to use this way back. The expense they were incurring did not quite justify my first fleeting impression that they must have seen a solitary L/C make his way over the top of the hill. The safest way seemed to be to travel under the crest of the hill, towards the road. Keeping along parallel with the road, it was easy to see why so little traffic was now on the road. Further along, answering a hail from the road, I found an 'R.A.M.C.' officer busy on the road trying to do something for four men who had seemingly divided a shell between them. They were horribly torn and shattered, but all were conscious. I helped him what little I could under his direction, and then we laid them in the shelter of the ditch at the roadside. The R.A.M.C. officer was working with a motor ambulance which he expected back along the road at any moment. He asked how things were further along the road. When I explained that the enemy were well through Proyart, and still travelling, he was quite upset at the thought that he would not be able to get so far up with his ambulance on its next run. The road was still being persistently shelled, though we were not then under machine gun fire. The ambulance was, shortly afterwards, seen coming along the road at a great rate, taking no notice of the shelling and bumping terribly over the broken road. We soon had the poor fellows on board and, after the officer had replenished his first aid requirements, the ambulance returned, leaving the Officer still carrying on his good work along the road. Before I left him I made my usual enquiry re Transport, mentioning my Battalion, Brigade and Division, but the only information he could give me was that he had seen a deal of transport passing through Harbonnieres very early in the morning. He pointed out the village across country. I did not like the look of it. It was only a very tiny place in the distance on the crest of another rise. What seemed unpleasant about it was a pall of smoke, that would have done credit to a large manufacturing town. Thanking him, however, I took the short cut across country towards Harbonnières. On my arrival there I found it extremely noisy for its size. It was only a small place of not more than twenty houses. The only occupants at that moment were a battery of 18 pounders and its personnel. They were playing a real devils tattoo, but were being badly shelled in return. I suppose they made so much noise with their own little battery that they did not notice the shells bursting round about, like an outsider would. There was no sign of any transport here but that belonging to the battery. I managed to make my everlasting enquiry, above the din, to a driver who was trying to hold a few horses down with one hand whilst he lighted a cigarette with his free hand. He said that they had only been there a couple of hours, and if they were there another ten minutes he would be somewhat surprised. These were not the exact words he used, as he used 'Artillery dialect', but the said dialect having some affinity to the 'Infantry dialect', I was able to gather his meaning.

Not wishing to be in the way when they were packing, I left, and made my way back towards the Amiens road. Before I reached it however, I noticed a solitary horseman galloping in my direction. In case he was looking for me, and not wishing him to tire his horse unduly, I went to meet him to ask him the usual question. He got in first however with his own query. I found he was an 'M.P.', but not for our division, and having a stripe or two more than I could boast of and also having a horse to add to his stature, his enquiry as to my destination was couched non too politely. Indeed I felt that with a horse and two more stripes I could have replied quite cuttingly. I tried to explain that I was doomed for the rest of my days to endeavour to track the transport of the 6th Cheshires. My attempt to brighten the atmosphere with a little pathetic humour fell pathetically flat. He demanded a pass, but I overcalled him with some of the contents of my despatch bag, further he was able to give, at least, a sense of direction to my search. He could tell me that the 39th Division transport had been seen moving towards Villers-Bretonneux and gave me the good advice not to make direct for Villers-Bretonneux by the high road, but go the roundabout way through Marcelcave, which route may not be quite so exciting but considerably safer.

Villers-Bretonneux itself was deserted save a few odd detachments of transport who seemed to be waiting orders to move at any moment. It was now growing dusk, and I was beginning to feel that I had rambled about enough for one day, when, turning a corner, I found a small party of drivers 'brewing-up' and cooking bacon. I had of course breakfasted at Proyart, but unfortunately in the hurry of our departure, the remainder of my rations had most likely gone to feed some perhaps equally hungry German. Transport men never really seemed to be short of rations, but they were for once actually short of bacon, but what an infantry man thinks is a shortage, of course differs considerably from what is considered shortage amongst the transport.

A mess tin of hot tea and a big slice of bread well 'dipped' and the War soon took on a brighter aspect.

It was quite dark when I left them, having gathered the further information that the 39th Div. Transport had passed through Villers B. in the direction of Cachy.

There were so many ways out of Villers, that it was sometime before I found the road out to Cachy. Getting clear at last I soon found the road lined with transport, some drawn into the fields at the roadside, others still moving along slowly in a seemingly endless line. Owing to the frequent halts, I was able to gain along the line of vehicles, but reached Cachy without having identified any unit belonging to our division.

The crossroads at Cachy were jammed with vehicles, and in the darkness it was quite an easy matter to get trodden on by a mule or two, or jammed between the vehicles whilst hunting for identification marks. It was quite impossible to make any verbal enquiries just here. Transport officers were busy swearing at the Sergeants, Sergeants were passing it on with interest to the drivers and drivers were passing it on with accumulated compound interest to the mules, and the mules would have bitten and stamped on anybody they could get at.

The enemy was also busy with their bombing planes, which added to the general gaiety.

I seemed to be able to find scraps of transport belonging to any known and unknown unit of the B.E.F. with the exception of the 39th Div., but as I heard that transport had been moving through Cachy all evening, I had still a chance of seeing some more. Leaving Cachy and making for Gentelles, the line of vehicles dwindled, till at last the road was clear. This made my search more difficult. The move had evidently stopped for the night, as the fields at each side of the road were full of transport unharnessing and settling down for the time being. I could not go on, but must now search the fields in the darkness. I gathered definite information however, that our Brigade transport was parked in a clearing in the Bois de Gentelles, about a mile through Gentelles.

For the last hour rain had been pouring down steadily which added greatly to the joys of my walking tour through France. By the time I reached Gentelles, I felt that the remaining one mile must have been like the last straw that gave the camel its permanent hump. The Bois de Gentelles did however loom up at last and looked anything but inviting in the darkness. After scrambling some distance in the wood I eventually found a clearing, and at last the long lost transport. Everyone seemed to be sleeping, but the horses seemed restive when I stumbled amongst them and tripped over their lines. One tent I found, but from the sounds coming from it I judged it contained Officers, or at least Sergeant Majors and was no place for a L/C. Exploring further I came across the huge trunk of a fallen tree and alongside it and as far as possible underneath it, were various recumbent forms wrapped in ground sheets and blankets, oblivious to rains, wars and other incidentals of the period. I could not recognise any of them under their coverings, and it was distinctly unwise to waken anyone who might be unsympathetic. I did actually tumble over the first man I found, but he was as insensible as the tree trunk itself.

By the side of the last figure in the row I stumbled over a package wrapped in a ground sheet. Investigation produced half a loaf of bread and half a tin of jam. Mentally promising my apologies to the owner in the morning, I cured an aching void, but thought it wiser not to lay me down to sleep next to the possible owner, in case he wakened first and looked upon it as an unfriendly action.

Groping round for a more sheltered spot, I found Pat's mess cart and, borrowing a harness blanket from some harness, made myself comfortable under the cart.

I had a faint recollection of Pat appearing during the night, and I seemed to wake up with more bedclothes than I had lain down with.

The first thing I heard on waking was a driver asking for the blood of the man who had purloined the blanket from his harness set. The next thing I heard was another voice enquiring for the unprintable, indescribable blighter who had pinched half a loaf and a tin of 'Pozzy'. I first of all disposed of the harness cover, where it would not be found in my possession, as I did not know the driver intimately enough to explain. To the owner of the voice enquiring for the bread and 'Pozzy' I explained that it was only half a tin. It was only my chum, Len, so I was able to further explain that if I had only known that his was the end form laid along the tree trunk, I would assuredly have wakened him and asked him for the 'Pozzy', had I not known quite well that he would rather have lost his 'Pozzy' than his sleep. 'Quarters' was there too, so we had the Orderly Room staff complete, and the war was in safe hands again.

Pat also turned up shortly afterwards, he had been out all night with the ration limbers.

Rations now were not being sent up to each battalion by its own transport. Battalions, for the time being, had ceased to exist, and composite companies were being formed of mixed troops, and transport was used to take up rations to certain points for troops who might or might not be there at a certain time.

29 March

We heard today (March 29th) that our Divisional General, General Feetham, had been killed and our own Brigadier-General Bellingham had been taken prisoner, along with one of our runners, who had been on duty with him.

During the day we found useful additions to our rations at a deserted farm close by where there was a fair assortment of only fair poultry, also a collection of rabbits. Two or three hens, a couple of rabbits, a plentiful supply of potatoes and onions gathered in the same neighbourhood made a stew the like of which we had not smelled or tasted for a long time.

In the wood was a smartly built stone shelter evidently used at one time as a picnic rendezvous. At present the picnic in occupation consisted of the Brigadier Major, Staff Captain, our man Captain 'Tubby', batmen and cooks, and a few pots and pans, trying to carry on as Brigade Headquarters.

30 March

The following day (March 30th) our 'C.O.' arrived with Capt. S ..., who was acting Adjutant, as the Adjutant was missing. Both the 'C.O.' and his companion were much the worse for wear, in fact thoroughly worn out.

We were ordered to move the next day, and as neither the 'C.O.' nor the Adjutant were able to walk, and no horses being available, both found room in a limber, carrying amongst other impedimenta, the big drum belonging to the band.

A pouring wet day it was as we tramped along with the transport. During a stop for a meal about mid-day, Pat won a derelict tent which someone had not bothered to move when they left the district. He could not, however, obtain permission from the Transport Officer to put it on any vehicle, so Pat had to leave it where it was.

He was anything but pleased later, to find that the 'T.O.' had changed his mind before leaving and had put it aboard a limber for his own use later. We finished up that evening, after trudging the whole day, at the little village of Fuscien. The place was deserted and looked as if it had been so for the last twenty years. A dirty little tumbledown place it was, with only one redeeming feature. That was a supply of potatoes we found in a cellar in the broken down cottage, where half a dozen of us found shelter for the night.

Even the potatoes were an unmixed blessing, as we were kept awake most of the night with enquiries calling about "Them Spuds".

31 March

We moved early again and heard that our division had been relieved, and at the end of another day of tramping we picked up what was left of the battalion at the village of Guignemicourt, where we had a busy night sorting out companies and reckoning up casualties.

1 April

We spent the morning resting a Guignemicourt, leaving in the afternoon and reaching Taisnil late at night to find the billeting party, who had left in advance, had not yet found billets. We were eventually tucked into a comfortable farm billet with plenty of straw. Here we learned that we were off to the North again. Ypres of all places, to which we had said a fond farewell, only a couple of months since, with not the slightest regret, nor the faintest wish ever to see the place again.

We also heard for the first time that the Germans were making a big attack up there.

Very cheerful and entertaining and all that, but nothing to miss a good night's sleep about anyway.

We were making for Eu, a railhead on the coast, so we evidently had some tramping still to do.

2 April

We left Taisnil early next morning, arriving at Thieulloy-l'Abbaye in the evening, but could not find the billeting party again. This 'B.P.' was getting a bad reputation. One of the party, however, soon arrived on a bicycle with the news that no billets could be procured in the village, but at Hornoy, five miles further on, good billets had been fixed up. ONLY another five miles.

3 April

We left Hornoy at 10 a.m. for Andainville arriving about 4-0 p.m.

For the first time since March 31st we were able to unload the orderly room boxes and typewriter, and get to work on the records, straightening up and getting up to date, while the rest of the battalion slept peacefully.

We stayed here for three days and had quite a good time. The villagers were very friendly, eggs and milk could be bought, and the two estaminets did a roaring business.

Pat introduced me to a farm house where the very best cider was kept, and where the cider was taken 'En famille', the local paper was also handed round, which we pretended to read.

It was at Andainville that a certain C.S.M returned late to his billet after discovering Crème de Menthe for the first time.

He appeared in a high state of hilarious inebriation asking "Whawhadyethink of me-hic-on-hic-on Peppermint".

7 April

We were quite sorry to leave the place early in the morning of the 7th, a gloriously fine morning and passing through Senarpont, Nesle-l'Hôpital and Bouttencourt we finished the day at the village of Ansennes. The Companies found billets in the village, while Headquarters found rather sumptuous quarters in a fine old Château some distance from the village.

Len and I hunted round the outbuildings for a place in which to settle down and get some work done. We found a low building, spotlessly clean with a tiled floor, divided into little compartments. We fixed ourselves up in one of the little compartments quite cosily and commenced work, after putting the Orderly Room notice board outside.

The building had puzzled us a little, we could not quite make out what it had been used for previously, but we settled down to work and found the low dividing walls quite useful for putting odd books and papers on, out of the way. Someone else, however, had evidently found out what the building was. Hearing peculiar noises outside we went to see what was the matter. The runners were sat outside evidently enjoying a good joke. Every time anyone passed, the runners gave a huge grunt and the passer-by replied with a grunt and a broad grin. We watched this with interest for sometime and, curiosity getting the better of us, we offered to buy the joke.

Before negotiations were concluded however, we saw 'Quarters' come striding round the corner of the building looking as if war had really broken out.

"What d'you mean by putting the Orderly Room in a ... piggery?" We had not heard of the breed of pigs he mentioned, but he was really upset. As we had been working hard however, while he had been having a really good time at an estaminet in Ansennes with various other Warrant Officers, we informed him that if he didn't like to be seen there we could do all the work without him, and so, being a man of peace, he returned to the little estaminet at Ansennes and left us alone in our piggery.

When we had finished and judged Pat was also through with his work at the Château, we looked him up and had a look through the Château. It was a really beautiful place, owned by 'Le Duc de something or other' but was in the charge of caretakers. All the treasures (if any) had of course been removed. This must not on any account be taken to infer that 'Le Duc' had heard that our Battalion intended visiting there. Later in the evening our band played in the Château grounds where all the villagers (with of course the exception of the proprietor of the estaminet) gathered to hear the music. Left Ansennes in the early morning and marched the day in drenching rain, finishing up late in the afternoon at the village of Bouvaincourt. A most depressing and dirty little village. The only enlivening incident of the evening being a glimpse of Pat, our staid Mess Corporal, walking down the village street with a rather pretty girl. Pat tried to explain later that she was helping him to find a place for H.Q. Mess. I forget now whether he said that she was the only girl in the village who spoke English, or the only person who could understand his French.

It was here that we first heard that our division (39th) was to be broken up, and its units scattered into other Commands. This disgusted us completely, as naturally our division was the finest in the 'B.E.F.' (the Guards next of course).

9 April

We left Bouvaincourt about 5.0 p.m., and a couple of hours brought us to the town of Eu, which is practically on the coast. This was evidently a garrison town, as we passed a huge barracks, where the guard turned out and gave the salute. It seemed ages since such a thing happened before.

It was quite a busy little place, and although the train did not leave till about two hours after we arrived, a good many of those lucky ones, who were able to leave the precincts of the station, nearly missed the train. The accommodation on the train was, as usual, as good for the men as for the horses.

10 April

We detrained at Arques near St Omer at 7.0 a.m. and spent the day resting and cleaning up. The following morning nine officers and 360 men of the battalion were sent off hurriedly to reinforce General Hubback's brigade defending Hazebrouck with the 21st Division. The remainder of the battalion moved to Holque near Watten, but on arrival there orders were received for the remainder of the battalion (less Headquarters) to also move up hurriedly to Gen. Hubback's Brigade. Headquarters went into billets at Ganspette.

Behind a little cottage we fixed up the Orderly Room in a little outhouse. It was mostly window along one side and looked on to a pleasant garden. It was soon evident that British troops had been here before, as most of the natives were fairly fluent in the B.E.F. patois. The old lady at the cottage was a good motherly sort, and at least three times a day would send coffee in by one or other of her two daughters.

The younger daughter, aged about 5, soon made her presence felt, and became known as our lady typist after the Adjutant had come in one day and found her sitting on 'Q's' knee, having her index finger jabbed on to the keys of the typewriter until she typed her name, the name of all her relatives and also those of her ancestors. Officers held no terrors for her, and while Sgt. Majors and Officers stood without the gate waiting audience of the Colonel, she would dash in without ceremony. The Colonel was unfortunate in drawing attention to himself by asking her whose little girl she was. He was met by the surprising retort "Oh la la Officer beaucoup swank eh?"

Our friendship nearly came to a tragic end one day. It happened thus.

After a deal of trouble she had made me understand that she was going to the village shop to buy "favours". I thought "favours" might be sweets, but found out that they were her hair ribbons. Things were quiet and I was immersed in an interesting book when she returned. She was not satisfied with my admiring her purchases, but climbed on my knee and tried to decorate me with her hair ribbons. Hearing a clink of spurs just at that moment, I put the young lady down hurriedly with her ribbons and my "allez" must have hurt her feelings, for she turned at the door and hurled the awful epithet "Boche" at me. It cost me a franc for chocolate later in the day to regain my nationality and her friendship.

The only news that we received here from the Battalion was a long list of casualties.

We could, however, tell that very heavy fighting was going on from the continual throbbing of heavy gun fire, and it was at that time that Field Marshall Haig's famous "Backs to the Wall" appeal was issued to the troops. This of course totally converted the few remaining optimists in the battalion.

21 April

Having more staff than work in the Orderly Room we arranged afternoons free in turn. Mine today. Went to look Pat up and tracked him down to a cottage, where he was trying to persuade an old lady to sell him some flour, against her will and the laws of France. He managed to get his own way, as usual. Then we adjourned to the kitchen, where I was introduced to the old man. The old man was delighted to see us. I gradually learned from Pat's "asides" to me that the old gentleman distinctly remembered us being billeted with him in 1915 at Armentières. We expressed our agreeable astonishment at his wonderful memory for faces. (We only crossed the channel in Dec 1916 and had not yet seen Armentières.) After being regaled with coffee, and the old lady promising to wash the table linen for the Officers' Mess on the strength of the old acquaintanceship, we had not the heart to tell them otherwise.

An American Division arrived during our stay here, and were billeted in the district. They seemed to be thoroughly fagged out when they arrived. Constituting ourselves immediately as experts, we decided there and then that the exhaustion was the result of wearing gaiters instead of puttees, and the ridiculous arrangement of their equipment.

Before dismissing to their billets however, they performed some little foot and rifle drill, which we felt was more for the benefit of onlookers than anything else. It was real music hall stuff.

We made their acquaintance in the evenings at the village estaminets. They were a particularly fine type of men, very likeable, but rather prone to explain how they were going to finish the war. The first thing that happened to them however, was that all their rifles were handed in to be exchanged for the Small Lee Enfield used by us, and they were immediately put through a new course of musketry by our N.C.O. They were, however, wonderfully keen to be seeing the war, some of them even enquiring if they could get a car, just to run up during the afternoon and look at the 'FUN'.

We had only two grudges against them. The first was that circulars were at once issued, illustrating the marks of rank in the U.S.A. army, and we had to immediately learn them carefully in order to avoid international complications, which might arise by our Saluting a U.S.A. Lance Corporal or calling a Colonel 'BUDDY'.

The second grudge developed over a much more serious matter. The pay in the 'A.E.F.' was extremely lavish compared with pay in the 'B.E.F.' and their expenditure in the estaminets and sweet shops was in proportion. The result was that the three staple luxuries of the 'B.E.F.' (beer, eggs and chocolate) soared in price until they were quite out of our reach.

We were soon, however, on sufficiently good terms with them to broach the matter of prices reigning in the village before their arrival, and the respective financial standings of the 'B.E.F' and the 'A.E.F.' having been discussed, matters were soon adjusted and everybody happy again.

25 April

Seemed to be some sort of Church Festival in the village. All the little girls were bedecked in white frocks, and the boys disguised in new suits and white collars. Every cottage in the village seemed to be having a party.

Orderly Room staff lucky again, Len and myself receiving invitations to have dinner in the house with the family. Receiving orders to change our billet during the afternoon, we were fixed up in the new billet in time to have tea with our new hosts. A much more convenient billet with a couple of wire beds. We had a front room to ourselves looking out on to a large front garden, and as it was in the centre of the village, the band played in the garden on fine evenings.

6 May

We received orders to turn out every available conveyance that could possibly be used for transport, to be sent forward to convey our detachment with Gen. Hubback's composite Brigade back to billets, as they were in too exhausted a condition to march.

At 3.0 a.m. the next morning they arrived in a sorry state, and we all got busy making them comfortable for the night. After a good rest next day, plus a bath and a visit to the Q.M. Stores they were fully recovered, though sadly reduced in numbers.

9 May

Had a day off, and accepted Pat's invitation to join him in a day's shopping at St Omer for the Mess. He turned up with an empty valise slung on his back, as a market bag. It was a beautiful morning for a walk, and I happened to mention it. He took his briar out of his mouth and glared. "Walk" said he "You've got it all wrong, you don't suppose I am walking eight miles to St Omer and eight miles back. You've got to jump it." Now if there was one thing I did not enjoy it was 'jumping' W.D. motors. No infantry man objects to a ride of course, it was just the preliminary jump that bothered me. A little explanation of the art of 'Jumping' may not be out of place for the benefit of the uninitiated. In the first place a W.D. motor never travels with its tailboard down, and when it was up, I could just reach the edge of it with my fingertips.

First you walk quietly along the road until you hear one coming behind you. You must appear to be totally unaware of its existence until the latest possible moment. If the driver suspects that you are the least bit interested in his vehicle, he immediately 'steps on the gas' and leaves you 'as you were'. As the rear of the wagon passes you make a wild dash at it. If you manage to get a good grip over the edge of the tailboard you have progressed well towards the second movement. If you have not, you will most probably have been rudely dumped onto an unsympathetic road, and need not bother further with the next movement.

No. 1 completed, hold on for dear life while working the legs with a frog-like motion till you can get a toe on the hinge of the tailboard. If luck (and your fingers) still hold, the rest is easy, you simply heave yourself over the tailboard and drop into the wagon. If your luck is out many things may happen between getting your toe on the hinge of the tailboard and getting inside the wagon. If the wagon happens to strike a hole in the road as you are passing over the tailboard, and you land inside the wagon instead of outside, you gain full marks. I barely had time to admire Pat's new breeches with brilliant yellow leather riding grips, when we spied our 'BUS'. We walked along unconcernedly and then dived at the right moment. Splendid!! We both gained full marks, we picked ourselves up from the bottom of the wagon and smiled at each other, well satisfied. The driver looked inside and also smiled. He was evidently agreeably surprised at our agility, or was it the sight of Pat's new breeches? No!! We had not noticed the devilish glint in his eye, for he immediately shot off the main road to St Omer into a side road, and then proceeded to shew us what his engine could really do. We climbed quickly back over the tailboard and hung on till we could gauge the speed that the road was leaving the 'BUS' and then let go. When we had stopped running, we sat by the roadside to regain our lost belief in the good feeling that was supposed to exist between all branches of the 'B.E.F.'. Pat's decision to ride to St Omer was still unshaken. With the persistence and bull dog tenacity that won the war (apologies to 'U.S.A.') we did actually arrive eventually by 'BUS' or various 'BUSSES' into the square at St Omer.

As it was hot and dusty, Pat thought that an immediate glass of beer would be a distinct aid to shopping. I pointed out that it still needed two hours for twelve o'clock, before which time no soldier was allowed to be served in any estaminet, and he could not get it. "Watch me" was all he said. We walked down a little narrow street from the square into a small grocery shop, and he winked portentously at three little beer pumps on a side counter. His first enquiry was for 'Semolina', but the lady behind the counter seemed to be under the impression that we had mistaken her emporium for a music store. Pat perspired in his efforts to explain that it was like rice, like tapioca, like sago, but not quite. The poor lady was inconsolable at her inability to grasp his meaning, so to relieve the strain he ordered two beers. She understood that immediately, but pointed to the clock and shook her head. Pat smiled, took my arm and walked through the shop into a little room beyond, then sat down after closing the door behind him. A minute later the lady followed with the beer, and secured an order for small groceries. We next walked along to a smart little dairy shop. It was beautifully fitted up in white marble. Trade seemed quiet, so Pat proceeded to take an inventory of the stock of tinned goods, much to the lady's amusement. Any labels on the tins that were not quite clear to him, the lady gave him a translation as far as possible. After learning quite a lot more French he bought some butter. Then walking round the shop again to make sure that he had seen everything there was to see, a serious look appeared on his face, and he commenced to sniff round like a terrier suspecting rats.

Suddenly he pounced on a package, drew it out and almost shouted 'ROQUEFORT'. "Ah" said the lady "Beaucoup stink monsieur, six francs". Out came six francs and the lady proceeded to unwrap the corpse with seemingly unwilling fingers, cut it gingerly, wrapped it up well and then washed her hands carefully in a white marble bowl, before she took the money.

Pat thought that the cheese might flavour the groceries in his valise, so he produced a sandbag, put in the cheese and gave it to me to carry. The next item required was crockery, a few glasses, cups and saucers. We found a splendid shop, shewing in the window just what we required, at what seemed quite a reasonable price, until we found out the price was 'per piece' and not 'per dozen'. We eventually found what we could afford, if not quite what we wanted, at a shop where they also sold second hand clothes and ditto bassinettes. Next we bought some fish. Pat wanted my opinion on his purchase, but as I was a bit doubtful whether gills should be judged by the same rule as railway signals, Red for 'danger' and Green for 'All clear' or vice-versa, I left it to him. I opened my bag for the lady to put in the parcel of fish, when she suddenly stiffened and commenced to sniff. Pat hurriedly apologised for the ROQUEFORT and put the fish into his valise instead, where the company was quieter, and transferred some bottles to my sandbag.

Shopping finished, we decided on something to eat, found a restaurant, and had quite a nice little lunch. Made us feel quite 'civilian' to call it lunch once more. Only one fly in the ointment, our waitress bore a frozen supercilious look every time she came near us. We suddenly remembered the ROQUEFORT and, deciding that explanations would not be dignified, we finished rather hurriedly and left quickly.

We found an 'R.F.C.' motor wagon in the square just about to leave for Watten, which was quite near home. The driver was evidently under the impression that everything belonging to the R.F.C. should fly, and I was quite pleased to find on reaching Watten that the bottles in my sandbag were safe and sound. It was not necessary to open the bag to see if the cheese was alright.

14 May

Our old friends the Black Watch left the village today, leaving our division for another command. The 39th Div. was breaking up after all. We had been alongside the 'Jocks' for nearly eighteen months, in the line, in camp and in billet, and would miss them.

There had been a riotous night or two of farewells in the estaminets. Many of us walked to Watten to see them entrain, and 'Auld Lang Syne' was rendered feelingly to the astonishment of the natives. So we said farewell to the merriest and best of fighters in France. On getting back to the billet I found Len looking very disgusted. For a few days now we had been very friendly with one of the hens at the billet, who had shewn her enthusiasm for the ENTENTE by coming in through the window into our bedroom, and laying an egg in the corner, where we had made her a nest. We had not disclosed this matter, fearing for the bird's reputation. I learned from Len, that, seeing the bird come in, he had left her to it as usual and gone out, closing the door quietly behind him. He returned on hearing the usual cackle, to find that she had only left her card. We gave her one more chance, but when she disgraced herself again next day, we ordered her off the premises and sent her nest after her. Len said it was our own fault for giving her soft food. Evidently Army stew was not the thing for laying hens.

Another catastrophe. Someone had left the garden gate open and we had lost the billet cow. Excitement was intense, and runners were out with the firm resolve to bring her back, or another cow. Who should bring her back, however, but the old lady from our last billet. We asked her if she had milked it before bringing it back, but she "No Compreed". We could obtain no milk for supper that evening, which was rather suspicious.

21st May 1918 – Tuesday 5 a.m.

Dear little sweetheart,

I had to be up at 4 this morning to get a runner off on a long trip, and as it is quite daylight I don't feel like getting to bed again. It is going to be such a glorious day again. I have such a glorious view from the window here, the mist is just rising, and a great filmy red sun is just peeping over a ridge right away in front. The grass is all shiny wet and glinting like myriads of wee diamonds, and diamond cobwebs in the bushes. The birds are all getting up and there surely must be heaps of little fluffy balls of babies in the nests as the chittering and chattering going on is immense. The old cock here has just been having a vocal argument with some old rooster further up the village, but has subsided and decided he will have another nod. Oh! and the smell with the blossoms and lilac (we have some lilac). One can hardly imagine there is a ghastly war on and that a lot of poor chaps are spitting and coughing out lyddite fumes and such like stinks after the usual morning hate has been hurled across.

Yours was a dear little letter yesterday. I know it must be hard for you little woman, a man's feelings anytime, though perhaps rougher, are never, and never can be as keen as a woman's. I am not wanting you like I do sometimes in the heat of the day, or the heavy sensuousness of the close of a hot day. As I went through the garden a few minutes since, a little leaf with the dew on just drew itself across my lips, oh so cool and sweet, just like your lips in your quiet moods. Just like you sitting up in bed early one morning, shaking your hair back and giving me one of those brushing kisses and saying "Oh lad what a glorious morning it is". This morning is just the sort of morning that you would say "Just let us have a look down the garden before we have breakfast" and argue that your slippers were quite waterproof when they were not.

Reveille is just blowing now and I must rattle Len out of it. He can see no beauty in an early morning.

Just eight little kisses, one for your hair, one for each dear eye, one for the top of your nose, one for each cheek, one on the chin, and as it is rather early and you may not be quite dressed, one for each of your sweet little breasts, from your loving husband Walter.

We had the battalion signal office fixed up in our room at this time, and as we had so little to do in the Orderly Room, I offered my services on the signals, so that we need not have a signaller on night and day.

We had only one wire to Brigade Headquarters, about a mile away. When the first message came through in morse, I found that I had got very rusty, or perhaps overestimated my abilities in tackling Brigade experts. I had only got three words down out of a fifteen word message. I modestly gave back "Repeat all after ..." expecting immediate trouble. I was pleasantly surprised to get in reply "Is that you Walt?" I had quite forgotten that two of our own signallers had gone on duty at Brigade H.Q. I had no further difficulty after this, as messages came through afterwards at a speed which I could negotiate, but would have made the Brigade Signal Officer gasp.

The Brigade General would have had apoplexy had he heard of the following dialogue being 'morsed', "Is that you Walt?" "Are you busy?" "Anybody in?" "Would you like some practice?" "Please" and for perhaps quarter of an hour, morse practice would follow.

25 May

Our holiday finished, we left Ganspette with real reluctance. Our division had now been completely disbanded, and we were to go down to the Marne, this time to join the 11th Batt. Ches. with the 25th Division. Whether we were to absorb the 11th, or the 11th were to absorb the 6th was not made clear.

The only evident advantage that seemed to accrue to us from the breaking up of the old division, was the fact that the Divisional and Brigade canteen stocks had to be liquidated immediately and what could not be sold was divided amongst the troops.

As we marched out of the village, villagers gave us a good send off and we gave them a feeling rendering of that pathetic ditty 'Goodbyee don't cryee' assisted by the band. At Watten station, where we entrained, we were served out with the remainder of the canteen stock, consisting of chocolate and biscuits. If we could only have foreseen what the next few days were to bring, we would not have sat on the station demolishing our share before the train left.

We left Watten about 3 p.m. and arrived at Étaples about midnight, passing the night in a large camp, which was chiefly remembered afterwards by the smell of the incinerators. Here we found W.A.A.C.s in numbers, who seemed to be chiefly employed in signal offices and depot work. There were of course none in our part of the camp, and much discontent was expressed when strict orders were issued that no one was to leave camp, and military police were posted at all exits to see orders were enforced.

26 May

Pat decided of course that he wanted to go into the town. I feel convinced that he would not have bothered his head about going if it had not been prohibited. We of course left the camp by the exit guarded by our own battalion police, who would understand that the H.Q. Officers Mess Corporal and the Orderly Room Corporal would not be going out on anything but of state importance. Our visit proved uninteresting. It seemed rather a dirty large fishing village. The tide was out in the estuary and a few fishing boats were laying about untidily in the mud. The quayside was deserted, and the shops chiefly given over to the sale of the everlasting silk postcards for Tommy. Estaminets were more numerous than in any place we had yet been, and most of them only seemed to be cleaning up from the night before. An hour in the place sufficed and we returned to camp to find dinner being served and moving orders issued.

We entrained again soon after dinner and were disappointed to find that our train had been changed from passenger coaches to the usual type for '40 hommes et 8 chevaux'.

Before setting off something gave us the feeling that our halt had not been expected and everyone felt that something had gone wrong somewhere.

We travelled slowly and uneventfully with many halts till about 5 p.m. Then we saw what appeared to us to be a big relief in progress. French troops, transport and guns making their way along all mixed up. Some along the fields, some along the roads. We had been in some reliefs that had been badly mixed up, but this had been in narrow trenches. It was not till some time later that we found out that this was another retreat in progress. Another cheerful outlook. We were now looking forward to some excitement. We still travelled forward slowly, then shells began to drop in rather close and uncomfortable proximity to the line. I happened to be in a wagon with H.Q. details. The Reg. Police with us, had in their charge, a man who was being held for trial on a charge of desertion. He was evidently a nervous breakdown case, and more fit for hospital than a court-martial. No sooner did he hear the shells dropping than he made a frantic dive for the door, but was dragged back and sat on during the remainder of the proceedings. Suddenly we found ourselves under rifle fire from somewhere close by in the fields by the line, but could not locate exactly where it came from. As bullets were coming right through the vans, we quickly laid on the floor. Some mathematician in the company suggested that if someone followed the line of the next bullet from its entry on the one side to its exit on the other side of the van, and extended the line indefinitely on the side the fire was coming from, we could soon find out where the fire was coming from. Two or three N.C.O.s, however, dashed from the train with drawn bayonets into a corn field by the side of the line, and immediately three Germans bobbed up with their hands up, and were bustled on board for an interview with the C.O.

The C.O. evidently obtained enough information to decide that our train was on the main line for Berlin if we proceeded any further, and that we actually were at that moment behind the foremost German troops on that sector.

In the meantime one of the French locomotive men had dashed from the engine, and bolted over the hills and out of sight. Two men with fixed bayonets were placed on the engine to make sure that the remaining locomotive man did not follow his friend, and orders were given to reverse.

Our train could evidently travel quicker backwards than forwards, as we made quite good speed for some miles back to the last station we had passed, Fère-en-Tardenois. We could find no staff on the station, so the C.O. went into the village to see if he could find any Military Representative to report to, but the place was deserted. We remained in the station till dark, when enemy planes arrived in the vicinity, having no doubt heard that the 'Cheshires' were trespassing in the district. We left the train rapidly and took shelter in a wood close by, and hoped that the train would be fit to travel later on. We did not detrain too rapidly however, to see that the ration wagon was also unloaded. We tried to make ourselves comfortable in the wood, but a downpour of rain damped the proceedings somewhat. We were comforted with the thought that the station was not nearly so comfortable, or as quiet. No touch could be obtained during the night with any other troops, and just before dawn we were packed into the train again, which same train was nearly intact. The engine driver was also intact, as he had been well looked after and entertained during the night.

28 May

After a weary journey we detrained again at La Ferté-Milon about mid-day. Things were very busy here, train loads of refugees passed through, and French troop trains were rushing to and fro. The C.O was off in the village in conference with some Military authority, while we stayed on the station from mid-day till we were bundled into a train about 7.30 p.m. Where that train went to during the night we never knew, but before darkness fell we occasionally caught sight of a broad river, which we took to be the Marne, and ran through some beautiful country. Then weariness overcame us and we slept.

29 May

At 1-0 a.m. we detrained at Dormans, cold and stiff. Dormans was just a name on a station as far as we were concerned. I obtained a glance at orders which were to hold a line from 1 kilo south of Romigny to 3 kilos north of Lhery. I wondered what the distance was between Romigny and Lhery, and what length of line the remnant of our battalion was to hold. Also where was the 11th Battalion that we were to join. It turned out that during our journey the enemy had opened up his big effort on the Marne, and the nice quiet place where we were to join the 11th battalion was, at the moment, somewhere about 10 miles behind the German line, so our amalgamation would be attended to later. At present we seemed to be an odd unit handy to be pushed into the first hole that presented itself.

With the aid of one map presented to the battalion, the position indicated was reached after 3 solid hours marching, passing long columns of civilians, old men, women and children leaving their villages and farms. Again we found ourselves out of touch with troops of any kind. We simply took up a line in a convenient ditch as far as the battalion would reach, hoping we were behind other troops of ours or French, and not left alone to win the War.

We were left in peace during the day, and towards evening H.Q. fixed up quarters in a barn close by.

30 May

The enemy attacked soon after dawn, and we were fairly swamped. I don't think the enemy even knew we were there at first, as later on we found German troops working a good distance in our rear at both sides. Of course we had to move quickly. With one map for the battalion and strange ground, a party going one side of a hill lost altogether the party that tried the other side. The afternoon found Headquarters and one company together, but the remaining 3 companies, lucky dogs, had dropped into the arms of the division we had come to join, and who were just being relieved. Our luck was out, as we managed to get attached to the Division that came in to relieve them. We fell back and took up a position on the edge of a forest known as the Bois de Courton, and that night slept in the woods.

31 May

We moved again at dawn marching through the forest, through the village of Champlat picking up stragglers of the 8th, 19th and 25th Divisions. We moved about from Bois de Courton to Bois d'Eclisse for some days, first under the orders of one division and then another. We were still a spare unit owned by anyone in a tight corner for a bit of help, but owned by no one as far as rations were concerned. When not wanted we seemed to take up quarters in the Bois de Courton, where we dug ourselves holes about three feet deep and wide enough to sit in when we were bothered by shells. In the wood we found a charcoal burners hut with a store of nice new charcoal bags about 6ft. by 3ft., which made comfortable sleeping bags. For three days here we were dependent on what rations could be spared from a stragglers post.

Our "Black Hand Gang" (signallers) got to work however, and after dark scoured a little deserted village in the valley below the wood. Pork, rabbits, vegetables, fowls and 'what not' began to appear on the signallers menu. Len and I were treated as honorary signallers for the time being and the officers' cook used to wonder, until he also joined in the foraging party.

Our original 'Old Bill' (Beswick) was leader of the gang, and his discoveries were sensational. His first special was a live pig, which was killed and cleaned down in the valley, in order to save trouble getting it home in the dark.

While on a search through what he presumed was an empty house, he actually found a poor old bedridden woman nearly starving to death. All Bill could make out from her ravings was that she was "tres faint", so Bill made her some hot soup, came back to his telephone, found the nearest ambulance station and got her moved within the hour.

6 June

The enemy evidently found out where we lived, as he shelled the wood all day, and what times we came out of our holes were not spent lounging about in the open. We lost four of our number, in addition to eighteen badly wounded and a few gas cases. We lived this Robin Hood life in and out of the Bois de Courton and Bois d'Eclisse until the 10th of June, when 5 officers and 160 men were organised as a company to join the 19th Composite Brigade, and 14 signallers off to the 58th Brigade at Nanteuil. The remaining officers and 26 men, comprising Headquarters, were ordered to the transport lines of the 58th Brigade at Hautvillers some six miles away. The six miles proved a heavy task as we had no transport, and between us we had to carry along cooking dixies, spare Lewis Guns and all sorts of spare impedimenta. Here we were again fixed up in a wood, a beautiful little spot overlooking the Marne river. Just below us was the pretty little village of Ay, and across the river we could see Epernay for the first time, without seeing a bottle. We did not bother to dig holes for ourselves here, but fixed up little Crusoe huts with twigs and branches, with beds of bracken and prayed for fine weather to continue. We had a good comfortable rest here. From a visiting staff officer we learned that 'Q' was safe with the 11th Battalion, and was again in charge of the Orderly Room, with the clerks of the 13th. This looked like Len and myself finding fresh jobs when we arrived there.

We had by now found out the chief difference between trench warfare and the present kind. In the old trench business if one felt a tickling sensation down one's neck we knew at once, without any doubt, the cause of it, but now it might be anything, possibly a butterfly, even an earwig, maybe a mosquito, why not a worm.

15 June

Major G and Capt. 'Tubby' left us here to join the 11th Batt., and we were evidently to follow when the remainder of our lads came out of the line.

19 June

On the 19th we left our rookery to meet our lads coming out from the line, marched to Germaine where we entrained about 7.0 p.m., we arrived at Fère-Champenoise at about 10.0 p.m. where our battalion cookers met us with a good meal. Then we were packed into motor wagons to St Loup to find the 11th Battalion which we should have joined on the 26th of May. We were only 24 days late. We were dropped about half an hour's walk away from the camp as our old band wanted to take us in. We cheered our old band like a lot of happy children and they did ditto, then they blew us with a non stop tune into the camp at midnight. The tune was one of our own unpublished ditties "I'm reet glad to see thee back again". Len and I quickly found the Orderly Room, 'Q' welcomed me with 3 weeks post from home, and now he had got rid of it there would perhaps be room to work. From the 21st of June to the 30th we spent in re-organisation with the 11th Batt. at St Loup. As the 11th possessed their own officers' mess staff intact, Pat returned to his old job on the signals, as a linesman.

Owing to the stress of work in the Orderly Room, Len and I were kept on the staff with the old staff of the 11th. 'Q' was in charge again, much to our delight, as we heard that the Orderly Room Sgt. of the 11th was no treat to work with. He had fortunately been already transferred to another battalion.

Our new friends on the staff are a weird contrast. A young L/C name of Tommy, a sweet cherub of a boy with a cupid bow of a mouth, all smiles and merry quips. Looks as if he need not trouble about shaving for another 10 years. Guessed straight away from his ladylike voice that he came from Liverpool. Any mother would simply love him. We christened him 'Tommy Tittlemouse' straight away. The other was a full corporal. Full of misery, stone deaf, or nearly so, wore blue spectacles and his chin was always blue. We found that young Tommy had already found the only fitting name for him, 'Bluebird' which eventually was reduced to 'Bluey', which was even better.

The new Colonel, very young, very smart and very keen. Soldiers Friend and Khaki Blanco very much to the fore. Even the rifles of the Orderly Room staff had to have a clear view down the barrel.

We are delighted to find out here that we are still to be called the 6th Battalion and not the 11th.

1 July

We left St Loup, evidently going North again. Whether we are marching it all the way seems in doubt. A terrifically hot day, marched via Linthelles, Pleurs, Ognes, Corroy to Euvy where we stayed the night.

2 July

Off again on foot, hotter than ever, the white roads unbearable. Via Gourgancon, Semoine. Cannot admire any scenery, everyone blinded with perspiration and dust. Worst march we have met yet. 'Bluey' commencing cursing soon after we left in the morning, he never could be cheerful in the best of times, and he cursed consistently, practically the whole day, when everybody else's lips were too parched and cracked to utter a sound. Halting for a short spell in one village, we looked such a dead beat lot that the villagers came rushing out with jugs of water, some even with beer and vin rouge. A sharp order was given by the 'C.O.' and officers drew revolvers, threatening to shoot any one giving drink to the troops. I don't think the threat was meant seriously, but it scared the villagers off. It may have been good discipline for the troops, but I don't think the new 'C.O.' endeared himself much by it. The 'Bluebird' however was still cursing. He commenced the march by feeling sure he could not manage his pack for a mile, at the second mile he wants to shoot all the officers, at the third mile the King himself must be assassinated, at the fourth mile the whole British Empire must be wiped out, and so it continues till his last complaint is that "his kidneys had gone". Tommy, who had evidently been somewhat in fear of the gloomy corporal before our arrival, was quite startled when Len started loud enquiries in the ranks, for two lost corporal's kidneys. My solicitous enquiries from the corporal himself as to where they might have gone, received no answer.

We eventually arrived at a large French Camp at Mailly. Baths were immediately available and, as there was a village close by where plenty of refreshment and entertainment was available, the march was quickly forgotten.

3 July

The next day we entrained at Mailly in the evening evidently bound for the North again.

After 23 hours on the train, we detrained at Pont-Remy only about half way to our supposed destination. We had however the pleasure of a glimpse of the sea from the train, at one part of the journey, "The same water wot touches Dover" as someone remarked. We were marched to a big camp here, and found Americans busy training on Machine Guns. It happened to be American Independence Day but nothing unusual was taking place. The only excitement during our stay in the camp being Mr Lloyd George's visit to the camp to see the American troops. As we were not paraded during his visit, we felt we were not respectable enough, and rather glad of it. The general opinion was expressed, however, that our hair did not need cutting as badly as L.G's did.

7 July

On July 7th we entrained again at Pont-Remy and arrived at St Omer the same evening, marching to Clairmarais and camping there in the fields for the night. The new C.O. evidently just picked what looked like a fairly comfortable field, and was marching us in when the farmer appeared gesticulating wildly and shouting at the C.O. in what appeared to us to be very bad language in French. The C.O. took no notice until the farmer caught hold of his horse's bridle.

Then the C.O. playfully produced his revolver and scared him off, but as he returned to attack he was pleasantly escorted off his own field by a couple of amused privates with fixed bayonets.

Early next morning orders were issued for an early parade of all ranks for inspection. In the Orderly Room this caused us no excitement beyond rushing the orders round to Company Commanders. We were aghast when our friend the R.S.M. looked in and warned us all for parade. We, of course, said it wasn't possible and all that, but he explained, in his sweetest tones, that cooks, officers' batmen, Orderly Room staff and 'all the rest of the riff-raff' were to parade with the battalion. 'Q' disappeared discreetly, so there was nothing for it but for Len and me to turn out as soon and as quickly as possible, especially as the R.S.M. added genially, that he would come round and shoot us up if we were not on parade. We were back on duty in the orderly room later when the R.S.M. looked in and grinned most ferociously, remarking that if he ever caught us on parade again in his lifetime, he would shoot us on sight. It is so difficult to please some people. What happened was that Len and I had 'fixed bayonets' on hearing the order 'Fix' instead of 'waiting for it' as we had learned in our first week in the army, but had long forgotten. The officer inspecting our rifles had looked down the barrels of our respective rifles, turned pale, but passed on lost for words. The R.S.M. following was evidently gratified at our 'passing' on the rifles, but was inquisitive enough to have a look down the barrels himself. Hence his visit to the Orderly Room later.

We stayed here two nights, and on the 9th July marched 22 kilos to St. Jans Capelle via Arques, Le Nieppe, Bavinchove, Oxelaere and St Marie Capelle.

10 July

Orderly Room established in the schoolmaster's house at St Jans Capelle. Very comfortable, but not room for a staff of five. The Colonel decided to have two orderly rooms. The present one to be used as the 'posh' orderly room, where he would hold office hours, 'Q' and Len to take charge there. Tommy, Bluebird and myself to find fresh quarters where we could do the office work. We found a room at the estaminet 'La Pomme d'Or'. Our room was divided from the estaminet proper by the house passage, really too near when work was on hand, but convenient enough at other times.

Not the least attraction of the estaminet was Madamoiselle, who officiated behind the little bar and looked the pocket edition of some panto fairy queen. She held sway over the room with a frosty smile for polite French, a stony stare for bad language and always made a point of speaking English. A polite murmur of "Biere Madamoiselle" always brought

"Beer Tommy Yees". Any hint of familiarity from our side of the bar was frozen in the bud by an icy stare. Mere (Ma), fat and dirty, only seemed to show her head at intervals over the top cellar step to hand up supplies.

Only once did we rise early enough to catch a sight of Madamoiselle before business opened at the estaminet. We wondered whether the grub reached the butterfly stage in one move before business hours, missing the chrysalis stage out altogether.

11 July

The day seemed full of Generals. The Corps, Division and Brigade Commanders appearing in turn, to see whether we were worth taking over. Separate parades for the benefit of each. They all seemed to take us on trust, for a while at any rate.

Pat has another grudge against the world in general. The officers are going up to the line in turn to reconnoitre the Godewaersvelde district, and he has been taken off the signals (where he had nothing to do at present), in order to look after their 'Messing' arrangements. That is not quite how Pat put it to me, but his respect for rank is not yet what it ought to be, despite my continual efforts to instil into his mind the sanctity of stars, or even stripes.

14 July

The bigger portion of the battalion detailed for working parties up the line, Tommy going along as clerk. Young Len has been detailed off for a fortnight rest at the seaside camp at Audresselles near Boulogne. This is a new departure, small parties to leave fortnightly. The young lady at the billet kissed him goodbye, which Len did not object to, but when she patted his head and murmured "Pauvre Piccanin" he was annoyed. I filled his place with 'Q' at the schoolmaster's house and left Bluebird to the tender mercies of the lady of 'La Pomme d'Or'.

'Q' seems to have made progress with the schoolmaster's daughter, and his French at the same time. The schoolmaster, his wife and daughters have to pass through our room to retire at night, and do it in procession each evening, the youngest daughter leading the way, with Pa and Ma bringing up the rear to make sure that there are no stragglers.

15 July

The old lady finds out that I make my bed with a couple of blankets on the tiled floor of the orderly room. Inconsolable, until I accept the loan of a spare mattress which I have difficulty in disposing of as orderly room furniture during the day.

The Adjutant today drew my attention to the fact that my trousers were not in a state of repair desirable in an Orderly Room, especially in an Orderly Room visited by ladies, and suggested a visit to the stores. A visit there found the Stores in the same parlous state 'Out of Trousers'. I was, however, supplied with a rather gay pair of riding breeches, but no horse.

'Q' and myself busy one morning in the Orderly Room (talking to Lucienne) heard a terrific din in the school yard, and looking through the window watched an interesting performance. The children were lined up in the yard with old 'P.H.' gas helmets slung over the shoulder. In front stood the schoolmaster with a little boy who held an empty biscuit tin and a big stick. On the order the boy beat the tin noisily, while the children got into their gas masks with wonderful smartness and precision, and marched round the yard until they were halted. They repeated the performance half a dozen times before disappearing into school again. They thoroughly enjoyed it as a game. If soldiers ever prayed, we sent up a silent one that it may never be more than a game to them.

The old lady here interested to find me wearing a wedding ring. Very strange. Any piccanins? Producing latest photo of Jim in my rookies hat and leather belt, Ma and all the girls (including Lucienne, 22) send him a substantial kiss. 'Q' wondering now how he can produce the photo of his little daughter, after having informed Lucienne, during a French lesson, that he was a single man. Gave him a homily on 'Truth its own reward'.

18 July

One of the schoolmaster's little girls had not been seen for a day or two. Ma in an anxious state asked if we would have a look at the little one. "Very sick, no doctor in the village". We put on our most professional air and were taken upstairs. We found the little one suffering agonies with a badly gathered face. Her face was very swollen and discoloured. Poor old Ma wondered whether our 'M.O.' would do anything for her. We knew, however, that he was away up the line with the working parties.

Then we thought of 'Bob'. Bob Cawley of Hyde was the M.O.'s factotum and battalion chiropodist, who, when out of 'number nines', will give you a No. 4 and a No. 5 with the desired result, and if you speak to him nicely on the quiet, and present him with a green envelope, he will find you a cure for anything, from a running nose to a galloping consumption. He came and was inducted upstairs in state. 'Q' was of the party as interpreter (though Bob did not think he needed one). What capacity I was required in I do not know, but as I had been to find Bob, the old lady evidently thought that on that account, I was entitled to a place on the team. Bob looked at the little girl's face and 'Q' asked him what it was.

Bob replied "Joost abeaut reep". The poor old lady nearly collapsed when she heard what it was, and it made 'Q' perspire freely to explain matters. Bob said he would be back in a minute or two and would they get some water ready "Tres chaud". 'Q' was not going to get all the honours, in French anyway. He appeared again very shortly with his Red Cross satchel and a small case of surgical lances. When he opened this the old lady turned pale, and 'Q' spent another busy five minutes explaining to her the meaning of Bob's "There's nowt geet t'wind up abeaut". Bob got to work deftly and had the little girl more comfortable in a very short space of time, sucking something mysterious and pungent. As Ma was thanking him profusely he gave her a final fright by looking gloomily at the little girl and remarking in a hopeless voice "Ool be awreet bi't morn".

Then I took him downstairs and paid his fee with a couple of green envelopes.

22 July

Just deciding that we could manage the war very well indeed from St Jans Capelle, but orders came in today for an early move in the morning.

24 July

After marching about in the rain for two days, we eventually settled down in a farm billet on the Steenvoorde-Eecke road, not more than 7 or 8 miles from St Jans Capelle. The boys who had been working up the line rejoined us here. We fixed up the Orderly Room in what appeared to be a cellar store for potatoes under the barn. Quite comfortable if not overclean. One company was billeted in the barn overhead. We had to move some of the boys, however, from over our ceiling, as a pair of legs suddenly appeared through one evening, covering us with dust and straw.

29 July

Len arrived back from the seaside rest camp at Audresselles, looking very different from when he left us. He gave glowing accounts of the bathing, the food and the general lack of anything in the way of work at the camp. He had evidently grown particular since he had been away, as he no sooner got settled in than he commenced to speak very disparagingly of our premises. After being suitably squashed, he settled down to work.

He paused a little later in the midst of a furious attack on the typewriter to moan pathetically "Well I have seen Blighty anyway". We put it down to a touch of sunstroke, but he would insist that he had seen Dover cliffs from Audresselles.

30 July

Pat and myself detailed for the holiday camp on August 2nd. Now praying fervently that no shells or bombs drop too near the billet before that date. We were given an afternoon off to find the nearest Divisional Bath, so that we might go away for our holiday nice and clean. We might also apply to the stores for a new shirt each (if any). We had no difficulty in obtaining the shirts after I had given the stores corporal my definite assurance that his name was near the top of the leave list. As a matter of fact, it was not a fact, my inborn veracity giving way before my anxiety to wear a new clean shirt for my holiday. The bath was a different matter. Even for a bath we could not find it in our hearts to walk six miles there and six miles back. Pat knew of a local pond which would do just as well, so we did our best with plenty of cold water, instead of a little drop of hot.

2 August

Pat and I left at 6.0 a.m. for the holiday camp at Audresselles as the battalion was preparing to leave Steenvoorde for Cassel. We reached the 2nd Army Rest Camp in time for tea. Audresselles was a small fishing village about nine miles north of Boulogne. The fishing industry, however, seemed to have been put on one side for the time being, the only industry at present being catering for the thirst and general amusement of that part of the B.E.F. at present located at the Rest Camp.

The camp was on the sand dunes just out of the village. The first evening we spent in the camp getting settled down. The next day, being thoroughly wet, we did not get further than the village. We were allowed as far as the village without belts and puttees. This was evidently part of the rest cure. The only daily parade was 9.30 a.m. This was a compulsory bathing parade, compulsory to the extent of marching down across the dunes to the beach carrying a towel. In addition to the compulsory bathing parade at 9.30 a.m., bathing could be indulged in during the afternoon and evening. A dozen men were detailed each day as 'Bathing Picket'. It is presumed they were there to see that no one deserted by way of swimming the Channel. If the weather was clear we could distinctly see the Dover cliffs, the temptation was actually there. In addition to the picket, there was also a guard boat manned by two fishermen, to cut off any such aspirants to Channel fame. This was all very discouraging to long distance swimmers. There were no regulations regarding costumes, for the simple reason that there were no costumes.

Being the only man amongst the 13 in our tent weighted with the dignity of a 'stripe', I was put in charge of the tent. My responsibilities were purely nominal, as everyone just pleased themselves. My chief duty seemed to be the evening lie to the Orderly Sgt. when he slapped the tent with his stick at 'lights out' "All present Corporal?" "Yes Sgt." I think the Sgt. himself was on holidays and would not have thanked me if I had informed him of the true state of affairs. We were always complete before dawn at any rate.

9 August

A Red Letter Day. Pat's sister, who was at one of the big hospitals in Boulogne visited us. We took her down to the rocks (well away from the bathing beach), and spent a most delightful afternoon speaking English instead of B.E.F. We were a little bit out of practice, but by going carefully, we managed quite creditably. The high point of the day came when Miss Nunn opened a delightful little tea-basket. As we packed the basket for her some time later, we sighed as we thought of supper out of the usual mess-tin.

11 August

Pat and I obtained passes for an afternoon in Boulogne. We promised ourselves a little treat in the shape of a nice little dinner, at some nice little place and, if funds ran that far, a little bottle of something more choice than the everlasting 'Vin Blanc'. We were doomed to disappointment. Each nice little place that we found was reserved for officers only. Looking through the windows we could see nothing below 2nd Lts or above Generals, barring the waiters. We eventually subsided into a Soldiers Institute, where we had a substantial meal, which Pat described as 'Feeding not Dining'. I offered him comfort by explaining that evidently one could not 'Dine' without getting the 'Pip', so to speak, and received an icy stare in reply, which I deserved. We spent the short remaining time looking round jewellers and curio shops, much to the discomfort and worry of the proprietors. We priced a few 'Objets d'art' (quite good that), but found the dot in the price was anything between two to four places further to the right than we could afford.

We finished up the evening by sitting at a little open air café and watching the last train leave that would have taken us a mile or two back on our way to camp. We did not of course know that it was the last train until we had finished our glasses.

Pat immediately suggested that we call on his sister at the hospital, who had promised to find him a bed if he happened to stay a night in Boulogne. Now I have never objected, nor has Pat, to our joining of a blanket anywhere under all sorts of circumstances, but two in a hospital cot, no not for me. Besides I am responsible for the evening lie to the Orderly Sgt. at 'Lights out' and I could not have it on my conscience that someone else would have to do it for me.

'My duty' I explained to Pat, "N.C.O. in charge of the tent and all that". My good counsels prevailed and we did eventually arrive back in camp before 'Lights out', aided by a surreptitious ride on the back of an Ambulance car.

15 August

All good things come to an end sometime and today found us marching back to the train. Find packs rather heavy after only using them for pillows during the last fortnight. Belts also prove evidence of a little extra adipose, which will no doubt disappear shortly. Find the battalion out of the line in bivouac at Steenvoorde.

21 August

'A Local Operation'

Half the battalion left camp at dusk, as did two other half battalions in the neighbourhood on the same errand. We soon divided up into smaller sections for obvious reasons, and wended our way across country tracks. There was still light enough to see the notices here and there "This track must not be used by daylight". The original reason of the notices was that troops using the track by daylight might give away the position of the tracks to enemy aircraft. In their present state it was easier to trace the tracks from the shell holes along them, than from any actual evidence of the tracks themselves. We eventually reached a high road which was in an even worse state.

The road took us through the village of Locre. When we were in Locre last in October 1917 it was the most pleasant of places, very few of the inhabitants had left, quiet little estaminets abounded. The only objectionable feature to the average Tommy, being the presence of numerous "Brass Hats" in the vicinity, and the consequent strain of exceptionally smart behaviour. It was so quiet and peaceful then, that it was rumoured that some of the elite of the War Correspondents had been allowed in the village.

Now all was devastation with the hideous reek of high explosives and unburied dead. The pretty cemetery, where Capt. Redmund (son of the great Irish patriot) was buried, was shelled away out of all recognition. The lovely old church was a heap of stone and rubble, a stark dagger of ragged masonry jutting into the dark sky, was all that was left of the great square tower. All round the district, that had been well known as the best of resting places for tired troops, had become almost like to the hideous no man's land that we had become accustomed to in those long months in front of Ypres. This devastation had all come about after the big German advance in March had been held up on the Somme, and the enemy had then turned his attention to trying to break through in the North of the line.

It is after midnight when we reach the line, we are evidently staying in the Support Line for the night. Accommodation of sorts has to be found along with the troops already in the line. Rations for the following day had been served out to the men before leaving camp, and a good soldier can always be relied on to find tonight's supper out of tomorrow's rations.

The art of living improvidently, one meal mortgaged, has here been brought to a science.

Everyone is busy next morning. Conferences of officers at the C.O.'s dugout, carrying parties bringing up wire, stakes and other impedimenta, inspections of rifles, bayonets, serving out bombs, shovels, etc. The telephone in the C.O.'s dugout seems one continual buzz.

Darkness arrives at last, rolls of wire, stakes etc. are continually passing our dugout, and over the top. Signallers are hanging 'Don threes' round their necks and getting inextricably enmeshed in coils of wire. Nobody seems to know what time 'ZERO' is to be.

'ZERO' is that mysterious moment, the close approach of which causes a strange feeling of tightness under the ears, and can even make a bald headed corporal fancy that his hair is standing to attention. The boys move up at last in the darkness, and those left at Headquarters make a feeble effort to be very casual in wishing 'Good luck' to a particular chum. The troops who have been holding the front line come in as our boys arrive up.

We all suddenly become interested in the weather. "Too much moon" "A mist coming up, good!" etc. Even the Adjutant strolls out, whistling softly (a sure sign of excitement), looks at the moon and peers at his watch. Hoping for some information as to 'ZERO' I ask him for the right time. As he is notoriously suspicious of his own watch and frequently pops in to refer to my watch often hung in the Orderly Room, he grinned understandingly. "Brigade Officer expected up any minute to synchronise watches" he replied. This officer arrived almost immediately and disappeared into H.Q. dugout, reappearing very soon waving a 'Cheerio' to the Adjutant and quickly disappearing in the direction of Brigade Headquarters. The Adjutant coming down to earth from gazing at the stars again, looks at his watch, "Correct time Corporal is ..." and in a lower voice "ZERO 2.15, time to dig in before dawn". He strolls off leaving me to marvel at the wonderful forethought of the great ones in thinking of these things. Dear old 'Tubby', if all Adjutants were as cheerful and easy to get on with, the war would not be so bad.

"Three minutes to go". A machine gun opened out and we thought they were too early, but the gunner was evidently just warming his barrel up for 2.15.

"Two minutes to go". "They are late" said someone. "Put it under a tram next time you see one" someone retorted.

"One minute to go". A dead silence, then someone started to speak, but no one heard what he said. The only man who made himself heard at all, was the man who yelled "They're off". The odds are that he was a Bookie in civilian life. One cannot quite truthfully say that we heard the barrage from our guns. Ear drums were never meant to cope with such a weight of noise, but one's flesh felt the peculiar sensation of being treated like the skin of a kettledrum for the introduction of the National Anthem.

The mist was now so thick that we could not see the flashes of our guns, nor the burst of shell. We peered through the mist to try to see the enemy 'S.O.S.' rockets go up, as we expected to find ourselves in a hot corner as soon as they went up. The mist was too thick however. The German's supporting artillery evidently could not see them either, as we seemed to get no reply. Telephones would be absolutely useless, as not a wire could have survived our opening barrage. By this time our boys would be in the enemy lines. In fact before the mist cleared, and the German's Artillery had found out where they were wanted, our boys were busy digging in and consolidating beyond the German's front line. The first news loomed out of the fog in the shape of a youngster with what looked suspiciously like a shattered wrist. He was quite cheerful about it, and was convinced that it was 'A sure Blighty'. He was shown into the Aid Post, while it was reported to the C.O. that a 'walking casualty' had come in. "Bring him in when he has been attended to". The C.O. was sat with his ear glued to a telephone, the other end of which was in charge of the signallers with the attacking party.

All the news the youngster could give when he returned to H.Q. dugout was "We've got 'em guessing Sir". Not much but quite satisfactory so far as it went. "Drink this and get down" was his dismissal and he quickly disappeared on his way to 'Blighty'. The next to turn up was a procession of 7 Germans carrying a machine gun between them, the rear being brought up by a rather diminutive Lance Corporal looking very businesslike and formidable. The prisoners did not need to understand much English to know what the L/C meant when he yelled "HALT" in the voice of a Guards Instructor. He walked into H.Q. dugout leaving his collection outside in quite good hands.

"Seven prisoners and one machine gun" he reported, clicking his heels at the C.O. The C.O. weighed him up and smiled. "How did you do it Corporal?" "Didn't Sir, I only brought them down, there were eight Sir" said the Corporal. "Where is the odd one?" enquired the C.O. "He didn't want to come Sir" explained the Corporal apologetically. "Poor chap" murmured the C.O. sympathetically. A few more questions and the Lance Corporal disappeared to pick up a few more machine gun teams. After the prisoners had been questioned by the C.O. they were taken to the M.O. to act as stretcher bearers. As other prisoners were brought in they were escorted back to Brigade Headquarters, after the Medical Officer's requirements had been met. About 6.0 a.m. the enemy artillery really woke up and, after putting down a heavy barrage, a heavy counter attack developed. Our artillery machine guns quite quickly decided that this was to be nipped in the bud. The attack was nipped so closely that not one man reached our new line.

Instead of taking the matter of his beating in a philosophic spirit, our friend the enemy simply got bad tempered and treated us to a good sample of Artillery hate for the next hour or two, which kept us all distinctly uncomfortable instead of being able to pat ourselves on the back in peace. Within the next 24 hours the enemy made various counter-attacks with unvarying failure, and those two or three half battalions eventually handed over their new line to the care of relieving troops.

The whole show seems to have been rather a fuss about rather little, but our sense of proportion was corrected later when we received our daily paper with the morning milk,

In the successful local operation carried out by us this morning south of Locre we captured 138 prisoners. [Actual newspaper cutting]

Some time before the relief, the Adjutant sent me off with my list of casualties (pleasantly light) and various other matters requiring attention, to find the Orderly Room with the transport, in the neighbourhood of Boeschepe. As all the roads in the vicinity were receiving a deal of attention from the enemy artillery, I decided to try my hand at cross country, if only to disprove Pat's often asserted contention that I could never find my way anywhere if left by myself. I eventually arrived at Boeschepe, but thought it wiser not to let Pat know how long it had taken me to find it. I am afraid he had his suspicions, as he seemed quite delighted that I had not gone due East and been well on the way to Cologne. Very nice and 'cushy' under canvas, under the shelter of the hill, the only fly in the ointment is a big gun close by. When the gun starts play, we close down work in the Orderly Room, as with each round fired the tent flaps about, bits drop off the old typewriter, open books shut up and closed books fly open, as if by magic.

23 August

The remainder of the battalion goes up to the line with Len as clerk, remainder of Orderly Room and details pack up to join the transport at Steenvoorde. Feeling very hot and tired on the way, dropped behind and lost sight of the rest of the party. I decided to have a rest before trying to catch up. Some hours later a search party, consisting of Tommy and two runners, sent out by 'Q', found me still asleep by the roadside only a couple of miles from Steenvoorde. Reported for duty very meek and subdued and spent most of the evening listening to various revised versions of the tale of 'The Babes in the Wood'.

27 August

'Q' introduces Corporal Billy Hunter, returned to the battalion after being on Brigade Headquarters since 1916. As the Orderly Room is now overstaffed, we expect there will soon be some transfers to companies. Billy Hunter goes up to relieve Len and as one of the Company 'Q.M. Sergts.' has been gassed rather badly and is not fit to take up his ration party at night, Tommy steps into the breach. We fear for Tommy's welfare, as he is only young and C.Q.M. Sgts. invariably carry a C.Q.M. Sgts. ration of rum in their water bottles to soften the hardships of night travelling. Perhaps Tommy knew this.

28 August

The weather breaks badly, torrential rain. Our French tent has door flaps back and front, neither of which meet by six inches – very nice for summer weather (if fine). We got so busy digging sump holes inside the tent to take the water, that we forgot to cover up the tables. All our stationery papers are reduced to pulp and artistically streaked with traces of copying ink pencil.

   Tommy and Len turned up in a sorry plight at 2.0 a.m. soaked through, dead beat and gassed. As things were quiet and no one about, Billy Gee (Q's batman) and I got them into a barn that we were not supposed to use, settled them down in the straw and by dint of systematic 'scrounging' we obtained a tin of condensed milk, a sufficiency (perhaps more) of rum and, boiling some hot water, we dosed them all with the concoction. We then purloined a couple of the post corporal's mail bags, shuffled Len into one and Tommy into the other, piled them over with straw and left them, confident in the result of our special treatment.

We peeped in at our invalids at breakfast time, but as they were sleeping like a couple of babes (more or less) we left them alone. Our treatment proved so successful that they wakened at dinnertime well enough to curse us roundly for not waking them for breakfast.

30 August

We hear that the enemy is retiring through Wytschaete and Messines, and we are on the move again, joining in the fighting for Dranoutre Ridge.

We suffered fairly heavy casualties and lost one of our best officers, Captain Nicholson. Young Harry Murphy, the little boxer I have mentioned before, had both legs badly shattered. He was soon being carried to the aid post by his big brother Jim, and being assured by him that one leg at least would patch up. Jim was badly wounded a few minutes after depositing his sad burden at the aid post.

31 August

In the same envelope received today from the Casualty Clearing Station, advising the death of Harry, was a field card from Harry to his brother Jim, with everything stroked through but the line "I am quite well". Harry never had a grumble about anything.

9 September

We move up to Kemmel Hill, any amount of dead French troops lying in the rank undergrowth, evidence of the terrific fighting that had taken place for the hill.

The place reeks of the dead, high explosive and gas. We suffered a few casualties from 'Mug Traps' left by the enemy, before official warnings were issued. After hearing of the man who found a bottle of beer in a dugout and who left no evidence of where he went to drink it, we look askance at German helmets, belts or souvenirs in any shape or form, and all turned 'T.T.', excepting of course official rum, officially issued.

Nights in the Orderly Room tent were not devoid of excitement. Leaving my tent in inky blackness with a message for the Adjutant on the first night, I tripped over a tangle of wires and measured my length in the mud; waiting for the end and counting up the times I had been accused of having a dirty rifle, being unshaved and many lesser sins, it slowly dawned on me that these were our own signal wires. Thereafter I fell over them each night regularly without a qualm.

We are here in support for the 89th Brigade and we hope they will need more active support as our location is distinctly disagreeable.

A Bosche plane shot down one of ours on our side of the hill today, but our anti-aircraft brought the Bosche down and we saw him come down in flames on the far side of the hill.

14 September

We relieve the Inniskillens in support on the Neuve-Église Sector, take up positions at Dead Man's Corner (sweet name) and down the Neuve-Église Road. Why had we grumbled at Kemmel. Headquarters find quite a good cellar on the roadside, big enough to hold H.Q. officers, runners, signals etc. Our artillery has a battery of 'heavies' just off the other side of the road, and every round rocks our cellar. The enemy artillery are trying to find the battery and, as they are short, we are not too comfortable. Their range improved so much, however, that the battery moved. We seriously think of sending a message to Fritz, to advise them of it, as they don't seem to know, and we are still getting it hot. Perish the thought but have they seen our new C.O. in his new lavender breeches entering our cellar? Our new Colonel is very 'posh', very regimental and expresses his dislike of living in such close proximity with the 'Other Ranks' of Headquarters staff. Not conducive to discipline etc. Finds a smaller cellar some distance along the road and there are dugouts round about it for signallers, runners, etc., I suppose I am an etc. Move up the road and find the so-called dugouts – just a few small shelter holes dug in the side of what looked like an old rubbish tip. Five runners squeezed themselves into one of the holes, that looked better than the rest, as it was lined with corrugated iron. Bobby (the R.S. Major's general factotum) and I had not got settled in when we heard it come. We dived down into the mud. When we picked ourselves up, half stunned, we saw that the shell had dropped right into the opening of the runners little shelter. We dug frenziedly with our hands while shouting for help and dragged out 'Jud' Foley, recognisable only by his black curly hair and medal ribbons. We carried him to the M.O., who was already on the spot, 'Jud' was still alive. With many helpers, Gamble and Bailey were pulled out, badly smashed, but also still alive. What was left of Lee and Birk was wrapped up as reverently as possible to wait the Transport. Gamble died before the M.O. could do anything for him.

The Adjutant found room for Bob and me in his sleeping quarters and, after we had seen the transport leave, we sat there, blood soaked and reeking of lyddite, feeling sore and bitter. All five of the runners were Bob's pals who had come out with him in 1914, then only young boys. I tried to persuade him to get down and sleep a bit, but he refused and, as he was becoming hysterical, I slipped out to find the R.S.M., I told him how things were and he exchanged water bottles with me. When I had settled Bob down I tried to get some work done, but I could not settle to it. As it had quietened down outside, I sat out of doors on an ammunition box and wondered why it should be a nice cool moonlit night.

15 September

Another bad day at Dead Man's Corner, the boys in the trench in front support have been shelled and gassed all day. Capt. Kenyon, one of our very best officers being carried past on a stretcher, stopped to discuss the position of the trench with the C.O. and says that it is untenable. C.O. says that orders are that the trench must be held as ordered, and wished the Captain "Good Luck". The Captain manages to salute and the stretcher bearers set off again. We hear later that the Captain died before the stretcher bearers had reached the Aid Post. Gas cases coming along now in a string.

Sergeant Speakman killed in the trench. Support lines lately are the very devil, can do nothing but hang about the trenches getting knocked about and gassed and not even firing a shot.

17 September

The companies change over and the same thing goes on. 'Q' is on leave in Stockport and has promised to call and see my wife. I can trust him to tell a good tale of the good times we have, and leave the rest alone.

22 September

We leave Dead Man's Corner with no regret, for a rest behind Mount Rouge. Good French dugouts in the hillside for the troops. Someone decides that the Orderly Room needs fresh air, so a tent is fixed up, actually with floor boards and rush chairs (souvenirs). The only drawback at night is having to blow the candles out every few minutes, when enemy planes fly over. Have now invented a patent shade, a biscuit tin with holes, only in the sides. When we hear the warning whistle we drop the tin over the candle, just leaves sufficient light to see by. If the 'all clear' whistle does not come quickly, however, the candles get soft and then there is trouble.

23 September

Went to Meteren for a bath and new undies, first wash all over since our seaside holiday. Feel quite cheerful and quite a lot nearer to godliness. The Band returns from some weeks playing at an Officers School, very posh, fix a bandstand up in the valley and play us all the latest. It is quite a good war at present.

27 September

The Padre holds a very early Communion Service in his dugout, it is well attended, and we do not seem to mind the fact that these celebrations in the forward areas usually precede some big move. The battalion moves up the same night, again to the same vile spot. The roads are blocked with transport, and going through Locre everything's an absolute jam. The enemy always seems to find out about these little matters and proceeds to shell the roads with disastrous results.

8 October

Since the 28th Sept. we have been travelling to some purpose, through Wulverghem (we knew it was Wulverghem by the sign post on a heap of rubble at the cross roads), and over Messines Ridge. Messines itself is only identified by the ruins of the old Hospice Mill. Desolation and mud everywhere with many signs of the enemy's hasty departure, but we are still very wary of picking up souvenirs. From Messines we moved along the top of Wytschaete Ridge to Wytschaete. The road here is lined with wonderfully built concrete dugouts, many of which have been pulverised by our heavy shell fire. We can now understand why we have had such an uncomfortable time in the valley between here and Mount Kemmel. The whole ridge is a perfect observation post. On through Oosttaverne, along tracks with queer German names, one a wooden road nearly two miles long called Zigzagweg. It was truly zigzag and turned abruptly about every hundred yards, first right and then left. It was a wonderful idea to reduce loss by shell fire. We rested a night in a huge German dump at the end of this road. We were now in sight of Wervicq, and could see the church plainly. What an observation post for the enemy. I am afraid if he stays there long the Church Tower is going to suffer. We have been relieved today and come out to Joye Farm in reserve. Joye Farm consists of a few trenches on the East side of Wytschaete Ridge with small dugouts and a huge concrete Pill Box in the valley. Where the farm was we never heard. We were not supposed to shew ourselves by daylight, but it is doubtful whether the shelling could have been worse if we had held pastoral plays in daylight in the valley. The chief target seemed to be the Pill Box, which had been used as a German H.Q.s and which the enemy must know would now be in similar use. There were two rooms and while the C.O. and H.Q. Officers used the larger room, the other room held the Orderly Room, cooks, signallers, runners and batmen, and we disobeyed orders frequently by sitting outside to get a breath of fresh air. It was a wonderful erection and wonderfully lousy inside. The sides and roof were three feet of solid concrete. On top of the concrete roof were alternate layers of wire brattice and lengths of steel rails, finished off with another solid layer of concrete on top. The Hun obtained one or two direct hits on it during our occupancy, but beyond giving us all a headache and making us feel slightly sick, and putting the lights out, very little damage was done.

We have great discussions on the respective merits of the German louse and the B.E.F. variety. After extensive tests it is proved beyond doubt that though the Germans can beat us for size, they cannot touch the B.E.F. for speed and staying power.

We received word that a bath and clean shirts were available at a certain map reference, which we made out to be somewhere between Wytschaete and Messines, and a few of us decided to get there somehow. A rendezvous was arranged, and for sometime previously a few figures might have been seen stalking off from the pill box in all kinds of queer positions, making for the rendezvous over the top of Wytschaete Ridge, where we hoped to be out of observation. After a long walk, enlivened by a shell or two, we eventually found where the bath had been. Like the rest of us even the Bath must have either advanced or gone back to reserve. We sat down in the mud to express our feelings more comfortably and then set off back. As some compensation for the loss of bath, we were treated to a deluge of rain on the way back in the darkness. No party is too small to contain the man who knows a short cut. Our party is no exception. Of course we got hopelessly lost, fell into shell holes and had a good time generally. To add to the gaiety of the evening we were compelled to don gas masks for the last mile home, as the Hun was dropping gas shells.

Sometime later in the pill box, when our four-foot something bugler, who had been with us and was scraping himself clean with a bayonet, remarked "There's nowt like a bath and a clean shirt to fresh a feller up". We fell on him and threatened him that if he dared to be cheerful about it, we would choke him with his own bugle the next time we saw him with it.

13 October

The powers that be have evidently decided that our present location is not a place to stay with the winter coming on. For once we agree with them. The drains are bad and we are sadly overlooked, and what Englishman likes his privacy destroyed. The roof of the pill box isn't what it was either. We were overlooked from all the higher ground over the River Lys. There was the tower of Wervicq church, Paur Bucq hill and beyond, all overlooking the ground we occupied. If Fritz would only mind his own business and get off home quietly, it would not be so bad. Beyond the river looked like the promised land, perhaps not flowing with milk and honey, but at least it looks better underfoot.

14 October

5.35 a.m. A wonderful barrage opens the proceedings. The smoke shells make a splendid cover for the attack. The Irish and the Londons lead the attack for our brigade, and quickly take all objectives except the River itself. The enemy will not budge from the high ground across the river which makes the crossing a problem, having blown up the bridges.

15 October

At dawn our battalion passed through the Irish and got one company across by the aid of a bridge hastily repaired under a smoke barrage by the R.E., a wonderful piece of quick work, the R.E. suffering heavy casualties, but carry it through. We feel a little conscious of the many nasty things we have said about them in the past. The lads have a hot job clearing machine gun nests out of Wervicq-Sud. The rest of the battalion push through Wervicq, but held up by heavy machine gun fire from Paur Bucq Hill. By late afternoon the boys are half way up the hill, but held up again by machine guns. After dark a battalion of Highland Light Infantry came up to relieve us, but our C.O. would not hand over until he could hand over Paur Bucq Hill, top included. We handed over the hill complete at 2.0 a.m. and made our way out, tired, wet and hungry to Tenbrielen, where we put up tents in a sea of mud.

17 October

Bobby, now L/Corporal in charge of runners, looking after me as if I was his father, brings me in a nice new German shirt, officer's by the look of it, and I am unpatriotic enough to get into it at once, although I have still enough of my old shirt left to polish my rifle with.

Great excitement in the camp, someone has a copy of the 'Sunday Chronicle' of the 13th October, from which we learn that Peace has been declared. Four days since and we never knew. Why on earth did we start the war off again on the 14th. We are served out with a substantial rum ration, that settles all doubts. The 'Sunday Chronicle' has got it all wrong. Guns are going through, all but the heavies are now out of range, even observation balloons are being towed along by motors with observers still up.

We get sudden orders to pack, and we are off up again to try to catch the front line troops, who are evidently on the run (Eastwards). Through Menin we go, so this is Menin. We had come to believe that there was no such place, and that the Menin Road only led to Blighty or the little Rest Camps where little wooden crosses grow. We don't like the look of Menin anyway, spikes of walls sticking up like daggers into the darkening sky, not a whole wall left in the place, nor a living soul. We push on through Ghelne and put up comfortably for the night in a big German camp.

18 October

Off again early, marching through Lauwe and Reckhem and got as far as Aelbeke, where we get in touch with the enemy just beyond the village, by 10am. 18 pounder field guns are put under orders of Battalion Commanders. The lads are not too comfortable with the guns following in the rear, afraid they might go off, but as it dawns on us that they don't travel muzzle forward, our fears are allayed. By late afternoon we had gone forward ten miles, the enemy only fighting a light rearguard action with machine gun posts, which were quickly disposed of by our own machine guns or bombs. If any proved stubborn we just sat round while a couple of the 18 pounders drew up and did a little practice, then we passed on again. We had only one killed during the day, a good man Sgt. Marsh. The natives insisted on digging his grave and promised to look after it.

In the evening we were relieved by fresh troops after we had passed over Coyghem Ridge. After we were fixed up comfortably in billets, we found, to our amusement, that all the girls and young women had been put carefully out of sight, as we found that 'Fritz' had grossly libelled our moral character. The old folks and the very young seemed to be reassured very quickly, and families were soon at full strength again. Most of the young ladies, however, would have been safe anywhere, and 'Fritz' need not have gone to so much trouble.

They have not seen British troops in these parts before, and we are soon made a fuss of, we seem to be subjects of interest and objects of rather embarrassing attentions. We could stand being kissed by the old ladies and some of the younger ones, but when the old men commenced to butt in we 'no compree'd'.

At the farm we used for a few hours for Headquarters, the old lady stayed up all night making coffee and roasting potatoes for us. Everyone that called in also had to have a basin of coffee and a potato.

One of our Company Q.M. Sgts., having had a heavy time of it bringing up his company's rations, had got lost on his way back and, being tired, slipped into a barn and laid himself down to sleep. He was wakened at dawn by an elderly dame tugging at his sleeve <u>and trying to coax him to a stiff glass of cognac.</u> After she had succeeded, she took him indoors to as good a breakfast as her house could provide.

An old chappie told us a good tale of how, when the Germans left, he was ordered to put his only horse in his only cart and join the transport, but soon after they had got on the move his cart collapsed. The baggage was quickly transferred and he was roundly cursed and left behind to mend his cart. Like a good raconteur he kept the point of his joke to the end. He had taken the axle pins out before he set off, and chanced his neck. It took him a long time to tell the tale, and we had no small difficulty in understanding him, until he took us outside and, with much vigorous pantomime, introduced us to the horse, the cart and even took the axle pins out. The difficulties of the telling did not detract a jot from the enjoyment of the listeners, or for that matter, of the teller.

22 October

Pat returned from Paris leave, bringing along a draft of half a dozen men, fresh from England. Since getting off the train it had taken them three days marching to catch us up. He seems to have been guide, philosopher, friend, cook, grub finder and nurse generally to the party. He swears he tracked us down by a trail of 'Cheshire' cap badges worn by the girls of the villages we had passed through. I thought he looked at me suspiciously, but I was able to produce mine for his inspection. He has had quite a good time in Paris, but <u>complained</u> that he did not dare put his face out of doors for fear of being kissed. We agreed with him that Paris had gone mad.

23 October

The great joke of the day. The old saying 'Down at the Transport Lines' is now out of date, as the transport nowadays is toddling along close in the rear. If we move across country they follow, if possible, by roads and by-roads. Today as we were moving across country the transport, fearing they might be left far behind, made good speed along the roads. Turning a corner through a village they suddenly found themselves close in the rear of the Germans and in front of us. They made a wild dash back into the village until we had well passed them. We have now christened them the Tank Corps.

We rest at Petit Turcoing whilst the 7th Royal Irish go through to cross the River Escaut, we hear that they failed at the first attempt but get across later in the evening.

26 October

'Fritz' is making a solid stand on the other side of the river, and we hear the Irish are having a heavy time of it, with their backs to the river.

Our worst enemy at present, however, is influenza. The villages we have been passing through were rampant with it, and we now have a hundred severe cases down with it, all fixed up in a big barn, one corner of which we are using as Orderly Room. The M.O. and his old factotum, Bob Cawley, are worked to death, and trying to attend to civilians as well. No chance of moving any to hospital. Late tonight an urgent message came from Bob Cawley's billet for the M.O. Before the M.O. reached there, Bob was dead. He had been busy in the barn a couple of hours before, making his patients comfortable for the night. Wherever he has gone Bob old man, he won't be happy unless he has someone to patch up and make comfortable. He could be gentle enough to mend angels' wings or strong enough to hold the devil himself still, while he straightened a crumpled horn for him. Medical Officers have come and gone, medical services have been reorganised, reduced, increased and changes of all kinds have occurred in his department, but Bob Cawley has gone on for ever (at least since 1914, before which nothing seems to have happened). He is buried in a nice little field at the back of the little estaminet in Petit Turcoing, and the husband of the lady who kept the estaminet carved a very special cross for his grave, for did not 'Bob' save madame's little girl from 'La Grippe'.

27 October

We leave quite a third of the battalion sick at Petit Turcoing and move up to St Genois on the west bank of the River Escaut. Not too comfortable along the roads in the darkness with gas helmets at the 'Alert' as 'Fritz' is shelling the roads with mixed shells. It is a sad sight to see the procession of civilians coming from St Genois, which is being heavily shelled. Imagine women pushing babies in bassinettes along shelled roads in the dead of night, little kiddies toddling along holding mothers skirts and sobbing with weariness and terror. Old women, some being wheeled in barrows, nuns and Sisters of Mercy helping all and sundry. One stalwart Sister of Mercy was seen trundling a heavy barrow with four small babies packed in safely and comfortably and seemingly fast asleep. To add to the terror of their journey they could not distinguish between the burst of German shells and the fire of our guns which were coming up, halting and firing off a few rounds, then moving up again and continuing the process. When we arrived at St Genois the civilians had all left and the place was being very badly shelled. The whole battalion was marched into the great cellar of the Hospice, while rations and fresh ammunition were served out. Headquarters remained at the Hospice. Dawn suggested an exploration of our quarters. It was a wonderful place built round a quadrangle, the walls of the quadrangle being painted with kindergarten pictures. There was a beautiful chapel and the remainder of the pile contained a big school, dormitories and huge kitchen premises, all in a state of damage and disorder. From the upper windows we could see over the River Escaut. A couple of shells went through another part of the building while some of us were in the upper premises. We did not bother too much about that, but when we found the windows being ranged by machine gun fire, we crept quietly down to the cellar again and proceeded with our various duties (if any).

Then the fun commenced. We could hear the buildings above us tumbling to pieces and shells dropping in the quad. The C.O. said that someone must have been moving about upstairs by daylight, we said nothing. We gazed at the great brick arches of the cellar and felt fairly comfortable. The C.O., however, decided that this was no place for Headquarters.

When there was a lull, our intelligent Intelligence Officer went out to see if he could find quieter quarters. He was back before long and had found a nice quiet farm just outside the village, so we were ordered to leave the Hospice, as and when we could and not more than two men at a time. For some time afterwards, at varying intervals, men in couples would appear in the open and dash out of the Hospice grounds, disappearing quickly out of sight. All that left the Hospice arrived safely at the farmhouse. Two 'Sanitary wallahs' decided that the Hospice cellar was safer and made it their own H.Q. until that evening when a 9 inch shell came through the cellar roof and embedded itself between their downy couches. It was a 'DUD'. It is said that they both kissed it affectionately and packed up their traps, then joined us at the farm in quick time.

The farmhouse had evidently been used as some Headquarters, and had seemingly been left in a great hurry, it was undamaged and quite well furnished. We even found a cupboard full of jam. The Adjutant found me a nice little room with a desk, a basket chair and a bed. The war improved daily. The little window of my room looked out on the back garden. The Mess had a piano in their room, but after an attempt had been made to play it, it was reverently closed again as a token of respect for its great age. I had just settled down to unpacking my stationery when the Adjutant hurried in and searched round hurriedly. He asked me if I had seen a bottle of 'Black & White' anywhere about. I thought he eyed me suspiciously, but confident in my innocence (and bad luck) I was able to assure him. He explained that he had brought it from the Hospice and put it down in this room, it happened to be the last bottle the Mess had got (or had lost), and Heaven help the man who had taken it. If it had met with an accident on the journey it would not have been so bad, but to land it safely and then a thing like that to happen. Sometime later a signaller came in with a message and asked me to go across and look them up at their billet. Not having stayed to look round on my arrival, I took the opportunity. Out of the front door we met the usual rectangular smell in the farmyard, but not so large as usual. One wall of the yard was built up to its whole height and length with rabbit hutches, many of them occupied. They were either huge rabbits or Belgian hares, my knowledge of natural history not being equal to the task of stating a case. My attention being distracted by a pleasant odour of cooking, I walked across the yard to the barns opposite and found the runners and signallers snugly ensconced in a brick cellar under the barn, evidently a huge potato store. They were busy with a big stew pot on a fire, and it smelled really good. Three rabbits, any amount of potatoes, carrots and turnips. I was promised a good plateful when it was ready. Stew was not the only thing I could smell. Who has got whisky I enquired. I was immediately invited to a tot of 'Black & White'. It was explained that a certain runner had found a bottle of 'B & W' left by the Boche in a little room in the house. They had not bothered to wonder how the Boche was importing 'B & W'. There was consternation when I told them that it was the last bottle belonging to the Mess, and that I had myself seen a solemn conclave in the Mess, where each officer had loaded his six-shooter for the first man who smelled of whisky and was not duly authorized to smell so. The tedious preliminaries of a Court Martial would be dispensed with. The remaining whisky was immediately disposed of and the bottle disappeared where it would not be found until even this war was forgotten. Everyone commenced to smoke furiously, and, for an hour or two afterwards, any signaller or runner who received a call to Head Quarters underwent a severe test from the rest on smell and appearance, if he did not pass the test safely a better candidate was sent in his place.

31 October

A big attack opens on our left at 5.30 a.m., a battery of 6 inch guns has been moved up not far from the rear of our farmhouse and joins in the fun. Of course the unexpected happens. We were all out in the back garden watching the enemy's efforts to range the battery when we heard it coming and, as one man, we went down into the cabbages and peas. When we realised that we had not yet finished with the war, we got to our feet and gazed at our farmhouse, from which one end had disappeared. That end contained my comfortable orderly room, my bed, my desk and my basket chair. I wended my way there sadly, and salvaged what I could of records, stationery and my equipment. Headquarters then moved into the cellars which, though safer, were neither so pleasant nor so comfortable.

1 November

The battalion is relieved by the 2/16th Londons and we go as far as Petit Belleghem to rest. Orderly Room, signallers and runners fix up in the front room of an empty estaminet, the only proof of its late identity being the sign outside and the little counter in the corner of the room with the rows of shelves behind.

Signaller McKnight has fixed up his instrument on the little counter and sits on a stool behind. In strolls a runner, lounges on the bar and leers at Mac.,

"Any Cognac M'selle?" "Cognac" protests M'selle in horror. "Yes, I'll have it in the back room" leers the runner.

"No compree Tomee, I'm married to ze poliss militaire on the cornaire" says M'selle.

The front door opens and in walk the C.O. and Adjutant. Mac becomes busy shouting down the phone "Hello Brigade, testing, all OK". The runner is standing to attention and the Orderly Room becomes suddenly busy. These constant sudden interruptions prevent our dramatic rehearsals developing on the right lines.

We got paid today for the first time in six weeks (one weeks' pay), but as there is nothing to spend it on, we are not bothered about it. What we don't like is piling up anything to our credit at the pay offices at Shrewsbury, where some girl clerk, while busy with a lipstick in her left hand looking into a mirror, will just pop the credit balance into the 'debit' column. We feel that it is safer to work on a 'debit', as just the reverse may happen through the same cause.

9 November

Great excitement. We have orders to move up, and rumour has it that we must move hard and fast if we are to catch up the troops that we are to relieve, and Armistice negotiations are being talked about.

10 November

We were on the move early leaving St Genois and, crossing the River Escaut at Escanaffles, we were soon clear of the ground that the enemy had been fighting hard to hold for the last few days. Then the march just became a quick step with the band in front blowing a gale.

The civilians were absolutely frantic. Flags everywhere and kiddies shouting patriotic songs at the tops of their shrill voices. Old men and women dancing like lambs in the spring. Young boys running to the horses and fastening little flags and flowers in their harness, and a little girl dressed up in the Belgian colours with a huge bunch of Chrysanthemums, who had evidently been hastily rehearsed, came solemnly out of a house, waited in the middle of the road and presented the bandmaster with the bouquet under the impression that he was the Commander-in-Chief, or at the very least a Colonel.

Almost every cross road had been mined and blown up, but the natives, mostly women, children and old men, had hastily filled in the holes and bridged them with anything handy. One corner had actually been made passable by two big farm carts being overturned in the hole and the wheels taken off, we passed over on the flat bottoms of the carts. The prime author of this engineering feat, an old greybeard, stood with his helpers at the corner with a big flag. The C.O. dismounted, shook the old gentleman's hand and stood with him while the battalion marched past, with the band playing 'Brabanconne' with great gusto.

If we happened to halt during the day near any houses, the occupants came rushing out with every available chair and basins of coffee, no milk or sugar, but what of that. At every halt little kiddies seemed to spring from nowhere with little flags and shriek 'Vive les Anglaises' at us, while poking our eyes out with the little flags.

We marched through Renaix, marching 'At Attention' and found the place seething with excitement, the narrow streets packed with people, cheering and singing, where all the little flags came from was a mystery. Mons. 'Le Maire' decked out in all his regalia, with what looked like the members of the Council, or the Watch Committee at least, stood on the steps of the Town Hall, or was it 'L'Hotel de Ville', and waved little flags, we dare not even laugh as we were marching 'At Attention'. We were tired and we wished Renaix had not such a long straggling main street. We were positively glad to get out of it and hear the order 'March Easy'.

We finished up the march just before dusk at a really bon village named Anseroeul. The band started off again on the 'Brabanconne' and as we turned into the square a terrible din ensued. In front of the big church stood 'Le Maire', the padre, school children and the village band, and it suddenly dawned on us that our band with its

'Brabanconne' was drowning the village band and the village choir, who were making desperate efforts to make themselves heard rendering our own National Anthem. Peace was soon declared and the Anseroeul Band and choir had a clear field.

There was no question of having to look for billets in the village, it seemed a wild scramble by the villagers who had any room, to make sure that they got their full share of soldiers. We fixed up the Orderly Room in an upstairs room, nicely furnished, in a nice house, with a couple of tables, comfortable chairs and best of all a huge bed, where Billy Hunter and I could sleep without being aware of each others presence. 'Q' found quarters with others of his rank, where they could make a night of it without being disturbed. We put in half an hours work on 'States' and then finished work for the night. Always when we stopped for the night we put outside our billet the little wooden sign with the crest and '6th Cheshires Orderly Room' so that we could be found when required. We were soon busy again. A knock would come to the front door, the lady would attend to it. In the meantime we had closed up the Orderly Room upstairs and joined the family downstairs. The lady would explain that Madame at the door had a 'petit enfant' (or feminine as the case may be) very ill. 'La Grippe' again. Had we a doctor with the troops? After the M.O. had been to half a dozen cases and found that his services were still in great demand, he took over the public room in the village as a dispensary, and after doing what he could for serious cases at their homes, he and his staff spent the biggest part of the evening making up medicines and pills, the only restriction being that those who required medicine must bring their own bottles. The poor M.O. was exhausted before long, not so much examining and dosing his patients, as by his efforts necessary to explain his instructions in French. He was called away later in the evening and it was sometime later that he reported that it was the most important case of all and that Mother and Son were doing very nicely, thank you. The Mess immediately drank a toast to 'The M.O.s Belgian Baby' but made amends by whipping round for a subscription for a present for the baby.

The people of the village could not do enough for us, coffee was on the boil all night in nearly every house and no one seemed to think of going to bed. The two little estaminets in the village, who had not great stocks in hand, soon became dry and kept going on coffee and music.

A little extra latitude in the matter of 'lights out' was allowed and the village made merry most of the night. We had even more than a suspicion that hostilities might cease at anytime. We had heard that the Germans had left Anseroeul three hours before we arrived, so the odds were that we had seen the last of him and we hoped that he would not waste any long distance shells or aeroplane bombs until matters were settled.

11 November 1918

Billy Hunter and I lay on the bed only partly undressed about 3.30 a.m., idly chatting and smoking with a candle firmly stuck on the bedstead, when it gradually dawned on us that all the other bedrooms in the house were entered from our room. There was a problem, should we get up and dress before the family, or wait till the family were all up. We need not have bothered about the matter as, when we heard 'Reveille', all the family were busy downstairs.

We found water laid out in a wash bowl for us, with a clean towel each, and when we were seen out in the back garden, polishing our shoes with a jack-knife, out came the family box of brushes and blacking.

We had already received orders to move at 10 a.m., but about 9.0 a.m. someone gave me a whisper. In fact in another two minutes everyone seemed to have heard the same whisper. The civilians seemed to feel something in the air and the coffee pots got boiling. We had no telephone running to H.Q., so I watched the door closely for a Brigade messenger arriving. As 'Quarters' 'P' was on duty in the room, I took up a strategic position near the door and was rewarded by hearing someone 'drop off a bike' and yell for Cheshires Orderly Room. Beating 'Quarters' by yards, I dragged the 'runner' indoors and slammed the door, as the crowd outside looked likely to overwhelm us. Signed the receipt and then read (while being crushed to death)

G.H.Q. wire begins –
AAA 'Hostilities cease at 11.00 hours' AAA

There were other details but these did not matter at the moment. Dead silence for a moment, then pandemonium. The two ladies had a good cry and the old man trickled a diamond or two down his white beard.

The C.O. and the Adjutant came in almost at the same moment and as I handed the message to the Adjutant he looked at his watch and groaned. He had lost 200 francs by two hours.

It was nearly time to march, but everyone in the room had to have a cup of coffee, while an order was put round to the companies that steel helmets were not to be worn and we hoped that we had now worn them for the last time. We got off prompt at 10.00 hours, after standing 'To Attention' while the band played the Belgian National Anthem. As we moved off we were showered with chrysanthemums and all the girls of the village tried to decorate us with Belgian ribbons. We stepped out briskly as we had to halt at 11.00 hours and report our location, and it was up to the battalion to get as far forward as possible in the time available. We were rather quiet until a rather gruesome joke started the rounds, it was to the effect that it would be a bit of bad luck if any man got hit with a shell before 11.00 hours. This seemed to liven the party up a bit, especially as odd shells could be heard passing over.

Ten minutes before the hour we passed through a little village with a little church that had a big hole in the spire, and out of the hole a large Belgian flag. On the steps stood the Curé, a silver haired picture in full vestments, who gave us his blessing as we passed by. We marched on through the village, out into the wilds again, uninteresting flat country, made doubly uninteresting by a depressing steady rain. We had hoped that when we halted at 11.00 hours, it would be in some comfortable, hospitable village, but when that hour arrived we found ourselves miserable, wet and cold, still in the wilds and last night's jollifications seeming like a memory of some long way back Christmas Eve celebration. Map reference was dispatched to Brigade Headquarters somewhere in the rear, and we awaited further orders while sitting on the roadside, wet and cold. Orders eventually came along per despatch rider, who arrived slightly 'woozled' owing to having to wait with the 'Signals', awaiting Brigade's reply to ours. 'Signals', as usual, had evidently found the wherewithal to celebrate with. Orders were to proceed to the next village, Ellezelles, for billets. As this place was still about 10 miles distant, cooks were ordered to 'serve dinner' as quickly as possible. Dinner was not a success, and we felt that the cooks must have been suffering from a hangover after last night's festivities. Ellezelles, a smaller village than Anseroeul and much more poverty stricken, did its utmost to make us comfortable. Orderly Room was billeted in a small house with an old man and his nephew. When we started to make a bit of supper out of the remains of our rations, the friendly old chap produced a jug of milk, a slab of cheese and some butter, and would take no payment. He then wanted to tuck Bill and myself into the only bed in the house, a great four-poster. We managed to stick out against it however, and we made ourselves very comfortable by the kitchen fire on a couple of German palliasses, we found them quite comfortable and F.F.V. (evidently officers' kit).

12 November

Slept like logs and awakened to brilliant sunshine, the young nephew appeared with two bowls of hot steaming coffee. Orders came in early and the Adjutant said that we were likely to have a few days rest. He looked at the weather, then looked at me and evidently thought the weather the better looking of the two, for he suddenly glared at me and said "Corporal Williamson, you are sacked, you can have half an hour to clean up, then if I see you anywhere nearby the Orderly Room before dark, I'll have you in the Guard Room". I dived to the kitchen and proceeded to 'posh-up' while the Adjutant stayed talking to 'Quarters' and Billy. Billy seemed to have appointed himself official timekeeper and kept popping his head into the kitchen, yelling 15 minutes to go, 10, 5 and so on. I eventually reported to the Adjutant with 3 minutes to spare. 'Quarters' and Billy were to have their day out later. Walked through the village and met Joe Hayes, batman to the Adjutant, must see their billet and be introduced to Madame (young) and her daughter Jeanne. I was introduced to Madame as "Mon ami, what the 'ell is French for Orderly Room Corporal – scrives for my boss l'Adjutant". Madame understood perfectly and brought in two bowls of coffee. I left soon after and walked on through the village and found the boys out on a shopping expedition, resolutely refusing to accept any change in German currency.

It was such a lovely day that I decided on a ramble on my own, took the road out of Ellezelles and, breaking the terms of the Armistice, the British Army, represented in the person of one Corporal (acting), advanced beyond the line of demarcation, taking the road towards Flobecq with Mons not far away. Roads full of Belgian civilians returning to their own districts, each party seemed to be led by their own village priest. All on foot, all vehicles and horses evidently having been commandeered by the Germans and everyone weighted under a great bundle, the priests bundle as big or bigger than the next best. Nuns trundled bundles of babies in wheelbarrows and small boxes on wheels. Suddenly remembering that I am the only member of the British Army visible, I saluted the Belgian Flag at the head of the procession and was rather flustered to receive a rousing cheer for 'l'Armee Anglaise' as represented by two stripes (one unpaid). A little later, passing a pretty roadside cottage, I scared a little girl who ran inside screaming to her mother. I felt a little abashed to be able to translate her screams into something about a little English Corporal. I was dragged in again for more coffee and a glass of vin rouge, the 'V.R.' still tasting like red ink.

15 November

After only three days peace, we turned westwards towards home, wondering how long it would be before we landed in England. Marching back by the route we had come, reached Moen (16 miles), found very poor billets, and the Belgians already cooling off in their enthusiasm for the British Army and padlocking their pumps again.

16 November

Off again, another 15 miles, to Belleghem, which place we passed through on October 20th during the advance. Orderly Room fixed up in an estaminet (empty). Got busy getting the lads away on the leave allotment just come in. Pat and I are included in the allotment, but I cannot get away till I have got the others off. Pat decided to wait and go along to see me safely as far as London. Adjt. 'Tubby' going into Courtrai for a night out, gave us a lift to Courtrai station where we caught up the leave party.

5 December

Met Pat at Euston coming from leave at Corton (Norfolk). Left 7.30 a.m. for Dover. Rough crossing. No room in the leave camp at Calais, so were put up in a P.O.W. camp adjacent and spent the night on corrugated iron shelves.

6 December

Turned out at 3.30 a.m., not too unwilling, breakfast at 4.00 hrs. and ready to move off at 4.45, but did not get any move on until 8–30 hrs., feeling ready for another breakfast. Marched to the Fontinettes railway siding to watch trains go by and shunting. At about 16.00 hrs. we were marched back again to camp, which was full again with leave men who had come in while we had been watching trains. We had to squeeze in ones and twos where we could manage. At 20.00 hrs. call came for us to parade again. As we had got down to 'bed', Pat and I decided to toss a coin to decide whether we should get up. As our trousers were being used as a pillow, we decided that it was too much trouble, so we rolled over and went to sleep again.

7 December

Up with the lark, 4.00 a.m., and had a quick look round to see if any of our party had been left behind with us, but could not find anyone. Nothing for it but to make tracks for the station. Luckily we had our movement orders with us. Managed to get to the station without being pulled up by any of the numerous military police knocking about. Found a train at 8.30 a.m. for St Omer, arriving noon. Made a bee-line for the Lord Robert's Club and found pork chops, chips and coffee quite nice after having had no breakfast. The R.T.O at St Omer station had given us the location of our Battalion at Wardrecques, about six miles away. Took our time so as to arrive about teatime. Found it a very nice village and the boys all 'poshed up', even to the extent of wires at the back of their caps. We heard that a Colour Party, consisting of Capt. Wood, Capt. Yorston, one Sgt. Major and two Sgts., left a few days ago to collect 'The Colours' from St George's Church, Stockport and bring them out to the Battalion. I expect there will be a big show in Stockport in this connection. Found the Orderly Room sunk in waves of voting papers, also studying first circulars re demobilisation. Find we are billeted in a bachelor establishment, Tommy tells me that he is the village miser and is reputed to be the richest man in Wardrecques, which fact does not prevent him from finishing off what we leave of our rations. In the evenings he will sit in the dark until we give him a candle, then he would immediately dive off to bed to save it, and then do the same thing the following evening.

10 December

10th December 1918 – Tuesday

Dear Kiddy,

Glad to get your letter of the 6th today, and to hear Granny has gone along for another holiday.

It is keeping like summer weather here, though today has turned out rather wet. I havn't been able to get out since Sunday as we are in the throes of getting miners away, and snowed under with forms of wonderful and weird questions over and over again in as many styles as a legal expert could devise with ice cloths on his head. My first effort today took me forty minutes to make one miners papers out.

We have opened an annexe to the orderly room and call it demobbing dept and of course yours truly has dropped into the job of looking after that department. We are increasing the department tomorrow. I have just got a nice pile of forms in front of me, filled in to the best of my ability, and am waiting to see the C.O.s face when he finds how many times he has to sign his name for five miners leaving in the morning. With all the big staffs at Army Pay Offices and such like, that have had such a good soft time during the war, it seems a rather dusty trick to put practically the whole of the demobilizing clerical work on to clerical staffs of the Battalions out here. When you find out that ten wonderful and weird forms have to be filled in for every man, you can fancy there is going to be something doing. As a sign that the war is over, all forms have to be filled in in ink.

All orderly room staffs in the Division had to attend a lecture on the work yesterday, given by a big nut from Div. HQ., but he didn't seem to be any wiser than we were on points that we were not clear about. I don't know whether this work is going to tie me down at all, but I don't think so, and if any application started by Mr. Bronnert comes through this way, I shall be in a position to see that it isn't pigeon holed.

Pearson is well away from it all and looks like getting his 10 days extended. He knows what he is about, as we shall be well into the swing of the work before he comes back.

The Adjt. is having a busy time of it too as the assistant Adjt. (Capt. Yorston) is away, but he is as cheerful as ever and getting through a big amount of work, he is a trump.

He, Billy Hunter and I had quite an important conference together today on the "demobbing" work and he has a wonderful grasp of things and helps us tremendously. He has already got the pioneers at work fitting our "Demobbing dept." with shelves and pigeonholes. It reminds me tremendously of my visit to Houldsworth Hall, though I am not getting 2/6 for each man whose forms I fill up.

I am keeping very fit and we are feeding like fighting cocks, having a new friend on the stores staff (one of the runners). Last night we had a nice bit of steak for supper, and tonight have got a nice chop each, so we are doing nicely.

We look like settling down here, as the powers that be, bustled by Adjutants and C.O.s generally, are getting billets fitted up with wire beds, recreation rooms going, and huts built for concerts and entertainments.

Glad to hear you are keeping the Flu away, as next time I come home I want to see you looking a deal better than when I arrived home last, as you havn't much to worry about now.

Sorry to hear Billikins has been doing jiu-jitsu on himself, hope his wrist will soon be alright again.

Give my love to everybody and bunches of kisses for yourself and the boy from Your loving husband Walter.

Opened an annexe to the Orderly Room for 'demob' dept., 'Quarters' said he couldn't possibly take charge as he would be one of the first to leave, in any case we feared that he would not be in any fit condition to study all the rules, regulations, amendments, priorities etc., which are enough to drive even a sober man to drink. So I have been put in charge with a small staff. Find that miners are first priority. I have evidently been misinformed in my early youth, when I was taught that Cheshire was an agricultural county, as I was surprised when a call went round the battalion for miners, about 50% reported to the Demob. Office. Then the fun started. When it was explained that they would be put into mines by the Govt. and would not be released until such time as their corresponding length of service men in non-priority classes were demobbed, there was a sudden reduction in the number of miners, and the 'Cheshires' reverted to a more agricultural flavour.

All demobbing staff of all units in the Div. ordered to attend a lecture by the Divisional Expert at Racquinghem. He didn't seem to know any more than we did about it.

14 December

Have just heard that the Colour Party has arrived at St Omer and will be here tomorrow, that means a big parade. We have seen a copy of the Stockport Advertiser splashing the ceremony of collecting the Colours from St George's Church, and giving details of the Battalion's record since 1914. Surprising what a thrill one can feel about it. I have not seen the Colours yet, as they were lodged at St George's Church when the Battalion left for France in 1914.

Adjt. 'Tubby' collared Bobby Howarth (erstwhile prince of runners – now retired to R.S.M.s batman) and asked him if he could cook. Now Bobby could cook a whale to taste like a lemon sole and assuring Tubby that the chef at the Savoy had nothing on him in the matter of cooking, Tubby asked him if you could spoil a goose in the cooking. Bobby declared that he would like to spoil one after cooking. 'Tubby' had bought a big goose for the runners (four of them). He gave Bobby the map reference of the farm where the said goose was strutting about in complete ignorance of the mercenary transaction which contracted for his early demise. Bobby soon checked on the map reference and the goose, and insisted on marking it on the feathers with a good copying pencil. The Orderly Room has been invited to partake in exchange for use of table and room for the party.

The Colours arrived quietly last night and were lodged in the Officers' Mess, awaiting today's ceremony. They were to be collected by a colour-escort and carried to the Battalion on Church parade. Half a company left the Battalion, who were on church parade and proceeded to the Mess to collect the Colours. We shut the Orderly Room down and cut down to the village to see the show. Lt. Jimmy Holt, one of our most enthusiastic young officers was in charge of the Escort company, and he had been digging into King's Regs. and procedure. We got to the square in advance of the escort and took up a point of vantage in an unobserved corner. Then 'Bandy' Hobbs appeared in all his glory with tasselled staff leading the band and looking as if they had spent six months ration of 'Blanco', 'Soldier's Friend' and 'Silvo' in one gorgeous flutter.

17th December 1918 – Tuesday

Dear Kid,

Got your letter of the 12th today. You promised in your last to write me about the procession you saw at Stockport, but as you don't mention a word about it in your letter, I am still left wondering whether it was our Colours you saw.

You seem to have had a pretty good rush round at Cheadle Hulme. I was rather amused at Mrs Lees account of rats in the bedroom. Is it possible she was trying to put the breeze up to prevent you wanting the house too early. Never mind, you could stand seeing rats in a strange dark lion house, and it won't be nearly as bad in your own house in the light. At the worst Dinah can live up there and then we shall feel safe enough.

We managed another couple of hours out this afternoon to watch a football match – Officers versus Sergeants – it was great fun. Sgts won 3-1. The Colonel was playing and scored the only goal for the officers – more by good luck than by good management. He headed it in, or at least somebody else's bad shot hit him on the head and it bounced in. Anyway he was a fine sport. No mercy was shewn on either side and the Col. buried himself in the mud as cheerfully as anybody and platoon officers and sergeants mutually got their own back for previous shortcomings.

Billy Hunter is off on a motor (W.D.) trip to Boulogne tomorrow with a party who are going to buy in the Christmas festivities.

Our Regimental S.M. left us the other day and forgot to take his canvas bath with him. Billy has collared it and as Tommy and he had a bath last night, it is my turn tonight. I have got a petrol tin of water busy boiling on the fire so I must be seeing to it.

Will write again tomorrow, Your loving husband Walter.

Tommy wishes to send his love to both of you and sends a very Merry Christmas to Jim and you too, he wants to be early with it.

20th December 1918 – Friday

Dear Mams,

Got your parcel safe and sound today, and the little cakes were just scrumptious. I say were, because we finished them at a sitting. Mother was quite right – they don't last. Except the parcel, I havn't had a letter from you for the last two days, though I got one from Madge today. Letters are very slow nowadays and take 5 days each way.

I am sending one or two photos along. Tommy and I went up last night to collect ours and we got quite friendly with the lady photographer and she got busy shewing us the negatives she had done during the day and prints she had finished. I am busy now making a collection of any photos I want and anytime I can slip up I can have a look at anything fresh that I may want. As the battalion seems to be having its photograph taken singly, in pairs, in platoons and in companies, and officers on mounts and off, I seem to be going to get some collection. The two gents with the bikes are – on the right with the stripe – Bobby Howarth, OC runners. The other old warrior is one of his worthy henchmen – George Clarke – alias 'Clarkey' proprietor of the "Black Lion" Hillgate, Stockport. As he is going on leave in a day or two, a good chance of a free glass of beer for you if you call in and put your head over the counter and shout "Runner" in a voice like mine. I don't think you know any of the officers, though Arthur T. may know most of them. The big fat Regimental Sgt. Major has just left us for England, he was a good old sort, but not our old original. We took him over with the 11th while ours went to train Americans. His companion is one of the 6th Cheshires men who came to France with them in 1914. He is a Company Sgt. Major on the photo, but since, has taken over the Regimental Sgt. Major's job which at present is chiefly concerned with seeing that the guard is very posh, and seeing that the footballers, boxers and cross country runners train regularly, and sees that the Sergeants Mess has plenty of beer on stock. Our football team is a fine one and hasn't been beaten yet by anything in the Division. They are after the 5th Army Cup, but that is a good way off yet.

Reverting again to photos, the little Sgt. Major in the middle of the group of Sergeants was one of the orderly room runners as recently as 15 months ago. In fact he got his first stripe a few months after mine. Talking of stripes, Bill Hunter puts his third up today. Of course we are as "Catty" as you say women are, and as it is only a Lance stripe and unpaid, we reckon it is only so that he can have his dinner in the Sgts Mess at Christmas. But Officers Mess and Sergeants Mess will not compare with a cut at the Runners goose and trimmings and perhaps a drop of something good to drink to good pals present and past.

Pearson is expected back tomorrow (perhaps), in any case we are sure of him being back for Christmas. He won't miss that, but I wouldn't be a bit surprised if he tells us that he hadn't finished "checking records" down at Rouen and want to go back again.

Demobilization is going splendidly, we havn't yet finished studying the second scheme of "demobbing" when we are startled to read of a 3rd in the papers, which hasn't reached us yet, but which we expect in any day now. If you know anyone that wants a good expert on points of law, military or boy scout, a K.C., a statistician, a man of infinite patience with multitudinous enquirers, for 2/6d a day (4d advance on my present screw), please don't forget to hand my name in for the job. Bill Hunter says it was a good job I started on the job bald.

Anyway I have got a room of my own for the job now and do no ordinary orderly room work. I have got a champion little assistant, a little Welsh lad who helps me tremendously with horrible Welsh addresses of a big Welsh draft we had one time from South Wales, he is a champion little worker, and as keen as mustard on his job, and we quite enjoy ourselves on it.

A sheaf of new instructions, memoranda and forms came in tonight and when Tubby came in tonight to give orders for tomorrow, I put them before him. He immediately picked his stick and gloves up, stood up and stroked his brow, sighed, looked at his watch and smiled "Let me know what you make of them in the morning" and walked off. However poor Tubby is going to give a lecture to all companies in turn on demobilization. It will beat a battalion smoking concert.

Well I must finish tonight, in case I am yet in time, another Merry Christmas to all of you and bunches of love and kisses from Your loving husband Walter.

December – 1918

Writing about photographs (part letter)

Len looks as if he wants to sneeze badly, or a least badly wants to sneeze, and Bill Wildgoose looks like a curate just waiting for his afternoon cup of tea, I'm getting badly mixed, I mean his cup of afternoon tea. You will be getting to know the background of the picture quite well soon. You will keep noticing I hope how very posh we are every time. Nowadays we look at a couple of inches of mud and walk round it, quite forgetting how our Birkenhead Sgt. Major used to yell at us for stepping over a puddle and threaten us with being up to our sanguinary necks in sang in a fortnight. We even put our belts on under our overcoats which is nearly getting to snobbishness. Still with all our 'poshity' I don't suppose the 6th will be seen marching under the Arc de Triomphe in Paris, or even having button holes presented to us by Queens when driving in our landau past their front door, but still …

Bill Hunter and Quarters have just 'made it the disappear' to the Sgts Mess and we have seen the last of them tonight, till Bill comes in (perhaps per runner) and perhaps wants putting to bed. Christmas has started already at the Sgts Mess.

A good old stick has gone on leave today and was a source of much merriment before we finally got him off. Old George Clarke (age 41) proprietor of the Black Lion, Middle Hillgate, Stockport, which fact he spent his last half hour drumming into us in case he didn't come back. He is the other 'lad' with Bobby H and the bicycles. This morning he went down to the stores to get some new clothes and the Quartermaster asked him to do him a little commission while home and then gave him something to keep the chill off the inside of his water bottle on the journey. George decided that his water bottle would take no harm during the present mild weather, so he transferred the stuff to a part of his physical equipment that he thought might need it more. He arrived here for his ticket in a peculiar state. He could walk as straight as on parade and he could almost say 'statistical' correctly. The only thing that seemed out of order were his eyelids. Everytime he blinked he had the utmost difficulty in lifting them again, and had the appearance of talking in his sleep. We learned quite a lot of his family affairs before we finally got him on his way. It appears that his niece married a man from Looker of Motor Car fame and lived next door to them. Evidently 'non bon' as a husband, as all she sees of him is 12/6 a week. It appears that old George heard some scuffling next door late one night, so went round and kicked the front door in and found him having a boxing match with his wife. He took him from upstairs, laid him in the gutter, then went back to collect his niece, lock up and she has lived with her uncle ever since. He hasn't seen him since and must have put the wind up him something considerable. It is more than any one could do to old George Clarke.

He is going to bring us something good back and if he doesn't come back we are to call sometime and find it on a shelf with the dust on it.

Tommy has just been warming a Machonachie up on the remains of the fire and I have got to shut up and have supper and then get to bed.

Bill Hunter has just come in. My apologies he is quite OK. It appears that a certain Sgt of ours in the mess was "blotto" and everyone else had to keep sober. This is how it worked out. The Sgt who was "so so" is a world famed bruiser and everyone wondered whether he was going to turn bad tempered, so kept themselves ready to do a sprint at short notice and did their best in the meantime to keep him pleasant.

Sorry to write such a lot of twaddle but things are very slow and I am sick to death of nominal rolls, dispersal stations, areas, pivotals, slips, cards and forms, schemes and other schemes. Nonsense is not so bad if it is amusing or attempts to be, but nonsense in the shape of army forms and schemes that keep men away from their homes when they are not required here, and spends millions of public money in keeping them, when they would be better employed keeping themselves – well it makes one tired. Hope Geddes will push 20 departments into 1 and sack thousands of officials and give men a chance to get home instead of strangling them with red tape thicker than the old German barbed wire. Now I am getting annoyed again, so I will shut up.

I really don't mind it a bit, but I havn't had a letter for two days and the last one was only a little one. Heaps of love and kisses for you and the boy from Your loving husband Walter.

December 23rd 1918 – Monday

Dear Kid,

Got two letters from you today, one has taken 7 days, the other 8 days to come, so I am not getting overdone with up to date news, you don't even let me know yet whether you saw the Colours. You say you saw the procession, but don't say whether you saw the Colours. Was there much of a crowd? I should like to have heard quite a lot about it from you. Of course I have read all about it in the papers, but I have wondered whether Stockport yet takes as much interest in its own and only battalion as it ought. Even you dismiss the matter in a line and a half and even then leave me in a fog whether you saw the Colours or not.

Have had a very busy day, as we have now got as far as statistics with demobilization. We start off so. How many men have you of group 1, then this goes on down to 43 groups. Then it starts again – how many men have you in group one for dispersal area 1. Then that goes on to the dispersal areas, which means we have about 750 names and particulars to wade through 43 times multiplied by 16, which means 688 times. Then we start again with men who want to rejoin. If they want to go home first, how many want to go to the various 16 areas and then again for men who require repatriation abroad. We have four forms to fill up with little squares, the forms would, with just about 2 of them, paper our scullery nicely. They are kind enough to point out that these returns are only needed for statistics. I fancy they are under the idea that as orderly rooms out here are not up to the eyes in work accounting for casualties, they ought to have their time filled in with something else to fill in the 24 hours.

I look like losing the orderly room shortly. Tubby has been suggesting that the orderly room shall be moved to one of some Nissen huts that are being put up near by, and we are to keep this billet going as the "Demobbing" dept. I don't think it will work as I am always wanting to get at some information from the orderly room and then again Tommy says he will pine away and die.

Have had a walk up to see the photo lady tonight to see if she had any new photos and enclose the results – at least not all the results, as she isn't above selling a bottle or two of vin rouge, very different stuff from what can be bought in the village. Of course I am not sending those home, they are to go with the goose on Christmas Eve (tomorrow). One is of the band – you will guess that of course from the big drum. Behind the drummer is Col. Stanway DSO. MC., our Colonel, at present acting Brigadier General. On the right of him looking at the photo is the famous 'Tubby', looking as if someone is sitting on his corns. On the other side of the Colonel is Major Rostron. Now for the equestrian statues. The one without the smile and trying to look an old warrior is Capt. Jimmy Holt, the other with the smile that won't come off is the irrepressible 2/Lt. WB Foden who has borrowed Jimmy Holt's horse for the occasion. The two gents on the door step are, the big chap on the lower step, Drum Major Poole, who teaches the drummers how to put their sticks to their chins and bring them down together. The little chap who has had to go up a step to look as big as his bosom chum, is the famous "Bandy Hobbs", the bandmaster, who looks the most important man on parade usually. It was "Bandy" who nearly got the C.O.s bouquet on the march through Renaise.

Must finish now, and you must excuse me if I don't write you tomorrow as we shall be very busy on the goose and other things tomorrow night, and as for Christmas, well I can't promise as we shall be busier than ever. I look like having to carve the goose tomorrow and it is a good job that you bought me that game knife when I was at home.

Well – goodnight Kid, wonder if you too are busy preparing for a big feed, I mean a good time of course not a big feed. Tommy and Billy are making themselves a nuisance, they have decided that 4 bottles are too much for tomorrow and are busy warming two bottles up out of the four. In any case we can get some more tomorrow. Tommy is a really fine singer and we havn't done half a bottle yet, but warmed and sugared (I should say mulled) it is a deal more musical stuff than cold. Hope we don't disturb the old man too much, but if he comes in here he will have to take 4th part in "Who Killed Cock Robin".

Well goodnight again Kid, and I know it is too late, but a Merry Christmas anyway, and if the next letter doesn't arrive in time, here's a great New Year to you and the feller.

Bunches of kisses and love from Your loving husband Walter

December 26th 1918 – Thursday

Dear Kid,

Wonder what sort of Christmas you have had. I suppose I should say that we have had a great Christmas as we have had big feeds, oceans of beer, no parades, and everything I suppose a soldier should have, and yet I never felt so fed up in all my existence and feel like nothing but grumbles and grouses (is the plural of grouse, grouses?) instead of Peace and Goodwill towards men I want to strangle the postman. I havn't had a letter for the last three days and not a Christmas line from anyone up to now, I suppose they are safely tucked away in a siding somewhere and they will follow us on about May or June, when we may be demoblized, that is if the postman has recovered sufficiently from his Christmas festivities by then to attend to his work. The battalion (with very few exceptions) has been completely 'Blotto' for two days. I claim no honour for being one of the few exceptions, for I tried hard enough, but the nearest I could get to Christmas elation was an uncomfortably distended stomach. Tommy annoyed me extensively by getting blotto 3 distinct times on Christmas day. What annoyed me about it was that I had to put him to bed 3 times. Billy H. and P started a day or two before Christmas and are still going strong. Christmas morning 'P' was found at 3am. in a ditch wanting to know what time zero was, sans hat and mud up to the eyes, with his beauty considerably spoiled by contact with the road before he found the front line.

Eight of us on Christmas Eve sat down to attend to the goose, and put 75 bottles into sandbags early next morning, at least I did. I was just getting a bit of work done Christmas morning when Bobby H looked in with a face like a bilious ghost and wanted to know if I had got a 'Teetotal book' as he wanted to sign every page of it.

Tommy has now finished up by completely losing his voice, says it is with singing carols. There isn't really much glory about our glorious Christmas.

And your letters recently have been most tantalizing. You have either had a nap and had to do a rush for the post, and going to write me tomorrow, or all the news is in a short P.S. with a promise to let me know all about it tomorrow, and when tomorrow comes you forget all about it.

Please blot out pages 1 & 2 as I am quite sweet tempered again and very sorry, please. The postman more or less sober, has just brought me two letters from you posted 19th and 20th, a card and a flag from Mother and a letter (with a diary) from Jack. Jack's is the first line I have had from anyone yet excepting Madge and yourself.

I didn't want to go back to the previous lines, but your first letter I opened has the following P.S. and I couldn't help smiling:-

" P.S. Of course it was the Colours. 20th December. What
a lovely surprise. Finest Christmas card possible.
Love Millie" (of course I love Milly) "writing you later,
just off to Stockport."

What was the lovely surprise and who was it from? Glad you liked the photo. If I can get a photograph of the lady photographer, I will send you one just to allay your anxiety. She is very 'taking' of course, but it would need a dark room to fall in love with her, it couldn't be done in the daylight, though she is very pleasant and, ought I to say it, homely looking. I am enclosing another photo. It is the Brigade H.Q. Staff. The Brigadier General is on the front row. If you are in any difficulty, Joe (or perhaps Mabel) can help you. Two of our officers are on the staff, on the back row, you can perhaps pick them out by their badges. The smaller of the two is Sydney Astle, son of the editor of the 'Stockport Echo'.

You mention that my Christmas of 1916 must have been a terrible one – well 1918 beat it. Tommy (oh he is quite OK now) sends his special love to Jimmy and says he simply dotes on fairies, and I quite believe him too. Now he has lost his voice his "Bon jour m'selle" has to be done with his best glad eye on all the fairies round about here.

You say that Ackrill is getting "married". Poor chap it looks like a horrid fate doesn't it. Got a 4th Manchester card from Arthur and

Madge today, it is a neat little thing. I think ours was spoiled by too much colour.

Statistics is still the biggest part of demobilization at present, but I ain't half kicking myself. If only I could have held on to my leave till Christmas, I could have been home for good by now. Goodnes knows when that good time is coming now. Rumours are knocking about however that we might move shortly nearer to the coast.

Hope Jim's toothache is better. Poor Kid. Give him a big kiss from me and a bunch of the same for yourself from Your loving husband Walter.

December 27th 1918 – Friday

Dear Kiddie,

Got your letter of the 21st today and like some of them here, you seem to have started Christmas early with crackers on the 21st. You are not the only folks however to have crackers, as on Xmas day most of the officers were invited to the Sgts. Mess for dinner in the evening, and they turned up with paper caps, pinafores and mob caps and all the usuals from crackers, but the atmosphere in the Sgts. Mess was much too moist for them to keep fresh, and they didn't last long.

Glad to hear Joe had a good time at the dinner and met a lot of old friends. I expect we shall have an annual at Stockport some of these fine days, and yours truly will have a night out on those occasions.

I havn't managed a trip to St Omer yet and don't look like managing it for a bit. Have been having a great day today working out some wonderful and useless statistics required by the Demobilizing dept., been at it from 8 this morning till 9 this evening and all is spick and span ready to be sent off tomorrow. It looks monumental, but for crass waste of time, ink and work, it can't be beaten.

Poor old "P" has been quite annoyed with me today, too vexed even to say "Before you came up, t'was thus." As he was spent up, he thought he would do a little work. He came in just as Tom and Bill H were both out on business. A bit of rush business came in, and not being as keen on work as he thought at first, he sent a bundle of work in to me. I immediately sent it back into his room by the runner that brought it, and to tell him that he had made a mistake, my room was not the orderly room, but was the demobilization dept. He came in and tried to play steam about it. I didn't miss the opportunity to tell him a few nice things and offered to do the work that he and Hunter did in a couple of hours in the morning, if he would take over my job. Tubby is away today, and he threatened to see him about the matter in the morning. I would much rather he did that, than do what he actually did, as after working half an hour, he said he didn't feel in form for work, so borrowed 5 fcs off me to go round to the Sgts. Mess and get a drink. Havn't seen or heard of him since. As it was Tubby who cut me off the orderly room work to attend entirely to demobilization work, I would rather have enjoyed hearing him complain about it.

There is a strong rumour in the air that we shall shortly move to the coast. Then perhaps it will take a fortnight to get a letter reckoning on the present state of affairs. When we were in the heart of Belgium we could get letters in three or four days, but now we are not far from the coast and up against a big railway centre, it takes 6 to 7 days. S'marvellous as Mr Veritas said.

I am enclosing another photo for the collection. The little bugler is little Fred Garlick, the battalion mascot. You will find him on the band too. The photo is "C" Coys. Guard. You can always tell whether "Freddy" has been teetotal that evening, when he blows "Last Post", if he hasn't his last few notes are heart rending. He reckons that it is the froth that gets into his bugle. At one time he did batman for the R.S.M. who has just gone home. This gent touched 6ft 2" and pulled about 16 stone. The RSM said when Freddy didn't do his work properly it wasn't any use trying to hit him, as he would only bolt through his (the RSM's) legs. The big Sgt. on Freddy's right in civil life is boss of a ducal horse stud farm. He once dragged an M.C. Officer out of his dugout by the scruff of the neck and threatened to thrash him if he didn't come and attend to his business while his lads were having a bad time of it. The Sgt. however, hasn't yet been awarded any decoration for the job.

The two boys on the top row on the left of the picture were two company runners when in the line and two little champions they were. They would always come through anything. The one of them on the outside is at present on Bobby's staff and was with us on the goose night, getting badly 'blotto' and was one of those missing at the last. Bobby and I found him eventually lying over the garden hedge like a piece of limp washing and carried him to bed. He was 'on parade' however early next morning. I am hoping to get a photo of Pearson in a day or two. I have seen the proof and it is a very good one, also a photo of the Sgts. of the battalion taken on Boxing Day, when most of them were distinctly so-so.

Glad you liked mine with Tommy. It is splendid of him, and I think it isn't half bad of me, or I should say I think it is very good. Anyway it is more respectable than the last.

I am trying to get up to the photographer's tomorrow night to make an appointment for our little picture with Tubby for Sunday, and may find some more photos that I want. I expect there will be a big post one of these days with Christmas cards, but not much doing yet.

Have you anything special in the way of news at all lately?

Bunches of love and kisses for you and the boy from Your loving husband Walter

December 29th 1918 – Sunday

Dear Kid,

No post today again and everybody is having sweet words to say about the postal arrangements, and the postman's life is pure misery to him, as every one gives him the benefit of it.

Things are very quiet with us except in the orderly room and the 'Demob' dept. We are up to our necks in it. All Army Forms connected with this department are numbered Z1 upwards. The highest we have reached yet is Z503. I don't know quite how many of them we have got in use up to now, but the way we are going on we shall have all the blanks from Z1 to Z503 shortly.

The weather lately here too is past words. Rain, day after day, and whenever it rains our chimney refuses to draw and puts a gas barrage up inside the house fit to asphyxiate anybody not well up in gas attacks.

Pat has gone off to St Omer today again despite the rain and a bad heel (which is evidently only bad enough to keep him off parades). He usually calls in to see me every morning, as he passes to have his heel dressed by the Doctor. The Doctor caught him a long way from his billet one day and played old Harry about it. I havn't been able to get my trip to St Omer yet and don't look like it, as I fancy we shall be moving this week.

All sorts of weird rumours are afloat as to where we are going and what we are going to do, but they vary so much that, like Asquith, I am going to "wait and see". One thing seems pretty certain however, and that is, that we are going to or near the coast.

I have really only one little bit of interesting news for you. "Tubby" gently informed me this evening that I had been recommended for

"M.I.D.". It looks a terrible thing, but it only means "Mentioned in Despatches". I ain't very excited about it yet, as it will be about March 1919 before we hear whether the C.O. has told a good enough tale, or enough fibs, which ever way you like it best. Anyway, if it doesn't come through it is pleasant to feel that somebody thinks I have at least tried to do my best at "Work of National Importance" or whatever I have been put to. I shall be very proud if it does come through seeing that, barring officers, I shall be only the 3rd "other rank" mentioned in despatches in the battalion since 1914. Young Billy Howarth is the second, he was "mentioned" in Douglas Haig's last despatch and we shall be the only two of less rank than Sgt. Major, to be "mentioned". I have lost mock modesty and do hope it comes through, and then I know my old woman will be pleased along with her old man.

I am enclosing two more photos. The small one reading from right to left reads – 1. The famous "P" who you will no doubt recognise. You will perhaps not recognise the smile as he was no doubt sober when you saw him. The centre piece is our Regimental Sgt. Major who always looks regimental, Christmas or no Christmas. On the left is Regtl. Quarter Master Sgt. Cooke, he also wears the Christmas smile. Another sign of Christmas is the manner in which he has rolled his puttees. Still another sign is the hat, 3 sizes too small for him. He had lost his own too, the same night Pearson was looking for Zero in a ditch near the Sgts Mess, he couldn't find a new one in stock big enough to fit the head he had next morning when he had the photo taken. Cooke is a son of a Mr Cooke of Rylands that perhaps father once knew. I hope the father was a better sample than the son, for whom nobody out here seems to have any admiration, and whose greatest misfortune will be to ever lose his present job. I think the dislike arises from the idea (not far from the truth) that the battalion rum ration usually runs to 4 jars for the troops and one for the R.Q.M.S. I have had various little tiffs with him and have usually carried the matter a bit higher, with the result that he has called me "Walter" till he breaks out again.

The larger photo was the result of a hasty decision in the Sgt's Mess. The R.S.M is "On Parade" as always, Pearson's smile is still the same and is evidently one that won't come off till the New Year is well set in, or till he is spent up, spoilt his credit or fallen out with Cooke. Cooke's hat looks worse than ever. On the second row from the top, third from the right with his hat nearly getting lost too, is Billy (pardon) Sgt Hunter, 'Tres Blotto'. Along the same row second from the left, with a smirk, is the famous 'Coll' (pardon) Sgt. Collier, DCM, MM, 1914 medal too. Once signaller with me on 'A' Coy station, who was wont to mend the wire when it wasn't broken, thereby gaining much kudos (or much rum) from Capt. Allen, whose motto was "Communication must be kept at all costs" (rum or otherwise). Overlapping Cooke's right arm is Jimmy (pardon again, bless me) C.S.M. Clarke who, within my time in the orderly room, was one of the orderly room runners. Marked with an arrow on the top row is Sgt. Langley, one time heavyweight boxing champion of the British Army. I believe there is some excitement in the Sgts Mess when he gets bad tempered, which is his stage before 'blotto'. One evening Bill turned in here wonderfully early and on Tommy and I making exhaustive enquiries, we were interested to hear that Langley was getting bad tempered. By 8.30pm. Pearson looked in too and thought he would have an early night. By 8.45 Sgt Langley was left in the Mess with the Physical Jerk Sgt. and four of the most stalwart members who were feverishly busy agreeing with every outrageous argument that Langley put out. By 9.15 p.m. Langley was past the bad tempered stage and the Mess filled up again quickly.

The hefty Physical Jerk instructor is on the bottom row on the extreme left. I have had to cut his hefty right arm off to get him into the envelope. Above Cooke, over his right shoulder, is little "Bandy Hobbs" trying to pose as Mackenzie Rogan. Find Billy Hunter again, on his right just behind him is Jack Steadman, who left us last week. A good pal of mine and a fine lad, who is the only pivotal man that the War Office has yet been able to advise us of. He is a quarryman and left last week. He is a fine cross country runner and has been coming in first every time, morning after morning, with our battalion cross country team, who have been training for the 5th Army Cup.

We should have had our photo taken with Tubby today, but the weather has been so bad that we have put it off till tomorrow.

Well Mammy, I must finish now and hope for lots of letters tomorrow. Bunches of love for yourself and the boy. Your Loving husband Walter.

January 5th 1919 – Sunday

Dear Kid,

Just a short line tonight as things are very busy just now. We landed here last night at the end of 3 days march. The first two days were not particularly interesting. The roads were very bad owing to the bad weather and the going was very heavy. As the runners had a couple of surplus "bikes", Tommy and Billy Hunter cycled each day. "P" as usual, playing at O.C., on WD wagon with the stores, and as I pointed out to them, there was only one soldier left in the orderly room. I could have managed a ride I expect, if I had wanted it badly, but I wanted to see anything fresh that there was to see. The first night we put the whole battalion up nice and comfortably in a big empty hospital at Arneke. The ground we covered we knew fairly well as back areas to the old Ypres front. On the next day the ground was much the same but we finished the march at a little place called Socx; the farthest north we have reached till then. When we arrived there we found the billeting party bad tempered at having to inform us that the villagers or even the farmers or bigger residents refused to billet us even in barns, stables or anywhere for the one night. Billets were eventually found for the lads beyond the village, part in a French Camp and the remainder at more willing farms outside. Tubby, who is rarely vicious, placed every estaminet, coffee shop, or any place that could make money out of the lads who had any – out of bounds – and their hopes of selling beaucoup bad beer at extortionate prices were lost. Tubby is brainy. The lads were pretty hard up, but what they did spend went just to the people who would billet them.

The third day was a deal more interesting and the roads such that you could hear the clink of your shoe irons and have the band going with some hopes of getting a good swinging march out of it. It takes more than a good band to play with mud up to its ankles and one foot in a foot deep rut and the other a foot higher. You see, the big drum loses its sense of the perpendicular and meets the drumstick sometimes on the off side, sometimes on the starboard, quicker than the drummer expects, which tends to syncopation rather than rhythm. Then the man with the big French Horn got wind up expecting to be impaled on it at any time. The man with the flageolet soon flagged badly too. Anyway on the third day we struck a fine hard high road running along the great Dunkirk-St Omer – goodness knows where to – canal, and for the first time for three days we marched, not squelched. The band then refused to compete with Flanagan's Discord Band and shewed the Continentals that Continental bands are not the only bands on earth, as some pre-war tourists wished us to imagine. I hope French kiddies can find their way home alright, as crowds of them followed us for miles. As there was no turning on the road for a number of miles they possibly found their way back alright. We passed through the most quaint little town I have seen yet over here and it was worth two days march to see what little bit of it we did see. The place was Berques. It is an old fortified town with a great moat all round it. Old drawbridges taking the main road through an old portcullis into the town. All the old walls are quaintly loopholed, and I could fancy the inhabitants pouring molten lead out of buckets on to the steel hats of the German invaders, or playing havoc with German aeroplanes with bow and arrow. A half hours bombardment with modern guns would have levelled the place, it looked so puny and yet so strong, like putting Jimmy's fort up against a 15 inch gun. There was a great belfry in the middle of the little place (that wouldn't look small against the Manchester Town Hall) with all the bells hung outside the belfry. The houses in the main street seemed to lean across to make visiting from the upper storeys safer than crossing the street. Most of the women folk at that time seemed to be "doing bedrooms" in various stages of déshabillé (of course I mean the women were, though I expect the bedrooms were not much better) and rather confidential utensils were emptied from upstairs windows at frequent intervals. I do the band the credit of believing it wasn't any objection to the noise they were making and put it down to the French idea of labour saving, but – well – but anyway we got safely through to the portcullis at the other end of the town and over the drawbridge again and away clear of the dear quaint dirty old Berques, but carried reminders a good way from the town in the shape of umpteen little gamins hanging on to us by any available haversack, strap or buckle. The only sign one meets with of French kiddies being mentally deficient is their hankering after "beesceets and bullie". Three hours later brought us into Dunkerke. A fine place as one gets into the centre of it, but like most towns and seaports, particularly French ones, goes off very badly at the outside edges. We got quite a good reception there, but whether it was what we hoped it was, but feared it wasn't, but was most likely delight under the mistaken impression that we were for the boat "en bloc" – well we are still in a fog about it. In any case I can assure you that our folks at home and your folks out here are not the only people who are getting fed up with our brilliant efforts at demobilization – er – speedy.

I notice in a paper a few days old that the first meeting of Parliament has been postponed for a fortnight. I suppose that is to give the demobilisation staff another fortnight to find where it is before there is steam to play at Westminster. However I had only just got to Dunkirk. We saw very little of it and passed through the dirty raw selvedge of St Pol out on to the dunes to – ye gawds – canvas and a wet January. Before we reached our camp we passed through a big camp, a very mixed business, big huts, little huts, tents, big notice boards and crowds of happy (I don't think) soldiers, mooning about glaring at notice boards with nothing on them (the boards I mean). We thought at first that it was a big leave rest camp, till we stumbled across men whom I have given demobilization papers to, and thought by now they would be having a miserable[?] time in "civvies" at home. I asked one poor chap what he was doing there. He smiled sadly and informed me that it was a "Demoralisation Camp". I am seriously thinking of making a slight alteration in the spelling of a long word in the heading of umpteen army forms that are now piled on my table. What was it that Lloyd George stood for?

There is only one good thing about this camp and that is the fact that the ground is sandy. It has rained every day since we marched into it and still keeps at it. The Brigadier here, however, is a good chap and our old Brigadier has looked us up, and between the two of them playing steam about it, we are likely to get better billets in a few days. Even Tubby looks glum and wishes he had learned to swim instead of play poker. Billy Hunter, Tommy and myself have a tent to ourselves with a table and chair each, all the orderly room boxes, typewriter etc., etc., etc., so you may guess we have lots of room to sleep. That is when the work is done.

Next door tent is where Pearson "supervises" Tubby "sign please", and sits looking sweet things about the weather, the Army and life generally, and wishing war would break out again to give some justification for our present predicament. Here also the C.O. holds office hours, and sits tapping his spurs what time he isn't scouring the neighbourhood and finding good billets, then going to the more or less Almighty and asking why we can't be put in there and asking why fighting troops of a victorious army (What!!) should live under worse conditions than Chinese coolies or German prisoners. Of course it serves us right for calling Wardrecques names. There is really nothing particularly hard about it of course, as we have stood 10 times worse conditions and the weather is really the worst offender. The fact of the matter is that we are bored to extinction now that the war is over.

However, here is a photo of "The team" at last. The reason that we all look so glum was that Tubby had just had us in a roar when the lady shouted "Stand to" or something like that and we all tried to look respectable on the instant. He had just been telling us how he thought we all ought to look. "P" had to look like he did at 3 a.m. Christmas, "Billy" had to look as if he had just heard that he was to be paid for his 3rd stripe, "Tommy" had to look as if all leaves were to be attended to at Brigade the same as officers, "I" had to look as at 10.0pm receiving an allotment from Brigade for 20 miners to leave at 8.0 a.m. next day, with no forms and just lost my pen and "He himself" was to wear a mournful air compatible with the dignity of office, with an added solemnity of mein that he would receive his pivotal papers, claim on the ground that he was his mother's son. He is very dissatisfied with the result of his stage management, and he reckons he is getting tired of seeing himself in front of that door. Poor chap, he didn't know that Tommy and I were wont to have a "vin rouge chaud avec sucre" occasionally there. Poor Tommy got wind up that day while Pearson was arranging with the photographers and Tubby telling him that it was all very well saying "Oui Oui" to everything she said as if he understood – "Never know what you are letting yourself in for" – while Pearson fervidly tried to explain what Madamoiselle was saying, wholly forgetful of the fact that Tubby, though he doesn't look like a Frenchman, can at least speak like one. While they were so busy, the old dame was screaming at Tommy in a whisper "Vin rouge apres" and Tommy was going frantic trying to shut her up with "Ce soir madame – ce soir sh sh sh – ce soir you old fool. And "ce soir" we did.

Got a nice long letter from you today dated the 2nd which means that about a week's letters are straying about looking for us. Hope they don't go and get demobilised before they find us. Thanks so much for a sample of the new note. After admiring the design I shall pass it on for further admiration in exchange for a few rather neat things in French silver coinage.

I am sending another photo of the team for Mabs. Take great care of mine please. I have put the key on the back each man to his department. Tubby treated us to ½ dozen each, but there has been such a demand for them that my stock has got down to two. The other photograph is from one of the old black hand gang (runners) and honours me by calling me "chum". He came on leave with me but failed to come back and we heard later that he was in Greek St. Hospital bad with heart trouble, through being gassed umpteen times I expect. One of the sort that doesn't know he is ill till his work is finished. He has been bedfast for a month now. He lost his best pals when that shell dropped but he was out on a run just then. Since he has been away he has been awarded the French 'Croix de Guerre' and it has been sent to Stockport for him. If ever you think you would like to look him up some visiting afternoon, take my next box of "James" to him, he knows the pink box well and likes them immensely – 266403 Pte George Ollerenshaw, 6th Cheshires at Greek St Hospital would find him alright. The 'Robey' that he mentions in his letter was one of the runners that was taken prisoner in March last on the Somme with Brigadier General Bellingham. From what we hear young Robey didn't have a very bad time of it and didn't wait till he was released when the Armistice was signed, and 'stood not on the order of his going' but went.

I really must finish now and get under my take. Billy and Tommy are long since under theirs. Keep writing nice long letters there's a good kid and tell the others it isn't fair to let yours count as theirs. As soon as they are ready to play 'slaps back' I can always find time (and ink now) for that. If there isn't the war or the weather to talk about tell Mabs, just talk anyway.

Give them all my love and bunches of kisses for yourself and Jim,
Your loving husband Walter

P.S. Madge's last two weeklies are evidently still on the journey somewhere, as, despite the bad example of her husband, I can still depend on her for one a week.

January 11th 1919 – Saturday

Dear Kid,

Got an hour or two to myself tonight before a big day tomorrow. This morning we weighed up possibilities of making a bit more room in the tent and after getting into such a state of mix up with tables, boxes, chairs, papers, our equipment, blankets and rifles that we thought we would never get out alive, we eventually simmered down and found our combined genius had resulted in getting two of our 3 table ends together so that we could work 3 at the two tables and one separate, with more room than the 3 of us had before. I got my young second in command at work and we got steam up to some purpose.

He is a fine kid to work with and tomorrow we shall make the papers fly. "Tubby" looked in this morning and asked "Well Pelman, how is it going?" That is my new name.

Demobbing after all is a bit of fun and if I can only get a bit more room to swing about, and a bit of warmth, it won't seem so bad. Everybody who seems to think they will be going first get bad shocks when they find chaps get orders to go who never dreamed that they stood a chance. I have been annoyed by chaps coming poking their heads in asking if it is true that they had to report to me in the morning. On asking who has told them to report and on hearing that the Orderly Sgt. had warned them, they have got their ears chewed off for daring to come and question the matter. The truth of the matter being that they have had such an awful shock hearing that they were off, and hadn't the least expectation of going. Folks have now got very chary of coming to me and wanting to know why so and so has gone before him. I have got a nasty habit of telling them that if they want to work 20 hours a day and sit here writing all day, day after day, instead of being able to play football nearly all day, and go down to Dunkirk every afternoon and the pictures every night, they might understand, or they might not, I didn't and I wasn't keen on trying to explain, but if they had any complaints to make, see the Adjt. and he would refer them to me, so there you are thank you.

Even the C.O. himself started grumbling today that the band kept dwindling one by one, and was it necessary. On my digging out a bundle of paper and proceeding to quote numerous orders, memoranda, notes etc., he ended the matter by saying he didn't know anything about it but as long as I knew it was alright, well, it couldn't be helped. Nobody will look into my department, especially if I want to shew them why so and so etc. etc. Anything smelling of demobilization is passed to me in deep silence. My little assistant has had a big day getting fifteen men off. It doesn't sound much, but it is.

But it is cold, no fire and little light. I have started chilblains now on nearly all my fingers. Tonight Tubby, who is very sympathetic, sent us a bit of comfort in and very comforting it has been too. If my letter seems a bit disjointed, it may be the effects of the bit of comfort, but not directly, only indirectly. What I really mean is that Tommy is very busy trying to say "The Leith Police dismisseth us" or "She stood at Burgesses and Smiths fish and sauce shop, smilingly welcoming him in" with indifferent success. Anyway we are warmer than we have been for a day or two.

I seem to have heaps of letters of yours to answer, your last was the 9th January. I haven't been able to keep up to date but I know you will excuse me. Like you, I am afraid I feel the tag end the hardest. It seems so hard to be doing nothing but what some old Grade umpteen workers of national importance could do in perfect safety. Let some of the old stagers who had such a fat and plenteous time during enlistment days come out, the authorities would no doubt find them a nice comfortable billet and beaucoup financial recompense, but overseas soldiers can do it in a tent, one man in midwinter at 2/2*d* a day with frozen feet and frozen fingers with his own breath freezing on his nose tip, can attend to the hysterical attempts to please the soldiers, the public and other phases of demobilization of 750 soldiers single handed. Billy is lucky if what you surmise is correct and he is likely to be out of khaki in a few days. It is quite what we out here expect. But when I came out here I decided that I wouldn't be beaten by anything in front of me. This job has been put to me and candidly I feel rather cocky carrying it on as a Lc Cpl. at 2/2*d* a day. I shouldn't say it of course, but without 'swanking' I could have 3 stripes in as many days. That won't do for me. I should then have to go into the Sgt's Mess and get over the line every night, which is just under seven times too many a week. I have caused enough vacancies this last week or two to fill me 'toute suite' up to Sgt, especially as I am by far the senior Lc Cpl in the Battalion, but every time 'P' suggests putting me through part II orders, I flare up and ask him if he thinks the Sgt's Mess is a proper place for me. I have such fun chewing Sgts up as a Lc Cpl that I wouldn't have another stripe for a good pension let alone a matter of an extra 3*d*.

The funny part about it is that they dare not give me another stripe, as I threaten to do something sufficient to turn me out of the orderly room if they dare put me up one more stripe. It is rather a unique experience I can tell you. Officers come to poor Tubby and enquire whether their Z32 or Z15a has come through and Tubby informs them that the man they want to see is L/C Williamson – next tent.

Poor me, I don't know how I am going to go on, I havn't heard anything yet from Mr Bronnerts move and can't do anything till I do, but Tommy's 'Guaranteed Employment' has come through, which means him going in a week or two at the most. I shall be wonderfully sorry when he does go, as he's one of those natures that "add to the gaiety of nations" and one is in bad need of such at the present time. Thirteen men went off today from here, after much ink slinging on my part, to a demoblizing camp close by and returned in an hour or two with the message that they could not be taken in, although we had distinct instructions to send them. As we have fifteen more for tomorrow to the same place, I don't quite know what is going to happen. "Ç'est ne fait rien" or "San Fairy Ann" as we say, "It doesn't matter", I shall send them and trust to luck.

Well Kid, I must say good night and get to bed as Billy and Tommy are long since down to it. Tomorrow two companies move to the other side of the town where I believe it is much nicer, and we shall likely follow with the other companies the day after. I hear that I am to have a hut and a little staff to myself for "demobbing", so we shall be quite OK.

Bunches of love and kisses for you and the boy. Your loving husband Walter.

January 22nd 1919 – Wednesday

Dear Kid,

Got letters of yours on hand, couldn't get time for a line yesterday as worked rolled in again, and busy again today. Just scribbling a line in between men coming in to fill up papers, so if it seems a bit patchy, you won't have to mind.

Things are very nice and comfy with us at present, which makes work much easier and pleasanter. Demobilizing in midwinter in a tent seems far away now we have a nice comfortable room, a nice stove, electric light, plenty of table room and shelves, and an odd five minutes on the piano in the Mess downstairs when the officers have all gone home.

Shall not see Pat again for a day or two as he is down on the docks again, but as I look like being busy for a day it is as well. I may have a slack afternoon to come in when he comes off duty again.

The little paper you sent from Bill was very useful, but why have they wasted ink on it. It is nice soft paper and would look quite well done in rolls with bathroom wallpaper to match.

(Later) Just finished work and got all ship shape, but the stove has gone out, so I have moved my quarters, sat by a nice big fire in the next room by candle light. Tommy has been a great help today, he hadn't much to do in his own dept., so he slogged into it with me, but he isn't hardened to it, and he started nodding at it about 10 o'clock, so I had to order him off.

I got young Bobby Howarth packed off home today, mixed between delight at getting off home and sorrow at leaving the team. Another man I got off was a man named White, a stud groom at Chelford. I asked if he knew George Williamson and he reckoned that he knew him very well, so I told him to call in and see him when he got home and tell him who gave him his ticket.

Tommy is 'sweating hard' on getting home soon now. I seem to be losing them one by one. I could nearly have it in my heart to put his papers out of sight a bit, but like us all, he is in a big hurry.

I have heard nothing yet from Mr Bronnert and shall write him in a day or two if nothing turns up, as I shall need something to hang on to, if I am not going to be left to carry the big drum home.

Billy has done well to get out so comfortably, and what with the nice fat couple of hundred pounds he will get and the nice fat time he has had in England, I am rather surprised that he should take any interest in the 'Tosh' that is suggested in the little bill. Like you I am a fairly peaceful sort, and that sort of rant runs to making Bolsheviks if it gets excited. Poor kid, you must have had a time of it, on occasions, to sit out some of his arguments. Anyway kid, we must have civilian politicians to add to the gaiety of nations, and a Parliament of soldiers is positively unthinkable. And a parliament should I suppose deal with some other odd matters besides soldiers. I have heard at one time, perhaps before the war, of babies, women, old men(!), I suppose we have an Army or had something under 10 million (to make myself safe), so if the population of Great Britain is anything like figures stated, there should be some other people in the country, and then surely one can vote quietly in ones own way without classing all civilian politicians under one heading. A nice hefty Sgt poor old Balfour would make, and I could positively weep to think of poor Mr Asquith in a labour battalion, but if we are to have Peace now we have won it, for goodness sake don't let Billy get Prime Minister or all will be lost. [PART LETTER]

January 26th 1919 – Sunday

Dear Kid,

No English post in today, but I have a little letter of yours yesterday not replied. I am sorry I havn't any bathing postcards left for you, but I sent you a 'wading' one last night, Joe has one he will perhaps show you if you ask him specially.

Things are still keeping busy in the demobbing dept and tonight I have done well finishing by 10.0 p.m. (swank of course). We are averaging about 10 a day. It doesn't sound much, but there is a wonderful amount of work to be done. An allotment comes in for about that number each afternoon and they have to be at a concentration camp about 4 miles away by noon next day. We usually get asked for, say ten men over perhaps nine different areas, perhaps ten. It is a lucky man from Scotland or Devonshire, or South Wales who somehow has drifted into the Cheshire Rgt. We have something like 400 men in the battalion from Lancashire and Cheshire, and about 150 of them with over 4 years service in, and say for South Wales we have perhaps 6 men who can't total 4 years between them, so the usual thing is to get an allotment of 2 men for the South Wales district and 2 for the Lancashire and Cheshire area and one each for some outlandish area where we have an odd one or two farmers' sons (Group 1 of course) who came out a few weeks after the colours arrived here. S'marvellous isn't it. When an allotment comes in the business starts. Everyman now on my register has all the necessary and unnecessary information on the nearly endless line his number starts off on, then his name, rank, Coy., what group he belongs to, when he joined the army, how long he has been out here, what his order of priority for release is (according to Demobbing Regulations), his trade, married or not, if he wants to go abroad, if his family does, his service category, his medical category, whether he is a specialist or not, and a few other odd items, each of which have to be duly considered in their due perspective, as affecting the priority of his release. Then we look at the allotment and find a man for Scotland. We have perhaps two, one with 3 years service, one with 2 months. The 3 years man is married, yes, but the two months man has his pivotal slip through. He is perhaps 18 years of age, licking stamps till quite lately in the office of some dept. of some Local or Public Authority, so his name is put down, and this business is done over perhaps 8 areas, and when we come to areas 3 and 4a (Lancashire and Cheshire) well there is something doing to pick 2 men out of 400. When the list of names is picked out I submit it to the Demob. Officer and he looks worried when he sees that 6 of the men together total perhaps 2 years service amongst them and the remaining 4 shew a total of 16 years, and murmurs something about questions at the next lecture. Then he submits it to the C.O. after making sure that we can't do any better at it. The C.O. starts to ask questions "How long has this chap been out, don't seem to know his name, What!!! 2 months, What the!!! Oh he is 'pivotal' is he, Lord bless me, what is he, a labourer in a quarry, Oh I see, no stone no roads, no roads no paviors and no streets, can't get anywhere, can't build houses, oh that's bricks isn't it, National Reconstruction and all that. What Good Gawd!!!! Oh here is old Dick ... been out since 1914, glad he has got his pivotal papers in, no , what, oh he is the 10% of the allotment that is allowed for long service men". The list however comes back to me about 3.0 p.m., all in order. I scribble a note to the company of each man to have him detailed at once to attend the orderly room 'toute suite' to sign forms. Ten minutes later a runner returns with 2 men out of the 10, 3 are on a guard at Berques seven miles away, 2 are on duty at Dunkirk docks, 3 can't be found – must be having the evening out in Dunkirk. However Tommy and I (if Tommy isn't busy) collar the 2. Take first one and stand him between us, Tommy with half a dozen small forms, me with that monumental and now famous form Z10 (dispersal certificate). Tommy snaps at him 'number' and I yell 'name' and he gets a crick in his neck and an impediment in his speech trying to answer us both at once. After Tommy has said 'bon' just to encourage him, I remember and stop the proceedings just to inform the poor chap that in view of the fact that General Demobilization has not yet been ordered, we cannot demobilize any man against his will and if he has any objection he must say so, if he is the usual 'pivotal' he says he has no objection and if he is an old soldier he starts to grin; but we cut him short – Tommy with "What's you Group number?" and I with "What station?" he tells me 41 and Tommy 'Stockport', but we manage to pick it up. Tommy's 'Have you a shirt?' usually meets my 'married or single?' The next I have to be careful not to put 'Sanitary man' down for reply to "Have you served with any other Regiment?" as Tommy's query is "Have you had any Regimental employment?" The questioning finished I can go on filling my forms up from the information I have got while I can hear Tommy at it, "Have you a pair of socks?" etc, then a pause, then the famous question "Have you anything wrong with you?" instead of "Do you wish to claim for any physical disability due to you military service?". Just about the time I get to the end of my form, I hear Tommy murmur "That's all, the corporal (that's me) wants to see you". Then I gather up all Tommy's little bits and fold them in my big one, and then the speech which I have now got word perfect and which you will doubtless hear me murmuring in my sleep one of these fine days – I mean nights of course. It runs thus "Take this form to the Regt Tailor, get him to fill in your measurements, you will decide at the dispersal station whether you will have a civilian suit or 52/6d in lieu of same. You will get from your company officer a certificate that your clothing and boots are in good condition, you will draw 24 hours rations, you will draw one week's pay, you will attend sick parade at 10.30 a.m. to be medically examined by the M.O. You will get from him a certificate that you are free from vermin and infection, you will parade here at 11.15 a.m. in full marching order with two blankets and jerkin, but without groundsheet, which will be handed in to your company store. That's all". As they pass out of the door feeling dazed, I usually yell "Don't forget – pay, rations, sick 10.30, here 11.15 with 3 papers".

Then a rush to the telephone "Hello Signals, I want Berques Supply Depot". Then I hear myself talking to the exchange at Dunkirk and get annoyed to hear Berques line is engaged and, after picking the telephone out of the fire and putting in on the mouth piece again and diving back to our room, I find Tommy busy making rude enquiries into another man's wardrobe and so get busy at the other side of him. Halfway through the telephone rings or I should say "buzzes" - "Berques?, hello can I speak to a Cheshire officer?" – " Haw who is that?" "Cheshire's orderly room, can I speak to a Cheshire Officer please?" – "Who is thaat?" Then I get on my top note and say something rude to find out I am speaking to an officer. There are then 2 courses open to me, and the other one is to apologise. He then gets off and a signaller comes on, that is evident from the fact that he gets rude too. Being at home with signallers of course I understand their code language. I never have found that Cheshire Officer I have asked for, but we generally manage to get the men down sometime that night. Once they left it till morning and there wasn't half a rush that morning to get them ready. We actually have some men staffing the demobilization camp at the other side of Dunkirk, then we have to send a runner for them, and after going through the mill, they go back through the same camp.

Next morning is spent getting umpteen documents away to different addresses and entering books up, right to 11.15 and then someone pops his head in and says the ten men are on parade outside. I grab 10 bundles of papers and rush downstairs and hand them a bundle each, and then give them another lecture on what has to be done with each form, where they are to hand it in, which they are to hand in and which they are to keep. Then one man will chip in that he hasn't got two little 'uns like the next man, then I find he has forgotten to get his louse – pardon – I mean medical certificate and clothing certificate, then I get excited in a calm way and fix him up with blanks to get signed on his way back past the camp. I then warn them to get dressed as the C.O. will come and say a parting word. I don't mean that they have forgotten to put their trousers on or anything like that, the weather is a bit too nippy for such forgetfulness, but just to get their equipment on again and button their pockets up.

By the time the C.O. has shaken hands with them all and assured them that they will all want to be back in the Army in a month, the post has come in with perhaps two for me and before I have found out from the first one how much you love me and how many curtains you have washed, a knock comes to our door and a voice asks for Cpl Williamson and then there is a procession handing in letters stamped all over by some Advisory Committee of some Labour Exchange. These have all to be entered up to the various recipients, then the post has to be attended to, pivotal papers, slips, RCVs and all sorts of horrible inventions of the Demobilization experts again to be entered up. Just ordinary letters too, asking for the immediate release of "my son" on some pathetic, compassionate, business or ridiculous grounds which all have to be replied to and advice given as to the proper channels through which to make the application. Before I have got half way through it, another allotment comes in for the next day and so the day goes on. Anyway at the rate we are going on there should be no battalion left in between two or three months, so in any case I look like being home before the summers sets in properly.

Old Cadger again. If you havn't already fixed me up with a birthday present, a nice little "Blackbird" with a fine nib would be a blessing, in a forgetful moment I passed my pen to a miner to sign with. I am not sure even now whether he thought it was a pick or a bayonet, but anyway at present it is equally as much use as a pick, bayonet or pen and I am losing words per minute writing with an ordinary dipping pen. If I am too late don't bother. I would have bought one here, but I refuse to be robbed at the prices they want out this way.

I am enclosing an official version of "a minor operation" which you will find interesting.

I am keeping in the pink and if nothing special comes through for me, I'll just get the Battalion demobbed "toute suite" and bring the pens and ink home. So love me till then and I'll tell you how nicely you have done the garden if I don't get home in time to make the start at it myself. Got another letter from Mabs on hand, so I must try and get her off my books tomorrow, she is trying to do it on me, she said she would.

Well goodnight Kid. Hope all the demobbing nonsense doesn't bore you. Heaps of kisses for you and the boy, from Your loving husband Walter.

January 28th 1919 – Tuesday

Dear Kid,

Got two letters from you yesterday, but none today. Sorry to hear the boy has got a cough again, but from what I hear of the weather in your quarter, I am not greatly surprised. We seem to be having much better weather than you. Nice sharp mornings, frost nearly every morning.

I am getting a habit now of taking half an hour off after seeing men away each morning, when I get down on the sands with Tommy and Pearson, and for half an hour we may be seen running for 3 minutes, walk for two, run again for 3 and walk two for the half hour. The transport men who have their horses on the front think the orderly room and demobbing staff is going "mental" through strain. We must look a queer trio walking along and on the instant breaking into a trot and after 3 minutes break into a walk without losing step and again breaking off in unison to a run, then to a walk and so on. Then down to work again like two year olds. There is "P" doubling with his nose up in the air trying to run with the dignity of a CQMS, MSM and 1914 ribbon, Tommy ambling along trying to keep his long legs in mind of what is due to a Quarter Master Sgt and a full corporal, and there is poor me putting in twenty to their fifteen, else springing an extra six inches every third step to pull up. Then we come back tingling and Tommy and I set to work again while "P" goes for a reviver. Better send Jimmy over, we would cure his cough for him.

Tommy and I had a couple of hours off last night and went down to Dunkirk for a little farewell dinner, as I expect he will be off very shortly, perhaps in a day or two. I shall miss him badly, but he reckons that he isn't going to finish pestering me simply because he goes home first, and wants to know if we will find him half of Jimmy's bed any time he comes and looks us up. You will like him when you meet him.

It is guest night tonight at the Mess downstairs, this is evidently going to be a Tuesday institution. The Brigadier, the Mayor of Dunkirk and various other personages in the district are doing the dine and the band is playing upstairs, next room to ours, and we can't do much in the way of work, so I have shut up the demobbing dept. for the night and trying to write a letter or two.

We are getting about seventy a week away and as we have not many more than 500 men in the battalion, things are running nicely and looking quite rosy for being home before long, even if nothing special turns up for me from Mr B. It will be nice too to be home for good and have the summer at Cheadle Hulme and perhaps a little holiday with you and the little feller. I have only seen him at the sea when his chief idea was to eat sand and do acrobatic feats in his go-cart to watch a sea-gull fly at the back of him, and have arguments with the bulldog. We must have a try for St Annes this year even if it is only for a week, even if I have to go in Khaki. Things however seem very disturbed at home just now, strikes and threats of strikes worse than ever, just when people ought to be feeling like a bit of peace. I see some folks who have only just been granted an 8 hours day are now out for a 6 hours day. What on earth are they going to do with the spare 18 hours? I am afraid a six hours day wouldn't do for me at present, firstly army pay wouldn't fit in, and then it fills in the time till coming home. You wouldn't find your old man causing any upheavals, striking and wanting revolutions.

Tommy and I had a taste of "civilization" last night and we dined next to evening dresses, and what with a nice white tablecloth and a serviette, well poor old Tommy looked into his mess tin and stirred the contents with his spoon and sighed, then looked at his wallet and found the odd franc note, and said "Well anyway last night was worth it". We had been saving up for it and hadn't much balance left when we had tipped the waiter, but it is pay day tomorrow. What with a tablecloth to every meal and not to have to clean up one's greasy mess tin after dinner with cold water, well – I don't know what folks want to strike about, do you?

Well here's to "The real day" Kid. Bunches of kisses for you and the Jim boy from your loving husband, Walter.

February 3rd 1919 – Monday

Dear little Woman,

Two lovely great long letters from you right on my birthday, and talk of a birthday month, what will you say if I am home before the month is out. It seems quite within the bounds of possibility as both the C.O. and Tubby have been particularly nice, and I shall get away before my proper turn, perhaps for the heavy work I have had. The demobbing officer tried to have a say in the matter, but I hurt his feelings considerably by laughing at him when he tried to explain that he was the demobbing officer.

I suppose we can find a corner somewhere to get in if we have to wait for the little grey house in Heathbank Road. So now you needn't think of packing up your best crêpe de Chine and toothbrush and coming this way, hardly worth while now, and the weather isn't exactly crepe de chiney, and anyway if it is to be a summer holiday this year at the seaside, I will see you have that swanky bathing costume, but only on condition that you get it properly wet.

I am wondering already whether you would like a good holiday away somewhere as soon as I come home, before I start work or would you like a summer holiday instead. If a holiday straightaway, I would take advantage of my 28 days furlough, or if you would prefer a summer holiday, a few days to get fitted up and spend with you and then get into harness and start keeping my own family again.

I can hardly grasp it yet. Nearly 3 years away from you out of five years married, I have a lot to make up to you little girl. You talk of making me happy when I get back, don't you think it is time I took a hand in that sort of thing too.

I want to see the old crochet work going again, as a sign of peace, of course you can do it in some nice soft stuff and stitch on bits of flannel and things, if luck goes that way. Then I'll read all those books to you and we will have some tremendous old arguments about them, then we shall find perhaps that some of our old arguments have got altered a great deal since the war started and finished. And the fire will twinkle on the table legs with that bit of extra polish on, and the old rose bowl will blink on the sideboard which looks swank, it doesn't matter much if the drawers won't open. That reminds me that the staff at Princes Street are buying Mr Bronnert something of that sort for his jubilee, and I have promised a guinea towards it. Don't know where the guinea is coming from, but that proves that your old man hasn't altered a bit.

There's to be a dinner afterwards too at the Grand Hotel, subscribers and wives (or ladies as the case may be) – that is really the way it was given to me, evening dress affair too, I suppose a guinea apiece too, which I am not particular about going to, and which the missus will be keen on, which is quite pre-war again.

Anyway let me get back home again reading to you, and when my voice gets tired (which will be quite often), you will drop your work and I my book, and you will come and sit with me and find my lips a change of occupation. Later I may be murmuring unconsciously "Have we any bread left for a bit of supper, or did we finish it for tea", or reckoning on a bit of tomorrow's and chancing a poor appetite for breakfast.

But isn't it all fine to look forward to in a short time. Then getting the old garden going again and having arguments as to whether the dog ought to sleep outside or not. And I hereby promise not to dig up any more Iceland Poppies in mistake for chickweed, that is, if you keep a sharp eye on me. And just think of all the joinering jobs I might do for you if they will only let me bring my entrenching tool home. I believe I could open that kitchen drawer with a single blow. But of course they won't let me bring it home, so I suppose it will be quite like old days, me standing watching you do it and being asked "Havn't you got a clever wife?" and I shall kiss you meekly and murmur "Yes dear, what about some tea, can I open the sardines for you?", and just fancy the sun shining too strongly on the tea table and drawing the blind just far enough to cast a shadow of the old greek key pattern across your nose, and Jim arguing that it is the correct thing to stir his tea sufficiently vigorously with a spoon to put it all into the saucer, or having him busy telling us an interesting tale while we are holding our breath watching him waving his cup far and wide to emphasise the point of the story. And in a few weeks too. I think I will get down to bed and shut my eyes and try and think it all out.

Good night little woman, we are on the last lap, and I can't help it. 'Oiseau' is French for 'bird'. Oasis is perhaps the word you were after. Of course a little green spot might possibly be a bird in the middle of the desert , or else the dinner got mixed, "An oiseau in the middle of the dessert" Tut Milly. Anyway a thousand kisses for a Happy Birthday with your two fine letters. Your loving husband Walter.

February 9th – 1919

Dear Kid,

Just having a jubilee night. Got a grand roaring fire, finished early, everyone gone to bed, and I am squatted on 3 chairs in front of the fire. Have already written Archibald, sent him his guinea, told him we won't be at the dinner, written Mother, Madge and am now on the last lap for tonight.

Had a little letter from you yesterday, but none today. If that is due to the strikes, then the strikers are in for trouble. The papers don't look at all nice, and it is not helping demobilizing any. The boys out here have some sweet opinions on the subject and if there is any trouble, they don't want to use home troops on the job, they should send here for them, and we would very soon have peace, am afraid there wouldn't be enough strikers left to make any more strikes. It was the Bolshevist in Russia that cost us dearly out here, and we have something of a grudge against that sort of thing. I do hope they will settle down and find what damnable fools they are making of themselves by showing Germany that they can be led by the nose by a few Bolshevist fire brands. The Englishman had a reputation once for being level headed, but they have evidently lost it, else all the Englishmen are still out here, and I wouldn't like to think that.

I must shut up however, as I get going in every letter I write lately, but it doesn't make one feel pleasant when one looks who are the leaders in these strikes. Not one has done anything for their country but try to bleed it, and 999 out of each thousand of the strikers have been bleeding the country at home for the last four years.

Am hoping to have a nice fat letter from you today, and must say I am surprised you keep so perky, a letter from you will do me good and make me think that things are not so bad as they look from the papers.

Well kid, things are not going at all badly out here, and I am getting nearer to coming home each day. Mr B's presentation is coming off on the 24th but am afraid I won't manage to be home just then, or for Jim's birthday, but I don't expect to be much later.

We have been having some grand frosty weather this last few days, but as it has come after a big fall of snow, it has made walking a wildly exciting pastime, especially in hob nails. I havn't been out for the usual little training on the sands in the mornings this last few mornings, but hope to get going again shortly.

Have you heard yet how Mr Lees is fixed about a new house. I suppose if they don't find one they will hang on till quarter day which can't be helped, but it would be nice if they could find something now and let us get back there as soon as I get home. I could just enjoy a few days helping you to straighten up there. Not too strenuous, say stop work by dinner time and half holidays each day.

I can't quite yet get level with the idea that we shall be together for keeps in an odd week or two. I have the same feeling that I had for a few odd weeks before we were wed.

I wonder what Jim will think of having me home for good, whether he will think me a bit of a nuisance for a bit, while he gets used to the fact that he is not the only man in the house, bless him. I suppose he will be teaching me all sorts of things, and I shall be teaching him kinds of things that I should not, and be getting both of us into trouble. But I suppose he will chance it with me and take his luck. But kid, it's fine to be thinking of, strikes or no strikes, and we shall have a great time together, so take care of yourself this next week or two.

Give the boy a big hug and beaucoup kisses for both of you.

Your loving husband, Walter.